The intellectual culture of the English country house, 1500–1700

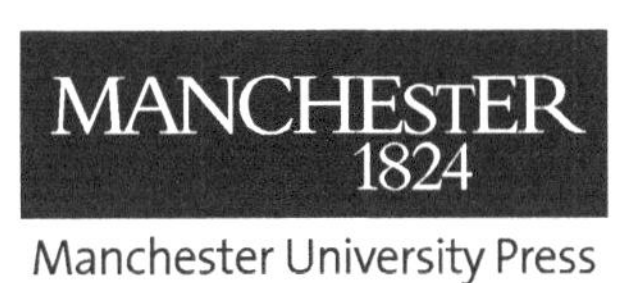

MANCHESTER
1824

Manchester University Press

The intellectual culture of the English country house, 1500–1700

Edited by Matthew Dimmock, Andrew Hadfield
and Margaret Healy

Manchester University Press

Copyright © Manchester University Press 2015

While copyright in the volume as a whole is vested in Manchester University Press, copyright in individual chapters belongs to their respective authors, and no chapter may be reproduced wholly or in part without the express permission in writing of both author and publisher.

Published by Manchester University Press
Altrincham Street, Manchester M1 7JA
www.manchesteruniversitypress.co.uk

British Library Cataloguing-in-Publication Data is available

ISBN 978 0 7190 9020 2 hardback
ISBN 978 1 5261 2712 9 paperback

First published by Manchester University Press in 2015

The publisher has no responsibility for the persistence or accuracy of URLs for any external or third-party internet websites referred to in this book, and does not guarantee that any content on such websites is, or will remain, accurate or appropriate.

Typeset by Frances Hackeson Freelance Publishing Services

Contents

Figures

Contributors

Hannah DeGroff completed her AHRC-sponsored doctorate, 'The Mental World of the Country House: The Textual Networks of the 3rd Earl of Carlisle' at the University of York in 2013.

Matthew Dimmock is Professor of Early Modern Studies at the University of Sussex. His work focuses on the field of cultural encounter and amongst other publications he is author of *New Turkes: Dramatizing Islam and the Ottomans in Early Modern England* (2005) and *Mythologies of Muhammad in Early Modern English Culture* (2013), and editor of *William Percy's* Mahomet and His Heaven: *A Critical Edition* (2006).

Alden Gregory is Curator of Historic Buildings at Historic Royal Palaces. He completed his doctorate, 'Knole: An Architectural and Social History of the Archbishop of Canterbury's House, 1456–1538' at the University of Sussex in 2011.

Andrew Hadfield is Professor of English at the University of Sussex, Visiting Professor at the University of Granada and Vice-Chair of the Society for Renaissance Studies. He is the author of a number of books on the literature and culture of Early Modern England including *Edmund Spenser: A Life* (2012), *Shakespeare and Republicanism* (2005) and *Literature, Travel and Colonial Writing, 1540–1620* (1998). He is also the editor of the *Oxford Handbook to Early Modern Prose, 1500–1640* (2013).

Tara Hamling is Senior Lecturer in the History Department, University of Birmingham. Her research focuses on the visual arts and material culture of early modern Britain, especially in a domestic context. She is author of *Decorating the Godly Household: Religious Art in Post-Reformation Britain* (2010) and editor (with Catherine Richardson) of *Everyday Objects: Medieval and Early Modern Material Culture* (2010) and (with Richard L. Williams) *Art Re-formed: Reassessing the Impact of the Reformation on the Visual Arts* (2007). Her next book, *A Day at Home in Early Modern England: The Materiality of Domestic Life* (co-authored with Catherine Richardson) is forthcoming.

Margaret Healy is Professor of English at the University of Sussex. She teaches many aspects of Renaissance literature, and is particularly interested in the cultural history of the body and the interfaces between literature, medicine and science. She is the author of *Shakespeare, Alchemy and the Creative Imagination: The Sonnets and* A Lover's Complaint (2011); *Fictions of Disease in Early Modern England: Bodies, Plague and Politics* (2001); *Richard II* (1998); and the co-editor with Tom Healy of *Renaissance Transformations: the Making of English Writing 1500–1650* (2009). She is literary editor of the British Medical Journal *Medical Humanities (BMJ)*.

Maurice Howard is Professor of Art History at the University of Sussex, was President of the Society of Antiquaries of London 2010–14 and subsequently President of the Society of Architectural Historians of Great Britain. He is the author of *The Building of Elizabethan and Jacobean England* (2007); with Edward Wilson, *The Vyne: A Tudor House Revealed* (2003); with Michael Snodin, *Ornament: A Social History since 1450* (1996) and *The Early Tudor Country House: Architecture and Politics 1490–1550* (1987).

Nicolle Jordan is Associate Professor of English at the University of Southern Mississippi, where she teaches eighteenth-century British literature. She has published articles on William Godwin, Anne Finch, Sarah Scott, Lady Mary Wortley Montagu, Elizabeth Montagu and Jane Barker. She is currently writing a book entitled *Prolific Ground: Landscape and British Women's Writing, 1700–1825.*

Elizabeth Zeman Kolkovich is an Assistant Professor of English at Ohio State University, where she teaches Shakespeare and Renaissance literature at the Mansfield campus. She has written articles on pageantry in *The Merry Wives of Windsor* and the political functions of Elizabeth Russell's entertainment at Bisham Abbey, which appear in recent issues of *Shakespeare Quarterly* and *English Literary Renaissance*. She is currently writing a book about Elizabethan country house entertainment in performance and print.

Andrew Loukes is National Trust Curator of Collections and Exhibitions at Petworth House, West Sussex, and a specialist in British art of the eighteenth and nineteenth centuries.

Alison McCann worked as an archivist at West Sussex for over forty years. During the majority of that time, she was responsible for the Petworth House Archives, and produced four volumes of the Catalogue of the Petworth House Archives, three published conventionally, the contents of the last volume being available online. After retiring in 2012, she became Archivist to Lord Egremont and the Leconfield Estate. Besides the catalogues, she has written more than thirty articles and pamphlets on various aspects of local history. She has also arranged and curated exhibitions on a number of subjects including Thomas Harriot, the Petworth Estate and the Petworth Emigration Scheme.

Anne M. Myers is Associate Professor of English at the University of Missouri, where she teaches courses in early modern English poetry and drama. Her articles include work on Anne Clifford and George Herbert, and her monograph, *Literature and Architecture in Early Modern England*, was published in 2013. In addition to literary and historical treatments of architecture in early modern England, her current interests include topographical writing, antiquarianism and the development of local history during the period.

Matthew Neely is an archivist at the Bodleian Library, University of Oxford, predominately working on early modern and modern historical collections. In addition to his research on Rycote Park, his recent work has included the cataloguing of the eighteenth- and nineteenth-century papers of the Earls Harcourt and their country estate Nuneham Park, Oxfordshire, and the cataloguing of the archive of the Townesend family, master masons in Oxford from the late seventeenth to mid-eighteenth century.

Louise Noble is Senior Lecturer in the School of Arts at the University of New England. Her research interests include the ways in which literature intersects with medical and religious constructions of the body and discourses of cannibalism; and the relationship between literature, culture and the natural world in early modern England and in post eighteenth-century Australia. She is the author of *The Healing Corpse: Medicinal Cannibalism in Early Modern English Literature and Culture* (2011).

Nicholas Pickwoad has been Adviser on book conservation to the National Trust of Great Britain since 1978, and was editor of the *Paper Conservator*. He is project leader of the St Catherine's Monastery Library Project based at the University of the Arts, London and is Director of the Ligatus Research Centre, which is dedicated to the history of bookbinding. He gave the 2008 Panizzi Lectures at the British Library and was awarded the 2009 Plowden medal for conservation. He has published widely on the history of European bookbinding in the era of the hand printing press.

Mark Purcell is Libraries Curator to the National Trust. He has published extensively on the history of books and libraries in early modern Britain and Ireland, including *The Big House Library in Ireland: Books in Ulster Country Houses* (2011) and, as co-author with David Pearson, William Hale and John Hammond, *Treasures from Lord Fairhaven's Library at Anglesey Abbey* (2013).

James Raven is Professor of Modern History and Director of the Centre for Bibliographical History, University of Essex and Senior Research Fellow of Magdalene College, Cambridge. He is the author and editor of a number of books, including *Bookscape: Geographies of Printing and Publishing in London before 1800* (2014); *Publishing Business in Eighteenth-Century England* (2014); *The Business of Books: Booksellers and the English Book Trade 1450–1850* (2007) and *Lost Libraries: The Destruction of Book Collections since Antiquity* (2004).

Richard Simpson is an architectural historian, Director of Publications at the Institute of Classical Studies, University of London and a Fellow of the Society of Antiquaries of London. He is co-author with Paul Drury of *Hill Hall: A Singular House Devised by a Tudor Intellectual* (2009).

Marta Straznicky is Professor of English at Queen's University, Kingston, Canada. She is the author of *Shakespeare's Stationers: Essays in Cultural Bibliography* (2013); *Privacy, Playreading, and Women's Closet Drama, 1550–1700* (2004), and editor of *The Book of the Play: Playwrights, Stationers, and Readers in Early Modern England* (2006). She has published on closet drama and early modern women's plays in *The Blackwell Companion to Renaissance Drama* and *The Cambridge Companion to Early Modern Women's Writing*. She is preparing an edition of the Huntington manuscript of Lady Mary Wroth's 'Love's Victory' for The Other Voice in Early Modern Europe series.

Edward Town is a Leverhulme Post-Doctoral Research Fellow at the National Portrait Gallery working on the artistic, artisanal and architectural practices of late medieval and early modern London. He is the author of a number of articles in *The Burlington Magazine, Country Life* and other journals.

Susie West is Lecturer in Heritage Studies at the Open University. Her research interests centre on the English country house, its landscape setting, and private libraries of the seventeenth and eighteenth centuries. She is the author of *Understanding Heritage in Practice* (2010) and guides to Hardwick Old Hall and Prudhoe Castle.

Acknowledgements

This collection developed out of a conference, 'The Intellectual Culture of the English Country House' held at the University of Sussex and Petworth House between 13 and 15 July 2011. We are very grateful to the National Trust for allowing us to hold part of the conference in the magnificent setting of Petworth House, and to Andrew Loukes in particular for facilitating the event. We would also like to thank The Society for Renaissance Studies, the School of English and the University of Sussex Heritage Research Theme Fund for supporting the conference. Simon Davies, as ever, played an indispensable role as the conference organiser. Our thanks also go to Brian Cummings, Rob Iliffe, Barbara Kennedy, Katrina Marchant, Catherine Parsons, Paul Quinn and Angus Vine for helping to make it such an informative and enjoyable event. We would also like to thank all the contributors to the volume for their hard work in preparing their work for publication, especially those who tracked down such a rich array of images to adorn the volume. It has been a great pleasure to work with Manchester University Press, and we would like to thank Polly Bentham, Matthew Frost and Kim Walker for all their help.

Matthew Dimmock
Andrew Hadfield
Margaret Healy

Introduction: the intellectual culture of the English country house

Matthew Dimmock, Andrew Hadfield and Margaret Healy

Between 1500 and 1700 large-scale changes took place in England. London grew from a significant conurbation of some 50,000 people to one of the largest cities in Europe, an imperial entrepôt of more than half a million people, a ten-fold increase.[1] The population of England had grown in the same period from about 3 million in 1500 to 5.5 million in 1700, just less than doubling in size. This is a staggering development, especially as the rate of London's increase was based on immigration because the death rate outstripped the birth rate for the whole of this period, so unhealthy was life for ordinary people in the capital.[2]

As England was changing, the nature of designing and building houses was changing with it, and there was a dramatic increase in the number of substantial houses built throughout the country. Not only did the aristocracy start to erect buildings designed for more comfortable living, but such transformations in architectural possibilities meant that the gentry was also able to sustain a wide range of projects so that by the early seventeenth century every third village had a 'resident squire'.[3] Put in the most basic terms, large provincial constructions were no longer designed primarily for defence and hospitality. Rather, they were designed with everyday living, comfort and taste in mind. The basic design of large houses with a central hall heated by one fire in the middle of the room was superseded through technological improvements in heating and insulation. Advances in chimney manufacture enabled flues to be built so that a number of rooms could be heated and smoke directed upwards more efficiently.[4] Windows became more common and larger, letting more light into more rooms.[5] It became possible to build houses that were more comfortable and more desirable.

The growth of such building stimulated an interest in and market for interior design. The grand houses of many of those families that rose to prominence in the sixteenth century were adorned with tapestries, paintings, elaborate fireplaces, mouldings, ornate ceilings, as well as expensive furniture.[6] Such work could, of course, contribute in vital ways to the intellectual nature of the individual house, and owners did have their houses designed and stocked with objects that suited their own tastes and interests. Many, especially those of wealthy Protestants contained paintings, textiles and wall hangings that told stories of favourite Bible stories, such as the pictures of Jeroboam in the Dryden home at Canons Ashby, Northamptonshire, and the wall paintings telling the story of Hezekiah in Sir Thomas Smith's house, Hill Hall.[7] As Nicholas Cooper has pointed out, having pictures and carefully designed objects in the house 'is evidence ... of the growing visual education that would lead knowledgeable individuals, by the mid-seventeenth century, to see buildings and works of art not so much in terms of meaning as of style'.[8]

Early modern country houses were often founded on existing structures, transforming them from relatively uncomfortable medieval manor houses into grand provincial palaces for the elite. Such developments played a significant role in stimulating change. The country house became an emblem of, and a centre for, new developments in intellectual culture, and enabled the wider diffusion into English culture and practice of domestic and continental innovations in art, architecture, animal husbandry, gardening and a host of other fields. A useful case study is Petworth House in West Sussex, the southern seat of the Percies, the earls of Northumberland, and a location of some importance for two of the chapters and the first part of the Afterword in this volume. The house that stands today, celebrated extensively by Turner in the nineteenth century, was largely the creation of Charles Seymour, the 6th Duke of Somerset, who rebuilt it between 1688 and 1696 in a slightly later era of great reconstruction. The fortified medieval manor house that occupied this site (elements of which were incorporated into the later comprehensive remodelling) was a less ostentatious affair, one that had been augmented and renovated from the simple house that was found to be 'greatly ruined' when Henry Percy, the 8th Earl, was confined to it from 1574 for conspiring against the Crown.[9] Thereafter, through the tenures of the 9th, 10th and 11th Earls, the extensive surviving household accounts demonstrate that Petworth was rendered able to entertain the nobility and the local gentry in lavish style when required.[10]

The Percies had long been associated with treason and the 'old faith', and their restriction to the south was the primary motivating factor for Petworth's Tudor and Stuart prominence. It was while he was imprisoned in the Tower of London for apparent complicity in the Gunpowder Plot that Henry Percy, the 9th and 'Wizard' Earl, began to draw up and annotate elaborate plans for an entirely new house at Petworth.[11] Although this new vision would never be built (the reasons for its abandonment are unknown), the plans reveal a nobleman engaging fully with the intellectual ideas and innovations that were transforming country house culture in the early modern period. This was not to be a gaudy construction built simply 'for envious show' like those derided by Jonson in his celebration of Penshurst, but instead shows Northumberland's determination to adhere to classical architectural models of scale and space in order to create an environment suitable for scholarly study and experimentation (as discussed further in Alison McCann's Chapter 7): the newly refashioned estate would house pursuits from alchemical research and wide-ranging literary study to horse breeding.[12] It would also continue to function at the centre of the wider community, opening through an elaborate gatehouse of 'hewn stone', with a clock and a battlemented roof, into the town itself.[13]

The ambition is extraordinary: the Earl planned a series of interconnected and enclosed quadrangular courts paved in stone (the first to be considerable: 360 by 400 feet) surrounded by open and closed galleries whose walkways were to be floored with marble and lined with Doric pillars. Square towers marked the ends of a space marked 'Gallery' or 'Library' that was to be a remarkable 315 feet long, with doors of 20 feet in height marking the entrance to the Hall.[14] Meanwhile the Earl's annotations on his plans indicate a care to address lines of vision from gallery windows and a keenness to use specific building materials and techniques to reduce noise and maintain heat. Finally, all exterior facing walls were to be battlemented and 'garnished', the walls clad with local Horsham stone. The total cost carefully estimated by Northumberland's steward Robert Flood was £2,810.[15]

These plans were not an idle aristocrat's fancy: like many later Tudor and Stuart noblemen Northumberland was keen for his house to be an instrument as well as a manifestation of his learning. He had already engaged in rebuilding his smaller house at Syon, south of London, and brought typically assiduous learning to his practical experience. A list of books he intended to send to his friend Sir John Holles from the Tower, reproduced by Gordon Batho, is a compendium of up-to-date and necessary architectural knowledge. It includes Vitruvius, 'father of all the rest', Vignola, Jacques Androuet du Cerceau, Lorenzo Sirigatti, Jacques Perret, Philibert de l'Orme, Sebastian Serlio, Wendel Dietterlin, Leon B. Alberti and Palladio – as Gordon Batho remarks, 'in short, all the best of classical and Renaissance writings on architecture'.[16]

The spatial development of the country house exemplified in Northumberland's plans for Petworth produced two apparently opposite but actually interrelated effects. On the one hand there was a growth in the possibility of privacy as the wealthy, at least, could have their own rooms and did not have to spend quite as much time in the company of others.[17] Beyond their libraries, it became possible for men and women to have their own rooms for study and private devotion, or where they would choose to be alone with important members of the household such as secretaries and stewards, often known as 'closets'.[18] The possibility of private study increased the likelihood of the development of an intellectual culture in the private house. Closets could also serve as studies, as is made clear when a letter written by an associate of Sir Francis Godolphin described the heartbreak caused when a fire burned down most of his house in Cornwall, including 'his closet wherein was most of his writings'.[19] In fact it was only in the 1570s that the word 'study' was commonly used in inventories of houses, indicating that the creation of this separate room was now recognised as a major innovation in household design.[20]

Although the 9th Earl of Northumberland's plans to realise a new Petworth do not detail the upper floors of the building, a detailed inventory taken at his death in 1632 does give a useful sense of the luxury a primary country house residence was expected to encompass, and reveals what this particular gentleman kept in his closet. There are a careful mix of public and private spaces, and the major chambers were adorned with Ottoman carpets and decorated to specific colour schemes with elaborate furnishings bound with the Percy crescent.[21] Given the Earl's intellectual pursuits it is not surprising – here as in many other noble houses – that 'the Library was one of the most important rooms', containing sixty-four chests of books (their display on bookshelves was a later innovation), four globes, seventy-eight pictures ('Turks', 'Emperors' and others) and a cupboard of mathematical instruments.[22] In keeping with other gentlemanly studies, Northumberland's closet led off his personal bedchamber. It contained forty-four folio volumes, twenty-eight vellum books, and thirty-three pamphlets, 'with maps and other writings in a wainscot box separately'.[23] This closet was indeed the working intellectual heart of his country house and estate.

As Northumberland's unique plans for Petworth demonstrate, a prolonged period of peace and relative stability, the widespread consolidation of estate incomes due to more sophisticated means of land management, and a new openness to new and classical architectural ideas from the continent meant that country houses started to develop their own particular nature and character, created by an owner who saw it as his – or her – duty to help develop the character of the area. While London dominated the life of the nation, country houses often tried to foster particular regional identities, drawing on local loyalties to do so.

This is particularly evident in the growth of the 'country house poem' genre.[24] Such poems, dating from the early seventeenth century, were inaugurated by Amelia Lanyer's 'The Description of Cooke-ham' which laments the break-up of the ideal female community established by Margaret Clifford, Countess of Cumberland in Cookham, Berkshire. Lanyer provides a description of the house as an (idealised) intellectual centre which determines the character and nature of the surrounding area as the women are left alone to practise their particular brand of religious devotion:

> In these sweet woods how often did you walke,
> With Christ and his Apostles there to talke;

> Placing his holy Writ in some faire tree,
> To meditate what you therein did see.
> With *Moyses* you did mount his holy Hill,
> To know his pleasure, and performe his Will.
> With lowly *David* you did often sing,
> His holy Hymnes to Heavens Eternall King.
> And in sweet musicke did your soule delight
> To sound his prayses, morning, noone, and night.
> With blessed *Joseph* you did often feed
> Your pined brethren, when they stood in need.
> And that sweet Lady sprung from *Cliffords* race,
> Of noble *Bedfords* blood, faire stem of Grace;
> To honorable *Dorset* now espows'd,
> In whose fair breast true virtue then was hous'd:
> Oh what delight did my weake spirits find
> In those pure parts of her well framed mind[.][25]

The poem suggests that a marriage in the family leads to the demise of the community, a painful reminder that the country estate was never self-sufficient and that it had to be maintained through interaction with an external world that was often indifferent to its merits. Estates could only continue to exist if they had sufficient finances to preserve their bucolic world, which generally meant complicated marriage alliances. In his only country house poem, 'To Penshurst', Ben Jonson praises the Sidney family at Penshurst but reminds his readers that it is marriage that makes the world go round when the Sidney tenants send tribute 'By their ripe daughters, whom they would commend / This way to husbands' (the poem is considered in relation to the house in Edward Town's Chapter 4).[26] Marriage is also the central thread by which Andrew Marvell charts the long evolution of Nun Appleton from monastery to country house (a trajectory followed by many Tudor houses), the seat and retreat of Lord Fairfax, in his celebrated 'Upon Appleton House'.[27] Lanyer, more so than Jonson or Marvell, commends the intellectual nature of the world she has lost, the women speaking directly to the biblical figures they worship who feature in the poem alongside the nobles who determine and shape their world. Readers understand that this community has the power and ability to create a self-contained pious retreat in which the women are free to worship properly, disrupted only by the unwelcome intrusions of the outside world. What the speaker especially enjoys is not the architectural beauty of the house itself, nor the carefully manicured gardens and grounds, but the intellectual stimulation of the household, a sense of belonging to a community that nurtures its own and in which individuals grow together in spiritual understanding. Lanyer is celebrating a particular space in which women can develop together and readers would have known that she was idealising this life. Nevertheless, the poem registers an acute sense of loss based on a Utopian ideal, an understanding of what a well-run country house could provide for those fortunate enough to live there.

The development and brief flourishing of a genre of country house poetry in the early and mid-seventeenth century marks and charts the new prominence of such 'prodigy' houses, showing how they became emblems 'of a society conscious of its own achievement of a civilised way of living, and conscious also of the forces that threatened to undermine and overthrow that achievement'.[28] New emphases on learning and display, on Arcadian abundance and on writing a natural and permanent aristocracy into the landscape played their part in the work of poets from Lanyer and Jonson, through Carew and Herrick, to Marvell as they presented the country house and estate as a synecdoche for the English state. As a result of this new prominence, the intellectual culture that generated and was generated by the early modern country house is central to our understanding of this period as a whole, but its study also offers new perspectives on the ways this past informs conflicted attitudes to the countryside and its heritage today.

The volume begins with a succinct overview of the field by the historian of architecture, Maurice Howard, who issues a timely reminder of the crucial significance of the visual aspects of great houses and their collections in the early modern period. The profound religious, political and social developments of this time encouraged a new ethos of what the country estate represented, ensuring that by the eighteenth century the role of great houses as topoi of the imagination and 'Temples of the Arts' was well established. These 'power houses' hosted gatherings of intellectuals, functioning as centres of political discussion and scholarship as well as religious devotion, enshrining and promoting the status and influence of their patron owners.

Following Howard's opening chapter, the volume is organised into four interconnected parts. In Part I, Reconstructing the English Country House, Alden Gregory's discussion in Chapter 2 of Archbishop Warham's sumptuous palace at Otford in Kent amplifies how such architectural edifices functioned symbolically, presenting a carefully constructed public face for the owner. At first sight, a damp, waterlogged position just off the main road from London to Canterbury might seem an inauspicious location to erect a showy new house that even boasted privy chambers; however, as Gregory demonstrates, it enabled the Archbishop to capitalise on the hagiographic value of the fountain associated with Becket located there – bolstering his image as a latter-day Becket – and, furthermore, to display his holiness in the form of hospitality and largesse to passing travellers. In this way, Gregory argues, the house formed a symbolic buttress to Warham's waning powers. While little is left today of this princely edifice in Kent, even less remains to evidence the splendour of a Tudor mansion that was once a dominant site in the Oxfordshire political landscape. In Chapter 3 Matthew Neely investigates the fascinating project undertaken by the Bodleian Library aimed at reconstructing Rycote, the seat of the earls of Abingdon and their forebears since the reign of Henry VIII. As Neely describes, saving the house from historical oblivion has meant the painstaking piecing together of the past from a wide selection of sources ranging from archaeological evidence to engravings, sales catalogues of interior goods and furnishings, privy council records, pay books, letters and antiquaries' descriptions. In the final chapter of this section, Chapter 4, Edward Town illuminates the networks of patronage between two Jacobean mansions, Penshurst and Knole, demonstrating in the process how a poem, in this case Ben Jonson's 'To Penshurst', can function as an invaluable source in the reconstruction of the intellectual history of the country house.

In Part II, The Culture of the English Country House, Tara Hamling's study in Chapter 5 of the interior decoration of the long gallery at Lanhydrock House in Cornwall demonstrates how this magnificent space with its decorative plasterwork and complex iconography played a key role in the piety and politics of the seventeenth-century house. As Richard Simpson's examination of Sir Thomas Smith's Hill Hall in Essex reveals in Chapter 6, a rather different space, namely the stillhouse, with its vast collection of alchemical books and distillation vessels, was the prime intellectual hub of this household where the 'strange, wondrous and incredible things of nature' were subject to experimentation and an abundance of medicines were manufactured. Henry Percy, 9th Earl of Northumberland, clearly shared Smith's pronounced interests in alchemy and new science generally; and in Chapter 7 Alison McCann surveys the library and archive at Petworth House in Sussex, piecing together the concerns and activities of Thomas Harriot, the talented astronomer and mathematician whom the 9th Earl maintained in his household. In chapter 8, country house poetry again comes under the spotlight as Nicolle Jordan brings ecocritical methodology to bear on the verses of Anne Finch, Countess of Winchelsea. Adopting this innovative approach, Jordan demonstrates how Finch's estate poems register significant changes in the political and natural landscape of post-Restoration England. As Elizabeth Zeman Kolkovich illuminates in her study of the Elvetham House entertainment for Elizabeth I in Chapter 9, printed accounts of newsworthy events, such as this one in Hampshire, can also function as important sources in the quest to reconstruct the once formidable but now sadly obscured intellectual culture of country estates.

In Part III, The Country House Library and its Intellectual Significance, James Raven provides an informative introduction in Chapter 10 to early modern book collecting and the relationships among books, their owners and households. He argues that bibliomania – the great passion for books that developed in the late seventeenth century – was motivated by a range of factors including intellectual interests, an urge to improvement, practical problem solving and entertainment; but prestige, family pride and the desire to bequeath a collection played significant roles too. A new emphasis on education in this period certainly meant that country house occupants increasingly comprised scholars and connoisseurs of books. In Chapter 11 Susie West addresses the material conditions of keeping a book collection within the early modern house using a methodology drawn from architectural history. In the process she offers important new case studies of pre-1700 book collecting by Norfolk gentry families, foregrounding the evidence for book rooms and other spaces that might have housed collections prior to the emergence of libraries. Hannah DeGroff's study in Chapter 12 examines book collecting by the earls of Howard and their families in Naworth Castle in Cumbria. She reminds us of the palimpsest-like mode through which nearly all aristocratic book collections were formed and of the variety of textual interactions that inevitably occurred in complex households. Her approach provides valuable insights into the personal library and reading habits of an aristocratic woman inhabiting the house in the late seventeenth century, namely the 2nd Countess of Carlisle.

The final Part of the volume, IV, Case Study: Wilton House, narrows its lens to focus on the estate bestowed by Henry VIII on Sir William Herbert, 1st Earl of Pembroke, at the dissolution of the monasteries. As these chapters reveal, the house and gardens of Wilton Abbey underwent cumulative early modern transformations, reflecting the particular intellectual passions of its successive owners – all famous patrons of the arts. In the celebrated re-design of the Wilton garden in the 1630s involving Inigo Jones, a cypress grove was laid out to resemble an amphitheatre and, as Marta Straznicky argues in Chapter 13, this feature suggests a rich interplay between architecture, landscape and the theatrical arts at Wilton – a prime site of English Arcadianism. Straznicky reflects that the most important function of the amphitheatre structure might well have been the prospect of the estate that it offered, transforming Wilton into a spectacle representing order, wealth and power at the height of the family's political influence. As Louise Noble writes in Chapter 14, Wilton served as a gathering place for writers, thinkers and scientists who shared creative and intellectual interests and Protestant convictions – the Wilton Circle. Noble's focus is on the scientific and technological preoccupations of the Circle, and in particular its concern with hydrological innovation and finding a practical solution for managing and distributing rural water. She describes how the art of floating meadows was both an aesthetically pleasing and pragmatic response to the latter need and illustrates how the 'progressive Pembrokes' enthusiastically embraced the new technology. In Chapter 15, Anne Myers demonstrates how Wilton House's status as both a converted monastery and an early English masterpiece of English Palladian style has made it particularly susceptible to the emphases of both antiquarian and aesthetic modes of architectural literacy; as she foregrounds, this elicits the same interpretive tensions between concerns about human history and others about visual experience that are registered in seventeenth-century country house poems.

The volume concludes with comments and reflections from a curator, a conservator and an archivist working for the National Trust today, a reminder that the intellectual history of the country house continues into the future.

Notes

1   E. A. Wrigley and R. S. Schofield, *The Population History of England, 1541–1871: A Reconstruction* (Cambridge: Cambridge University Press, 1981), Appendix 5.

2   Steve Rappaport, *Worlds Within Worlds: Structures of Life in Sixteenth-Century London* (Cambridge: Cambridge University Press, 1989), pp. 67–76.

3   Nicholas Cooper, *Houses of the Gentry, 1480–1680* (New Haven, CT: Yale University Press, 1999), p. 5; Olive Cook and A. F. Kersting, *The English Country House* (London: Thames and Hudson, 1974), Chapters 2–4.

4   Maurice Howard, *The Early Tudor Country House: Architecture and Politics, 1490–1550* (London: George Philip, 1987), p. 17.

5   Howard, *Early Tudor Country House*, pp. 134–5.

6   For one especially impressive collection, see Santina M. Levey, *An Elizabethan Inheritance: The Hardwick Textiles* (Swindon: National Trust, 1998).

7   Tara Hamling, *Decorating the Godly Household: Religious Art in Post-Reformation Britain* (New Haven, CT: Yale University Press, 2010); Anon., *Canons Ashby* (Swindon: National Trust, n.d.), pp. 20–1; Paul Drury, with Richard Simpson, *Hill Hall: A Singular House Devised by a Tudor Intellectual* (London: Society of Antiquaries, 2009), pp. 180–213.

8   Cooper, *Houses of the Gentry*, p. 319.

9   Carole Levin, 'Percy, Henry, Eighth Earl of Northumberland (c.1532–1585)', *Oxford Dictionary of National Biography* (Oxford: Oxford University Press, 2004), www.oxforddnb.com/view/article/21938.

10   See G. R. Batho (ed.), *The Household Papers of Henry Percy* (London: Royal Historical Society, 1962) and Lord Leconfield, *Petworth Manor in the Seventeenth Century* (London: Oxford University Press, 1954).

11   Detailed and reproduced in Gordon Batho, 'The Percies at Petworth, 1574–1632', *Sussex Archaeological Collections*, xcv (1958), 1–27, especially pp. 22–5. The original plans are now sadly lost.

12   As represented in the scale and classifications of library as well as the plans: see Gordon Batho, 'The Library of the "Wizard" Earl: Henry Percy Ninth Earl of Northumberland (1564–1632), *The Library*, s5–XV, 4 (1960), 246–61.

13   Batho, 'The Percies at Petworth', p. 22.

14   Batho, 'The Percies at Petworth', p. 23.

15   Batho, 'The Percies at Petworth', p. 25.

16   Batho, 'The Percies at Petworth', p. 25.

17   See Lena Cowen Orlin, *Locating Privacy in Tudor London* (Oxford: Oxford University Press, 2007).

18   Alan Stewart, 'Epistemologies of the Early Modern Closet', in *Close Readers: Humanism and Sodomy in Early Modern England* (Princeton, NJ: Princeton University Press, 1997), pp. 161–87.

19   Cooper, *Houses of the Gentry*, p. 300.

20   Cooper, *Houses of the Gentry*, p. 300.

21   Batho, 'The Percies at Petworth', p. 19.

22   Batho, 'The Percies at Petworth', pp. 20–1.

23   Batho, 'The Percies at Petworth', p. 22.
24   Alastair Fowler, *The Country House Poem: A Cabinet of Seventeenth-Century Estate Poems and Related Items* (Edinburgh: Edinburgh University Press, 1994).
25   Aemilia Lanyer, 'The Description of Cooke-ham', in David Norbrook and Henry Woudhuysen (eds), *The Penguin Book of Renaissance Verse* (Harmondsworth: Penguin, 1992), lines 81–98 (p. 416).
26   Ben Jonson, 'To Penshurst', in Norbrook and Woudhuysen (eds), *Penguin Book of Renaissance Verse*, lines 54–5 (p. 422).
27   Andrew Marvell, 'Upon Appleton House, To My Lord Fairfax', in Nigel Smith (ed.), *The Poems of Andrew Marvell* (London: Pearson Longman, 2007), pp. 210–41.
28   G. R. Hibbard, 'The Country House Poem of the Seventeenth Century', *Journal of the Warburg and Courtauld Institutes*, 19:1/2 (1956), 159–74, p. 159.

1

'The Lordship of the Eye': country houses as the setting for intellectual enquiry in the early modern period

Maurice Howard

This chapter will make the case for the importance of the visual aspect of the great house, in terms of both the building and the things within it, as a prerequisite for the intellectual activity that flourished there. The building and furnishing of country houses were the result of complex processes, through the constraints of time and money, and in the self-fashioning of patrons who negotiated deference to the past with the pressures of current fashion. It would be wrong of course to suppose that the house as the centre of intellectual engagement was entirely new to the early modern period, but the political, religious and social developments of the time encouraged a new ethos of what the country house represented. The increasing dominance of London as the centre of business and pleasure made the sense of the house on a landed estate as a place not quite of retreat but as somewhere with a view towards posterity that was different from the continual upgrading of lifestyle in the metropolis. By the eighteenth century the role of great houses as 'Temples of the Arts' was well-established.[1]

The literature on the country house stresses two principal ways in which the intellectual life was expressed, one symbolic, the other practical. On the one hand they have been characterised as 'power houses', no longer defensible structures as in times of internal conflict during the medieval period, but as centres of political discussion, and as the expression of the high status and influence of their owners.[2] On the other hand, the evidence of increasingly significant areas of private, internal space led to the provision of rooms such as closets, studies and libraries where objects were gathered for their curiosity and intellectual value, and scholars encouraged to discourse and write about them. The visual appearance of these country houses always bore witness to decisions that had been made to engage the mind and delight the eye. What follows here will engage with four aspects of the way in which that visual *persona* of the house was embodied in the outward aspect, the interior spaces and the objects gathered within them. First, external appearances, the 'architecture' of the building, absorbed new and fashionable styles but these co-habited with, indeed engaged in a dialogue with, features from the past that were deemed to demand respect and understanding. Second, the daily practice of religious devotion within the house, once through the intercession of the priest (and thus for the domestic congregation a fixed and obedient experience) was now in the post-Reformation world a very different practice. Individuals of the Protestant household sought their own salvation, still sometimes with a designated place of worship but also through a range of visual prompts in the daily spaces of their lives. Devotion became more of a spiritual and intellectual exercise through a daily reminder, and thus under constant review. Third, collections of objects became new reflections of pretensions to scholarship, becoming the focus of ongoing discussion through a dynamic between past and present. A verifiable national past was constructed through the making of family genealogies for display, heraldic portraits and the collection of archaeological artefacts, while an international identity came from the buying of ancient Greek and Roman antiquities, along with modern paintings of great classical stories. Finally, the representation of the house and estate itself was a thinking and demanding exercise; the capturing of the house in paintings, estate maps and book illustration involved an imaginative choice of viewpoint that depended on visual recall and often represented the building in ways that were physically impossible to experience.

The historiography of writing on the concept of the country house is now huge and each phase of interpretation has reflected the preoccupations of its age. Country houses have long been assumed of course to have 'a life' and the traditional way of grasping that life was to see it in terms of the domestic. The great volumes put together from H. Avray Tipping's articles in *Country Life* and published by that journal in the 1920s and 1930s were collectively called *English Homes* and reached a market that only owners of such places and their friends could ever imagine, so relatively inaccessible were these huge buildings to general public at that period.[3] When after the Second World War many great houses first opened their doors to the public either under the new ownership of the National Trust or through their private owners, the idea of 'home' was still retained. Visitors from the 1940s through to the 1970s were shown a range of rooms sometimes rather randomly displayed and set out; the pervasive sense of the owner just having left this or that space was born and often remains in these houses today, even though the expectations and demands of tourism have changed radically over the years.[4]

From the 1970s, and particularly from the moment of the publication of Mark Girouard's *Life in the English Country House: A Social and Architectural History* in

1978, there grew a new enthusiasm for the investigation and presentation of the house from top to bottom, from the servants' domain below stairs to the attics, across gender roles and opening up the consideration of these buildings as the centres of great estates.[5] The term 'machine for living in', coined by the modernist architect Le Corbusier with regard to everyday housing, was adopted as a useful way of looking at all domestic structures in terms of their functionality, suitability and use. The great houses were no longer 'timeless' and their collections simply accretive but were viewed as historically subject to changes over the centuries, both in the social structure (in master–servant and gender relationships) and in the habitual use of the house (such things as the times of formal dining and the places of recreation). It was an image of the country house as a more inclusive place, even if the truth was that as the last half-century or so of pre-Second World War houses came into public viewing (the homes of industrialists and newspaper tycoons, like Cragside of the 1870s to 1880s in Northumberland, or Castle Drogo of 1910–30 in Devon, both owned by the National Trust) in the world of the post-1960s, the pre-war systems of deference were now remote, although only a couple of generations in the past.[6] Recent developments in this social history of the house have encompassed huge political and social questions, most notably the issue of slavery as a means of paying for these buildings.[7] This kind of research will continue and we are all the richer for it.

Country houses were arguably at the forefront of debates about architectural style in the early modern period and in their time they carried forward the most profound debates about architecture's purposes and objectives. Amongst the plethora of European nations, and even amongst the countries of the Protestant north, Great Britain has a singular architectural history in that between the Reformation of the 1530s and 1540s and the coming of the Industrial Revolution the occurrence of great public building projects (that is to say churches, palaces, places of public assembly such as town halls) was relatively rare and often resulting from the accident of fire.[8] Most notable of course was the rebuilding of St Paul's Cathedral and the City of London churches after the fire of 1666. There were determined building campaigns at royal palaces between the building mania of Henry VIII (mainly in the second half of his reign, from 1529 to 1547) and the passion for building of George IV (from his coming of age in the 1780s until his death in 1830). But there was no Versailles, no focus of absolutist royal authority. In general, with the abbeys gone by the Acts of Dissolution of 1536 and 1539, great cathedrals were first neglected and then restored, and only a small percentage of medieval parish churches entirely rebuilt. That is to say that there is a case for arguing that for three hundred years, the country house was the forum for intellectual debate about architectural decorum in a way no other category of building could claim. It is significant the small body of published material on buildings that could fall under the broad category of 'treatise' in the sixteenth and seventeenth centuries mainly engages with debate on the house, from the practical advice of Andrew Boorde in the 1540s to the writings of Sir Henry Wotton and Sir Roger North.[9] Other than the royal palaces (where often they are preoccupied with the description of ceremony and its physical trappings) foreign observers travelling the country record great houses, especially if they are new and built by some present incumbent of power, far more often than other buildings.[10] Within the carapace of the great house, collections of books and manuscripts, the gathering of scholars around enlightened patrons, the writing of poetry and drama about the house in the guise of classical example were allowed to flourish. For learning and understanding the heritage of literature and political debate is nurtured by the visual, by the perceived equivalence of rationality and visual proportion, and of the acknowledgement of a frame of reference for the building's style, whether aspiring to be classical or redolent of the British past, which owners, guests, literary dependants all shared.

In turning to the visual aspect of the house, simply experiencing its architecture required a knowledge of shared example and vocabulary, most notably in the sixteenth and seventeenth centuries when first heraldry and then classicism, initially introduced to support and frame heraldic achievement, expected an understanding of certain ground rules. Heraldry is a practice which puts a concept that is simple and instantly communicative to a subtle effect through demanding complex hard-wired knowledge on the part of the viewer.[11] Its colours are bright, immediate and fully saturated, their juxtaposition making for intense but instantly recognisable patterns of ornament. But the message is highly sophisticated; the viewer has to know the intricacies and the peculiarities of the owner's coat of arms or personal badge in order to appreciate and acknowledge a sense of shared rank and status, of the network of intermarriage and local identity, of seeing what belongs to whom. In sixteenth-century England heraldry was apparent throughout the household, on objects both static and sometimes brought out purely for display (furniture, plate and textiles) and constantly on the move (most notably on the clothes of servants). On the actual fabric of the country house however the message of heraldry was twofold. The display of the coat of arms over a gatehouse or entry to the screens passage was an instant affirmation of ownership and command of power (Figure 1.1). Some Tudor courtiers were careful to put the royal arms above their own so as to underline the fact that they held power under the sovereign. Whenever the use of heraldry infringed convention or the message was at all ambiguous the situation became dangerous for the perpetrator; the fall from power of both the Duke of Buckingham in 1521 and the Earl of Surrey in 1546 engaged with evidence at their trials from their country houses that they had overstepped their claims to royal title through the misuse of heraldry.[12] The second message that was a particular feature of building was the way in which heraldry defined notions of space, or rather the liminal points at which the traveller through

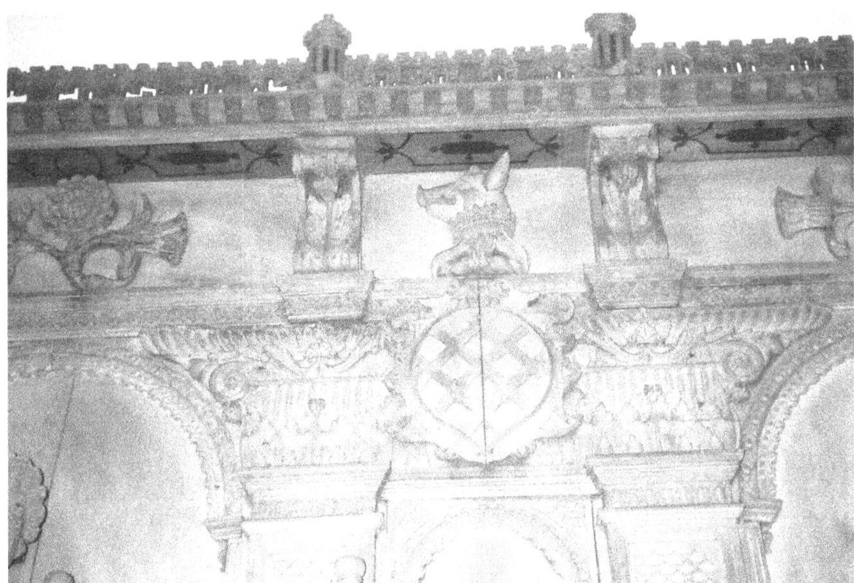

1.1 Haddon Hall, Derbyshire. Panelling, c.1600 in the Long Gallery. Family arms and crests were among the new language of the classical articulation of the interior.

the house was expected to perceive changes of purpose from public to private, using the owner's personal arms as a physical sign that a barrier was before them beyond which they could not venture. The understanding of colour and design principles through heraldry was the preamble to a sophisticated understanding of ways to interpret differences and inferences within the house. In many country houses the very decoration of the room space either side of a door will mark a difference of domestic purpose, the door frame invariably belonging to the decoration of the room it is in, rather than that is leading to, underlining the entity of the space in which the viewer is standing.

The visual language of classical architecture first appeared in order to frame and support the heraldic device.[13] The use of paired columns, half-columns or pilasters to frame coats of arms could physically separate the message conveyed by heraldry from the rest of the wall or give a frame to the overmantel. With its obvious likeness to the title-page of a book, there was a sense that this was something to be 'read' and thereby understood. This selective use of classicism continued at many houses in the development of the classical stone or plastered porch before an otherwise plain – perhaps brick – façade and, by the later sixteenth century, by the coming of the 'frontispiece', still essentially heraldic even if the bravado of the complex use of the classical orders now overwhelmed the heraldic shield.[14] The wider and more consistent application of the language of classicism across whole façades of buildings emerges with the knowledge of a

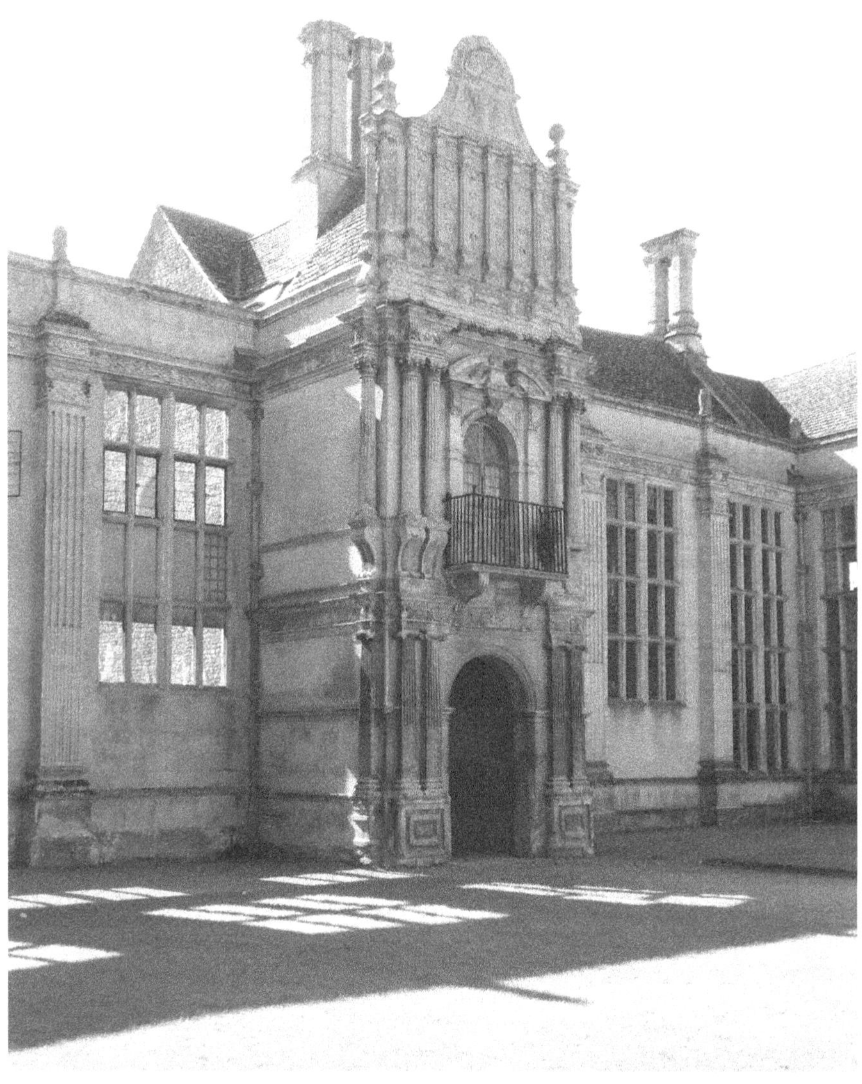

1.2 Kirby Hall, Northamptonshire, courtyard completed c.1575. The continuous applied pilasters around the court give unity to the different facades and the porch is replete with both classical and biblical allusions.

group of sixteenth-century patrons who commissioned highly articulate houses, with a grasp of classicism embraced with enthusiasm but only fully understood by degrees. The classical language imposes order not only by underlining symmetry but also by instilling the governance of proportion, so that a window embrasure relates proportionally to its bay, and the choice of Order reflects function and purpose. The final result should impose a general organisation to a given façade that overrides the various spaces and room heights behind it. Three houses of the period 1550–75 demonstrate different ways of understanding and using this classical language. By the rules of engagement that would demand a strict application of proportion and order, the façade of Longleat, as completed in the 1570s, is imperfect because the window openings are too big; the continuous giant order around the inner façades of the courtyard of Kirby Hall (as shown in Figure 1.2), finished by about 1575, still pays respect to the differing functions of hall and service areas either side of the entrance porch; and only Hill Hall, which began to be rebuilt by Sir Thomas Smith in the 1550s and was still undergoing change at his death in 1575, with its very particular French sources, comes close to the appearance of a singular design.[15] But all these great houses have one thing in common: they demonstrate the consultation with the book, namely the architectural treatise since by direct transcription or at one or two stages of imaginative 'remove' they all have direct sources in treatises from Italy and France, and pattern books from the Netherlands. We have very little evidence of the discussion between patrons and architects but considerable indications of debates between the patrons themselves, both at the level of exchanging books and knowledge and through the sending of skilled craftsmen from one to the other in order to realise their various conceptions of their individual buildings. The process was always individualistic and imaginative, betraying individual choice which might well override the tyranny of the book as authority. Nor did the language of the classical stand still; it was modulated by changing fashions and adaptation to local interpretations of its idioms. The architect Robert Smythson's work at Longleat in the 1570s was one species of getting the language right, applying the three major Orders of architecture through three floors and consistently across the building, if applied in quite shallow relief. When he moves on to Wollaton Hall in the 1580s the language has been infused with recently published ornament by Flemish artists; now the ornament is more crowded and exuberant and while symmetry is still dominant it is expressed now much more through the light and shadow of boldly projecting corner towers and a broken but echoing skyline.[16] Within these houses, we discover the first invasions of architectural panelling where a consistent dado and applied pilasters around the room bring an order into which doors and fireplaces have to be fitted, to take their consigned place. Eventually the interior order of architecture became the framing device for formal arrangements of furniture and the 'outer' frames of collections of pictures but it is notable that some of the earliest architectural interiors were meant to be viewed in their uncompromising and often bare entirety. The famous room called the 'Haynes Grange', now at the Victoria and Albert Museum, may have originally been such a space. It is as if the book of architecture is laid open for us, to admire the patron's understanding and claims to erudition.[17]

On first thought it might seem that the role of the country house in the post-Reformation world was part of the secularisation of so many aspects of daily life. The despoiling of the monasteries, the greater proportion of which became domestic dwellings large and small, might seem a very deliberate act of vandalism and all the evidence shows that on the whole the highest classes did not desist, or feel any qualms about destruction and adaptation. But not only did many houses continue to have chapels for private, domestic worship, it could be argued that there was a new responsibility of the owner to lead and guide the family in prayer and beyond the immediate family, the household altogether. The father as 'priest' was necessarily authoritarian but also encouraging of personal responsibility. The chapel itself took on different guises, indeed different situations within the body of the house over time. It moved from the isolated situations of the late middle ages, at the ends of wings of the rambling courtyard house of the time to the enfolding of chapels within the heart of the house in the Elizabethan period. Then, in the early seventeenth century and in the grandest, most aristocratic houses, it returned to a place at some distance from the hall and the everyday working spaces of the house and often was decorated with splendour.[18] This makes the appearance of the few Puritan (or often designated 'Cromwellian') chapels that survive all the more surprising. But that is only one half of the story. The notion of religious observance, of catching the eye and through that the mind to rehearse the central biblical stories was placed all over the house, on overmantels (e.g. Figure 1.3), on textiles, in plasterwork on ceilings, on the objects handed around and used in everyday rituals such as dining.[19] Sitting beside an overmantel with a biblical narrative on it might prompt unspoken daily prayer or simply be the object of the daily reminder of faith. It is hard for us now to fully understand the simple presence of these aids to devotion; art historians have sometimes been hooked on establishing sightlines and optimum places for 'reading' the plasterwork of a Long Gallery, perhaps underestimating the sense of contemporaries' familiarity with these stories and their ready duplication in printed texts for an immediate reminder of their significance.[20]

The extent to which British patrons understood and engaged with the literature on the visual arts emanating from Italy and elsewhere in the early modern period is a hotly debated issue. If part of that debate has been about conceptions of architecture, it is also to do with moveable objects within the house, decorated with classical symbolism, dependent on the configurations of the pattern book but leading in the end to the possession of objects that have primarily been gathered together because they are stimulating, referential, even beautiful (by whatever common currency of such value determined that). The emergence of the kind of collecting that we would now recognise as indicative of the owner's discrimination and taste is equally contested.[21] However, if the evidence of inventories is one significant marker of the practice of collecting (and letters between patrons, between patrons and their agents, that define and

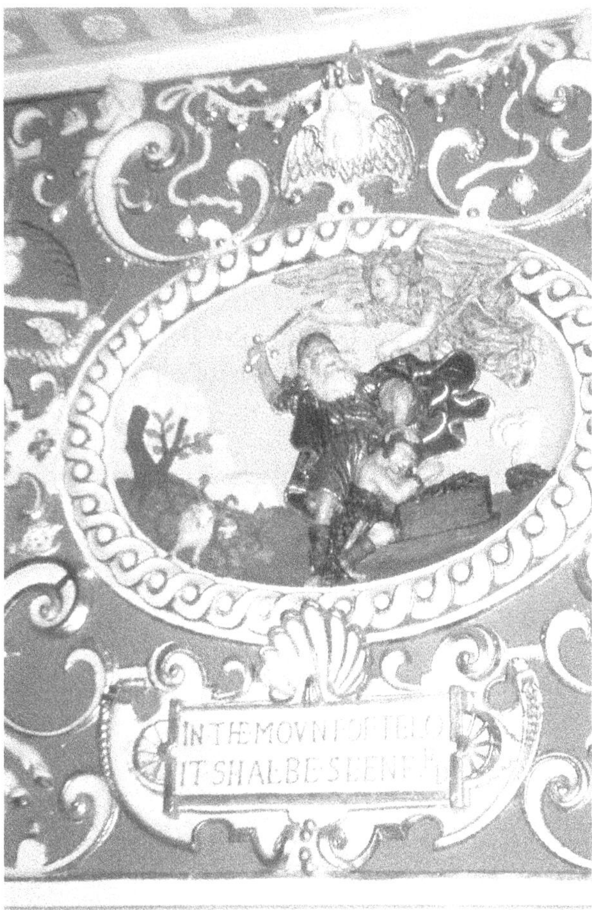

1.3 Boston Manor, west London. Overmantel of the Sacrifice of Isaac in the Great Chamber, 1623.

explore an ongoing dialogue and the circumstances of commissioning really only begin to appear in the seventeenth century) there is a marked shift over the course of a century from one kind of gathering objects to another. All collections are to some extent serendipitous but there is certainly a perception amongst certain early seventeenth-century patrons that particular examples of this or that artist, this or that subject-matter, is missing from the collection. Early and mid-sixteenth-century inventories record images of religious themes that are largely a residue of the past, but even after the Reformation, portable and now idolatrous images are not only sometimes retained but even sometimes clearly newly commissioned.[22] Then increasingly there are portraits of owners and their families, their contemporaries and increasingly copied images of the great and famous from across Europe, and sometimes these are copies by artists of international renown. The development of sets of portraits, originating probably in royal palaces in the middle ages in large-scale, and often sculpted, form, into the kinds of sets we still see surviving in some Elizabethan long galleries were part of one very significant contemporary debate, that of inventing a historical record of the country's past which bolstered prevailing political regimes.[23] In Elizabethan times there are many examples of what we might call discriminating taste, with certain patrons buying to order abroad, commissioning a special and famous painter, such as the portrait demanded of the Venetian artist Paolo Veronese by Robert Dudley, Earl of Leicester of his nephew Sir Philip Sidney. Leicester's collecting habits reflected his political tasks at Court, notably his interest in the art of the Low Countries in the last phase of his life when he was active there.[24] In the seventeenth century buyers were interested in collecting in a way that manifestly was competitive but also sought to echo the collecting habits of the ancient world through knowledge of texts about them. Great patrons such as the Earl and Countess of Arundel, the Duke of Buckingham and Charles I worked through ambassadors and agents, seeking opportunities to buy already-formed collections as others disposed of them, and accepting and presenting works of art internationally as the acknowledgement of a shared identity with other collectors.[25]

When the antiquary and librarian John Leland described the buildings he encountered in the England of the 1540s he did so as the traveller on foot, walking over bridges into towns, passing beneath the gate of country houses, seeing just one experience at a time, one façade at a time.[26] As the sixteenth and seventeenth centuries progressed owners of country houses needed both textual and visual means to complete the full 'view' of the house and ultimately enable that view to be carried in the head and reconsidered when absent from the site. The sense that country houses had become a *topos* in the imagination is shown by the emergence of the country house poem which recognised the values of the past when faced with the transient glamour of the present and inculcated a sense of the virtue of the owner through the life, the behaviour that was carried on at the country property.[27] Visually the house, especially if it was a post-Reformation family acquisition, needed to be set down in terms of its dimensions and those of the land around it. Estate plans fulfilled this function and the more sophisticated of them drew the house not in an abbreviated, symbolic way but with particular distinctive features to the point where they really do record complexities of the structure; in the case of some ex-monastic transformations they are our only record of immediate, post-dissolution adaptation and repair.[28] Between patron and architect the new house, or substantial refurbishment of an old one, had to be plotted with some exactness, both to make the intentions clear to those who were to build it, and as a kind of legal document whose precision became a point of reference.[29] The orthogonal projection of façade and plan provided this and a form of precise orthogonal precision would have been evident to patrons who saw an early edition of Palladio's *I Quattro Libri* of 1570, where he regularised and corrected the idiosyncrasies of his own achieved buildings to provide the template of good order and decorum. From this point though there was a necessary leap into the imagined view, and the development of techniques of perspective that helped give the viewer a sense of the real experience of viewing the house or entering, then being enclosed by, a room.[30] John Smythson's drawing of the marble closet at Bolsover, from the beginning of the seventeenth century, may be the earliest perspectivised view of a room, and revealingly, it is a room vaulted and clad with expensive – or mock expensive – materials, a room where the space is small but the concept grand. John Thorpe's imagined houses seek to express through perspective a full external and volumetric quality, with swelling bay windows and complex, faceted surfaces.[31] Crucially, these are seen from a further leap of the eye, that of the bird's-eye view, here only slightly raised off the ground, but on the path to later seventeenth-century views of actual great houses in their landscapes, painted by such masters as Jan Siberechts and engraved in the volumes of Kyp and Knyff. This seeing of the house from afar was a way of stretching the power to see through the imagination and thus of thinking of the house as a whole in its landscape. Such a concept would have been the starting-point for many in-house discussions of the ability of the eye and the thinking mind behind it. Seeing the house with such imagination was something that Henry Wotton describes in his 1624 book, pushing the eye to see further than it really could to contribute to the growing debate about the place of the country house in its broadest intellectual context:

> Some again may bee said to be Optical? Such I meane as concerne the *Properties* of a well chosen *Prospect*: which I shall call the *Royaltie of Sight*. For there is a *Lordship* (as it were) of the *Feete*, wherein the Master doth much ioy when he walketh about the *Line* of his own *Possessions*: So there is a *Lordship* likewise of the Eye which being a raunging, and Imperious, and (I might say) *Usurping Sence*, can indure no narrow *circumscription*, but must be fedde, both with extent and varietie.[32]

Notes

1　The phrase is taken from the title of the article by Gervase Jackson-Stops in Gervase Jackson-Stops (ed.), *The Treasure Houses of Britain: Five Hundred Years of Private Patronage and Art Collecting* (New Haven, CT and London: Yale University Press, 1985), pp. 14–21.

2　Mark Girouard, in Jackson-Stops (ed.), *Treasure Houses of Britain*, pp. 22–7.

3　H. Avray Tipping, *English Homes*, 9 vols (London and New York: Country Life, 1921–29).

4　See especially, Peter Mandler, *The Fall and Rise of the Stately Home* (New Haven, CT and London: Yale University Press, 1997).

5　Mark Girouard, *Life in the English Country House: A Social and Architectural History* (New Haven, CT and London: Yale University Press, 1978).

6　On Cragside, see Nikolaus Pevsner and Ian Richmond, *The Buildings of England: Northumberland*, 2nd revised edition (Harmondsworth: Penguin, 1992), pp. 244–6; on

Castle Drogo, see Bridget Cherry and Nikolaus Pevsner, *The Buildings of England: Devon*, 2nd revised edition (Harmondsworth: Penguin, 1989), pp. 245–7.

7   See Madge Dresser and Andrew Hann (eds), *Slavery and the British Country House* (Swindon: English Heritage Publications, 2013).

8   These dates are the parameters of John Summerson's seminal book, *Architecture in Britain 1530 to 1830* (Harmondsworth: Penguin, 1953) with many subsequent editions. This is not to deny the great number of exisiting and lost public buildings, first surveyed by Malcolm Airs, *Tudor and Jacobean: A Guide and a Gazetteer* (London: Barrie and Jenkins, 1982) and discussed in Maurice Howard, *The Building of Elizabethan and Jacobean England* (New Haven, CT and London: Yale University Press, 2007).

9   Andrew Boorde, *A Compendyous Regyment or A Dietary of Helth made in Mountpyllier, compiled by Andrew Boorde of Physycke Doctour* (London, 1542); Henry Wotton, *The Elements of Architecture collected by Henry Wotton Knight from the Best Authors and Examples* (London, 1624); Roger North, *Of Building, Roger North's Writings on Architecture*, eds H. Colvin and J. Newman (Oxford: Oxford University Press, 1981).

10   Notably *Thomas Platter's Travels in England, 1599*, ed. C. Williams (London: Cape, 1937), 'Diary of the Journey of Philip Julius, Duke of Stettin-Pomerania, Through England in the Year 1602', eds G. von Bulow and W. Powell, *Transactions of the Royal Historical Society*, n.s. 6 (1892), and Hentzner's *A Journey into England in the Year 1598*, ed. H. Walpole (Edinburgh, 1881).

11   See Maurice Howard and Tessa Murdoch, '"Armes and Bestes": Tudor and Stuart Heraldry', in Olga Dmitrieva and Tessa Murdoch (eds), *Treasures of the Royal Courts: Tudors, Stuarts and the Russian Tsars* (London: Victoria and Albert Museum, 2013), pp. 56–67.

12   Barbara J. Harris, 'The Trial of the Third Duke of Buckingham, a Revisionist View', *American Journal of Legal History*, 20 (1976), 15–26, and her subsequent monograph, *Edward Stafford, Third Duke of Buckingham 1478–1521* (Stanford, CA: Stanford University Press, 1986); Peter R. Moore, 'The Heraldic Charge against the Earl of Surrey, 1546–7', *English Historical Review*, 116 (2001), 557–83.

13   Vaughan Hart, 'A Peece Rather of Good Heraldry, than of Architecture: Heraldry and the Orders of Architecture as Joint Emblems of Chivalry', *RES: Anthropology and Aesthetics*, 23 (1993), 52–66.

14   Maurice Howard, 'From Gatehouse to Frontispiece in Sixteenth-Century England', in Monique Chatenet and Claude Mignot (eds), *Le Génie du Lieu: La Réception du Langage Classique en Europe (1540–1650)* (Paris: Picard, 2013), pp. 175–88.

15   On Longleat and Kirby, Mark Girouard, *Elizabethan Architecture: Its Rise and Fall 1540–1640* (New Haven, CT and London: Yale University Press, 2009), *passim*; on Smith's house, Paul Drury with Richard Simpson, *Hill Hall: A Singular House Devised by a Tudor Intellectual* (London: Society of Antiquaries, 2009).

16   See Girouard, *Elizabethan Architecture*, *passim*.

17   For the latest discoveries on the complex setting for this room, see Manolo Guerci, 'John Osborne, the Salisbury House Porticus and the Haynes Grange Room', *The Burlington Magazine*, 148 (2006), 15–24.

18   On this topic, Annabel Ricketts, *The English Country House Chapel: Building a Protestant Tradition* (Reading: Spire, 2007).

19   Tara Hamling, *Decorating the Godly Household: Religious Art in Post-Reformation Britain* (New Haven, CT and London: Yale University Press, 2010); Richard L. Williams, 'Collecting and Religion in Late Sixteenth-Century England', in Edward Chaney (ed.), *The Evolution of English Collecting: Reception of Italian Art in the Tudor and Stuart Periods* (New Haven, CT and London: Yale University Press, 2003), pp. 159–200.

20 Tara Hamling, 'To see or not to see? The Presence of Religious Imagery in the Protestant Household', *Art History*, 30 (2007), 170–97.

21 On collecting, see Chaney (ed.), *The Evolution of English Collecting*.

22 Susan Foister, 'Paintings and Other Works of Art in Sixteenth-Century English Inventories', *The Burlington Magazine*, 123 (1981), 273–82, and Williams, 'Collecting and Religion'.

23 Of published material, see Susan Foister, 'Edward Alleyn's Picture Collection', in A. Reid and R. Maniura (eds), *Edward Alleyn: Elizabethan Actor, Jacobean Gentleman*, exhibition catalogue (London: Dulwich College Picture Gallery, 1994), pp. 33–61. I am also indebted to the current researches of Catherine Daunt at the National Portrait Gallery.

24 Elizabeth Goldring, 'A Portrait of Sir Philip Sidney by Veronese at Leicester House', *The Burlington Magazine*, 154 (2012), 548–54.

25 Robert Hill, 'The Ambassador as Art Agent: Sir Dudley Carleton and Jacobean Collecting', in Chaney (ed.), *The Evolution of English Collecting*, pp. 240–55.

26 The standard text for Leland's work remains L. Toulmin-Smith, *The Itinerary of John Leland in or about the Years 1535–43*, 5 vols (London: Centaur, 1964). John Chandler's introduction to *John Leland's Itineraries: Travels in Tudor England* (Stroud: Sutton, 1993), gave a useful new analysis of the dates of the journeys.

27 The major texts in the large literature on the country house poem are William A. McClung, *The Country House in English Renaissance Poetry* (Berkeley, CA: University of California Press, 1977) and Alistair Fowler, *The Country House Poem* (Edinburgh: Edinburgh University Press, 1994).

28 On estate plans, Paula Henderson, *The Tudor House and Garden: Architecture and Landscape in the Sixteenth and Early Seventeenth Centuries* (New Haven, CT and London: Yale University Press, 2005). One interesting case study is that of Woburn Abbey; see Dianne Duggan, 'Woburn Abbey: The First Episode of a Great Country House', *Architectural History*, 46 (2003), 57–80.

29 The significance of their legal quality is summarised in Howard, *Building*, pp. 167–8.

30 Laura Jacobus, 'On "Whether a man could see before him and behind him both at once": The Role of Drawing in the Design of Interior Space in England c.1600–1800', *Architectural History*, 31 (1988), 148–66.

31 This development is summarised in Howard, *Building*, pp. 168–71 and the Smythson and Thorpe drawings discussed more fully by Girouard, *Elizabethan Architecture, passim*.

32 Wotton, *Elements of Architecture*, p. 4.

I

Reconstructing the
English country house

2

'In his own image': architectural patronage and self-symbolism in Archbishop Warham's motivations for rebuilding the palace at Otford (c.1514–26)

Alden Gregory

The ascent of William Warham (c.1450–1532) to Canterbury's archiepiscopal throne happened suddenly (see Figure 2.1). Already into his fifties when he was promoted to the office in 1504 he had, for much of his long career, served the Crown as a dependable and distinguished but, nonetheless, middle-ranking official. Despite holding a doctorate in canon law, until 1502 Warham had held a series of mostly secular offices. A short spell in the Court of Arches was followed by overseas diplomatic missions to Rome (1490), Antwerp (1491) and Burgundy (1493) until, in February 1494, he was promoted by royal preferment to the Mastership of the Rolls. Here, drawing on his shrewd abilities as a politician and negotiator, he flourished and marked himself out for further advancement. In October 1501 he was provided to the see of London (although his enthronement was not until the following September) and in March 1504 he was translated Archbishop of Canterbury, primate of all England. In the same breath he became Keeper of the Great Seal (1502) and Lord Chancellor (1504) and now, though already in relatively old age, Warham had achieved the highest ecclesiastical and lay positions that royal government could offer.[1]

Although his professional ascent is relatively easy to trace there are many other aspects of his early life and career that remain unknown. Since what follows sets out to consider Warham's interest in architecture and the motivations that encouraged him to devote much of his new-found wealth to its pursuit, it should first be remarked that, aside from evidence of a short period in the household of the bishop of Ely, little is known of his domestic situation in the years before his arrival in Canterbury.[2] Warham's income must have been sufficient to afford him a reasonable property since he had been awarded several profitable livings; but if he, like so many others, was inspired by the places he had visited on his travels to indulge in architecture – or indeed in the other arts – then any evidence of it

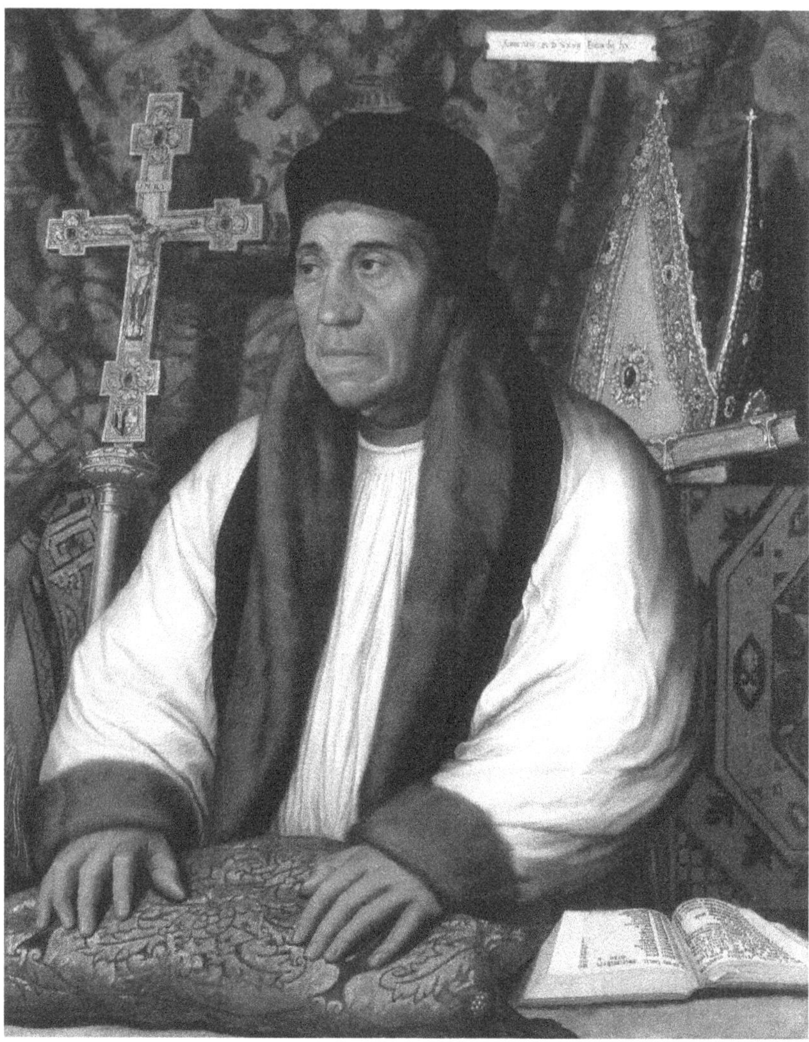

2.1 William Warham, after Hans Holbein the Younger, oil on panel, early seventeenth century, National Portrait Gallery, London. Warham is shown surrounded by the symbols of his office and with fabrics and cushions that may have been similar to those furnishing his new house at Otford.

has long since disappeared. Yet, by his death in 1532, nearly twenty-nine years after he had risen to the archiepiscopacy, Warham had developed a reputation as a builder having spent vast sums of money on his houses – £30,000 by his own estimation[3] – and had created one of the largest and grandest palaces of the early Tudor age at Otford in Kent (Figure 2.2). Today the scale and magnificence of Warham's house can only be guessed at. All that remains of Otford Palace

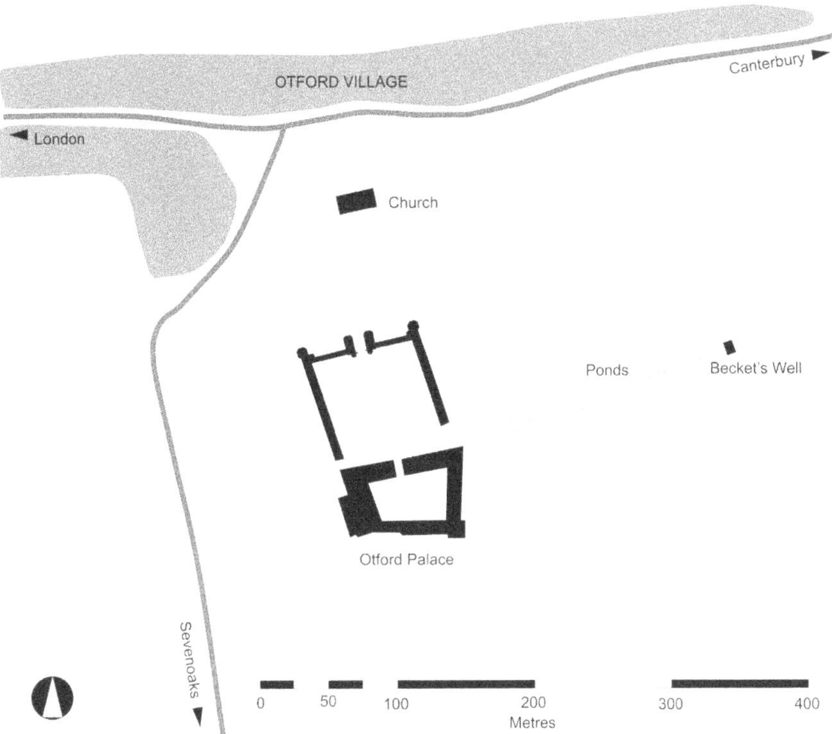

2.2   Schematic site plan showing the relationship between Otford Palace and its landscape.

is a single lodging tower and the stump of a gatehouse (Figures 2.3 and 2.4). Such ruination masks the fact that this was undoubtedly the great material achievement of Warham's life for there can be little doubt that in its day Otford rivalled most of the great royal, ecclesiastical and aristocratic houses. It was certainly sufficiently well-regarded to be recognised on a European scale and led one English observer in 1536 to remark of the margravate castle at Pforzheim in south-west Germany, 'I do rekon it to be as gret as my lord off canterbery place at otfford but it is not so goodly'.[4]

Not all observers were so charitable in their opinions of Otford. Writing slightly later in 1570 William Lambarde remarked, in a begrudgingly anti-Catholic tone, that,

Warham (not contented to continue it a plaine house, fit to withdrawe himselfe unto for contemplation and praier) had so magnificently enlarged the same, that it was now become meete, to make a Palaice for a Kings habitation and pleasure.[5]

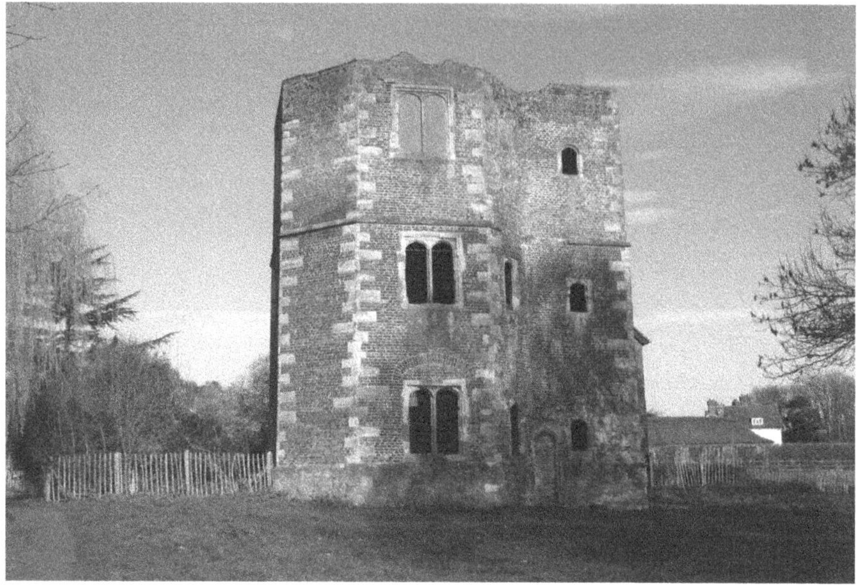

2.3   The surviving tower formed the north-west corner of the base court of Warham's Otford Palace. The tower contained suites of lodgings for the archbishop's visitors.

The king in question was Henry VIII, but he like many others was well aware that, in fact, Otford was an unattractive and unsuitable place to live. Henry who, during one of his many avaricious moments forced Warham's successor to cede ownership of Otford to the Crown, nonetheless compared it unfavourably with the archiepiscopal house at Croydon.[6] In his opinion the site at Otford on which the archbishop had chosen to build was too waterlogged and 'rheumatic', making it somewhere he could not stay 'without sickness'.[7] To this day it is often wet under foot and Henry's opinion was not surprisingly echoed by many of the palace's contemporary visitors.[8] Otford was, however, only three miles to the north of Knole, another of the archiepiscopacy's great Kentish palaces and a further concession to Henry's avarice, and so, he reasoned, while he resided at Knole he could, at least, put his household up at Otford.[9] This was far from a glowing indictment of Warham's achievement.

Why then should Warham, who as Archbishop of Canterbury held one of the largest landed estates in the country, choose to build in such an unsuitable location? Why, when before his promotion to the archiepiscopacy he had shown little apparent interest in architectural patronage, should he decide to commission such an impressive property at all? In theory such questions may be answered simply with the assumption that it was the product of the exuberance of a man with new-found wealth but a beginner's naivety about the importance of a well-chosen site. To do so, however, would be to miss completely the

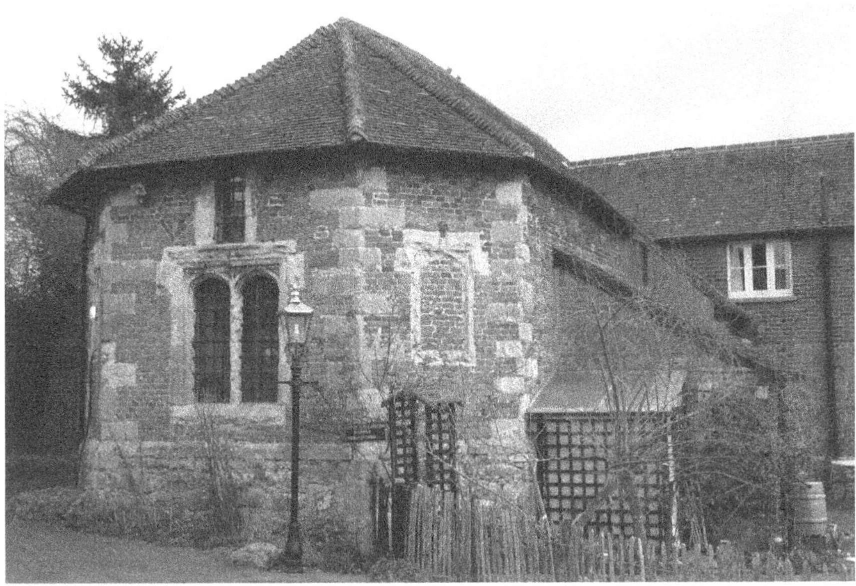

2.4   The remains of the palace's outer gatehouse, now much reduced in height. After the demolition of the palace the gatehouse and adjoining range were used as farm buildings and cottages.

complexity of the stimuli that encouraged Warham's choice. His house was to be more than just a place of showy habitation, work and leisure. Instead, far more importantly, it was to act as a tangible representation of his own self-image and a symbolic buttress to his increasingly waning power. The site at Otford, for all its literal shortcomings, suited these high-minded ambitions perfectly.

The lands around Otford had been in the possession of the archbishops of Canterbury since the 820s and a manor house had been established there before Domesday.[10] Warham's chosen location was not, therefore, a new site and when he took office he inherited with it a relatively substantial moated house with an impressive – but mostly apocryphal – associated history. In truth little is known about this early house since Warham's builders demolished it, save for the fourteenth-century Great Hall and Chapel, to make way for his new palace.[11] Excavations carried out in the 1970s confirmed that the old house stood at the south end of the palace site, beneath what would become Warham's inner court (Figure 2.5), and that it had been substantially rebuilt and enlarged in the second half of the fourteenth century.[12] It seems likely, therefore, that it was heavily damaged during the 1381 Peasants' Revolt by rebels who saw it as representative of the authority of the unpopular Archbishop Simon Sudbury for building accounts record that in the years immediately following the revolt a local mason, Stephen Lamberhurst, was at work at Otford building

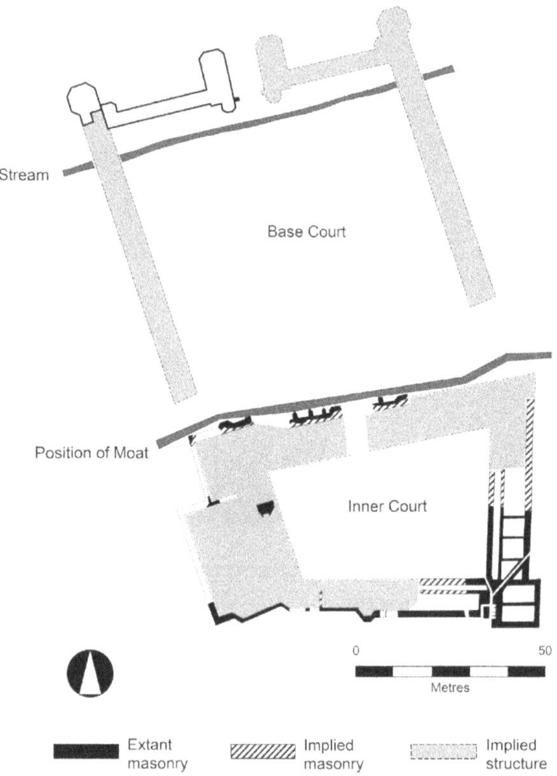

2.5   The layout of Otford Palace as excavated by the Kent Archaeological Rescue Unit in 1974.

the battlements and buttresses of a 'new hall'.[13] The archaeology is inconclusive about what this house looked like and while it might tentatively be compared to Ightham Mote, since it is nearby and of a similar age, the size of the moated enclosure at Otford (estimated at between 1 and 2 acres) indicates that it was on a much larger scale.[14]

Workmen seem to have begun the process of demolition and rebuilding by 1514. Building accounts for Warham's works do not survive so it is difficult to trace the progress of his project with any certainty. However, in 1514 Warham wrote to his friend Desiderius Erasmus, who at the time was suffering from gallstones;

> what is the point of stones in your frail physique? What could one build upon this rock? You are not, I imagine, building fine houses, or anything like that. Wherefore, since stones are not your line of business, be sure to get rid of your superfluous burden as soon as you

can; spend money to have these stones taken away; unlike me, who am spending money every day to have stones brought to my buildings.[15]

The letter is not specific about the buildings to which he referred. It is clear that Warham undertook work at several of his properties concurrently, including at Knole, yet the scale of the work at Otford outweighed any of his other projects and it is probably reasonable to assume, as others have done, that Otford was at the forefront of his mind when he wrote his letter to Erasmus.[16] Certainly by 1518 enough had been achieved at Otford for the house to play host to Cardinal Campeggio as he made his way through Kent to negotiate the Treaty of London.[17] Building work was still ongoing two years later when Henry VIII and Katherine of Aragon stopped there on their way to the Field of Cloth of Gold, since, only weeks after they had departed, masons working at the palace narrowly escaped a violent assault by a gang of local men.[18] Payments totalling £80 10s 7d were recorded for unspecified works in 1524–25 suggesting that construction continued, if on a reduced scale, and indeed it was not until 1526 that Warham himself announced of his achievements at Otford that it was, 'sufficiently repaired and enlarged and now a great house has been built with galleries and towers, and various new gardens have also been created'.[19]

Warham's new house was a vast palace of brick, stone and timber sprawling over an area of three acres. Approached through the village from the north it presented an imposing façade centred on a tall brick gatehouse with polygonal towers, similar in appearance and plan to the surviving early sixteenth-century gatehouse at nearby Lullingstone, though much larger in scale and with the plan reversed (Figure 2.6). At Otford diapered brickwork rises from a sturdy stone plinth – a concession to the damp soil perhaps – and what remains of the gate suggests that it conformed to the prevailing architectural fashions of the day (Figure 2.4). However, the depth of the gatehouse from front to back is quite extraordinary when compared to the flanking ranges. It projected forward from the surrounding buildings by almost ten metres, making a significant and prominent architectural statement.

The courtyard that was entered from the gate was bordered by guest lodgings – fifteen in the gatehouse and corner towers, twenty-one along the west side and more to the east[20] – and was a huge expanse of open ground designed, no doubt, to impress the visitor with its scale (Figure 2.5). On its far side was a moat and a second gatehouse flanked by ranges that separated the outer court from the inner. This building once again conformed to fashion, presenting a façade that was broken up by the regular projecting bay windows of a long gallery.[21] Here, however, according to contemporary surveys, the predominant building material was not brick but stone.[22] Beyond it the inner court was surrounded by open galleries, forming a domestic cloister, and enclosed by the mass of great chambers, galleries, lodgings, kitchens, a school house and the fourteenth-

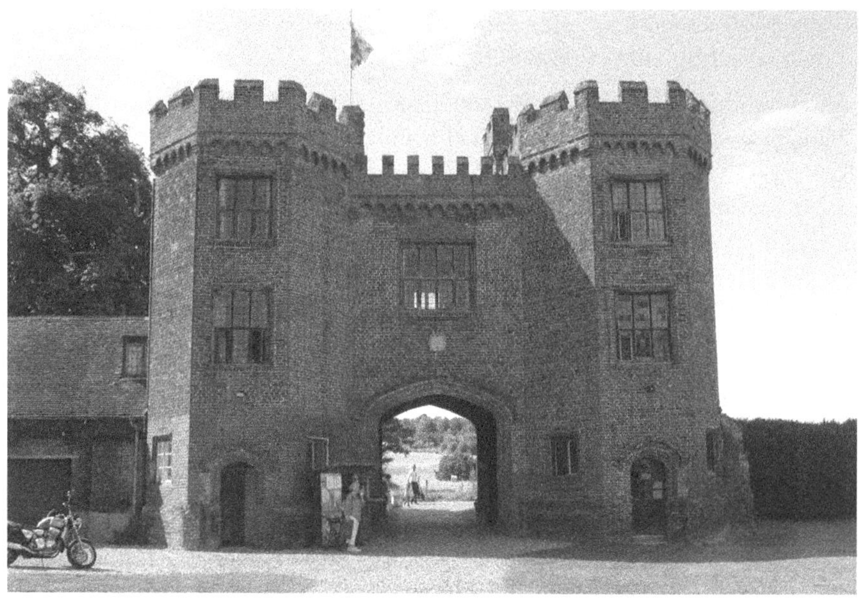

2.6   The early sixteenth-century gatehouse at Lullingstone Castle, a few miles to the north of Otford, shares the same plan form as the gatehouse of Otford Palace itself. It is, however, smaller in scale and reversed. This view is taken from the rear.

century hall and chapel; all the trappings of a 'renaissance' great house.[23] A survey made during the reign of Edward VI records that in addition to a Great Chamber, Otford also had privy chambers set aside for the King and Queen.[24] It is possible that these rooms were only set up to fulfil this function after the property transferred to the Crown in 1538 since Henry VIII certainly spent substantial sums of money on unspecified works at Otford during his tenure.[25] It is equally possible, however, that these state rooms were part of Warham's design and that he intended to provide a ready-made suite of royal apartments just as Cardinal Wolsey was doing at Hampton Court Palace.[26]

Despite the contemporary misgivings about Otford, Warham's new house attracted an unlikely voice of praise in Erasmus. Warham and Erasmus were closely associated. The Archbishop was a generous patron to Erasmus, supporting him financially and giving him lodgings during his visits to England. It is almost certain that Erasmus visited Otford and stayed with Warham there since he wrote of the house as though he had seen it in person. In a letter to Francis I dated 1523 Erasmus remarked, 'Nor should I have found [Otford] very attractive before William Warham […], had built there on such a scale.'[27] On the face of it grand architectural patronage of the type undertaken at Otford seems, to quote J. J. Scarisbrick, 'a distinctly un-Erasmian activity.'[28] Naturally, he was vehemently opposed to the abuses of clerical privileges and on occasions he expressed these views as an attack on excessive spending on building. So, for example, he railed against the fortune lavished on the Certosa di Pavia built, in his opinion, for the benefit of a few monks and their visitors, 'who go there merely to see that marble church'.[29] Nonetheless, Erasmus could appreciate a good building, recording in a letter of 1529 that, 'as the blind man is said to be especially drawn to things that can be seen, so the small man as I am is delighted by the great buildings and cities'.[30] He was, therefore, a lot kinder about the architectural and artistic patronage of individual clerics and more forgiving of their apparent excesses. Just as he had praised Warham's endeavours at Otford so too did he comment favourably on a house in which he stayed in Konstanz belonging to a canon there. Having described its painted interiors Erasmus exclaimed,

> And in the whole house, exquisite as it is in every part, there is nothing more exquisite than our host himself. He keeps the Muses and Graces more in his heart than in his pictures; they are more at home in his character than on his walls.[31]

Erasmus's words are an eloquent articulation of the view that art and architecture could represent a symbolic expression of the self-image of their patron, a view to which Warham's Otford seems consciously to subscribe. While Erasmus could, on the one hand, justify his criticism of the Certosa di Pavia on the grounds that it was an unnecessary and overtly exuberant manifestation of wealth and bad taste on the part of the monks who commissioned it, he could, on the other hand, appreciate Otford as a suitable and purposeful house fit for the many roles of a man of Warham's position. Although a palace on the scale of Otford was, amongst other things, simply a crude tangible representation of wealth and power – both no doubt fine motivations for Warham, if not for Erasmus – it could also be much more, and the genesis of the building lay in Warham's understanding of the symbolic importance of its function and in the significant hagiographic resonance of Otford itself. It was undoubtedly the emphasis of these noble characteristics, rather than of the sin of conspicuous consumption, that stirred and appeased Erasmus's humanist sensibilities.

It is telling that Erasmus preceded his description of the canon's house in Konstanz by remarking how hospitably he had been received there.[32] It is equally telling that when critical rumours about Warham's successor as archbishop, Thomas Cranmer, were circulating at Court in the early 1540s they were on the basis that Cranmer did not offer hospitality, 'correspondent with his revenues and dignities'.[33] All good Christians are, of course, expected to be hospitable hosts; it is, after all, written in the Book of Hebrews, 'be not forgetful to entertain strangers; for thereby some have entertained angels unaware'.[34] However, the Bible is even more explicit about these requirements in a bishop. Several times St Paul recorded the characteristics required of a bishop, each time emphasising sobriety, moderation, good behaviour and that he should be 'given to hospitality'.[35] A bishop should, opined St Paul, also be, 'One that ruleth well his own house […] (For if a man know not how to rule his own house, how shall he take care of the church of God?)'.[36] Such pronouncements weighed heavy on ecclesiasts like Warham who were surrounded by the excesses of courtly life and pulled in opposite directions by the forces of Pauline moral rectitude and earthly easy luxury. Posthumous eulogistic portraits of Warham by Erasmus and of his successor Cranmer by John Foxe both draw on the strictures of St Paul's epistles to extol their subjects' virtues and both, therefore, illustrate the extent to which the late medieval archbishop was expected to conform.[37] It is difficult to know whether the eulogy really reflects reality but, nonetheless, of Warham Erasmus wrote;

> Although he sometimes had bishops, dukes and earls as his guests, yet dinner was always finished within the space of one hour. In the midst of a sumptuous table, as his dignity demands, it is incredible to say how he abstained from all delicacies.[38]

For 'sumptuous table' we may equally well read 'sumptuous house' for it is evident that conspicuous spending on apparently excessive luxury could sit comfortably alongside the required sobriety and moderation. While on the one hand a great palace might act as a foil to the Archbishop's own image of humility, it could on the other hand provide the stage on which to both fulfil, on a grand and symbolic scale, his social obligations of hospitality and to display his ability to 'rule his own house'.

Such considerations were not necessarily the primary motivation behind Warham's decision to build at Otford but they certainly justified it. Otford was a worldly expression of wealth and power but it was also the grandest of stage sets on which to display his virtues. It was here that Warham would entertain his most important guests. Cautiously it might be described as his 'pleasure palace', although in truth the phrase is probably too suggestive a moniker to do justice to its multifaceted nature. However, what Hampton Court Palace was for Cardinal Wolsey, Otford was for Warham. It was his great house outside of London at which to entertain. With its huge hall and chambers, large numbers of guest rooms and vast hunting parks it could happily accommodate the biggest of retinues. It was also fairly easily accessible. While Hampton Court is twenty-one miles from Whitehall by river, Otford is about the same distance by road and it stood next to one of the principal overland routes between London and Canterbury, and thence to the Channel ports. This was a strategic location for it put Warham in a position to offer hospitality to the most important of travellers. Thus in July 1518 when Cardinal Campeggio was making his way through Kent from the coast at Deal to the capital to negotiate the Treaty of London it was at Otford that he and his retinue of a thousand horses were most lavishly hosted. Warham met the Cardinal at Canterbury and escorted him via Sittingbourne and Boxley Abbey;

> On the Tuesday he [Campeggio] went to the Archbishop's place at Otford, where the Archbishop received him, and there he remained two days; during which time the Archbishop made him good and great cheer, and divers pleasures and goodly pastimes.[39]

Henry VIII also stayed on several occasions including with Katherine of Aragon while *en route* to the Field of Cloth of Gold in May 1520. It may be the case that Warham had built the separate suites of royal apartments recorded in later surveys for just this sort of occasion.[40] If so then any comparison with Hampton Court Palace appears even more relevant.

That Otford held this position as a place of entertainment is emphasised by its dichotomous relationship with nearby Knole. It also helps to explain why these two great houses could exist so close together. When Warham was promoted to the archiepiscopacy in 1504 Knole was still relatively new, having been built predominantly in the 1460s and 1470s. It was already well appointed and of a reasonable size – although not as large as Otford was to become – and Warham even undertook his own campaign of building works there between 1508 and 1525 that probably included the creation of a new Great Chamber and private rooms.[41] Despite this and despite Knole's undoubted grandeur it was not used for receiving royal or ambassadorial guests. While for Otford these visits are easy to demonstrate, to date no convincing primary record has come to light with which to evidence equivalent events occurring at Knole. The palace at Otford stands on the edge of the village, next to the parish church and alongside the main road. It is a visible and accessible location. Knole, on the other hand, is isolated. It stands in the middle of a hunting park, a good half a mile from the town of Sevenoaks. In this regard Knole is unusual since the archbishop's other great houses conform to the pattern seen at Otford; they are almost exclusively in villages adjacent to the church. Indeed if there is one characteristic that seems to define archiepiscopal houses it is that they were usually built next to churches and certainly his major houses at Lambeth, Croydon, Aldington, Charing, Maidstone, Mayfield and Slindon all fit this pattern. William Horman's *Vulgaria* of 1519 uses as a grammatical example the sentence, 'The bysshops palayce is harde by the churche', thereby suggesting that this was something of an accepted rule.[42] It is Knole, therefore, and not Otford that is remarkable in this sense, but the difference that this implies helps to justify their proximity to each other. Knole was grand and luxurious, but it was not a 'pleasure palace' *per se*. Rather it served the archbishops as an isolated retreat; a place to escape to, as far as was possible, from some of the stresses of official life.[43] Warham's predecessor Archbishop Bourchier (c.1411–86) had spent most of his last decade in retirement at Knole and both he and Archbishop Morton (d.1500) had died there. Warham probably continued to see this as Knole's primary role. Otford could comfortably coexist so close by because it fulfilled an opposite function.

Wolsey's rebuilding of Hampton Court Palace is often quoted in the secondary literature as one of the primary motivations behind Warham's decision to rebuild Otford so lavishly.[44] Both houses were conceived and constructed at about the same time; Wolsey's Hampton Court between 1515 and 1525 and Warham's Otford from about 1514 to 1526 and both were on a similarly large scale. Otford's size has, therefore, been seen as Warham's response to Wolsey's achievements and power and, if this is so, then regardless of any pretensions to Erasmian humanism or aggrandised social responsibility in his motivations, it is also clear that Otford was born in part from vanity and pride. There may be some truth to this.

Certainly the relationship between Warham and Wolsey was, at best, tense.[45] Despite Warham's primacy in the see of Canterbury and his supposed seniority over Wolsey it was Wolsey who wielded the political and, increasingly, the spiritual power while Warham was pushed to the sidelines. 1515 was a difficult year for Warham; to compound serious political defeats he also suffered the indignation of presenting the red Cardinals' hat to Wolsey, despite not being a Cardinal himself, and later in the same year he resigned the Lord Chancellorship in Wolsey's favour.[46] Although Thomas More wrote that Warham was happy to give up the office and devote himself to his books, Polydore Virgil characterised Warham's demotion as evidence of Wolsey's thrusting and ruthless ambitions. Surely in this context Virgil's view seems the most likely.[47]

Out of these tensions sprang their architectural arms race. The competitive element of their building works is not, unfortunately, explicitly expressed in any surviving sources, so the temptation to overemphasise the significance of the point must be avoided. However, when the two buildings are compared or the correspondence between the two men is read, signs appear that their rivalry played itself out in their patronage of their great houses. Otford and Hampton Court were very similar buildings; both were vast moated multi-courtyard brick houses conforming to the styles of the day and both developed around the core of an older property.[48] Although Hampton Court has triumphed in terms of longevity, in their time it was Otford that won in terms of scale. Both palaces occupy sites of a similar size, but their outer courts, the part of the buildings that presented the impression of scale to visitors, were quite different. Hampton Court's Base Court was certainly large at 140ft by 166ft but it was dwarfed by the c.246ft square of Otford's corresponding base court.[49] (Figure 2.7)

It seems fair to assume that both Warham and Wolsey considered their own house to be the finer. In 1522 Warham invited Wolsey to visit him at Otford, apparently for the first time. Using all the cloying rhetoric expected in letters of the period, Warham wrote; 'If it myght please yor good grace to take the payne to see my power [for which can be read 'poor'] house at Otford when I retorne thither I wole think me self greatly bownd unto yor goodnes therefor.'[50] Perhaps we should not read too much into this passage – it is rhetoric after all

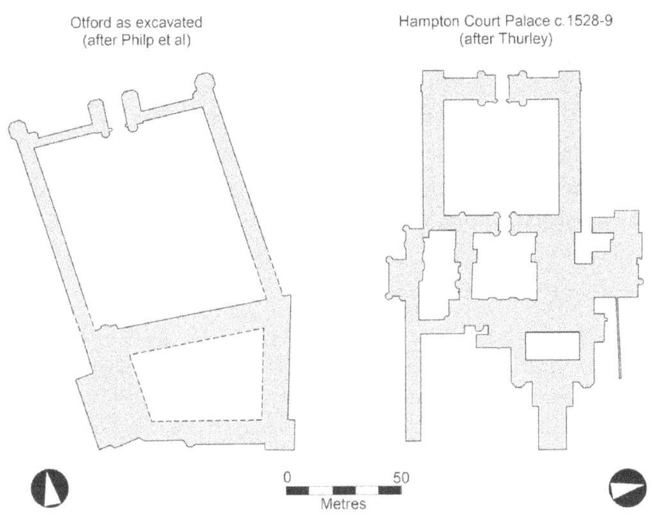

2.7   Comparison between the size of Otford Palace and Cardinal Wolsey's Hampton Court Palace.

– but nonetheless Warham's invitation to, 'see my poor house at Otford', seems to deliberately hide his excitement at being able to surprise his rival with the grandeur of his new palace; a palace that was, after all, anything but poor.

It is not recorded whether Wolsey ever accepted Warham's invitation but subsequent letters suggest that he knew the place.[51] More specifically he knew of Otford's waterlogged location and resulting damp problem, although this may have been by reputation only. While suffering from ill health in January 1523 Warham received a letter from Cardinal Wolsey inviting him to recuperate at his, 'mooste holsome Manor of hampton courte' and suggesting that he, 'make [his] abode in hiegh and drye growndes as knoll and suche other'.[52] Of this exchange of letters only Warham's polite response survives but it is easy to imagine that Wolsey's invitation was a sneering, if veiled, criticism of Otford's wet, and therefore, unhealthy position. Early sixteenth-century instructional literature was vocal about where to locate houses in order to promote good health; the soil should be well draining and the air fresh.[53] This was not the case in Otford's waterlogged hollow and it is therefore noteworthy that Warham's letter was indeed written at Knole.

Warham could have built his show-piece palace almost anywhere else; the Archbishop of Canterbury had one of the largest landed estates in the country and there were other houses in his possession that were ripe for redevelopment.

However, in fact, it seems to have been the source of the dampness at Otford and the story that accounted for the waterlogged soil that drew Warham to it. To the east of the palace site there is a natural spring flowing into a medieval conduit (Figure 2.2).[54] This provided valuable clean drinking water for the palace, but it also established a connection with Saint Thomas Becket. In the 1440s the spring was known as St Thomas's fountain and to this day it retains the name Becket's Well (Figure 2.8), closely linking it to one of the miracles of Warham's sanctified predecessor.[55] The story of Otford's illustrious past was later recounted by William Lambarde, whose critical anti-Catholic analysis is, nonetheless, worth quoting in full;

> It was long since fancied, and is yet of two [*sic.*] many beleeued, that Thomas Becket lay at the olde house at Otford (whiche of long time belonged to the Archebishops, and whereof the hall and chapell onely do now remaine) and sawe that it wanted of fit spring to water it: that he strake his staffe into the drye grounde (in a place thereof nowe called Sainct Thomas Well) and that immediately water appeared, the whiche running plentifully, serueth the offices of the newe house till this present day: They say also, that as he walked on a time in the olde Parke (busie at his prayers) That he was much hindered in deuotion, by the sweete note and melodie of a Nightingale that sang in a bushe besides him, and that therefore (in the might of his holynesse) he inioyned, that from thenceforth no byrde of that kynde shoulde be so bolde as to sing there aboutes: Some men report likewise, that for as muche as a Smithe (then dwelling in the towne) had cloyed his horse, He enacted by like authoritie, that after that time no Smithe should thriue within the Parishe. Inumerable suche toyes, false Priestes have deuised, and fonde people (alas) haue beleeued, of this iolly Martyr, and Pope holy man: which for the unworthynesse of the thinges them selues, and for want of time (wherewith I am streightned) I neyther will, nor can, nowe presently recount.[56]

There can be little doubting that these tales were in general circulation in Warham's own time; the identification of the spring as St Thomas's fountain in the 1440s suggests so and indeed Erasmus himself knew of a connection, perhaps having had the stories recounted to him during one of his stays at Otford.[57]

Stories of the miracles performed there made the link between the house and the saint indelible and it was a link that Warham exploited for its own symbolic value. Becket was a popular, if increasingly divisive, saint and even on the eve of the Reformation his shrine at Canterbury continued to attract pilgrims.[58] The well, therefore, must have been a site of some interest to passing travellers, particularly those making the journey to the shrine, and the road from London to Canterbury conveniently passed through Otford. There may have been an associated chapel, although one is not recorded, and certainly in the 1530s the parish church of St Bartholomew contained an image of St Thomas.[59] Now, alongside the well and highly visible to passers-by, Warham had enlarged Becket's house and created a new monument to emphasise his own links with the saint. It is perhaps also significant, therefore, that Warham kept the great hall and the

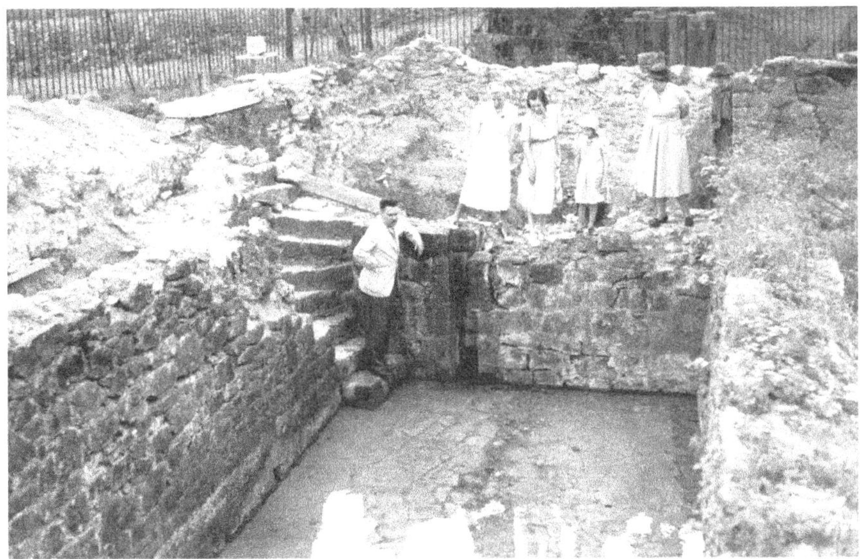

2.8   The remains of Becket's Well, Otford, photographed in 1953 following excavations in 1950. Today the site is largely inaccessible.

chapel of the earlier building. It is easy to imagine, although once again it is not explicitly stated, that these were the parts of the house most closely associated with the saint. Lambarde's statement in the passage quoted above that, 'Thomas Becket lay at the olde house at Otford, [..] whereof the hall and chapell onely do now remaine', cannot have referred to the state of ruination at the time of writing in c.1570 since sufficient survived to have been recorded in a survey dating to 1596 so must instead imply that Lambarde believed the hall and chapel to be remnants of the house Becket knew. The idea that these were Becket's hall and chapel – even if not strictly true – undoubtedly held an exploitable symbolic cachet and in this light Warham's Otford may be characterised as a sort of vast reliquary containing the architectural remains of his forebear.

Warham was devoted to St Thomas and the record of his archiepiscopacy suggests that he took a closer interest in the martyr than many of his immediate predecessors had.[60] He often quoted or invoked Becket in his writings and speeches, he tried always to attend the feast days in Canterbury and he pushed hard to secure a bull to celebrate the 350th anniversary of the martyrdom in 1520.[61] Moreover Warham also identified closely with the saint. Not only was he himself increasingly sidelined by his peers, but like Becket he was an archbishop overseeing a church losing its powers and subjugated by the secular authorities. Warham had risen to power under Henry VII, who he had served loyally, but when Henry VIII succeeded him the Archbishop found himself frequently at odds with the King.

The similarity between his own situation and the stories of Becket's antagonistic relationship with an earlier King Henry was painfully clear for Warham to see and increasingly he drew on it in defence of his own position. From the outset of his tenure Warham had been vocal in defence of church liberties but his efforts to secure them were largely unsuccessful. In 1512 a new act removed the right of clergy in minor orders to be tried in the church courts for serious crimes. Initially the act was to run for a three-year trial period but, by the time it was due for renewal in 1515, the issue had come to a head and Warham stood openly in opposition to the King and his ministers, chief amongst whom was Wolsey. A crisis meeting was convened at Baynard's Castle, over which Henry officiated. Warham, in a show of great bravery, reminded the assembled audience that his predecessor Becket had died a martyr in defence of church liberties. Henry was incensed, declaring that no king of England had ever had any superior, 'but God only', and Warham was left defeated.[62] His increased subservience to Wolsey and his attendant demotion from the Lord Chancellorship followed quickly thereafter.

Warham did not, however, disappear quietly and More's characterisation of him as a man happy to give way to Wolsey and retreat into his books does not ring true.[63] He continued as an outspoken advocate of church liberties and although his relationship with Wolsey may have warmed in later years, the two men continued to clash. Writing to the cardinal in 1519, for instance, Warham complained that despite Wolsey's promises not to threaten the jurisdictional rights of the archiepiscopal courts, his officers were still interrupting the work of the Court of Audiences and the other church courts in Canterbury.[64]

In the early 1530s Warham faced up to his greatest challenge. Chosen by Henry in 1527 to examine the case for his divorce from Katherine he was initially seen as a reliable judge and likely to find in the King's favour. However, as the issue became more complicated and the jurisdiction of Rome was called on Warham became uneasy and increasingly hostile to Henry's case. He is reputed to have told the papal nuncio in January 1531 that he would never disobey Rome in the matter and a year later he made a public announcement to the same effect. He went further, however, standing up in the Lords and publicly denouncing Henry's conduct.[65]

It is not hyperbole to suggest that against the backdrop of political conflict that shaped most of his primacy, Warham began to prepare himself for martyrdom. His tomb, which was commissioned early in his archiepiscopal term, while he was still alive and before his troubles started, was placed as close to the site of Becket's martyrdom at Canterbury as it was possible to be. Richard Scarlett's heraldic record of the monument reveals that in 1599 one of the six shields on the front of the tomb-chest bore Becket's coat-of-arms (today three

of the six shields are emblazoned with the saint's arms).[66] It can be assumed
that the configuration of arms witnessed by Scarlett had survived from 1532
and therefore indicates quite strongly that the tomb was indeed intended to
emphasise Warham's identification with St Thomas. Furthermore, as his own
troubles grew Warham may have hoped that the added resonance that his
political battles began to give the tomb would suggest to passing pilgrims that his
life and death should be contemplated alongside that of the saint's. Then in 1532
Warham found himself in more troubled waters. While the prospect of his own
martyrdom had previously probably seemed more abstract concept than reality,
it suddenly began to look like a dangerously real possibility. Faced with trumped-
up charges of *praemunire*, resulting in no small part from his disobedience over
the divorce, he composed an explosive speech in his own defence, choosing once
again to quote Becket at the King. In no uncertain terms the speech declared
that he considered the articles brought against him to be the same as those that
Becket had died for. With the prospect of his own martyrdom undoubtedly at
the forefront of his mind Warham prepared to address the Council;

> for this article and others made agenst the liberties of godd*es* churche [St Thomas] was
> rewarded of god with the grete hono[r] of martirdom, which is the best deth that can be,
> which thing is thexsample and comforte of other [who] speke and doo for the defense
> of the liberties of godd*es* church […] And in case ye shuld be so noted by other folk*es*
> instigation and ungodly meanes to drawe yo[r] sword*es* in this case and to hewe me to small
> pec*es* (which god forbede you shuld doo) yet I thinke it were bett*er* for me to suffre the
> same than agenst my conscience to confesse this article to be a preminure for the which
> Sancte Thomas dyed.[67]

These were deeply confrontational words seemingly designed to provoke Henry
VIII into ridding himself of his own turbulent priest.

As it was, Warham died naturally on 22 August 1532 before his inflammatory
speech could be delivered. His will, prepared in 1530, is notable for two reasons;
first because it called on St Thomas for intercession – not in itself an unusual
request in the wills of the late medieval archiepiscopacy, but of particular
interest in the context of the fate Warham appears to have been envisaging –
and second because it emphasised and justified in the broadest terms his vast
expenditure on building works.[68] Once again facing up to difficulty, in this case
his own mortality, it was these two preoccupations that Warham drew on for
support and comfort. Both in their own way acted as a symbolic buttress to his
inherently unstable position and in the palace at Otford the two were powerfully
combined. While his situation elsewhere seemed increasingly fragile, at Otford
Warham could consolidate and present a carefully conceived public face. It was
his seat of power, a vast image of lordly authority, and it was the place at which he
could show off his wealth, his hospitality and largesse, and his intellect to royal
and ambassadorial guests alike. In itself this gave him a tool to help maintain his
position at Court and retain his political influence but, as these slipped further

away from him, and as his attempts to exert his own voice in the increasingly fractious relationship between church and state came to little, Otford's symbolic significance grew. Now Otford's connection with St Thomas paid dividends for it allowed Warham to tangibly emphasise his self-identification with the martyr and gave him a house in which to position himself as a latter-day Becket, protecting the rights of his church.

Notes

1   J. J. Scarisbrick, 'Warham, William (1450?–1532)', *Oxford Dictionary of National Biography*, vol. 57 (Oxford: Oxford University Press, 2004), p. 411. Hereafter *ODNB*.

2   Scarisbrick, 'Warham, William', p. 411.

3   Kew, National Archives (hereafter TNA) PROB 11/24.

4   London, British Library (hereafter BL) Cotton Vitellius B/XXI f.155.

5   W. Lambarde, *A Perambulation of Kent: Conteining the Description, Hystorie, and Customes of that Shire, Written in the yeere 1570*, printed by W. Burrill (Chatham, 1826), p. 464.

6   J. Gough Nichols (ed.), *Narratives of the Days of the Reformation, chiefly from the Manuscripts of John Foxe the Martyrologist; with two contemporary biographies of Archbishop Cranmer*, Camden Society, Old Series 77 (London, 1859), p. 266.

7   Gough Nichols (ed.), *Narratives*, p. 266.

8   A survey of Otford undertaken by commissioners of Elizabeth I in 1596/7 concluded, 'And we the saide comissioners doo further certifie in our opynione that if the said howse shoulde be repayred that nevertheles the same woulde not be fytt for her majestie to lye in for that yt standeth in a verie wet soyle uppon springes and vawtes of water contynually comynge under it. And comenly the flowers and walles thereof in the winter time are very moyste and wett, and in the somer they are hoary and mustie, And besydes there are no woodes to any purpose upon the said manner other than those before mentioned and they nothinge nere sufficiente to ayer the saide howse', TNA E 178/1165.

9   Gough Nichols (ed.), *Narratives*, p. 266.

10   F. R. H. Du Boulay, *The Lordship of Canterbury* (London: Nelson, 1966), p. 28; D. Clarke and A. Stoyel, *Otford in Kent: A History* (Otford: Kent Archaelogical Society, 1975), p. 47.

11   Erasmus, *The Correspondence of Erasmus*, trans. R. A. B. Mynors and D. F. S. Thomson, 15 vols (Toronto: Toronto University Press, 1974–2012), ep. 1400.

12   B. Philp, 'The Archbishops of Canterbury's Palace at Otford', *Excavations in the Darent Valley, Kent* (Dover: Kent Archaeological Rescue Unit, 1984), pp. 159–60.

13   London, Lambeth Palace Library, ED 835.

14   Philp, 'Otford', pp. 159–60.

15   Erasmus, *Correspondence*, ep. 286.

16   Clarke and Stoyel, *Otford in Kent*, p. 100.

17   T. F. Mayer, 'Campeggi [Campeggio], Lorenzo (1471/2–1539)', *ODNB*, vol. 9, p. 871; *Letters & Papers of Henry VIII*, vol. II, ii, 4348 (hereafter *L&P*).

18   Oxford, Bodleian MS. Ashmole 1116 (f. 100r); TNA STAC 2/31/147.

19   London, Lambeth Palace Library, Estate Documents 1362 (f.3v); Canterbury, Christ Church Canterbury Reg. T. (f.272).

20   Sevenoaks, Sevenoaks Library, Gordon Ward Notebooks: Otford, vol. II. This survey is undated but on the basis of the evidence it contains must date to the first part of the

sixteenth century. The original is lost and it survives now only as an early twentieth-century transcript said to have been made from an original document in a private London collection.

21   Gordon Ward Notebooks: Otford, vol. II.

22   Gordon Ward Notebooks: Otford, vol. II.

23   TNA E 178/1100.

24   TNA E 101/497/4.

25   H. Colvin (ed.), *The History of the King's Works*, vol. IV (London: HMSO, 1982), pp. 217–19.

26   S. Thurley, *Hampton Court: A Social and Architectural History* (New Haven, CT: Yale University Press, 2003), pp. 27–9.

27   Erasmus, *Correspondence*, ep. 1400.

28   Scarisbrick, 'Warham, William', p. 414.

29   Erasmus, 'Convivium religiosum', trans. in *Collected Works of Erasmus: Colloquies*, ed. C. R. Thompson (Toronto: Toronto University Press, 1997), p. 199; see also E. Panofsky, 'Erasmus and the Visual Arts', *Journal of the Warburg and Courtauld Institutes*, 32 (1969), 211.

30   Erasmus, *Correspondence*, ep. 2195.

31   Erasmus, *Correspondence*, ep. 1342.

32   Erasmus, *Correspondence*, ep. 1342.

33   Gough Nichols (ed.), *Narratives*, p. 260; see also F. Heal, 'The Archbishops of Canterbury and the Practice of Hospitality', *Journal of Ecclesiastical History*, 33:4 (1982), 544–63.

34   Hebrews, 13:2.

35   I. Timothy, 3:2–5; II. Timothy, 2:24; Titus, 1:8.

36   I. Timothy, 3:4–5.

37   D. Erasmus, *Pilgrimages to Saint Mary of Walsingham and Saint Thomas of Canterbury. By Desiderius Erasmus, with the colloquy on rash vows, by the same author, and his characters of Archbishop Warham and Dean Colet*, ed. J. Gough Nichols (Westminster: 1849), pp. 159–60; J. Foxe, *The Acts and Monuments of John Foxe*, vol. 8, ed. S. R. Catley (London, 1839), pp. 3–44.

38   Erasmus, *Pilgrimages*, pp. 159–60.

39   *L&P*, II, ii, 4333.

40   J. G. Russell, *The Field of Cloth of Gold: Men and Manners in 1520* (New York: Barnes and Noble, 1969), p. 209; Henry VIII had previously stayed at Otford on 24 September 1514, *L&P*, II, ii, p. 1465; For the royal apartments at Otford see TNA E 101/497/4.

41   For a history of Knole see A. Gregory, 'Knole: An Architectural and Social History of the Archbishop of Canterbury's House, 1456–1538' (Unpublished DPhil thesis, University of Sussex, 2010).

42   W. Horman, *Vulgaria*, ed. M. R. James (London : Roxburghe Club, 1926), p. 352.

43   Gregory, 'Knole', pp. 168–72.

44   For example Philp, 'Otford', pp. 165–7.

45   Scarisbrick, 'Warham, William', pp. 412–13.

46   Scarisbrick, 'Warham, William', pp. 412–13.

47   Sir Thomas More, *The Correspondence of Sir Thomas More*, ed. E. F. Rogers (Princeton, NJ: Princeton University Press, 1947), ep. 31; Polydor Vergil, *The Anglica Historia of Polydore Vergil: AD 1485–1537*, ed. and trans. Denys Hay, Camden Society, 3rd series, 74 (London, 1950), pp. 230–1.

48   Thurley, *Hampton Court*, p. 17; Philp, 'Otford', p. 160.

49   Thurley, *Hampton Court*, p. 17; Philp, 'Otford', p. 160.

50   TNA SP 1/26 f.140.

51 Wolsey's itinerary as compiled by Dr Neil Sammon does not record any visits to Otford; N. Sammon, 'The Henrician Court During Cardinal Wolsey's Ascendency, c.1514–1529' (Unpublished PhD thesis, University of Wales, 1988), pp. 393–437.
52 TNA SP 1/26 f.273.
53 M. Howard, *The Early Tudor Country House: Architecture and Politics 1490–1550* (London: George Philip, 1987), p. 19.
54 F. R. J. Pateman, 'St. Thomas À Becket's Well, Otford', *Archaeologia Cantiana*, LXX (1956), 172–7.
55 London, Lambeth Palace Library, ED 868.
56 Lambarde, *Perambulation*, pp. 460–1.
57 Erasmus, *Correspondence*, ep. 1400.
58 R. E. Scully, 'The Unmaking of a Saint: Thomas Becket and the English Reformation', *The Catholic Historical Review*, 86:4 (October 2000), 584, 586.
59 Clarke and Stoyel, *Otford*, pp. 107, 121.
60 Scarisbrick, 'Warham, William', p. 415.
61 Scarisbrick, 'Warham, William', p. 415.
62 Scarisbrick, 'Warham, William', p. 412.
63 *The Correspondence of Sir Thomas More*, ep. 31.
64 TNA SP 1/18 f.42.
65 Scarisbrick, 'Warham, William', pp. 413–14.
66 BL Harl. MS 1366 f.14.
67 TNA SP 1/70 ff.214–214v; see also P. Roberts, 'Politics, Drama and the Cult of Thomas Becket in the Early Sixteenth Century', in C. Morris and P. Roberts (eds), *Pilgrimage: The English Experience from Becket to Bunyan* (Cambridge: Cambridge University Press, 2002), p. 201.
68 TNA PROB 11/24; see also for example L. L. Duncan (ed.), 'The Will of Cardinal Bourgchier, Archbishop of Canterbury, 1486', *Archaeologia* Cantiana, 24 (1900), 248.

3

Rediscovering a lost Tudor mansion through archives and manuscripts: The Rycote Project at the Bodleian Library

Matthew Neely

On 1 June 1807 Montagu Bertie, 5th Earl of Abingdon, held an extraordinary auction at Rycote Park, near Thame, in Oxfordshire. Rycote House, once one of the dominant seats in the Oxfordshire political landscape and host to six monarchs, was sold off brick by brick and demolished. The only part of the house to survive to the present day, presumably due to its failure to attract a buyer, is a remnant of the south-west tower. The mansion house demolished by the 5th Earl of Abingdon was a Tudor creation, built at some point between the early to mid-sixteenth century.

Rycote had been the seat of the earls of Abingdon, and their forebears, since the reign of Henry VIII. It came to the family via John, Baron Williams of Thame, who acquired Rycote from Giles Heron in 1539.[1] The Rycote that Williams acquired in 1539 was comprised of two manors: Rycote Magna and Rycote Parva. In December that year he was granted licence by the King to create the 200-acre Rycote Park from the two manors.[2] In August 1540 Williams entertained Henry VIII and his new bride Katherine Howard at Rycote during their summer progress.[3] It was the first of a succession of royal visits to Rycote that would stretch to the entertainment of James, Duke of York, and his daughter Anne, in May 1683. Williams died without a male heir in October 1559 and his estates were divided between his two daughters Isabel and Margery. Rycote Park descended to Margery and her husband Henry Norris. The Norrises enjoyed a warm relationship with Elizabeth I and entertained the Queen at Rycote on four occasions. Henry Norris was ennobled as Baron Norris of Rycote in May 1572.[4] Each of Henry and Margery's six sons fought with distinction in the Elizabethan military. Five of the six brothers died in the Queen's service, all within the lifetime of their parents. The male line of the Norris family defaulted upon the suicide of Francis Norris, Earl of Berkshire, grandson and heir of Henry, 1ˢᵗ Baron Norris of Rycote, in 1622. Rycote Park then descended through two female heirs until it came into the possession of the Bertie family, through the marriage of Bridget Wray, *suo jure* Baroness Norris, to Montague Bertie, 2ⁿᵈ Earl of Lindsey, in 1648.[5] Their eldest son, James Bertie, was created Earl of Abingdon by Charles II in 1682.

Despite the dominant position Rycote held in Oxfordshire during the sixteenth and seventeenth centuries, its place in the historical record has become obscured. The physical destruction of the Tudor mansion is undoubtedly a major factor, but the real reason perhaps lies more in the loss of substantial parts of its archival legacy. The papers of the Bertie family were acquired by the Bodleian Library in various tranches between 1925 and 1955. They comprise the surviving records relating to the administration of the family estates. This would seemingly be the natural place for material relating to the mansion. However, following the demolition, the mansion's archive was deemed to be of no lasting value and was destroyed on a bonfire.[6] The only Rycote material to survive in the Bertie archive is within estate account books. There is nothing earlier in date than 1753.

Yet a house of the influence and importance of Rycote cannot have been completely expunged from the historical record. Traces of Rycote's past are to be found in many disparate archival and manuscript collections. In 2007 the Bodleian Library began a project to identify these formerly fragmented sources and to bring them together in one online resource.[7] The project has largely focused on the Bodleian's own collections. The *Rediscovering Rycote* website draws on material identified in over fifty different Bodleian collections, formed by antiquaries, families and historical figures, to reveal Rycote's past from the medieval period to the present day. This essay focuses on the early modern period and examines how far the surviving primary sources can enrich our understanding of Rycote's lost Tudor mansion.

The central question concerning the mansion at Rycote is for whom was it built? To date no definitive documentary evidence regarding the precise date of construction has been identified. Architectural historians differ in their interpretation of the mansion's probable date, with suggestions ranging from the early to mid-sixteenth century. This places the mansion's possible construction date within the ownership periods of three individuals: Sir Richard Fowler; Giles Heron; or John, Baron Williams of Thame.

Sir Richard Fowler came into the possession of Rycote Magna, and possibly Rycote Parva too, in 1483.[8] During Channel 4's *Time Team* excavation of the mansion, broadcast in 2001, Simon Thurley suggested a construction date of not earlier than 1500 but no later than 1530. The *Time Team* conclusion was that the mansion was built by Fowler. Citing John Leland's claim that Fowler 'was very onthrift' and was forced to sell all his lands, they reasoned that the expense of the building had financially ruined him.[9] A possible objection to

Fowler having commissioned the mansion is to be found in Chancery and Exchequer records. These records suggest that Fowler was already experiencing financial difficulties in the early sixteenth century. It is possible that he did not possess the means to build on a grand scale.

Sherwood and Pevsner, however, date the architectural style of the mansion to the 1520s.[10] It is a dating supported by Garner and Stratton in the 1929 edition of their *Domestic Architecture of England during the Tudor Period*.[11] If this dating is correct, then the mansion can only have been the work of the Heron family. Sir John Heron, treasurer to Henry VII and VIII, purchased the manors of Rycote Magna and Parva from Richard Fowler in 1521.[12] Upon his death, the following year, Rycote passed to his son Giles.

Writing in the 1740s, Thomas Delafield, compiler of an unpublished history of Rycote's owners, recorded that 'it has been said, that the most antient part of the present great House at Rycote, was the work of the Quatremaynes [late fifteenth-century owners]: And the Remainder seems to have been built, or eminently repaired, by John Lord Williams of Thame, his Arms appearing on the Portal in the grand front'.[13] There is archaeological evidence of a medieval manor house at Rycote dating from the thirteenth to fourteenth century.[14] John Goodall has put forward a persuasive argument in favour of Lord Williams. Goodall argues that architecture has always been the privilege of the few and that the building of a house on the scale of Rycote requires substantial wealth and good connections to the Court.[15] Williams possessed both of these. As Master of the Jewels, and then Treasurer of the Court of Augmentations, Williams was superbly positioned to take full advantage of the opportunities created for personal enrichment by Henry VIII's suppression of the monasteries. A consummate survivor, he was able to negotiate the reigns of Henry VIII, Edward VI, Mary and Elizabeth I and retain royal office throughout. Goodall also contends that the architectural style of the mansion is indicative of the mid-sixteenth century.[16]

Our understanding of the mansion's architectural style is confined to five views. The earliest identified view of Rycote is an engraving by Henry Winstanley. Winstanley dedicated his engraving to 'James Lord Norreys Baron of Ricott & Lord Lievtenant of the said County of Oxford.' This dates the engraving to between 1674 and 1682. Lord Norris was appointed Lord Lieutenant of Oxfordshire in March 1674 and created Earl of Abingdon in November 1682. Figure 3.1 is a copy of Winstanley's engraving drawn in the early 1740s by William Delafield for his father Thomas's unpublished history of Rycote.

Figure 3.2 is an engraved view produced by Leonard Knyff and Johannes Kip in the early eighteenth century. It was published in the first edition of Kip's *Britannia Illustrata* in 1707. Another view by Pieter Van der Aa was published in James Beeverell's *Les Délice de la Grand' Bretagne et de l'Irelande* in the same year. It was probably produced using the Knyff and Kip view which it closely resembles. The Knyff and Kip engraving is the only view, of any date, to offer a

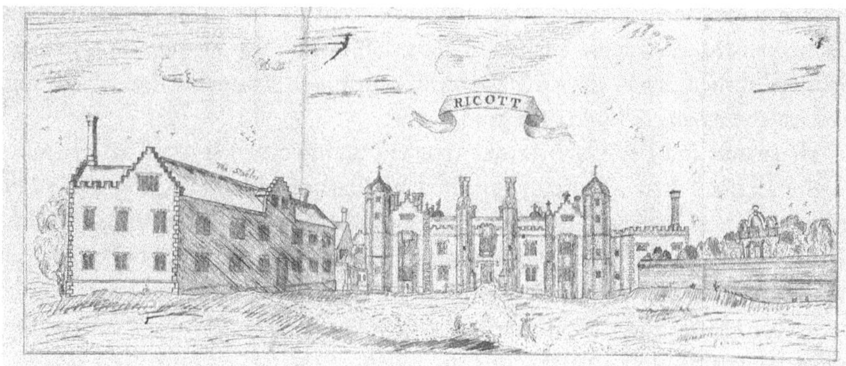

3.1   Henry Winstanley's engraving, which dates from between 1674 and 1682, is the earliest known view of the Tudor mansion at Rycote. This copy of Winstanley's view was drawn by William Delafield, probably in the early 1740s.

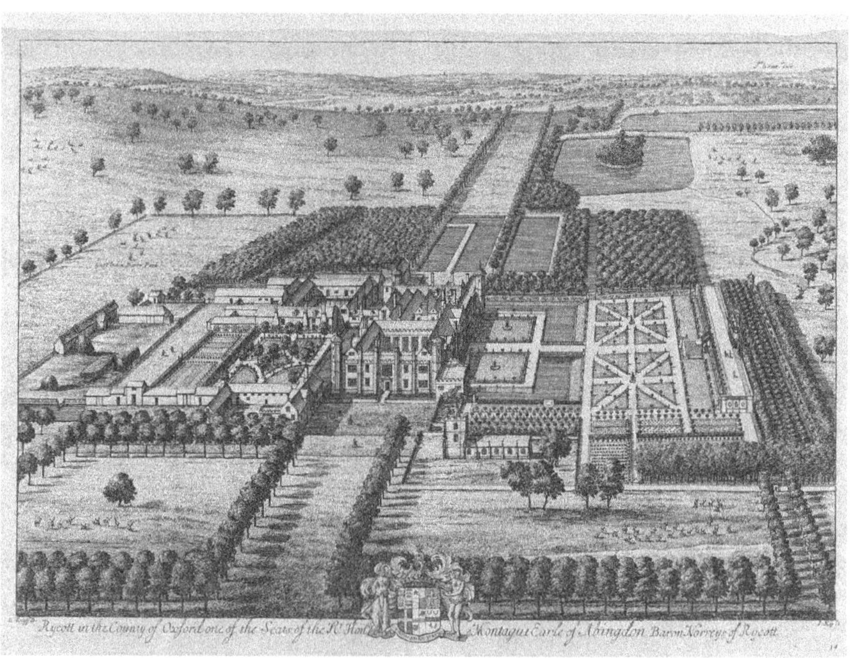

3.2   Engraved view of Rycote Park by Leonard Knyff and Johannes Kip, 1707. The formal gardens shown here are said to have been designed by Inigo Jones and date from the 1630s.

perspective of the Tudor mansion, the outbuildings and surrounding parkland in their entirety. Sir Roy Strong has dated the Jonesian Italianate formal gardens depicted in this view to the 1630s.[17] That Inigo Jones was the architect of the Rycote gardens shown here appears to be confirmed by a passage in the journal of John Loveday. During a visit to Rycote, as a guest of the 2nd Earl of Abingdon in 1736, Loveday was informed that the colonnade and terraces, seen on the eastern side of the mansion, were constructed by Jones to shelter the house from a 'mischievous Wind'. The 'mount', as it was known in the family, was topped by a 'light open kind of Alcove' which served as part of an ornamental approach.[18] The Inigo Jones gardens were obliterated by re-landscaping works undertaken by Lancelot 'Capability' Brown in the 1770s.[19]

Later views of the mansion depict stark alterations to the original Tudor building. On the night of 11 and 12 November 1745 a fire broke out at Rycote.[20] The fire is said to have started in the kitchens and destroyed much of the building.[21] Figure 3.3 is an engraving of the refurbished mansion published by Conrad Martin Metz and James Heath in *The British Magazine and Review* in 1783. When compared to the Winstanley view, the differences between the Tudor and refurbished Georgian mansion are clear to see. The turrets seen either side of the main entrance in the Winstanley engraving, for example, have been removed during the post-fire renovations. The windows have also been radically

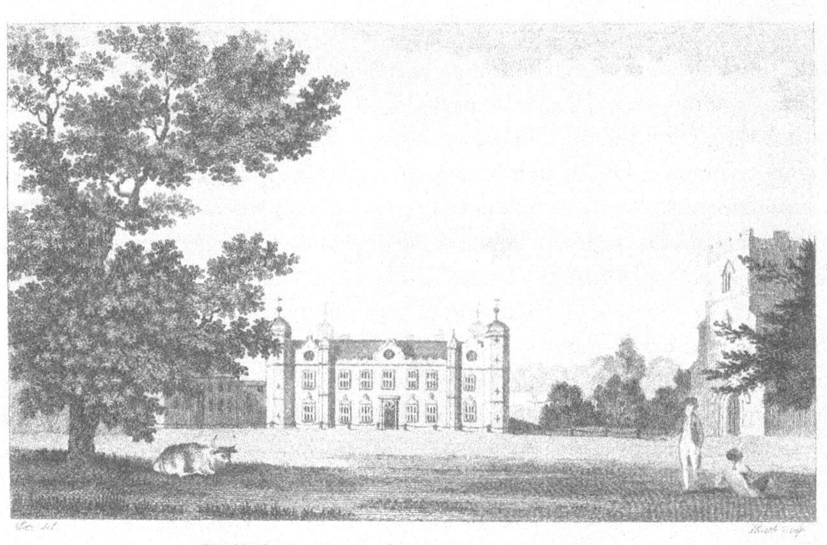

3.3   Engraved view of Rycote by Conrad Martin Metz and James Heath, 1783. The mansion depicted here had undergone extensive renovation following a fire in 1745.

altered. Metz and Heath's engraving does not afford us a detailed perspective of them, but the ground floor windows show the 'gothick' features castigated by Viscount Torrington during his visit of 1785.[22] Another engraving of Rycote, almost certainly produced from the Metz and Heath view, was published by J. Sewell in the November 1799 edition of *The European Magazine and London Review*.

Very few documentary sources provide any information concerning the internal arrangement of the Tudor building and its fittings. For an understanding of the mansion's interior we are wholly reliant upon eighteenth-century sources. Their usefulness for the study of the mansion before the fire of 1745 is highly questionable. Archaeological excavations, and the standing remains of the original Tudor buildings, help to fill the documentary void. The 2001 *Time Team* excavation located the great hall on the northern wing of the quadrangle, with an entrance way found on the eastern wing. *Time Team* also uncovered the remains of an orange and green chequerboard tiled floor dating from the second quarter of the seventeenth century. The hall is depicted as a two-storey structure in the Knyff and Kip view. We can also establish the position of the bakery from substantial surviving parts of the bread ovens, fireplace and a bent chimney flue. These are preserved in a house which still stands on the estate. On the Knyff and Kip engraving this is the building shown with three chimneys to the north-west of the great hall, on the west side of the moat. The Tudor stables, which are clearly labelled in the Winstanley view, form part of the present Rycote House.

It is clear from eighteenth-century documentary evidence that Rycote housed a gallery and a substantial art collection. The content of the pre-1745 fire collection is, however, difficult to ascertain fully. The earliest information that we possess is John Loveday's account of his 1736 visit. Loveday records the pictures in both the gallery and the billiard-table room. The pictures that he describes are mainly portraits of family members descended from Richard Bertie. The gallery and billiard-table room are each noted as containing portraits of Richard Bertie's wife Katherine, Duchess of Suffolk. A portrait of their son Peregrine Bertie, 13th Baron Willoughby, was in the billiard-table room. Portraits of Robert Bertie, 1st Earl of Lindsey, were also found in both rooms. Loveday records that the gallery also contained other family portraits of Montague Bertie, 2nd Earl of Lindsey, probably with his second wife Bridget, *suo jure* Baroness Norris; John, Baron Williams of Thame, and his wife; as well as unspecified members of the Norris family. Loveday also noted the presence of two portraits by Sir Anthony Van Dyck of James Stewart, 4th Duke of Lennox and 1st Duke of Richmond, and his wife Mary. Loveday records two further portraits of George Monck, 1st Duke of Albemarle, and Colonel John Cromwell as then being present in the gallery.[23]

Loveday's account of the gallery is corroborated by Thomas Delafield's history of Rycote. Delafield's description of the gallery contents was probably compiled around the same time as Loveday's and certainly before the 1745 fire. It is apparent, however, that Delafield did not personally view the gallery. In addition to the portraits listed by Loveday, Delafield also claimed that the gallery contained a portrait of the four-year-old Charles I. He surmised that the portrait was produced in 1605 to commemorate Francis Norris, Earl of Berkshire's creation as a Knight of the Bath in the same ceremony as Charles. Delafield also identifies the portraits of the members of the Norris family. He specifies that these were of Sir John Norris and his five brothers; Francis Norris, Earl of Berkshire; Elizabeth, *suo jure* Baroness Norris; and her husband Edward Wray. He also locates a portrait of Lord Williams and his wife in the gallery but, like Loveday, neglects to mention whether it is of Williams's first or second wife. Delafield's account, however, differs from Loveday's in that he places the portrait of Peregrine Bertie, 13th Baron Willoughby, in the gallery.[24]

Two sales catalogues of interior goods and furnishings of 1779 and 1780 provide further information regarding the picture collection. These catalogues, however, describe the mansion renovated after the fire of 1745. It is clear that the refurbished Georgian mansion did house a gallery. Its contents, though, are not known. A room known as the 'brown gallery' is listed in the 1780 catalogue but it states only that it contained forty-two landscapes and other family paintings which were not for sale.[25] We can discern from the 1779 and 1780 catalogues that four of the pictures described by Loveday and Delafield did survive the fire. Van Dyck's portrait of the Duke of Lennox and Richmond is listed in the sales catalogues as then being located in the large drawing room.[26] The portrait of the Duchess is listed in the library.[27] One of the portraits of the Duchess of Suffolk, the full-length portrait that Loveday saw in the gallery, also appears to have survived and been moved to the large drawing room. The 1779 and 1780 catalogues attribute it to Van Dyck.[28] The two sales catalogues also describe a portrait of the 1st Duke of Albemarle in the 'Egyptian hall, staircase and passage'.[29] This is possibly the portrait that Loveday viewed in the gallery in 1736.

The sales catalogues also describe further Van Dyck portraits. Whether they were at Rycote prior to the 1745 fire is impossible to know. The large drawing room is described as containing two Van Dyck portraits of Robert Bertie, 1st Earl of Lindsey, and John, Earl of Oxford.[30] The Earl of Lindsey's portrait appears to be different from the two recorded by Loveday in 1736. Both of the versions seen by Loveday were head and shoulders portraits whereas the Van Dyck is listed as a full length. Amongst the other portraits contained in the two sales catalogues is a Holbein of Henry VIII in the library.[31] Its provenance and authenticity are not known.

The evidence for the library and manuscript collections at Rycote is similarly rooted in Georgian sources. The 1780 sale catalogue of interior goods provides the earliest evidence for what the contents of the library may have been (Figure 3.4). It lists 350 printed books.[32] Another catalogue drawn up in 1801 lists over

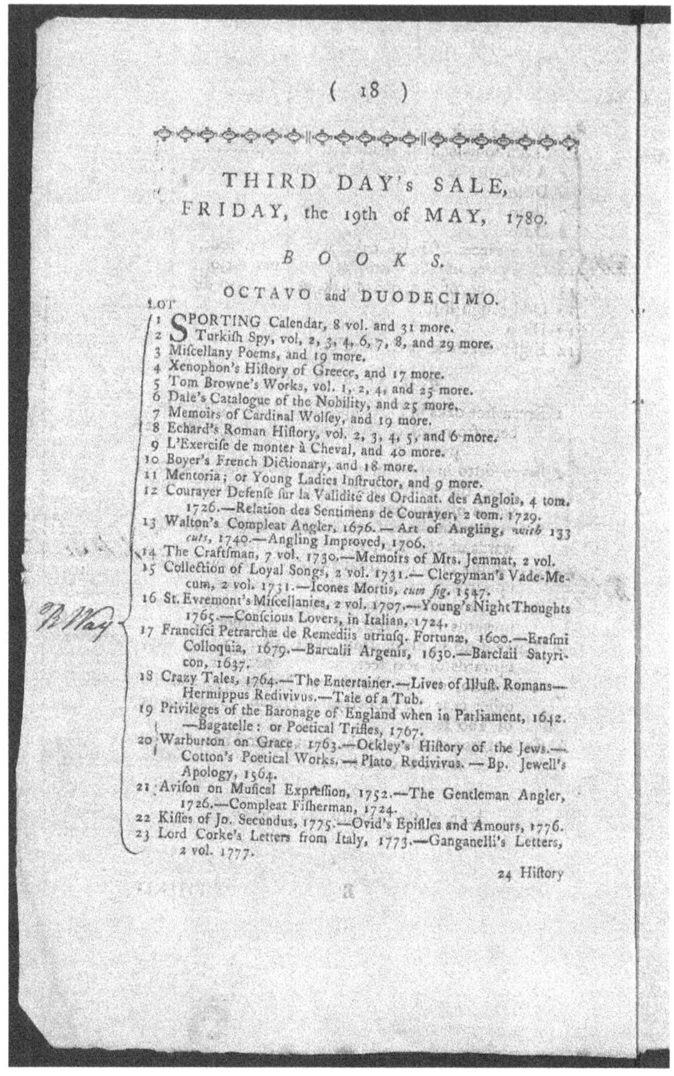

3.4   Part of the 1780 inventory of the Rycote library. This listing, which forms part of a sale catalogue of interior fittings and furnishings, records 350 books and two manuscripts.

one thousand titles.[33] The books in both catalogues range in date from 1506 to 1788. The earliest publication is a 1506 *Commedia di Dante*.[34] It does not appear in the 1801 catalogue. Some 531 of the books were published prior to 1700. Due to the dispersal of the library it is impossible to know if the pre-1700 titles were collected by Rycote's Tudor and Stuart owners. Neither of the two catalogues offer any information regarding provenance. We cannot rule out the possibility that the library they describe was created after the fire of 1745.

In addition to the collection of books, we also possess evidence of a small manuscript collection at Rycote. Only two manuscripts, however, can confidently be said to have been at Rycote prior to 1700. Henry, 1st Baron Norris of Rycote, is known to have possessed a cartulary of Abingdon Abbey in 1594.[35] It has been suggested that Norris may have acquired the cartulary upon his acquisition of the manor of Cumnor, a former possession of the abbey.[36] An alternative hypothesis is that the manuscript may have come to Rycote via John, Baron Williams of Thame. Williams was a participant in the dissolution of the abbey in 1538.[37] The manuscript was acquired by James Lyell in 1938 and was bequeathed to the Bodleian in 1948.

The second manuscript known to have been at Rycote prior to 1700 is an address, composed in Latin, probably delivered to Elizabeth I during her entertainment by the University of Oxford in 1566. A copy of this manuscript is now in the Bodleian Library, and includes a note that it was copied from the original at Rycote in 1576.[38]

In March 1733 the antiquary Thomas Hearne noted in his diary that a cartulary of Notley Abbey was in the possession of the 2nd Earl of Abingdon at Rycote.[39] It is not known how or when the cartulary came to Rycote, but in 1610 it was owned by Sir John Dormer.[40] According to H. E. Salter, this cartulary was destroyed on the same bonfire as the mansion archive in 1807.[41] There is no evidence of it having survived.

The 1780 catalogue lists two manuscripts. The first is the middle English poem 'Pearce Plowman's Visions' on vellum.[42] The catalogue provides no details regarding the manuscript's date or provenance. It does not appear in the 1801 catalogue. The second manuscript described in the 1780 catalogue is 'collections out of the journals of the House of Lords'.[43] Again there is no information regarding its date or purpose. It is possible that this manuscript survived the 1780 sale. The 1801 catalogue lists three very similar manuscripts, together with a treatise on nobility, but does not reveal their date.[44]

The 1801 catalogue of the library includes a manuscript titled 'Beda de ymagine Mundi'.[45] The date of the manuscript is not given but a 1366 catalogue of the Carmelite friary of Hulne, near Alnwick, includes a manuscript of the same title.[46] K. W. Humphreys claims this to be a misattribution to Bede of Honorius Augustodunensis's *Imago Mundi*.[47] A thirteenth-century manuscript in the library of Exeter Cathedral also uses the same title.[48]

The final manuscript reference, contained in the 1801 catalogue, is to a 330-volume collection of music.[49] These volumes, which are described as being chiefly in manuscript, are likely to have been collected by the 4th Earl of Abingdon in the second half of the eighteenth century.

To gain an insight into the functioning and political influence of Rycote during the early modern period, recourse is necessary to surviving personal papers of its owners and accounts of royal entertainments. Preserved accounts of royal progresses and entertainments at Rycote are fragmentary. The evidence relating to Henry VIII's progress in August 1540, for example, resides solely in privy council records indicating the length of the King's visit.[50]

Of Elizabeth I's September 1566 visit to Rycote we know little other than that she arrived following her progress to Oxford University, and knighted Henry Norris.[51] Details of her 1568 and 1570 visits are preserved in a pay book of building charges of the Queen's progresses. The 1568 account records the work of carpenters occupied in making a press for the Queen's robes; costs of 'planch-boards' and 'sengle quarters' for flooring; 'stock-locks'; and the transportation of the tent from Bicester to Rycote.[52] The account for 1570 (Figure 3.5) is more detailed and records more extensive building works such as 'carpenters occupied not onelye in daminge upp of dores and windowes and mending of Flowers as alsoe in makinge of presses and tables for the Robbes and mendinge of the stayers' and labourers employed 'in brekinge hols throwge a walle'.[53] It also records expenditure on a cellar, buttery and wardrobe of beds for the use of the royal household. These two accounts form the earliest written evidence of building works at Rycote.

The Queen's visit of 1592, however, is the only one for which we have any evidence of the more ceremonial aspects of the progress, in the form of a contemporary account published by the Oxford bookseller Joseph Barnes.[54] Jean Wilson has remarked on the very personal nature of the Queen's entertainment by the Norrises.[55] John Nolan has also drawn attention to the Norrises' careful exploitation of the presence of the Queen and her privy council to advance the careers of their soldier sons.[56] Lord Norris's speech, welcoming Elizabeth to Rycote, is a carefully orchestrated oration of family loyalty:

> Vovchsafe dread soueraigne, after so many smooth speeches of Muses, to heare a rough hewen tale of a souldier, wee use not with wordes, to amplifie our conceites, and to pleade faith by figures, but by deedes, to shew the loyalty of our harts, and to make it good with our liues. I meane not to recount any seruice, all proceeding of duety, but to tell your Maiesty, that I am past al seruice, saue only deuotion. My horse, mine armour, my shielde, my sworde, the riches of a young souldier, and an olde souldiers reliques, I should here offer to your highnesse, but my foure boies haue stollen them from me, vowing themselues to armes, and leauing mee to my prayers, fortune giueth successe, fidelitye courage, chance cannot blemish faith, nor trueth preue[n]t destinye, whateuer happe[ns] this is their resolution, and my desire, that their liues maye, be imployed wholy in your seruice, and their deathes, bee their vowes sacrifice. Their deathes, the rumour of which, hath so often affrighted the Crowe my wife, that her hart, hath bene as blacke as her feathers.[57]

Lord Norris's speech draws heavily on the family's sacrifices and personal connections to Elizabeth. The lives of two of the Norris brothers had already been lost in the Queen's service by the time of her entertainment in September

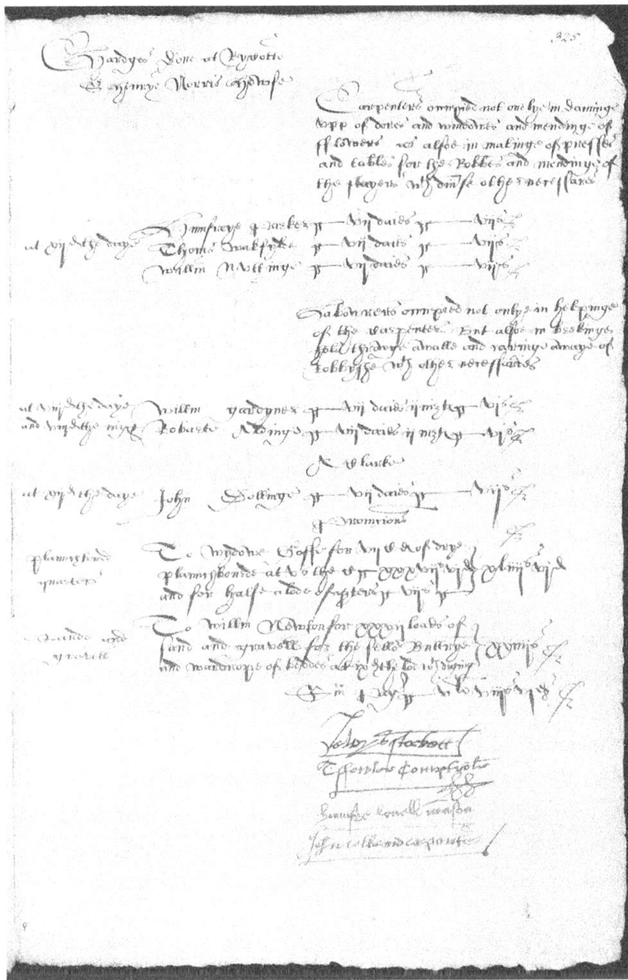

3.5 An account of charges for carpenters and labourers occupied at Rycote in preparation for the progress of Elizabeth I, August 1570.

1592. To reinforce the family connection to Elizabeth, Lord Norris makes explicit reference to 'the Crowe my wife'. This was a nickname given to Lady Norris by the Queen in respect of her dark complexion. Five years after this entertainment, Elizabeth wrote a personal letter of condolence affectionately addressed to 'myne owne crow' to comfort Lady Norris on the death of her son Sir John.[58]

The display of family loyalty and service was reinforced the following day with the arrival of letters and gifts from each of the four surviving Norris brothers. An 'Irish lacque' delivered a gold dart set with diamonds and inscribed, in Irish, 'I fly only for my sovereign.'[59] The gift was almost certainly sent by Sir Thomas Norris, then serving as vice-president of Munster. His accompanying letter again plays on personal sacrifice, claiming 'I am a stranger in mine owne countrye' and that 'I should accuo[n]t my ten years absence a flatt banishment, were I not honoured in her Maiesties seruice.'[60] Sir Edward Norris, governor of Ostend, sent a gold key set with diamonds and inscribed 'I only open to you.' The accompanying letter described it as the 'key of Ostende, & Ostend the key of Flaunders.'[61] Finally, a French page arrived with gifts of a gold sword set with diamonds inscribed, in French, 'drawn only in your defence' and a truncheon set with diamonds with the motto, in Spanish, 'I do not command but under you.'[62] The two gifts came from Sir John and Sir Henry Norris in Brittany. Sir John was the commander of Elizabeth's army in Brittany aiding Henry IV. Sir Henry was serving under his brother's command. The locations from which the gifts were sent, demonstrate the range of a family military network which spanned the major Elizabethan theatres of war. On the day of Elizabeth's departure, a messenger arrived from Jersey bearing a further gift of a gold daisy set with rubies from Lord Norris's daughter Catherine.[63] Catherine was the wife of Sir Anthony Poulett, governor of Jersey.

In comparison to the progresses of Elizabeth, the surviving archival evidence for the more numerous visits of James I is far less detailed. James made a total of five visits between 1612 and 1619. Aside from records documenting the creation of new knights at Rycote, only a single letter sheds any light on the nature of the the King's stay. Writing to Sir John Holles, after the 1614 progress, a resentful Francis, 2nd Baron Norris of Rycote, complained that James had not created any new knights at his house and had barely left his bedchamber throughout the visit.[64]

The documentary accounts for the visit of Charles I in July 1625 are equally fragmentary. Through State Papers and the issuance of a proclamation for the removal of the exchequer, we can state definitively that the King was at Rycote on 30 and 31 July.[65] A letter of Edward, Lord Conway, indicates that Charles's stay was intended to be for two days as he was due to be at the royal manor of Woodstock on 1 August.[66] We know nothing regarding the precise nature of Charles's entertainment at Rycote but it is said that the domed south pew in Rycote Chapel was installed for the King's use.[67]

Of the surviving personal papers of Rycote's early modern owners, none demonstrate the links between Rycote, the Crown and Oxfordshire politics more emphatically than those of James Bertie, 1st Earl of Abingdon. Appointed to the lord lieutenancy of Oxfordshire in 1674, he was the dominant force in the county for much of the final quarter of the seventeenth century. Tory in his political inclinations, Abingdon was a firm supporter of the restored Stuart monarchy and was at the forefront of efforts to suppress Whig influence in

3.6 Letter, 20 June 1685, from Henry Hyde, 2nd Earl of Clarendon, to James Bertie, 1st Earl of Abingdon, authorising the recruitment of volunteer militia in Oxford during the Duke of Monmouth's rebellion.

the county. He was steadfast in his loyalty to the Crown when the Duke of Monmouth instigated a rebellion against his Catholic uncle James II in June 1685. His correspondence network and the political nuances of his position in Oxfordshire are vividly captured both in his own surviving papers and accounts compiled by contemporary witnesses. The political situation in Oxford required careful handling. The interests of the city and the University often diverged. During the last years of the reign of Charles II, Abingdon had been at the centre of a protracted dispute over the issuance of a new city charter. At the outbreak of the rebellion the University sought a special commission from the King to raise its own volunteer militia. Ever keen to preserve its autonomy, the University wanted its militia to be free from the Lord Lieutenant's command.[68] Abingdon criticised the University for 'being jealous of I know not what punctilio of privilege, which I am afraid may spoil the whole design.'[69] However, in an obvious gesture of goodwill, the University proceeded to commission the Earl's twelve-year-old son, Lord Norris, to the command of its militia.[70]

It is clear that the Crown placed great importance on Abingdon's influence in the county. To his great frustration, the Earl was ordered to remain in Oxford by the King and not join the royal army marching to engage Monmouth.[71] The Lord Privy Seal, the Earl of Clarendon, maintained a constant stream of correspondence with Abingdon throughout the rebellion (Figure 3.6).[72] Commissions for the Earl's brothers, Henry and Richard Bertie, were also expedited.[73] Henry Bertie's letters from the front provided Abingdon with an essential source of news.[74]

Following the defeat of the rebellion, Abingdon hosted a celebratory dinner at Rycote for the University troop. The troopers are said to have returned to Oxford 'well fuz'd'.[75] Celebrations at Rycote appear to have formed a regular part of entertainments held by the city of Oxford and the University for visiting dignitaries in the second half of the seventeenth century. Entertainments held in Oxford for the heir to the Danish throne, the Moroccan ambassador, and the Duke of York all concluded with visits to Rycote.[76] Precise details of these entertainments at Rycote, however, remain tantalisingly elusive.

This is highly indicative of much of Rycote's early modern history. The surviving documentary evidence affords us only glimpses into aspects of the mansion's history. We are never presented with the full picture. This is very much the case regarding our knowledge of the royal entertainments. Joseph Barnes's account of Elizabeth I's 1592 progress is the only one to provide any substantial details of the nature of the entertainments staged for the monarch. Even then, as demonstrated by Jean Wilson, it is only a small excerpt from a much longer visit.[77] The question of the mansion's construction date also remains unanswered.

Yet the glimpses afforded by these surviving sources serve to reveal a country house of significant local and national importance. The Bodleian Library's Rycote Project has created a unique opportunity to bring together the fragmented resources to rediscover a lost part of Oxfordshire's history. Incorporating more than one hundred fully digitised sources, the Rediscovering Rycote website aims to encourage further research into a long-neglected story.

Notes

1   J. S. Brewer, R. H. Brodie and James Gairdner (eds), *Letters and Papers, Foreign and Domestic, of the Reign of Henry VIII: Preserved in the Public Record Office, the British Museum, and Elsewhere* (Vaduz: Kraus Reprint, 1965), vol. 15, p. 215.
2   Brewer, Brodie and Gairdner (eds), *Letters and Papers*, vol. 14, pt. 2, p. 300.
3   Brewer, Brodie and Gairdner (eds), *Letters and Papers*, vol. 15, p. 499.

4   George E. Cokayne, Vicary Gibbs and H. A. Doubleday (eds), *The Complete Peerage of England, Scotland, Ireland, Great Britain and the United Kingdom, Extant, Extinct, or Dormant* (London: St Catherine Press, 1910–59), vol. 9, p. 644.

5   Bodleian Library (hereafter Bodl.), MS. Gough Oxon. 30, fol. 274.

6   Charles Edward Doble, David Watson Rannie and H. E. Salter (eds), *Remarks and Collections of Thomas Hearne* (Oxford: Printed for the Oxford Historical Society at the Clarendon Press, 1885–1921), vol. 11, p. 166.

7   http://rycote.bodleian.ox.ac.uk.

8   Frederick George Lee, *The History, Description and Antiquities of the Prebendal Church of the Blessed Virgin Mary of Thame* (London: Mitchell and Hughes, 1883), pp. 294–5, 299–300.

9   Bodl., MS. Top. Oxon. e. 9, fol. 9ᵛ.

10 Jennifer Sherwood and Nikolaus Pevsner, *Oxfordshire, Buildings of England* (Harmondsworth: Penguin, 2001), p. 748.

11 Thomas Garner and Arthur Stratton, *The Domestic Architecture of England during the Tudor Period: Illustrated in a Series of Photographs & Measured Drawings of Country Mansions, Manor Houses and Smaller Buildings* (London: B. T. Batsford, 2ⁿᵈ edn, 1929), p. 144.

12 British Library, Arundel MS 26, fol. 76b.

13 Bodl., MS. Gough Oxon. 31, fol. 216ʳ.

14 Katie Hirst, 'Thame, Rycote House', *South Midlands Archaeology*, 31 (2001), p. 71.

15 John Goodall, 'The Tudor mansion at Rycote' (Bodleian Libraries: Rediscovering Rycote: A symposium on the history of Rycote Park, 31 October 2012).

16 John Goodall, *The English Castle 1066–1650* (London: Yale University Press, 2011), p. 457.

17 Roy Strong, *The Renaissance Garden in England* (London: Thames and Hudson, 1998), pp. 185–6.

18 Sarah Markham, 'The Tours of John Loveday of Caversham 1728–1756' (Unpublished transcript, 2010), p. 283.

19 Dorothy Stroud, *Capability Brown* (London: Country Life, 1950), p. 142; Peter Willis, 'Capability Brown's account book with Drummonds Bank, 1753–1783', *Architectural History: Journal of the Society of Architectural Historians of Great Britain*, 27 (1984), 384.

20 Bodl., MS. Gough Oxon. 31, fol. 215ʳ.

21 Katie Hirst, 'Thame, Rycote House', *South Midlands Archaeology*, 31 (2001), 71.

22 C. Bruyn Andrews (ed.), *The Torrington Diaries, Containing the Tours Through England and Wales of the Hon. John Byng (Later Fifth Viscount Torrington) Between the Years 1781 and 1794* (London: Methuen & Co. Ltd., 1970), vol. 1, p. 213.

23 Markham, 'Tours of John Loveday', pp. 283–4.

24 Bodl., MS. Gough Oxon. 31, fol. 244ᵛ.

25 Bodl., MS. Top. Oxon. b. 121, fol. 71ᵛ.

26 Bodl., MS. Top. Oxon. b. 121, fols 36ᵛ, 71ᵛ.

27 Bodl., MS. Top. Oxon. b. 121, fols 38ᵛ, 71ʳ.

28 Bodl., MS. Top. Oxon. b. 121, fols 36ᵛ, 71ᵛ.

29 Bodl., MS. Top. Oxon. b. 121, fols 38ᵛ, 71ᵛ.

30 Bodl., MS. Top. Oxon. b. 121, fols 36ᵛ 71ᵛ.

31 Bodl., MS. Top. Oxon. b. 121, fols 38ʳ, 71ᵛ.

32 Bodl., MS. Top. Oxon. b. 121, fols 73ᵛ–75ᵛ.

33 Bodl., MS. Top. Oxon. c. 382, fols 57ᵛ–103ʳ.

34 Bodl., MS. Top. Oxon. b. 121, fol. 74(a)ʳ.

35 Albinia Catherine De La Mare, *Catalogue of the Collection of Medieval Manuscripts Bequeathed to the Bodleian Library, Oxford, by James P. R. Lyell* (Oxford: Clarendon Press, 1971), p. 37.

36 C. F. Slade and Gabrielle Lambrick (eds), *Two Cartularies of Abingdon Abbey* (Oxford: Oxford Historical Society, 1990–92), vol. 1, p. xlii.

37 Brewer, Brodie and Gairdner (eds), *Letters and Papers Henry VIII*, vol. 13, pt. 1, p. 176.

38 Bodl., MS. Top. Oxon. d. 238, fols 33–6.

39 Bodl., MS. Hearne's diary 138, fols 129–30.

40 G. R. C. Davis, Claire Breay and Julian Harrison (eds), *Medieval Cartularies of Great Britain and Ireland* (London: British Library, 2010), p. 146.

41 Doble, Rannie and Salter (eds), *Remarks of Thomas Hearne*, vol. 11, p. 166.

42 Bodl., MS. Top. Oxon. b. 121, fol. 74ᵛ.

43 Bodl., MS. Top. Oxon. b. 121, fol. 75ᵛ.

44 Bodl., MS. Top. Oxon. c. 382, fols 62, 77, 97.

45 Bodl., MS. Top. Oxon. c. 382, fol. 65.

46 K. W. Humphreys, *The Friars' Libraries* (London: British Library, 1990), p. 169.

47 Humphreys, *Friars' Libraries*, p. 169.

48 Neil R. Ker, *Medieval Manuscripts in British Libraries* (Oxford: The Clarendon Press, 1969–2002), vol. 2, p. 822.

49 Bodl., MS. Top. Oxon. c. 382, fol. 97.

50 Brewer, Brodie and Gairdner (eds), *Letters and Papers Henry VIII*, vol. 15, pp. 498–9.

51 John Nichols, *The Progresses and Public Processions of Queen Elizabeth* (London: John Nichols and Son, 1823), vol. 1, p. 250.

52 Bodl., MS. Rawl. A 295c, fol. 266.

53 Bodl., MS. Rawl. A 295c, fol. 325.

54 Joseph Barnes, *Speeches Deliuered to her Maiestie this Last Progresse, At the Right Honorable the Lady Rvssells, at Bissam, the Right Honorable the Lorde Chandos at Sudley, at the Right Honorable the Lord Norris, at Ricorte* (Oxford: Joseph Barnes, 1592).

55 Jean Wilson, *Entertainments for Elizabeth I* (Cambridge: D. S. Brewer, 1980), p. 52.

56 John S. Nolan, *Sir John Norreys and the Elizabethan Military World* (Exeter: University of Exeter Press, 1997), p. 198.

57 Barnes, *Speeches to her Maiestie*, p. c.ii.

58 Bodl., MS. e. Mus. 18, fol. 168.

59 Nichols, *Progresses of Queen Elizabeth*, vol. 3, p. 169.

60 Barnes, *Speeches to her Maiestie*, p. c.ii.

61 Barnes, *Speeches to her Maiestie*, p. c.iii.

62 Barnes, *Speeches to her Maiestie*, p. c.iii.

63 Barnes, *Speeches to her Maiestie*, p. c.iii.

64 Royal Commission on Historical Manuscripts, *The Manuscripts of His Grace the Duke of Portland, Preserved at Welbeck Abbey* (London: HMSO, 1891–1931), vol. 9, p. 145.

65 John Bruce, William Douglas Hamilton and S. C. Lomas (eds), *Calendar of State Papers, Domestic Series, of the Reign of Charles I: Preserved in the State Paper Department of Her Majesty's Public Record Office* (London: Longman, Brown, Green, Longmans & Roberts, 1858–97), vol. 1, pp. 77–8.

66 Bruce, Hamilton and Lomas (eds), *State Papers Domestic, Charles I*, vol. 23, p. 38.

67 Sherwood and Pevsner, *Oxfordshire*, p. 748.

68 Samuel Weller Singer (ed.), *The Correspondence of Henry Hyde, Earl of Clarendon and of his Brother Laurence Hyde, Earl of Rochester: With the Diary of Lord Clarendon from 1687 to 1690, Containing Minute Particulars of the Events Attending the Revolution: and the Diary of Lord Rochester during his Embassy to Poland in 1676* (London: Henry Colburn, 1828), vol. 1, p. 133.

69 Singer (ed.), *The Correspondence of Henry Hyde*, p. 134.

70 Singer (ed.), *The Correspondence of Henry Hyde*, p. 134.
71 Bodl., MS. Top. Oxon. c. 325, fol. 46.
72 Bodl., MS. Clarendon 128.
73 Bodl., MS. Clarendon 128, fols 20–1.
74 Bodl., MS. Eng. hist. c. 51, fols 147–61.
75 Bodl., MS. Wood D. 19(3), fol. 79[v].
76 Bodl., MS. Wood D. 19(3), fols 4[v], 50–8.
77 Wilson, *Entertainments*, p. 52.

4

'To Penshurst' and to Knole – networks of patronage between two Jacobean country houses

Edward Town

Ben Jonson's poem 'To Penshurst' is perhaps the most important of all country house poems, and has provided the inspiration and a model for a host of subsequent authors. Writing in 1984, Don E. Wayne argued that the poem addressed the anxiety that was felt by some in the early seventeenth century that traditional forms of hospitality and reciprocity were in terminal decline.[1] The central thesis of Wayne's study was that the improvements made to the house in the mid- to late 1570s by Henry Sidney (1529–86) were intentionally sympathetic to the existing medieval fabric, which engendered a sense of continuity that might otherwise have been lost by new building. Wayne drew a parallel between the character of this building campaign and Jonson's grand poetic survey of the Sidney estate, which styled the house and its owner as a model of social community, free from the competitive and callous nature of Court and urban life.

In Jonson's depiction of Penshurst, the house itself was imbued with moral attributes that reflected the happy symbiosis of the owners and the estate, encapsulated in lines 45–6: 'And though they walls be of the countrey stone, / They' are rear'd with no mans ruine, no mans grone'. Although this idea is only fully expressed approximately halfway through the poem, it is one that is introduced in the opening lines:

> Thou art not, PENSHURST, built to enuious show,
> Of touch, or marble; nor cast boast a row
> Of polish'd pillars, or a roofe of gold:
> Thou hast no lanthorne, wherof tales are told;
> Or stayre, or courts; but stand'st an ancient pile,
> And these grudg'g a, art reuerenc'd the while.[2]

Through this method of comparison, Jonson defined Penshurst in terms of what it *was not*. The touchstone, marble, polished pillars, gilded roofs and lanterns listed in the opening lines can be seen as the manifestations of the 'enuious show' of Court and city, which were, by Jonson's estimation at least, not to be found at Penshurst.

This chapter offers an alternative account of the building history of Penshurst Place and by extension Jonson's poem, through an exploration of documentary evidence relating to the changes made to the house during the period 1594–1612. This is a phase of building which has often been overlooked, but which provides the immediate context for Jonson's intellectual conception of the house in 'To Penshurst'. This chapter also situates this campaign of building within the broader context of local politics, with particular reference to Knole, a country house situated approximately five miles north of Penshurst. Knole was acquired in 1604 and subsequently remodelled by Thomas Sackville, 1st Earl of Dorset (c. 1536–1608) between 1605–08.

These two houses have traditionally been defined against each other, with Knole seen as the epitome of Jacobean largesse, and Penshurst as the model of modest accretion. However, this conception not only masks the complexities in the development of these two houses, but also narrows our understanding of how political rivalries at Court played out at a local level through the acquisition and renovation of country houses. Within this context, Court and country were inextricably linked, as materials and personnel travelled back and forth, accelerating the exchange of skills, knowledge and expertise between the two locales. This brought the prevailing court style to the country houses of the elite, and in turn, materials and workmanship from the country to the Court and the city.

Given their proximity, it is unsurprising that there were numerous links between Penshurst and Knole. As it happens, both Henry Sidney and Thomas Sackville enjoyed short periods of ownership of Knole during the 1560s and 1570s, something that has often been overlooked in histories of both houses. What is also rarely mentioned is that prior to his acquisition of Knole in 1604, Thomas Sackville made a series of attempts to acquire the former archbishop's palace at Otford in Kent. This was a Sidney possession by virtue of their family's role as royal stewards of the house and park at Otford, a position that they had held since the reign of Edward VI.[3] According to gossip circulating at Court, Sackville had tried to obtain Otford for his son and political heir, Robert, who 'hath a great Mind to it, in Hope of a better footing in Kent', a clear statement of Sackville's intent to expand his influence in the north-west of the county.[4]

To that end, Sackville petitioned Robert Sidney (1563–1626) to release his interest in Otford, and aimed to outmanoeuvre Sidney at Court by raising anxieties about the Crown's ability to maintain the property.[5] The series of surveys of Otford made over the course of Elizabeth I's reign chart a steady decline in the house's fabric, and by 1600 Otford was in a serious state of disrepair.[6] Nevertheless, the Sidneys refused to relinquish their interest. A memorandum attached to a survey of the house in 1596 notes that they themselves had tried to obtain the fee-farm of the house and park at Otford, and were willing to bear the costs of the reparations so long as they were permitted to remove two large lodging ranges in the base court of the palace.[7] As an alternative to Otford, Sidney offered Leeds Castle in Kent to Sackville, although the lease drawn up in 1603 between the two was never signed.[8]

Matters were complicated further by the fact that as Governor of Flushing (Vlissingen), Robert Sidney was frequently abroad. In his absence, his principal secretary Rowland White conducted his affairs at Court.[9] On 11 January 1600, White wrote to Sidney telling his master that the Queen was under considerable pressure to sell Otford. Reluctant to do so, she instead issued a second survey to assess its state of repair.[10] Predicting his master's response, White added 'it is now full time to take the allarum, for it must surely be my Lord Treasurer or Lord Cobham, and in your Absence they will goe about to get it away'.[11] White was alive to the impact that this would have on local politics: Sackville and Henry Brooke, 11th Baron Cobham (1564–1619) both had considerable land holdings in Kent and Sussex, and their efforts to seize Otford were a direct affront to Sidney. White was also right to raise these fears because as he reported, two of Sackville's servants had travelled to Otford 'and viewed it', no doubt with a mind towards developing plans for its reconstruction.[12]

With tensions running high, White was quick to report to Sidney that there had been 'some unkindness between 900 [Sackville] and 400 [Lord Cobham]'.[13] Sackville also faced stiff opposition from Sidney's wife, Barbara, who visited Sackville at his London home and 'discreetly with some little vehemency, delivered her mynd'.[14] Undeterred, Sackville continued in his efforts. On 2 April 1600, Rowland White recalled a conversation that had taken place between himself and Sackville in Sackville's chamber at Richmond Palace.[15] Firstly, Sackville asked him whether White was Postmaster of the Court and the Queen's servant. He answered that he was, and Sackville gave White parcels to send for him. As he was leaving, Sackville called him back into the room and pressed him on the subject of Otford. He reprimanded White for advertising the conversations that he had held with George Wood (Sackville's gentleman of the horse), which Sackville alleged had been conducted without his knowledge. In this discussion, Wood had related that Sackville had 'fought to have some Parke or other neare London, but could not compas it; that all [Sackville's] Parkes and Landes were 28 Mile of, fowle Way'.[16] Having heard this, Sackville then conceded to White that he 'did greatly desire Oteford Parke', and admitted 'it is true that I have no Place neare to London to retire unto, and therefore shuld be glad of it, if Sir Robert Sidney wold part with it'.[17]

According to White, Wood had also suggested that his master was willing to pay more for Sidney's interest than it was worth, and that Sackville would procure a property of greater profit than Otford for Sidney from the crown in exchange. White was also promised a sweetener for his troubles.

In the end, a compromise was found. On 23 January 1604, Thomas Sackville purchased the lease of Knole for £4000, buying Sampson Lennard out of the fifty-one years that remained on his lease.[18] Just over a year later, on 5 April 1605, the Crown (unknowingly) granted the lordship of Knole in Kent to Rowland White, Robert Sidney's representative and agent, and other unnamed individuals for the sum of £220 6s 8d.[19] On 12 April, Rowland White and the London goldsmith and financier John Williams granted the lordship of Knole with the mansion house and the park to Thomas Sackville for the sum of £2500.[20] This complex series of transactions, whereby White and Williams purchased the freehold from the Crown only to sell it to Sackville days later, was a premeditated plan, which was orchestrated by Sackville himself with all parties fully complicit. For Rowland White, who was instrumental in the success of this operation and probably had a hand in its planning there was the obligatory kickback: on 8 June 1605 he received the reversion on the demesne lands at Otford.[21] Rather than continuing in his attempts to oust the Sidneys from Otford, Sackville rented the lodge and the park from Sidney: a remarkably civil resolution to what had been an acrimonious squabble.[22] However, although a compromise had been found, Sackville's acquisition of Knole and his foothold at Otford represented a clear challenge to Sidney's influence in the area.

An important reason why Penshurst, Knole and Otford were so highly prized by magnates such as Sidney, Sackville and Cobham was that they had amenities and resources that would have been attractive to any member of the ruling elite. Easily accessible from the court at London, the houses were no more than a day's ride from the capital, although leisurely travellers often stopped off overnight at Knole en route to Penshurst. The estates also sported sizeable manorial lands with large hunting parks, a prerequisite for any significant country house of the period. Their lands also contained large stocks of timber: an instant draw for both Sackville and Sidney, who both had a long-standing involvement in the Wealden Iron industry. Buoyed by the influx of foreign expertise, the industry's growth created a demand for woodland suitable for coppicing, which frequently led to disputes between landowners. It was probably this demand for timber stocks that proved the motivation for Thomas Sackville's short-lived acquisition of Knole in 1569: a tenure that had been unpopular with a host of local landowners, the Sidneys included.[23]

The manors were also well provided with large deposits of stone, and skilled quarrymen and masons. Knole and Otford lie on the belt of Lower Greensand stone that traverses the county from Folkstone to beyond Sevenoaks, and yields the stone known commonly as ragstone, which was the principal building material used at Knole for both the medieval great house and the subsequent transformation of the building of 1605–08. Some of this stone was quarried in the pits just north of Knole in the town of Seal. When Archbishop Thomas Bouchier bought the manor of Knole in 1456 from William Fiennes, the deeds of sale noted that he was entitled to 'alle tymbur woode ledde stone and breekebeing or lying wythine the saide manore landes and tenements And at the Quarree of John Cartiers in the parsshe of Seall'.[24]

Unlike Knole, the principal building material at Penshurst was the local sandstone from the Hastings Bed, a superior stone easier to work than the brittle ragstone. When he came to rebuild Knole in 1604, Thomas Sackville also had access to the sandstone quarries at Buxsted in Sussex, situated near to his ancestral seat at Buckhurst. During the first decade of the seventeenth century the quarries at both Buxsted and Penshurst supplied worked stone for the ambitious building project at Salisbury House, Westminster begun by Robert Cecil, 1st Earl of Salisbury (1563–1612). In August 1601 Barbara Sidney wrote to Cecil, informing him that she had allowed his workmen to help themselves to any of the stone at Penshurst.[25] In 1608 ashlar blocks and pillars from Buxsted were carried along the road from East Grinstead to Godstone and then through Croydon to Vauxhall where they were wharfed along the river to Salisbury House. The payments for this work at Buxsted were set out in a schedule written by Thomas Woodgate, keeper of Buckhurst Park.[26]

The hewing and the carving of the stone for Salisbury House in 1608 was undertaken at the quarry by a team of masons working under the supervision of John Killner and William Wilson, all of whom appear to have been local to the area. Their work, which came to £55 17s 8d, was then appraised and valued by Simon Basil, Surveyor of the King's Works, and Cecil's household steward Thomas Wilson.[27] The Sussex masons would have worked to designs and templates supplied by Cecil's architects, and in this way the latest stylistic innovations of London made their way to the quarries of south-east England.

The Kerwin family of north-west Kent played an important role in the building campaigns at both Penshurst, between 1594 and 1612, and Knole, between 1605 and 1608. The best-known members of this family are William Kerwin, Freemason of London (active 1560–84) and Andrew Kerwin, Freemason and paymaster to the Office of Works (active 1593–1617). Although it cannot be proved, William may have been one of the two brothers named as overseers to the will of John Kerwin, freemason of Seal in 1585.[28] However, the links between the London branch of the family and their relatives in Kent are confirmed by a bequest in the will of Andrew Kerwin's widow in 1619 to John Kerwin of Penshurst.[29]

The London Freemason William Kerwin is recorded in 1560 as part of a team of masons working at Greenwich Palace.[30] In 1562–63 he supplied stone for rebuilding at Christ Church Hospital,[31] and in 1567 was paid £4 3s 4d by the Grocers' Company for 135 feet of stone (at 8d the foot).[32] In 1577 he was elected as a sworn viewer of the City of London and, following the death of Phillip Paskyn, was made city mason.[33] In 1580–81 Kerwin was employed by the Office of Works at Greenwich,[34] and in 1584–85 he was paid 73s 6d for 147 feet of Purbeck paving 'wrought and laid at 6d the foot' for Somerset House.[35] Between 1584 and 1586 he rebuilt Ludgate to his own design.[36] His assessment at £50 in the lay subsidy of 1582 as a parishioner of St Ethelberg, Bishopsgate attests to his wealth and growing status.[37] In 1587 he was granted a coat of arms that described his father as 'John of Yorkshire, descended from Curwen' which was probably untrue, and based on a tenuous link to another family.[38]

He later moved to St Helen Bishopsgate, where his wife Magdalen (25 August 1592), his maid Clemens Kerwin (11 March 1596), his son William (3 May 1586) and his son Benjamin (30 July 1621) were all buried. 'William Kerwyn ffremason' was buried on 26 December 1594 'in the vault w[hi]ch he made.'[39] Administration of his estate was passed at the Prerogative Court of Canterbury in 1595.[40] His tomb monument, erected by his son Benjamin and his siblings, survives at St Helen Bishopsgate. Succeeding William Kerwin as City Mason, Andrew Kerwin undertook work at the city Guildhall in 1593,[41] and worked at the Royal Works until he formally received the paymastership in 1604, which seems to have required him to surrender his positions as City Viewer and City Mason.[42] At Knole in 1605–08 Andrew Kerwin supplied Sackville with choice materials such as Purbeck marble and Oxfordshire stone.

At Penshurst, Robert Sidney used his household servant and the woodward of Otford, Robert Kerwin (active 1582–1616), to manage his work at the house.[43] In a letter to his wife in May 1594, Robert Sidney reported that the extensive works at the house were well in hand and that they were being closely supervised by his servant Robert Kerwin.[44] In a similar vein, Thomas Sackville used his manorial bailiff, Thomas Holmden to supervise and manage the work at Knole, and his keeper Thomas Woodward to oversee work at Buckhurst. This suggests that even wealthy patrons such as Sidney and Sackville understood the practical and financial benefits of utilising local knowledge and expertise. In his letters to Sidney, Robert Kerwin demonstrated knowledge of local stocks of timber and stone and also the prices of materials such as lead that were sourced from London. His first surviving letter to Sidney, dated January 1600, stated that he had recently completed the covering on the chancel of the church in the nearby village of Leigh and was planning further work on the terrace in the gardens at the house.[45] Although by this point some work at the house was already in hand, preparations for the most substantial aspect of this phase of work were only beginning. Kerwin's letter of 19 January, sent to Robert Sidney, relates that Lady Sidney had given order for the masons to begin their work. Some 880 feet of stone had been wrought for window dressings, cresting and gable vents, with 100 foot still required. 5,000 boards were needed, as were four fothers of lead from London. By 13 February 1600 Kerwin had begun his work in earnest, having levelled the base court according to Sidney's orders.[46] The windows, doors, gable vents, cresting and corbel stones had also all been carved. Although Kerwin's correspondence is never entirely clear, it appears that the main objective of this campaign of building was to create a large corner tower at the south-west corner of the house, accessed by two galleries (one on top of the other). Traditionally this work has been associated with the previous phase of building at Penshurst, which was undertaken by Henry Sidney, Robert Sidney's father. However, Kerwin's correspondence makes it clear that this corner tower and gallery was the product of Robert Sidney's campaign of building, begun in earnest in around 1600 and largely complete by 1606.

Subsequent letters between Robert Sidney and Robert Kerwin detail that the cost of building the stable and tower was estimated at around £500. Alongside these specifications for building, Kerwin also included a ground plot (presumably drawn himself) of the stable and the tower, which was sent to Robert Sidney for approval.[47] It was in this manner that decisions on the build were made: Kerwin would assess the viability of each phase of the building project, estimate a cost, and then send plans to Sidney for consideration. Many of his letters include requests for funds, and it appears that Kerwin had to put his hands in his own pockets in order to sustain the momentum of the work.

There is a large gap in the correspondence relating to the building work at Penshurst after September 1600, but it is clear that work was well in hand and continuing at a slow but steady pace. By January 1605 the tower must have been largely complete because Thomas James, a surveyor and another of Sidney's servants, wrote complaining that Kerwin lacked funds to pay for lime wash. In the same letter James wrote that the gallery had been glazed, although there was still some confusion as to how the window overlooking the garden should be made. Once glazed and plastered, the gallery (Figure 4.1) could then be paneled, and for this important aspect of the room's decoration, Kerwin and Sidney employed one Herman Scholier.

Referred to simply as 'Mr Herman' by his Kentish employers, Herman Scholier was a native of Xanten (now part of Germany). He was resident in London by 1585, which was where he would to reside until his death in 1619.[48] Like many foreign joiners and carvers, Scholier lived for a period on the south bank of the Thames, firstly in the parish of St Mary Magdalen and later in St Olave Southwark.[49] However, at some point between 1593 and 1598 he moved north of the river to the parish of All Hallows Staining in Mark Lane, which was where he was living when he made his will in 1617.[50]

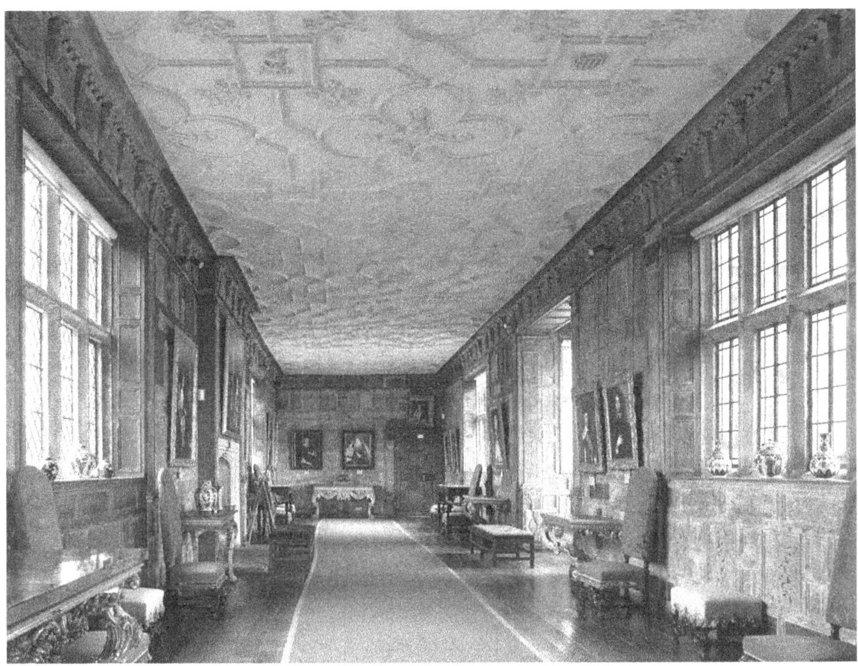

4.1   The Long Gallery at Penshurst Place, Kent, with the panelling installed by the Dutch joiner Herman Scholier in 1606.

Scholier's work at Penshurst involved the construction of the wainscot panelling in the Long Gallery, which measured 294 yards, for which he charged 3s 6d the yard. Scholier also worked in the 'open roome next the garden' (probably the enclosed loggia where the library is now situated) where he made 71 yards of panelling at 2s the yard. He also reset old panelling in the 'low gallery'. An initial payment was made to Scholier on 18 November 1606, and full payment of £44 4s 6d on 5 December 1606. Scholier wrote in receipt of the first of these payments 'Ontsangen van mesiter golding dan 18 dach November 6li 4s 6d ... bii min herman scholier'.[51] A second bill, from 'Mr. Harmon the Joyn[er]' in the same series of accounts sought payment for repairing various items of furniture in the house, seventeen days' labour setting up the old wainscot in the lower gallery, and twenty-five days' work by his man. The final payment included the 'making of viij frames for viij pictures and ffastening them to the frames xs'.[52] Although simple in design, Scholier's work in the gallery at Penshurst was in a fashionable Northern European style with full-height neo-classical pilasters set either side of the windows. An inventory of 'the great Matted Gallery' of 1623, lists an exceptionally fine suite of furnishings of a couch with a gilt frame upholstered in a russet-coloured cloth of gold, with matching chairs and stools. There was also a Persian carpet wrought with silver and gold thread, a square table with a gilt frame painted with various coloured flowers, and a host of portraits of European dignitaries and monarchs, Sidney's peers and various members of his family.[53]

Around this time a certain 'Mr Treswell' appears in the Sidney correspondence. He is first mentioned in a payment made to Thomas James, and Robert Treswell, for helping 'Mr Treswell measure Otford park'. This Treswell can readily be identified as Ralph Treswell, painter-stainer of London (active 1567–1616 or 1617), famous for his numerous surviving surveys of country estates and London tenements.[54] Like many other London Painter-Stainers of the period, Treswell owed his success to his versatility. Not only did he collaborate with Sidney's servants in surveying the large park at Otford (a job which took a week to complete), he also undertook decorative work at Penshurst. The first record of Treswell's work at the house comes in the form of a fascinating letter written in May 1607 by the household steward to Robert Sidney, describing his work.[55] At this point he had not yet finished painting the panelling in the lower gallery, and had only set the Sidney device of a broad arrow head in the middle of each panel.

Although Treswell's work no longer survives, Golding's description provides important clues as to how decorative work of this type was planned and executed. Golding's letter relates that Treswell was in two minds as to whether he would place the letters R – for Robert, B – for Barbara, and L – for Viscount L'Isle, in each of the panels.[56] Once dried, this work was to be varnished to an effect that Golding predicted would make the room 'a very pleasant and lightsome place'.[57]

Golding's following letter described the work that Treswell planned for the banqueting house.[58] Again, the banqueting house no longer survives, but the description of the decorative work undertaken by Treswell and his painters gives a good sense of Penshurst's appearance at the time that Ben Jonson came to write his famous poem. After restoring the sizeable number of paintings in the house, Treswell took it upon himself to paint the wooden pillars of the banqueting house to imitate marble.[59] To do so, he called upon two painters who were then at Knole to complete this work. Remarkably, some sections of the original polychromatic scheme at Knole survive in situ, and part of the decoration of the great stair at Knole includes a series of pillars painted to imitate Purbeck marble, as can be seen in Figure 4.2.

It is worth considering this work in relation to Jonson's poem, because the decorative work that Golding described in his letter to Sidney seems to directly contradict Jonson's depiction of the house in 'To Penshurst'. These were not the noble walls of an ancient pile but a wooden banqueting house painted in *tromp l'oeil* by one of London's most fashionable painters, while his servants were down the road at Knole, itself currently being renovated in the most comfortable and up-to-date style.

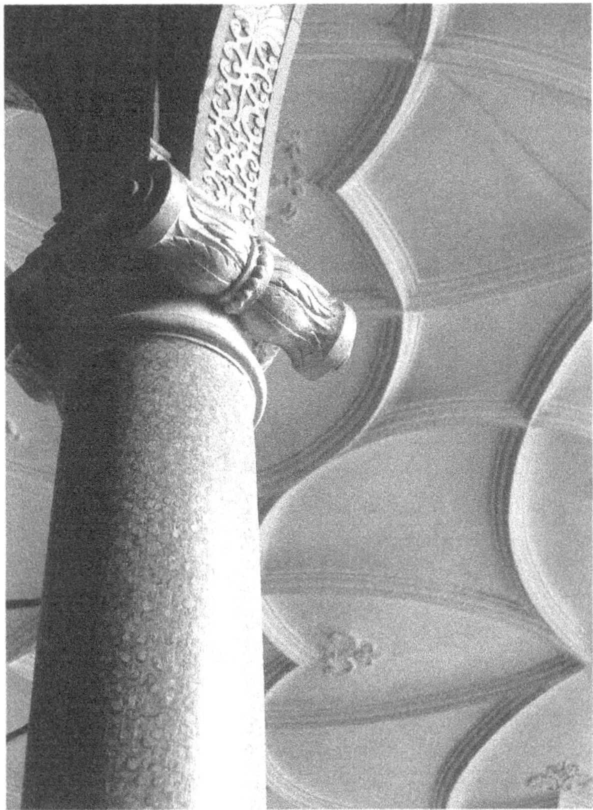

4.2   Detail of painted tromp l'oeil decoration on a wooden column on the Great Stair at Knole, Kent of c.1607 by an unknown artist, possibly Paul Isaacson.

While it is clear that the decoration of the two galleries and the banqueting house was important, the most ambitious aspect of this phase of building was the renovation of the stables at Penshurst. Unfortunately, the seventeenth-century stables were completely destroyed in the nineteenth century when the entire service wing of the house was rebuilt. However, it is clear from Sidney's correspondence that they were built at a scale to rival the stables of the other two leading magnates in Kent. Here, Robert Kerwin's comments are especially revealing:

> I had writton to your Lordsheepe the last weeke, but Gyles Roger had not [then] been att Cobham and at Knoull to see that Knoull stabell is the fairest and that you Lordshepe will like that best.[60]

The stables at Knole were almost entirely gutted through fire in the late nineteenth century, but the shell of the building remains intact. Today, it is difficult to get a sense of its former glory, but as Thomas Golding's letter relates, it was obviously an impressive structure, yet one that Sidney's agents were confident could be surpassed.

Although much of the material evidence at Penshurst has now been lost, Sidney's correspondence gives a good sense of what he aimed to achieve. To maintain his standing at Court, Sidney needed a country house that could accommodate the King and his courtiers as they travelled to hunt during the summer months. To this end, Sidney equipped his house with the requisite state rooms and created two long galleries, wainscoted by a foreign craftsman and filled with portraits of his contemporaries at Court. He also completely rebuilt his stables as the final part of this ambitious phase of building. To ensure that they would impress, Sidney sent his agents to view the stables of rival magnates at Cobham Hall and Knole. These court rivalries, played out in the decoration of the Kentish houses, suggest that, contrary to Jonson's assertion, Penshurst was a house built to envious show.

Through his employment of skilled craftsmen such as Herman Scholier and Ralph Treswell, Robert Sidney brought the latest fashions in interior decoration from London to his country seat in Kent. If there was any of the continuity suggested by Jonson, it was in Sidney's employment of Robert Kerwin, a member of an established family of Kentish masons, as his foreman, but even he had ties to the leading family of Freemasons in London. Identifying such links between the Court, city and country helps further our understanding of how ideas, skills and techniques travelled back and forth between the metropolis and the provinces. The proximity of Kent, Sussex and the other Home Counties to the capital ensured that this interchange took place more regularly than elsewhere, and it is for this reason that some the best examples of London craftsmanship from this period can be found in country houses such as Penshurst and Knole.

Notes

1	Don G. Wayne, *Penshurst: The Semiotics of Place and the Poetics of History* (London: Methuen, 1984).
2	'To Penshurst', Ben Jonson, *The Poems of Ben Jonson*, ed. George Burke (Cambridge, MA: Harvard University Press, 1985).
3	Dennis Clarke and Anthony Stoyel, *Otford in Kent – A History* (Otford: Otford and District Historical Society, 1975), pp. 121–2. For the grant of the park at Otford to Henry Sidney in 1568 see *Calendar of the Patent Rolls, Elizabeth I, Volume IV, 1566–1569* (London, Public Record Office, 1964), p. 235.
4	Arthur Collins, *Letters and Memorials*, vol. II (London: 1776), p. 197.

5   On 14 March 1552, Henry Sidney was made High Steward of Otford and Knole, and gained a lease of the Little Park of Otford. *Acts of Privy Council Volume IV, 1552–1554* (London: 1892), p. 242. The lease for the Little Park was renewed on 26 March 1568. *Calendar of Patent Rolls, Elizabeth I, Volume IV, 1566–1569* (London: Public Record Office, 1964), p. 235.

6   The 'Inquisition and survey of the Queen's mansion-house and park at Otford' of 13 December 1596 estimated the cost of the repairs at £1868 2s 3d. British Library (hereafter BL) Lansdowne 82/117 The Survey of Otford made in February 1597 recommended that even if the house was repaired it would still be unsuitable for the Queen's use due to its unhealthy location. The National Archive (hereafter TNA) E178/1165.

7   BL Lansdowne MS 82/117. There were further suitors to the house and park at Otford. On 21 June, an unknown suitor (possibly William Brooke, 10th Baron Cobham 1527–97) wrote to Burghley seeking his preference for Otford. 'Otford being so near to my house, I have long desired to have some estate in it, and once moved you in the matter, and you wished I had it. I will buy it of the Queen … if I may have a good estate in the park, I will build a pretty house at my own charge'. TNA SP12/259/54

8   Kent History and Library Centre (hereafter KHLC) U1475 E63A.

9   For White's life and career see, Lisle C John, 'Rowland Whyte, Elizabethan Letter-Writer', *Studies in the Renaissance*, 8 (1961), 217–35.

10   *Report on the Manuscripts of Lord De I'Isle and Dudley preserved at Penshurst Place, Kent, Volume Two* (London: HMSO, 1934), p. 428.

11   Collins, *Letters and Memorials*, p. 141.

12   Collins, *Letters and Memorials*, p. 451.

13   *Report on the Manuscripts of Lord De I'Isle and Dudley, Volume Two*, p. 432.

14   *Report on the Manuscripts of Lord De I'Isle and Dudley, Volume Two*, p. 435.

15   Collins, *Letters and Memorials*, p. 141.

16   Collins, *Letters and Memorials*, p. 183.

17   Collins, *Letters and Memorials*, p. 183.

18   KHLC U269 T1 Bundle B [A:8:14].

19   TNA SP14/60/46.

20   KHLC U269 T1 Bdl B [A:8:16]; TNA C 54/1822.

21   *Calendar of State Papers Domestic Series, James I, 1603–1610* (London: 1857), p. 222.

22   KHLC U269 A1/1. Sackville paid an annual rent of £40 9s to Sidney for the park and the lodge.

23   Edward Town, 'A House Re-edified – Thomas Sackville and the Transformation of Knole 1605–1608', Unpublished PhD dissertation, University of Sussex, 2011, pp. 51–66.

24   Alden Gregory 'Knole: An Architectural and Social History of the Archbishop of Canterbury's House, 1456–1538', Unpublished PhD dissertation, University of Sussex, 2011, p. 20 quoting from KHLC U1450 T4/17.

25   Hatfield House Archive (hereafter HHA) MS CP 87/138.

26   HHA Accounts 8/13; Edward Town, 'A House Re-edified – Thomas Sackville and the Transformation of Knole 1605–1608', Unpublished PhD dissertation, University of Sussex, 2011, p. 170.

27   HHA Accounts 8/13.

28   KHLC DRb/Pwr 17 f. 75. For other wills of the same family from the period see KHLC DRb/Pwr 8 f. 32 (Will of George Kyrwyn of Mereworth 1526); KHLC DRb/Pwr 8 f. 49 (Will of William Krywyn of Mereworth 1526); KHLC DRb/Pwr 12. 380 (Will of John Kywin of Tonbridge and Mereworth 1570).

29 TNA PROB 11/133/653. Kerwin's widow, Margaret Swarland, who he married at St Michael Cornhill on 22 July 1571 was also from a Kentish family. Her will cites relatives in Horton in Kent.
30 TNA E101/464/3.
31 Guildhall Library (hereafter GL) MS 12819/2.
32 GL MS 11571/6 f. 231r.
33 W. J. Williams, 'Masons of the City of London', *Ars Quator Coronati*, vol. XLVI, 1932, p. 152.
34 TNA E 351/3215.
35 TNA E 351/3219.
36 Betty R. Masters (ed.), 'Chamber Accounts of the Sixteenth Century', *London Record Society* (1984), p. xix.
37 R. G. Lang (ed.), 'Two Tudor Subsidy Rolls for the City of London', *London Record Society* (1993), p. 152.
38 Arthur J. Jewers, 'Grants and Certificates of Arms', *The Genealogist*, 21 (1905), 64.
39 LMA MS P69/HEL/A/001/MS06830, Item 001.
40 C. Harold Ridge (ed.), *Index to Administrations in the Prerogative Court of Canterbury Volume III 1581–1595* (London, 1954), p. 92.
41 Kerwin was charged with completing a pinnacle on the west end of the Guildhall for which he was paid £16. Caroline Barron, *The Medieval Guildhall of London* (London: Corporation of London, 1974), p. 49.
42 Howard Colvin, *History of the King's Works, Volume III, 1485–1660*, Part I (London, 1975), pp. 97, 107; Marc Fitch (ed.), *Index to Administrations in the Prerogative Court of Canterbury, Volume V. 1609–1619* (London: HMSO, 1968), p. 74.
43 Kerwin had entered into Sidney's service by at least 1582, the year in which his wife Anne was buried in St John the Baptist, Penshurst. The parish registers also record the burials of Mercy Kerwin, the wife of Robert Kerwin, on 21 January 1603. Robert Kerwin himself was buried on 9 February 1616. In his will, proved in the Prerogative Court of Canterbury on 27 February 1616, he made bequests to the poor of Penshurst, his cousin John Kerwin of Seale, and his brother Andrew Kerwin, TNA PROB 11/127/241.
44 KHLC C81/36-8. Cited in Michael G. Brennan and Noel J. Kinnamon, *A Sidney Chronology 1554–1654* (Basingstoke: Palgrave Macmillan, 2003), p. 141.
45 *Report on the Manuscripts of Lord De I'Isle and Dudley, Volume Two*, p. 426.
46 *Report on the Manuscripts of Lord De I'Isle and Dudley, Volume Two*, p. 437.
47 *Report on the Manuscripts of Lord De I'Isle and Dudley Preserved at Penshurst Place, Kent, Volume Three* (London: HMSO, 1936), pp. 147, 151, 482.
48 R. E. G. Kirk and E. F. Kirk, *Returns of Aliens in the City and Suburbs of London 1523–1571*, The Publications of the Huguenot Society of London, vol. X, Part II (Aberdeen: The University Press, 1902), p. 279; R. E. G. Kirk and E. F. Kirk, *Returns of Aliens in the City and Suburbs of London from the Reign of Henry VIII to that of James I*, The Publications of the Huguenot Society of London, vol. X, Part III (Aberdeen: The University Press, 1907), pp. 146, 159, 176.
49 His daughter Lydia was buried at St Olave on 24 April 1593. LMA MS P71/OLA 009.
50 He gave all of his goods to his 'beloved wife Rebecca', 40s to the Dutch Church and 10s to the poor of Mark Lane. LMA MS DL/C/B/007/MS09172/030 fol. 278.
51 KHLC U1475 A62/A, bound volume of receipts V, f.170.
52 KHLC U1475 A62, bills and receipts 1587–1608, unfoliated bundles.
53 KHLC U1500 E120.

54 For Treswell see Edward Town, 'A Biographical Dictionary of London Painters', *Walpole Society*, 76 (2014), 175–6.

55 *Report on the Manuscripts of Lord De I'Isle and Dudley preserved at Penshurst Place, Kent, Volume Three*, p. 374.

56 The title that Robert Sidney was granted in May 1605.

57 *Report on the Manuscripts of Lord De I'Isle and Dudley preserved at Penshurst Place, Kent, Volume Three*, p. 374.

58 *Report on the Manuscripts of Lord De I'Isle and Dudley preserved at Penshurst Place, Kent, Volume Three*, p. 386.

59 All the pictures in the house are listed in the inventory of 1623. See KHLC U1500/E120.

60 *Report on the Manuscripts of Lord De I'Isle and Dudley preserved at Penshurst Place, Kent, Volume IV, Sidney Papers, 1608–1611* (London: HMSO, 1942), p. 302.

II

The culture of the
English country house

5

Decorating the Godly Gallery: piety and politics in plasterwork at Lanhydrock House, Cornwall[1]

Tara Hamling

The decorative plasterwork of the long gallery at Lanhydrock House in Cornwall, dating from c.1636–42, is an outstanding example of interior decoration from the first half of the seventeenth century. Through analysis of this artwork, this chapter examines the key role of the gallery as a grandiose setting for contemplation and discussion by individuals and groups in the intellectual culture of the English country house during this period. At Lanhydrock this established function of the gallery was augmented and enhanced by the addition of a comprehensive scheme of iconography representing divine, natural and social order to articulate the particular religious and political concerns of its owner at a time of heightened divisions and growing instability within the nation. The discussion that follows demonstrates the importance contemporaries attached to visual expression and communication in considering the intricacies of theological and political points of difference. It also establishes the ongoing presence but modification of traditional religious imagery in country houses as a tool for spiritual endeavour in post-Reformation England.

By the time Lanhydrock House was built the gallery was an accepted, indeed, expected feature of the houses of the gentry.[2] The gallery as a dedicated space for retreat from the hubbub of the house, pastime and gentle exercise probably developed from the covered walkways of the greater houses of early Tudor England, combined with the influence of Renaissance fashion. Two factors in particular influenced the character of this room; an association with illustrious individuals and affairs of state, and the awe-inspiring impact of its exaggerated physical proportions. The scale and grandeur of the space evidenced the wealth and position of the owner but also contributed a monumental quality that could be enhanced through its decoration. The space apparently proved useful not only for show and recreation but also for conducting potentially sensitive transactions in relative privacy for, as Lena Cowen Orlin has discussed, the spatial properties of galleries offered a rare opportunity for intimate conversation at enough distance to prevent being overheard by others present.[3] This room certainly would have provided a greater sense of calm and quiet as a place withdrawn from the activities and distractions of domestic life, which could facilitate contemplation of weighty matters.

Decoration of galleries responded to the epic quality of its form and illustrious associations; in his description of an ideal building based on classical models, Sir Henry Wotton offered advice on the disposition of pictures, recommending 'Graver Stories in Galleries'.[4] The use of galleries to display statuary and pictures is well known, but the range of subjects depicted in surface decoration is further evidence of the way in which this room was not only associated with intellectual enquiry but was actively exploited to represent a sense of universal, social and natural order. At Little Moreton Hall in Cheshire the gallery built in the 1570s is decorated with two allegorical designs in plasterwork, contrasting the sphere of destiny, ruled by knowledge, with ignorant belief in the wheel of fortune.[5] The lost gallery built in the mid-1570s by Nicholas Bacon, Keeper of the Great Seal, was painted with thirty-seven pairs of Latin *sententiae*, while another lost gallery of around the same date created by Lord Burghley at Theobalds displayed the coats of arms of all English gentry families set within a landscape representing the country.[6] At Blickling in Norfolk the gallery is decorated with a plasterwork ceiling dating from 1620 depicting allegorical figures including the Senses and emblems. The emblem, a combination of image and text, was a rhetorical device intended to encapsulate profound wisdom and the decoration reflects a vogue for printed complications of emblems.[7] Such decoration was aimed at the owner's social equals, equipped with the education and cultivated taste required to appreciate such intellectual devices.

The gallery at Lanhydrock is extraordinary, however, in the extent and cohesion of its scheme of imagery. It reflects a more general fashion for biblical imagery in interior decoration at the gentry and middling levels of society and is one of a group of West Country houses with biblical scenes depicted in high-relief plasterwork of the 1620s and 1630s.[8] It is, nevertheless, the most comprehensive and elaborate example of this design trend in England (certainly in a single room) which raises questions about the particular motivation and purpose behind such an ambitious work.

The decoration of the gallery at Lanhydrock has been presented and understood in relation to the vast library of sixteenth- and seventeenth-century texts it now contains. This direct link between physical space and literary pursuit has been severed by Mark Purcell's meticulous examination of the collection in which it is established that the library as it stands was compiled by at least four individuals and may not have come together as a single collection at Lanhydrock until 1677 or even 1685.[9] Purcell also calls attention to the fact that the use of the gallery to house the library is a relatively modern development; its installation there is placed between 1799 and 1808.[10] What follows, however, draws a more general comparison between the spirit of intellectual and theological enquiry and debate reflected by the collection of early printed books at Lanhydrock and the content, meaning and function of the scheme of decoration as an expression of puritan piety and political ideology on a grand scale.

The magnificent decorative plasterwork can be dated to c.1636–42 and was almost certainly created for John, Lord Robartes (1606–85), who inherited the Lanhydrock estate in 1634.[11] John Robartes is described as 'politician and army officer' in his entry in the ODNB but his biography is rather more complicated than this description suggests, reading almost as a character and career of two contradictory halves separated by the Interregnum.[12] The first half of John's life reflects the puritan outlook instilled through his upbringing and education at Exeter College, Oxford, and cemented by his marriage in 1630 to Lucy Rich, second daughter of the Earl of Warwick who was 'the most visible and consistent supporter of the Puritan cause among the English nobility in the first half of the seventeenth century'.[13] This family and religious alliance influenced John's political position and career prior to and during the civil war. An advocate of godly reform in the Church of England and a leader of parliamentary forces in the 1640s, he has been characterised as 'a man of conscience'.[14] Despite his beliefs and active political and military opposition to Charles I, however, John had a remarkable political comeback when the monarchy was restored. John withdrew from national affairs at a crucial juncture and prior to the execution of Charles I. He managed to navigate the turbulent decade prior to the Restoration despite apparent disillusionment with the Commonwealth, and paved the way for a full and active, if not always successful, political career under Charles II – including the office of Lord Privy Seal between 1661 and 1673.[15] While he conformed to the Church of England and was able to distance himself from presbyterianism, he remained a strong advocate of toleration towards protestant non-conformists. The compliance and careful politics of his later career appear far removed from the robust ideologies and allegiances of the 1630s and 1640s, when the decorated ceiling at Lanhydrock was created and viewed. But the stand he took in 1648 in withdrawing from political affairs and the moderation displayed in his subsequent career can help inform a reading of its iconography as representing the priorities and dilemmas that framed John's biography and weighed on his mind during this earlier period of his life.

The mansion house at Lanhydrock was founded following the purchase of the manor in 1620 by John's father, Richard Robartes.[16] A wealthy merchant and money-lender, Richard profited from the Cornish tin trade and benefited from James I's profligacy with honours, acquiring a knighthood in 1616, a baronetcy in 1621, and a peerage in 1625.[17] John succeeded his father as Baron

Robartes of Truro in 1634 and while the establishment and design of the house may reflect Richard's ambition and meteoric rise in position, it is clear that John was responsible for at least some of the construction.[18] Much of the present house at Lanhydrock is a Victorian rebuild following a major fire in 1881 but set within the exterior walls of the north and south wings are two granite door lintels with the dates 1636 and 1642 and the initials ILR. These may have been repositioned, but John must have engaged in substantial building work in some part of the property to merit date stones with his signature and this sort of building work to stamp an individual's mark on a newly inherited property is characteristic of the period. It is not clear if the creation of a gallery, which occupies the length of the north wing on the first floor, was part of the work undertaken for Richard or John but it forms an integral part of the architectural design as realised. This north wing, which escaped the 1881 fire, formed one side of a traditional quadrangular house arranged around an enclosed courtyard, and it connected the entrance frontage with the main block containing the formal reception rooms of the house.[19] This lateral position permitted a gallery with sizeable proportions at 116 feet in length and 20 feet wide, which is consistent with other new galleries in the greater houses of the elite.[20]

Inside, the room is decorated with an elaborate barrel-vaulted ceiling in lime plasterwork with moulded and hand-modelled imagery contained within a geometric pattern defined by enriched ribs (Figure 5.1).[21] Depicted in high relief within the main body of the ceiling are thirty-six scenes from the book of Genesis, starting with Adam in the Garden of Eden and progressing through a series of scenes from the story of Adam and Eve, Cain and Abel, Noah and the Ark, the Sacrifice of Isaac and the life of Jacob.[22] In addition there are two plasterwork overmantels depicting specific scenes from the life of David; Saul throwing the spear at David (1 Samuel 18.11) and David taking the pitcher and spear from Saul's tent (1 Samuel 26.12). In the tympanum at the west end of the gallery is a scene depicting the victory of David over Goliath, illustrating 1 Samuel 17.49 (Figure 5.2).

The sheer number of separate episodes depicted in one room – thirty-nine in total – is an enthusiastic response to the potential of the gallery as an exhibition space for a programme of imagery. The main body of the ceiling is devoted entirely to scenes from Genesis and this emphasis suggests a particular interest in the first book of the Pentateuch, a preoccupation also evident in contemporary literature. During the sixteenth and seventeenth centuries a great number of exegetical commentaries on Genesis was published in Europe. While this output reflects a general increase in scriptural exegesis characteristic of this period, a concentration of texts dealing with the book of Genesis has been identified as a distinct and substantial sub-category.[23]

A number of factors influenced this literary and theological concentration on the book of Genesis. The episodes described in the first book of the Bible

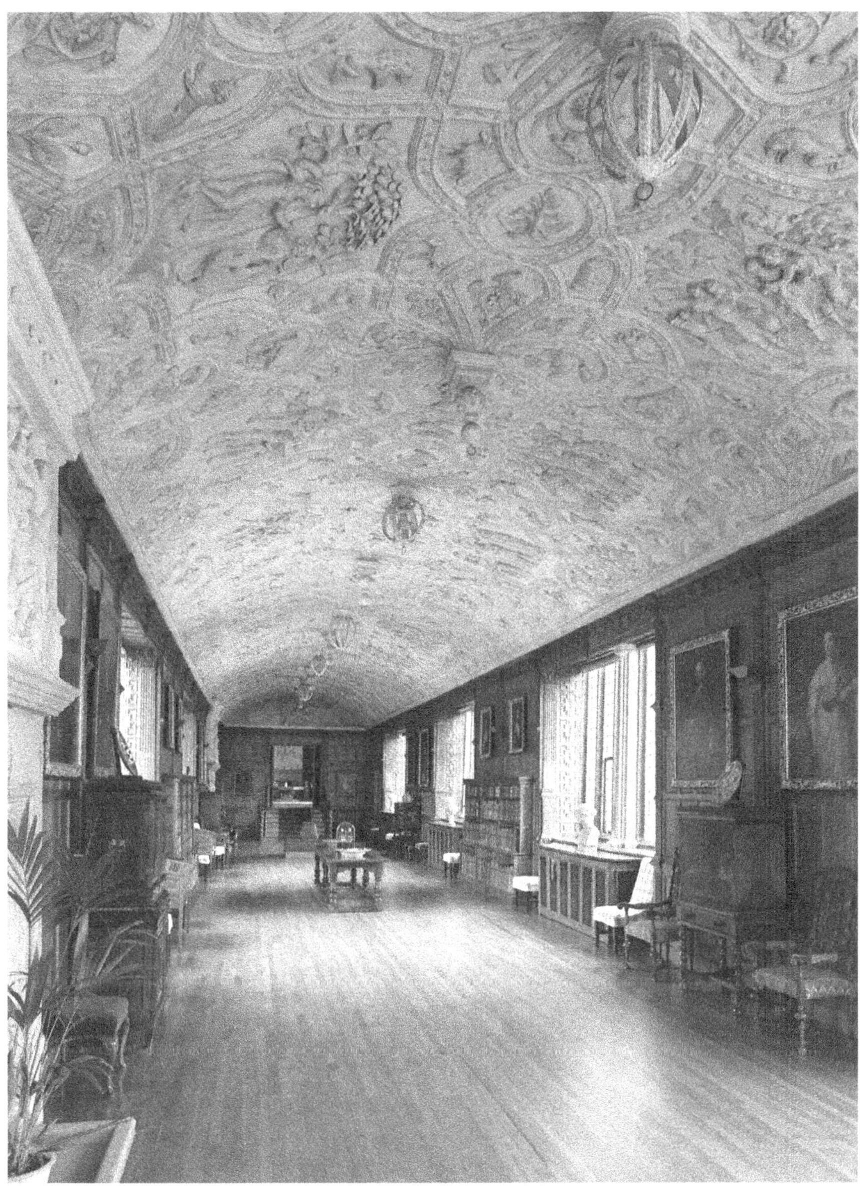

5.1 View of the plasterwork ceiling of c.1636 in the long gallery of Lanhydrock House, Cornwall.

satisfied a popular demand for information about the creation of the world and the beginning of life. In theological terms Genesis describes some of the most significant episodes for the Christian faith. The story of Creation attests the omnipotence of God and that the universe was created for the purposes

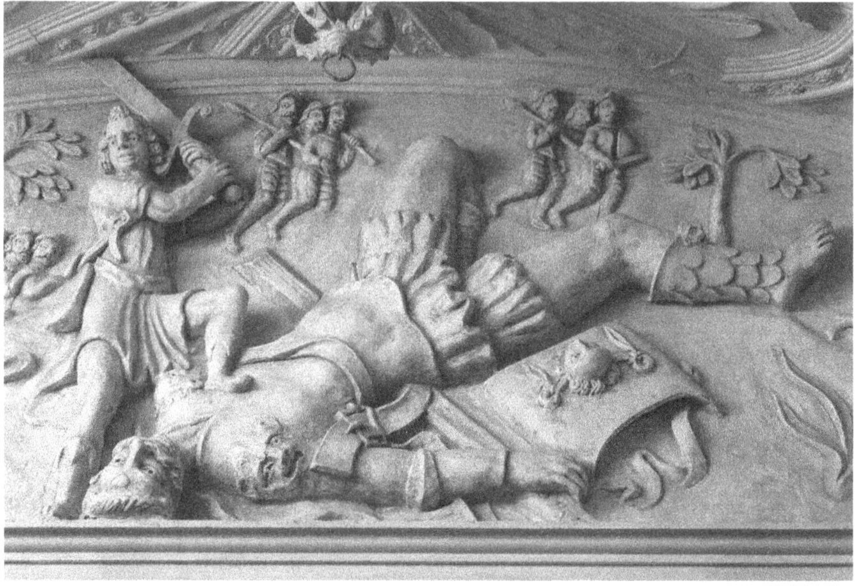

5.2   David victorious over Goliath, detail of the plasterwork in the long gallery at Lanhydrock House, Cornwall, c.1636.

of His design for mankind. Adam and Eve's fall from grace is one of the two crucial points of Christian history, with the sacrifice of Christ on the cross as the other. The narrative of the Flood, and the histories of the patriarchs Abraham, Isaac and Jacob establish God's covenant with his chosen people, providing the foundation for the whole of Christian history. Theologians on both sides of the religious divide separating Catholicism and Protestantism utilised the stories in Genesis to support their own doctrinal concerns.

Two commentaries on Genesis in English are still part of the collection of books at Lanhydrock today; Henry Ainsworth's *Annotations upon the First Book of Moses Called Genesis* (1616), and William Whately's *Prototypes, or, The Primarie Precedent Presidents out of the Booke of Genesis* (1640). Both texts are typical of their genre in the application of stories in Genesis to doctrinal and moral issues, and as illustrations of the scheme of salvation, the foundation of the church, the operation of election and grace. The mysteries described within Genesis were understood to reveal the ultimate divine plan for, as Ainsworth explains, 'in the histories, are implied Allegories, & in the laws are types and shadows of good things that were to come: the body whereof, is of Christ.'[24]

In the left-hand section of the ceiling (when viewed from the original entrance to the gallery), twelve scenes depict some of the most theologically significant episodes in Genesis, covering chapters 2 to 22, including the creation of Adam and Eve, their fall and expulsion from paradise, the stories of Cain and

Abel, Noah and the Flood and the Sacrifice of Isaac. The Adam and Eve and Abraham and Isaac narratives were popular in early modern decorative art more generally, depicted separately and together. The Sacrifice of Isaac, for example, is depicted in a plasterwork overmantel in another country house in Cornwall, with an inscription to emphasise the importance of obedience.[25] Meanwhile there are other comparable decorative schemes with a series of biblical scenes; very similar images of Adam and Eve, Cain and Abel and the Sacrifice of Isaac feature in the carved wood decoration of the Bluett family pew in Holcombe Rogus church in Devon (c.1614) and, further afield, in the exterior facade of the town house associated with Bishop Lloyd in Chester (1615). What these and the additional scenes at Lanhydrock share in common is the theme of election, the mystery of the operation of divine will in choosing some people in preference to others. It was Adam and Eve's sin of disobedience that led to God's grace being withdrawn from all mankind. Cain and Abel both made offerings to God but it was Abel, the younger brother, whose offering gained His favour, resulting in Cain's jealousy and murderous rage. Both episodes are treated sequentially in the ceiling. Noah and his family were chosen to survive the flood while the rest of mankind was destroyed. God's covenant with Abraham and his progeny was renewed after he demonstrated his unquestioning fidelity to the will of God in being willing to sacrifice his son, Isaac, in response to divine command.

These scenes therefore reflect the central place of the doctrine of election in the form of Protestantism adopted in England, which had absorbed Calvinist principles. Calvin had made the doctrine of predestination one of the cornerstones of his system, asserting that certain persons are pre-elected by God wholly without relation to faith or works and that Christ's sacrifice was intended only for the elect. While the doctrine of election was affirmed by the Anglican Thirty-Nine Articles of 1563, commitment to an uncompromising predestination as defined by Calvin was one of the indicators of puritan conviction.

It is therefore significant that there is also a particular emphasis on the life of Jacob in the ceiling at Lanhydrock. The right-hand section of the ceiling depicts twenty-four separate episodes, covering chapters 27 to 35. In order to accommodate this number of separate scenes, the design of the ceiling changes in the section running the length of the north side of the gallery so that each star-shaped narrative panel contains two separate episodes (see diagram in Figure 5.3). It is clear that the story of Jacob must have been of particular interest for John Robartes to have endorsed this asymmetrical design. An explanation for this interest lies in the application of the story of Jacob as an exemplar for the operation of election. Jacob had cheated and lied in order to steal his father's blessing from his brother Esau, and yet it was Jacob and his lineage that God chose for his covenant. According to Calvin in his own commentary on Genesis, this illustrated that election and grace was not achieved through works, but through God's will.[26] Calvin further elaborated on this theme in his thirteen sermons 'Entreating of the Free Election of God in Jacob, and of Reprobation in Esau' which was published in an English translation by John Field in 1579. Following Calvin, Whately opens his discussion of the 'example of Jacob' with the observation;

> and in them [Jacob and Esau] the Lord did manifest the freedome of his Election, seeing he choose the younger before the elder to inherite the promises, and that before they had done good or evill, that the purpose of God according to election might remaine (or be firme) not of works, but of him that calleth.[27]

It is clear from the choice of scenes that the ceiling at Lanhydrock was not an indiscriminate or comprehensive pictorial rendering of the book of Genesis. Instead, the content represents a systematic investigation and illustration of the nature of election. The quantity and content of scenes from the life of Jacob, in particular, indicate a specific interest in episodes relating to Jacob's calling and his covenant with God. This same emphasis is evident in Protestant literature on this subject and is entirely in keeping with the puritan faith of the patron. This imagery could therefore serve to instruct and edify as an extension of the godly patriarch's role to promote the reformed faith and instil spiritual understanding.

A puritan form of piety determined not only the choice of particular subject matter from the book of Genesis, but also affected the content and iconography of the pictorial scenes. Some of the scenes in the main body of the ceiling have peculiar and awkward compositions. The scene of Adam in the Garden of Eden is especially odd, as Adam's body is depicted at a strange angle with his limbs oddly contorted (Figure 5.4). He cannot be described as standing or lying down but instead his body appears to be half-propped against a tree. This makes the precise identification of the scene difficult; is it a depiction of Adam naming the beasts? If so, why is Adam depicted in such a strange position? An answer is provided by comparison with printed illustrations in bibles. In her study of the illustrations contained in the official Elizabethan Bible of 1568, known as the *Bishops' Bible*, Margaret Aston describes how the woodcut blocks by Virgil Solis employed for these illustrations were also used in Lutheran and Catholic bibles printed on the continent.[28] Crucially, for the 1568 English Bible these blocks were altered to accommodate the particular demands of the Elizabethan Church so that the image of God the father as a robed and bearded ancient was 'edited out' of several pictures, and replaced with the Hebrew tetragrammaton. While there was a range of positions on the question of the validity of religious images, there was a consensus among Protestant theologians that the image of God the father was unequivocally forbidden by the Second Commandment, so that for the 1568 *Bishops' Bible* an attempt was made to expunge the image of God the father wherever he occupied a central or substantial part of the composition. This required the physical alteration of the woodblock, so that

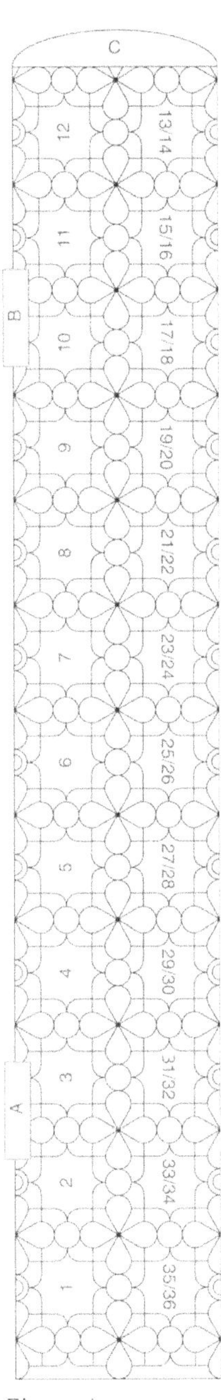

1. Adam in the Garden of Eden
2. The Creation of Eve
3. The Temptation and Fall from Grace
4. The Expulsion from Paradise
5. Adam and his family toiling after the Expulsion
6. Cain and Abel making altars to God
7. Cain killing Abel
8. Noah building the Ark
9. Boarding the Ark
10. The Flood
11. Noah and his family give thanks to God
12. The Sacrifice of Isaac
13. Rebekah speaking to Jacob
14. Jacob catching kids
15. Esau hunting
16. Isaac blessing Jacob
17. Rebekah speaking to Isaac
18. Isaac speaking to Jacob
19. Jacob praying
20. Jacob's dream of the ladder
21. Jacob anointing the stone
22. Jacob meeting Rachel at the well
23. Jacob speaking to Laban
24. Jacob working for Laban
25. Jacob with Leah and Rachel
26. Jacob, with his wives on camels, leave Laban
27. Laban searches the tent for Jacob
28. Jacob and Laban setting up a pillar
29. Jacob wrestling with an angel
30. The man of God and Jacob
31. The meeting of Esau and Jacob
32. Hamor and Jacob
33. The slaughter of Hamor and Shechem
34. Jabob leaving for Bethel
35. Jacob pouring oil upon an altar
36. The burial of Isaac

A. Saul throwing a spear at David
B. David taking the pitcher and spear from Saul's tent
C. David and Goliath

5.3	Diagram showing the position of biblical scenes in the plasterwork ceiling of the long gallery at Lanhydrock House, Cornwall (not to scale).

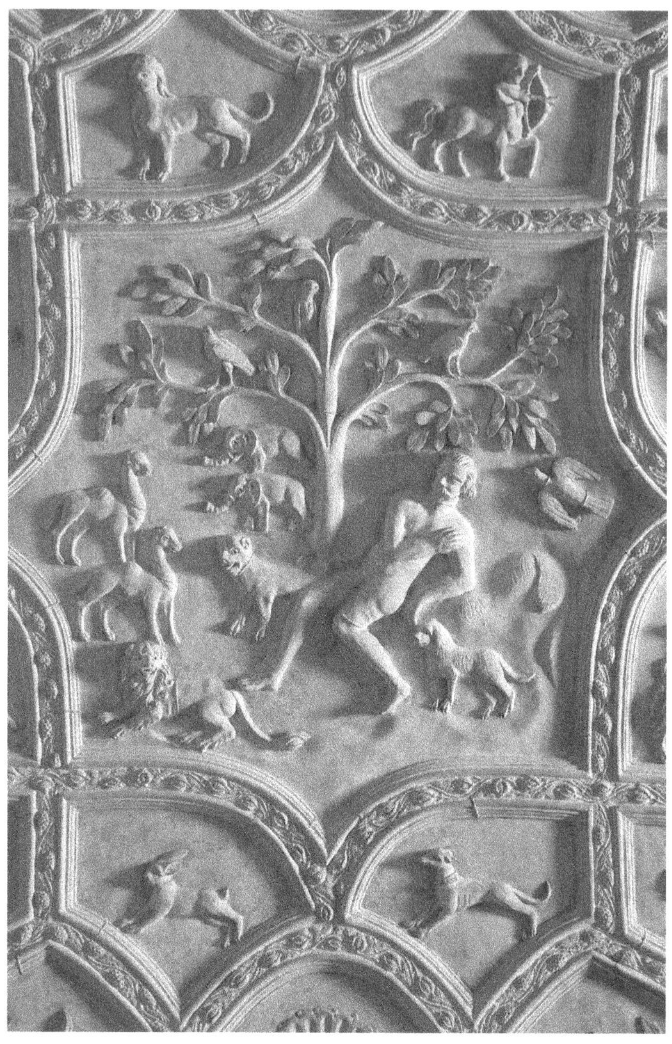

5.4 Adam in the Garden of Eden, detail of the plasterwork ceiling of the long gallery at Lanhydrock House, Cornwall, c.1636.

the part depicting the offending figure was removed and substituted with a fresh wooden insert carved with the tetragrammaton. As Aston describes, the censorship is most evident in the first two woodcuts for the book of Genesis, illustrating the Creation of the World and the Creation of Eve.

Nevertheless, this process of censorship was not comprehensive, and many of the illustrations incorporating a smaller figure of God were not changed. This oversight provoked the outrage of the puritan lobby so that the Second Admonition to Parliament in 1572 criticised the 'sight of blasphemous pictures of God the father' in the first Bishops' Bible.[29] In the subsequent edition published in 1572, the process of censorship was comprehensive. A new set of illustrations eliminated all depictions of God in human form, with the tetragrammaton deployed instead.

This censorship resulted in several unusual and pictorially incoherent compositions, and one of the most anomalous outcomes is the illustration of the Creation of Adam. In medieval iconography, the figure of God the father as a robed and bearded man is depicted in the Garden of Eden reaching out to give life to the inert Adam. This is the incident depicted in the iconic scene from Michelangelo's painted ceiling in the Sistine chapel. In the 1572 *Bishops' Bible* illustration of the Creation, the previously central and substantial figure of God is missing, so that there is no visual explanation for the strange position and posture of Adam's body (Figure 5.5). This 1572 illustration is very similar to the corresponding scene in the ceiling at Lanhydrock with the same awkward positioning of the body of Adam propped against a tree, though reversed, so that Adam is on the right-hand side of the scene rather than the left. This suggests that the figure of God has been 'edited out' in a similar manner to the process employed to expunge the offending subject in the bible illustrations. It is certainly apparent from comparison with the corresponding illustration in the 1572 *Bishops' Bible* that the first scene in the gallery ceiling is also intended to represent the Creation of Adam, an identification not obvious from the image alone. The second scene in the ceiling, the Creation of Eve, has also been subject to censorship. Again, comparison with the *Bishops' Bible* illustrations is instructive. The large figure of God the father shown extracting Eve from the body of Adam in the woodcut included in the Lutheran and Catholic Bibles, is conspicuously absent from the version of the same illustration included in the 1568 English Bible. Instead, the figure of Eve emerges from the side of Adam and looks upwards towards the tetragrammaton (Figure 5.6).[30] In the Lanhydrock version, even the tetragrammaton is absent, so that Eve emerges as if spontaneously from the body of Adam, presenting an edited, and thereby simplified, version of the traditional iconography (Figure 5.7). Other scenes in the ceiling at Lanhydrock show signs of similar expurgation and adaptation. The scene of Jacob's dream of the ladder, for example, lacks the traditional figure of God in heaven included in the 1568 *Bishops' Bible* illustration, and instead the ladder ascends into a swirl of clouds and stars.

These interventions to remove the figure of God the father from the otherwise conventional iconography depicted in the ceiling at Lanhydrock proves that the choice of particular imagery for the decoration was carefully considered and, where necessary, adapted to expunge any offensive elements. This level of critical attention to the pictorial content of so-called 'ornament' demonstrates that decorative art was understood to be subject to the same controls and prohibitions as other forms of imagery. The decoration of the

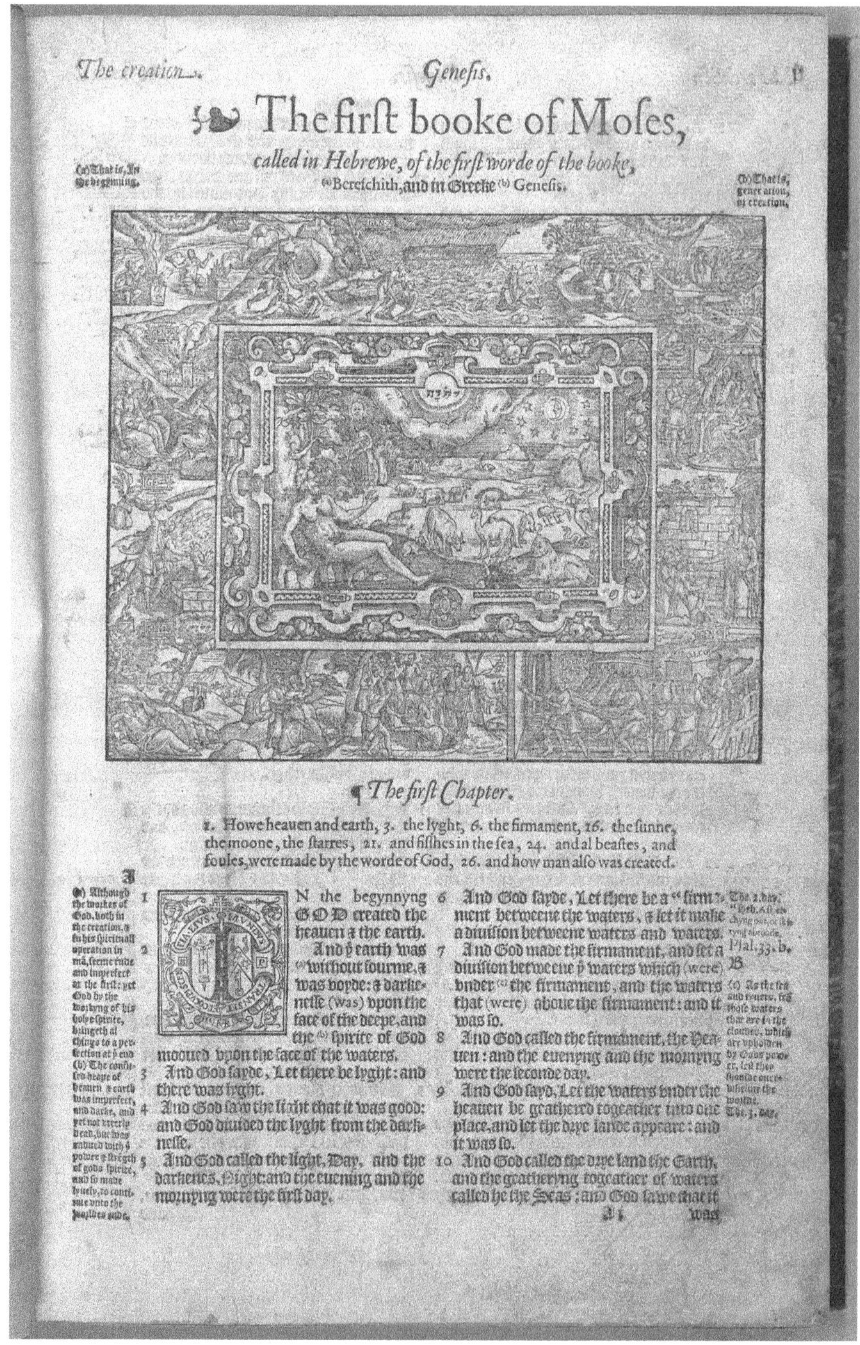

5.5   The Creation of Adam, woodcut illustration from the 'Bishops Bible' of 1572.

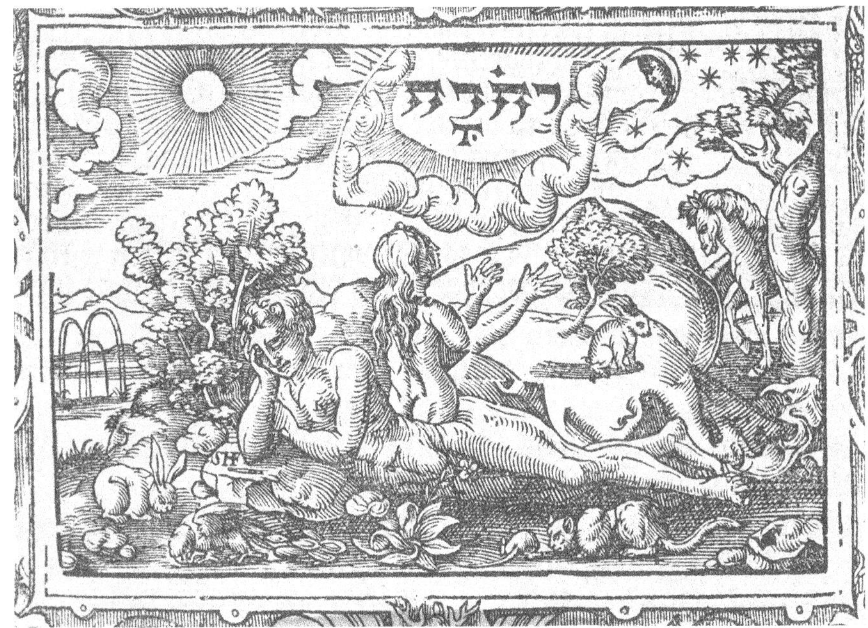

5.6   The Creation of Eve, woodcut illustration from the 'Bishops Bible' of 1568.

gallery at Lanhydrock with a scheme of biblical scenes demonstrates that even a committed puritan like John Robartes approved of large-scale religious imagery within the domestic sphere. However, the steps taken to ensure that the imagery was purified of objectionable elements underlines that patrons were concerned that such imagery had the potential not only to edify and inspire but to corrupt the thoughts and behaviour of its audience.

No single printed source has yet been identified for the scheme of scenes included in the main body of the ceiling at Lanhydrock. The similarities with the *Bishops' Bible* illustrations of 1568 and 1572 are striking, but there are various omissions and discrepancies that rule these illustrations out as a single source. It is likely that a number of different printed sources were employed to construct such an extensive programme. Indeed, the range of imagery employed in the lesser panels of the geometric design is drawn from other sources, including Edward Topsell's *Historie of Foure-Footed Beasts* (1607). The design also features various heraldic badges, birds, flora and fauna. Topsell explained his spiritual purpose in publishing his volume, claiming that only a divine or preacher should do so as, 'the knowledge of the Beasts, like as the knowledge of the other creatures and works of God, is Devine … seeing that at the first they were created and brought to man as we may read Gen.1. 24, 25'.[31] The encyclopaedic quality of Topsell's natural history is also present in the Lanhydrock ceiling, as a comprehensive

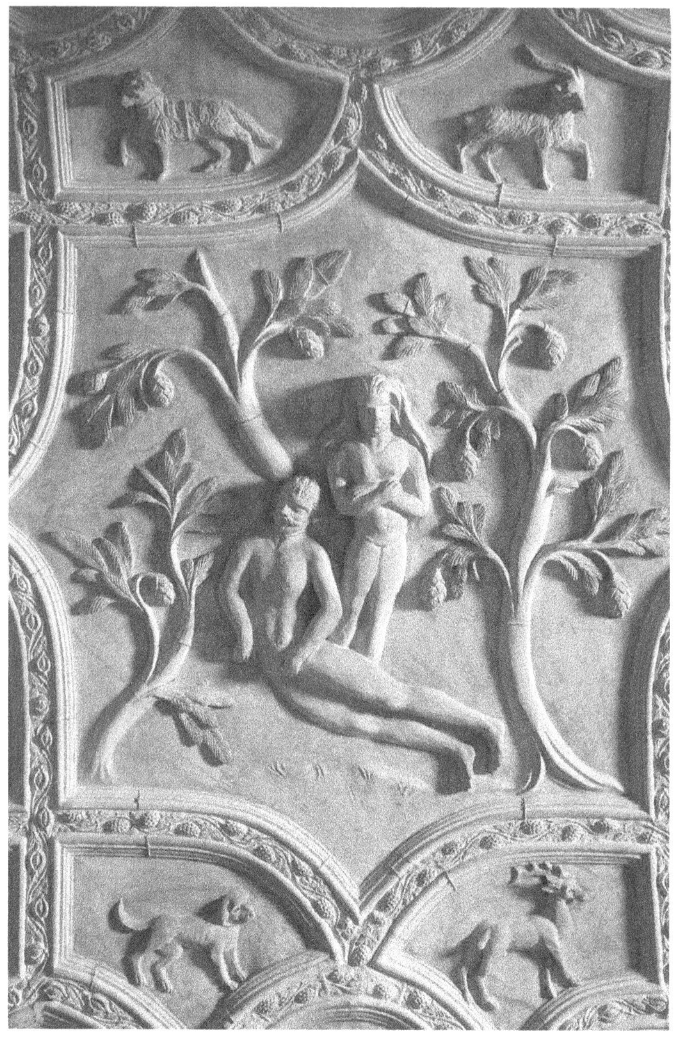

5.7   The Creation of Eve, detail of the plasterwork ceiling of the long gallery at Lanhydrock House, Cornwall, c.1636.

representation of the foundations of Christian history, the mystery of God's divine plan of election and reprobation and the wondrous variety of the natural world He created for that purpose.

The three scenes depicted in the fireplace overmantels and in the tympanum are not directly related to this scheme, however, and appear to reflect a separate project and purpose. As Anthony Wells-Cole has demonstrated, these scenes are all copied from the *Thesaurus Sacrarum Historiarum Veteris Testamenti* published by Gerard de Jode in Antwerp in 1585.[32] All three scenes are

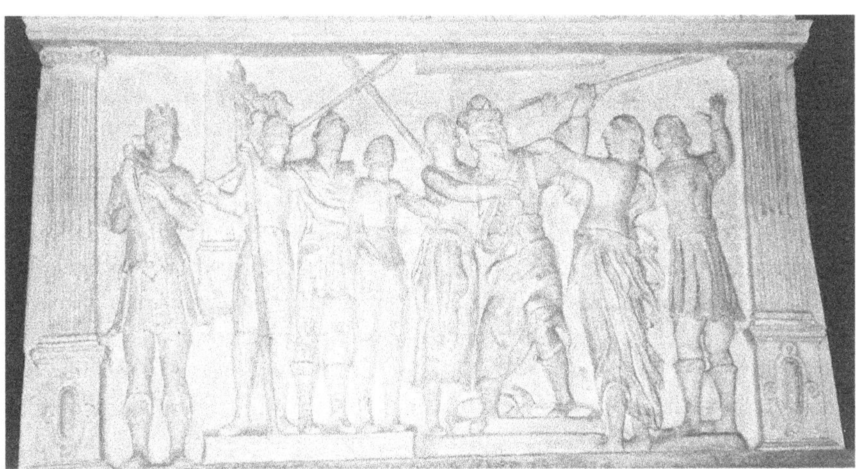

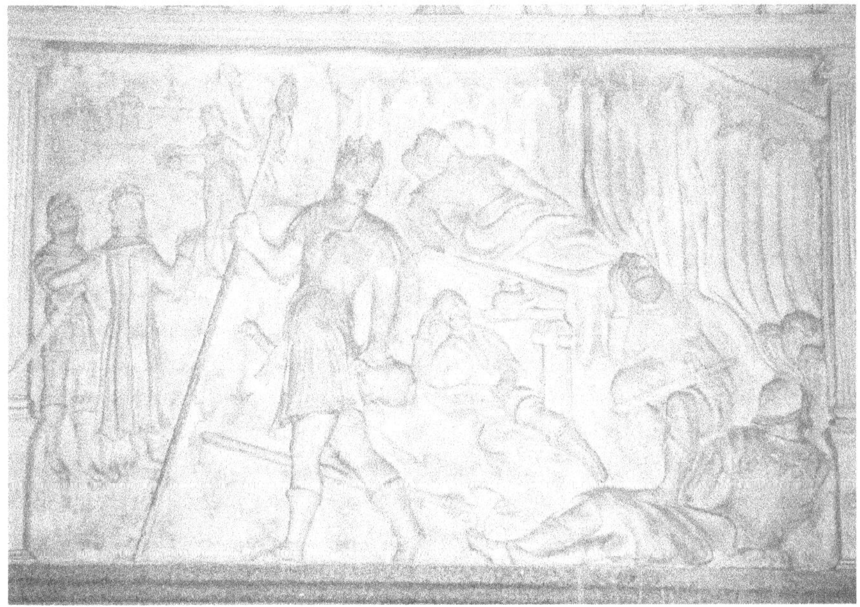

5.8   Saul throwing the spear at David (above) and David taking the pitcher and spear from Saul's tent (below). Plasterwork overmantels in the long gallery at Lanhydrock House, Cornwall, c.1636.

concerned with incidents from the life of King David, a particularly popular character as a subject for decorative art during this period. Then understood to be author of the Psalms, David is often shown playing his harp, serving as an example of legitimate music-making as a vehicle for praising God.[33] In one of the overmantels in the gallery at Lanhydrock, King David is shown playing his harp to entertain King Saul (Figure 5.8).

King David playing his harp is also the subject of a carved overmantel of c.1624 in the long gallery of Apethorpe Hall in Northamptonshire. An inscription underneath extols the virtues of music to dispel melancholy and 'foule spirits'. But the iconography at Apethorpe also has an allegorical meaning. The statue of David has features not dissimilar to King James I and the harp alludes to the harmony brought about by his reign. The central figure of David playing his harp stands in a niche and is flanked by reclining female personifications of Justice (on the left) and Fortitude (on the right). In low-relief on the panel above Justice is the head of Goliath pierced through with David's sword and above the figure of Fortitude is the sling and stones used by David to defeat the giant. The overmantel in the long gallery at Apethorpe is part of a programme of allegorical decoration throughout a newly built state suite of apartments for the use of the King and is a vehicle for royal propaganda. King James I was often compared to King David in the literature of the period, and the James-as-David iconography in the long gallery at Apethorpe celebrates the benefits of the King's rule by a loyal supporter.[34]

The selection of three particular scenes from the life of King David in the gallery at Lanhydrock also suggests a political message, but represents the other side of the political divide. The imagery in the chimneypieces and in the tympanum, taken from the first book of Samuel, stand apart from the series of scenes in the main body of the ceiling. The subject matter for these three scenes is taken from a different book of the Old Testament and the imagery is copied from a set of printed engravings not employed for the other scenes in the main body of the ceiling. When considered together, these three scenes suggest an allusion to contemporary politics.

When the decoration of the gallery at Lanhydrock was created, around 1636–42, the personal rule of Charles I had exacerbated the political and religious divide between the Puritan Parliamentary faction and the Crown. The conflict between King Saul and the young David as illustrated in the two overmantels at Lanhydrock can be understood as an allegory of this growing rift. The choice of particular scenes emphasises Saul's tyranny (Saul throwing the spear at David) and David's diplomacy and military restraint (David taking the pitcher and spear from Saul's tent). David's resolution not to retaliate against the deranged King Saul, who was trying to kill him, was widely understood as a scriptural endorsement for the divine right of kings. Indeed, as Gwyn Howells has pointed out, in the Elizabethan Homily, *An Exhortation concerning good Order, and obedience to Rulers and Magistrates*, the same two episodes from the book of Samuel are recounted as evidence that no amount of tyranny or persecution can justify the overthrow of an anointed king by his subjects:[35]

Holy David also teacheth us a good lesson … who was many times most cruelly and wrongfully persecuted of king Saul, and many times also put in jeopardie and danger of his life by king Saul and his people, yet hee neither withstood, neither used any force or violence against king Saul his mortall and deadly enemie, but did ever to his liege Lord and Master king Saul, most true, most diligent, and most faithfull service … when the most unmercifull and most unkinde King Saul did persecute poore David, GOD did againe give king Saul into Davids handes, by casting of king Saul and his whole armie into a dead sleepe, so that David and one Abisai with him, came in the night into Sauls host, where Saul lay sleeping, and his speare stacke in the ground at his head: then said Abisai unto David, GOD hath delivered thine enemie into thy hands at this time, now therefore let me smite him once with my speare to the earth … And David answered and said to Abisai, Destroy him not, for who can lay his hands on the Lords anointed, and be guiltlesse? And David sayd furthermore, As sure as the Lord liveth, the Lord shall smite him, or his day shall come to die, or he shall descend or goe downe into battaile, and there perish, the Lord keepe me from laying my handes upon the Lords anoynted. But take thou now the speare that is at his head, and the cruse of water, and let us goe … Here is evidently prooved that we may not withstand, nor in any wise hurt an anointed King, which is GODS lieftenant, vice-gerent, and highest minister in that countrey where he is King.[36]

In creating a pictorial version of this subject for his gallery Robartes was perhaps expressing his dismay at the political and religious policies of the King during the personal rule, while underlining the need for appropriate restraint and trust in providence. As the scenes in the two overmantels illustrate, God and righteousness was with David (the godly) but the godly must not take action against the King, as God's anointed, but should trust in divine will. However, the large scene of David victorious over Goliath in the tympanum, a traditional allegory of Virtue over Vice, serves as a reminder that God assists the righteous to triumph over the forces of oppression (Figure 5.2). This fusion of political and religious belief expressed through biblical metaphor is typical of the age. As Christopher Hill has demonstrated, during the seventeenth-century Revolution the Bible was used to justify both resistance to and defence of the King.[37] The use of imagery in the decoration of the gallery at Lanhydrock is part of this trend in referring to biblical precedent, and testifies to the function of the gallery as a tool for communicating the character, beliefs and intellectual interests of the owner.

There are two periods in which John Robartes was in the best position, geographically and ideologically to invest in large-scale decorative work at Lanhydrock: between 1634 and 1642 (although from 1640 he would have been engaged with parliamentary matters in London) and between 1648 and 1660, when he withdrew from national affairs. The reminder that only God has the right to punish tyrannical rulers could have sounded a warning in response to growing discontent among the puritan faction at the Personal Rule in the later 1630s, but equally the cautionary perspective on regime change expressed in the selected biblical scenes from the book of Samuel is consistent with John's disassociation from parliament following 1648 and during the Commonwealth, and his immediate resumption of political service under Charles II. While the style of the ceiling is characteristic of the 1630s, it is possible that the three scenes from Samuel represent a second phase of work; their message does seem especially pertinent to John's stance in 1648.[38] Whether the plasterwork decoration was created in its entirety around 1636–42 or in two separate phases, with the further addition of the chimneypieces and tympanum in the period following 1648, its presence in the gallery places the iconography in the context of a room associated with affairs of state and greater truths, to persuade as well as to impress contemporaries with this show of piety and principles.

The intellectual world of the country house in the early modern period embraced visual as well as textual forms. An exchange of views during the religious and political divisions of the mid-seventeenth century was not limited to sharing and annotating scholarly books; doctrine, opinions and agendas were also expressed visually. The plasterwork decoration of the gallery at Lanhydrock is a supreme example of the power of this space and this medium to encapsulate and communicate religious and political views. It offers a unique perspective on the vacillations in forms of piety and government that defined this period of English history.

Notes

1   This chapter provided an opportunity to revisit research on Lanhydrock published in my book, *Decorating the Godly Household: Religious Art in Post-Reformation Britain* (New Haven, CT and London: Yale University Press, 2010), pp. 182–91. I am grateful to Yale University Press for permission to reproduce some of this material in the present volume. A Philip Leverhulme Prize supported the cost of reproducing images.

2   The architectural evolution, form and functions of the gallery in the English country house have been discussed extensively elsewhere and so only a short summary is provided here. The definitive work is by Rosalys Coope, 'The "Long Gallery": Its Origins, Development, Use, and Decoration', *Architectural History*, 29 (1986), 43–72. See also Maurice Howard, *The Early Tudor Country House: Architecture and Politics* (London: George Philip, 1984), p. 116; Mark Girouard, *Life in the English Country House: A Social and Architectural History* (New Haven, CT and London: Yale University Press, 1978), pp. 112–16 and Nicholas Cooper, *The Houses of the Gentry, 1480–1680* (New Haven, CT and London: Yale University Press, 1999), pp. 300–4.

3   Lena Cowen Orlin, *Locating Privacy in Tudor London* (Oxford: Oxford University Press, 2007), Chapter 6, pp. 226–61.

4   Sir Henry Wotton, *The Elements of Architecture Collected by Henry Wotton Knight from the Best Authors and Examples* (London, 1624), pp. 99–100.

5   These figures are copied from the title-page to Robert Record, *The Castle of Knowledge* (London, 1556).

6   Elizabeth McCutcheon, *Sir Nicholas Bacon's Great House Sententiae*, English Literary Renaissance Supplements 3 (Claremont, CA: University of Hawaii and Sir Francis Bacon Foundation and Library, 1977); J. M. Sutton, 'The Decorative Program at Elizabethan

Theobalds: Educating an Heir and Promoting a Dynasty', *Studies in the Decorative Arts*, vii (1999–2000), 33–64.

7   The figure of 'Doctrina' in the Blickling ceiling is copied from Henry Peacham's, *Minerva Britanna* (London, 1612), as identified by Anthony Wells-Cole, *Art and Decoration in Elizabethan and Jacobean England; The Influence of Continental Prints, 1558–1625* (New Haven, CT and London: Yale University Press, 1997), p. 165.

8   Described and discussed in detail in Tara Hamling, *Decorating the Godly Household: Religious Art in Post-Reformation Britain* (New Haven, CT: Yale University Press), esp. pp. 130, 154–5, 159–62.

9   Mark Purcell, 'The Library at Lanhydrock', *Book Collector*, 54 (2005), 195–230.

10   Purcell, 'The Library at Lanhydrock', p. 218.

11   A date in the mid-1630s is most likely based on the style of the plasterwork compared with similar examples in the region. The assumption that the work was executed during the period 1636–42 is informed by two pieces of physical evidence. First, a lintel above a ground-floor entrance to the north wing housing the gallery is carved with the initials I: L: R: L. and the date 1636, referring to [J]ohn, '[L]ord [R]obartes'. The extra 'L' may refer to Lucy Rich, his first wife or Lanhydrock, i.e., J[ohn &] L[ucy] R[obartes] L[anhydrock]. This may have been repositioned, however, as a description of Lanhydrock as it appeared early in the nineteenth century describes the lintel dated 1636 as being carved 'over the entrance' of 'the principal front'; C. S. Gilbert, *An Historical Survey of the County of Cornwall*, 2 vols (London 1817–20), p. 636. There is another carved lintel on the south wing with John's initials and the date 1642. These dates and signatures obviously mark important phases of building work showing John's investment in the building at this time. Secondly, the arms of John Robartes impaling those of Warwick, for his first wife Lucy Rich are depicted in the tympanum at the east end of the gallery. They married in 1630 and Lucy died before 1646.

12   Anne Duffin, 'Robartes, John, first earl of Radnor (1606–1685)', *Oxford Dictionary of National Biography* (hereafter *ODNB*) (Oxford: Oxford University Press, 2004), www.oxforddnb.com/view/article/23707, accessed 31 August 2013.

13   Sean Kelsey, 'Rich, Robert, Second Earl of Warwick (1587–1658)', *ODNB*, www.oxforddnb.com/view/article/23494, accessed 31 August 2013.

14   As, for example, by David Keep, 'Works by Zurich Reformers in the Library at Lanhydrock', in Gervase Jackson-Stops (ed.), *The National Trust Year Book* (1976–77), 73–80, p. 73.

15   He was unsuccessful in the offices of Deputy Lieutenant and Lord Lieutenant of Ireland.

16   Paul Holden has raised the intriguing possibility that Richard Robartes utilised an existing Tudor manor house at Lanhydrock, which then formed the core of the north wing, in '"Situation, Contrivance, Receipt, Strength and Beauty": The Building of Lanhydrock House, 1620–51', *Journal of the Royal Institution of Cornwall* (2005), 32–44.

17   Duffin, 'Robartes, John'.

18   There are no extant documents from the period relating to the building of Lanhydrock House. It is therefore impossible to determine the relative roles of father and son in the design and construction of the house. But John's involvement is clear from the carved dates and initials on the lintels discussed above (which suggests the house was constructed in phases) and on the gatehouse (1651). For a useful discussion of some of the more puzzling aspects of the building history see Holden, 'Situation'.

19   According to William Borlase's description of the house in 1756, the east wing (demolished in c.1784) was 'one large anti-chamber a handsome apartment communicating with the Gallery which is the length of the whole Eastern Front' (Borlase MSS book, 1756, Courtney Library, Truro).

20 The new gallery wing added c.1600 at Haddon Hall in Derbyshire is 110 feet long; Blickling's gallery is 123 feet long.

21 Claire Gapper's doctoral thesis, 'Plasterers and Plasterwork in City, Court and Country 1530–1660' (University of London, 1998, 2 vols) provides a comprehensive account of the English tradition of lime plasterwork. An updated version of the thesis is available online: Claire Gapper, 'British Renaissance Plasterwork', http://clairegapper.info/, accessed 3 September 2013. The identity of the craftsmen responsible for the work at Lanhydrock is not known; an association with an 'Abbott family' of plasterers is unproven.

22 The series of scenes in the ceiling was meant to be viewed on entering the gallery from the east wing, as the sequence begins with Adam in the Garden of Eden at the eastern corner of the gallery, directly above the original doorway connecting with the east wing.

23 Arnold Williams, *The Common Expositor: An Account of the Commentaries on Genesis, 1527–1633* (Chapel Hill, NC: University of North Carolina Press, 1948). Williams examines thirty-five commentaries on Genesis in Latin and six in English.

24 Henry Ainsworth, *Annotations upon the First Book of Moses Called Genesis* (Amsterdam, 1616), Preface.

25 Hamling, *Decorating the Godly Household*, p. 238, fig. 167.

26 Calvin's commentary on Genesis in Latin was first published in Geneva in 1563 and was translated into English by Thomas Tymme as *A Commentarie of John Calvine, upon the first Booke of Moses* (London, 1578).

27 William Whately, *Prototypes, or, The Primarie Precedent Presidents out of the booke of Genesis* (London, 1640), p. 41.

28 Margaret Aston, 'The Bishops' Bible Illustrations', in Diana Wood (ed.), *The Church and the Arts, Studies in Church History*, vol. 28 (Oxford: Blackwell, 1995), 267–85.

29 Cited in Aston, 'Bishops' Bible', p. 272.

30 Interestingly, the woodcut was subsequently altered back to reinsert the figure of God for publication in later bibles. See Aston, 'Bishops' Bible', pp. 278–9, for comparison of the various states of the woodcut, from the version printed in the German bible published in Cologne in 1565, the changed version as included in the first *Bishops' Bible* in 1568, and then changed back to reinsert the figure of God, as illustrated in a Bible published in Antwerp in 1570.

31 Edward Topsell, *The Historie of Foure-Footed Beasts* (London, 1607), the epistle dedicatory.

32 Wells-Cole, *Art and Decoration*, p. 162.

33 See for example, illustrations in Hamling, *Decorating the Godly Household*, figs 78 and 107.

34 Adam White, 'The Iconography of the State Apartment at Apethorpe Hall', *English Heritage Historical Review*, 3 (2008), 63–85. See also Graham Parry, *The Golden Age Restor'd: The Culture of the Stuart Court, 1603–42* (Manchester: Manchester University Press, 1981), pp. 231–2.

35 Gwyn Howells, 'The Great Creation Ceiling in the Long Gallery', *Lanhydrock House Journal*, 2 (2002), 4–17. In pointing towards the connection between the overmantels and the homily, Howells sees such an unambiguous declaration of obedience to the monarch as more in keeping with the views of Richard Robartes, but acknowledges the possibility that they were put up by John after 1649 to express outrage at the execution of Charles I.

36 *Certaine Sermons or Homilies appointed to be read in Churches, In the time of the late Queen Elizabeth of famous memory* (London, 1623, STC 13675), ed. Ian Lancashire, www.library.utoronto.ca/utel/ret/homilies/elizhom.html, accessed 15 January 2015.

37 Christopher Hill, *The English Bible and the Seventeenth-Century Revolution* (London: Allen Lane, 1993).

38 As suggested by John L. Thorp, 'The Ornamental Plasterwork of the Long Gallery at Lanhydrock, Cornwall', *Apollo* (National Trust Edition) 434 (April 1998), 30–4.

6

Sir Thomas Smith's stillhouse at Hill Hall: books, practice, antiquity and innovation

Richard Simpson

Sir Thomas Smith's library at his Essex country house, Hill Hall, as known from his own list of books 'found in my gallery' in 1566, has had a recognised place in English historiography since the list was printed in 1698 in John Strype's *Life of the Learned Sir Thomas Smith*.[1] The biography of Smith was part of Strype's series of studies of the English reformers, printed with supporting documentary evidence, and the list of books, divided into eight categories, could be specifically related to Smith's life.[2] The collection of philosophical works, with its many Greek texts, reflected Smith's early interests: a young scholar at Cambridge in the 1520s and 1530s he was one of the proponents of the revived study of ancient Greek.[3] His work from about 1542 as the first known Regius Professor of Civil Law at Cambridge is witnessed in his collection of legal texts. As a humanist scholar of law, he urged his students to read widely in ancient history and literature if they were to understand the true meaning of the Roman law, and he had substantial collections of works in these categories.[4] His library was rich in theology – he had been Secretary of State to Edward VI during the Protectorship of the Duke of Somerset in the late 1540s when he had worked with Cranmer on the first English Prayer book.[5] Collections on mathematics and medicine suggest even wider intellectual interests. So it was a collection reflecting Smith's scholarly, professional and personal interests, a library of close to 600 books – substantial for 1566 when a private scholarly library of 300 books can be considered large.[6]

But the list printed by Strype only gives part of the story of Smith's library. Four lists are now known.[7] The list Strype printed had been drawn up by Smith in 1566 on his return from four years on embassy in France, and another copy of this list has additions to each category. These new entries, it seems from the books listed, were made between 1566 and 1569. Then, in 1576, fearing terminal illness, putting his affairs in order and writing his will, Smith made another list of books. These lists present Smith's collection as considerably more extensive than Strype had disclosed, suggesting a library closer to 1,000 volumes. The lists also show Smith's book collecting as dynamic, developing over the years from 1566 to 1576. It was the decade when his career reached its summit. While on a further embassy to France in 1572 he was appointed Chancellor of the Order of the Garter and on his return became Principal Secretary to Queen Elizabeth.[8] It was the decade when he recreated Hill Hall itself in two transformational campaigns of building. These lists, and the books that they have made it possible to identify, have provided key evidence for Smith's developing intellectual engagements, including his Platonic and neo-Platonic thinking in ethics and on the nature of the human soul, suggesting the larger understandings which can be seen to have informed his choices in the iconography and style of the comprehensive scheme of wall, tile and glass painting in his newly built house.[9] And the book collection itself can also be seen to have had a place in Smith's evolving Hill Hall. Both the 1566 and 1576 lists identified the location of the books in the house: in 1566 in Smith's gallery, in 1576 in his study. But where those spaces were within the house is not certain. The Hill Hall of 1566, between Smith's rebuilding of 1557–58 and 1568–69, is only known from archaeological survivals which allow a partial reconstruction of the plan at ground floor level, although this suggests a gallery in the west range which could have been where Smith kept his books.[10] If so, they were housed in one of the larger spaces which Smith had created on the site of the modest, medieval structure he had acquired in 1556.[11] They were spaces which appear to have formed a suite of high-status rooms linked to the high end of the Hall itself, and also to the main stair, which gave access to what was possibly the best apartment on the first floor. In 1576, Smith's inventory identified shelves in his study on both east and west sides, on the west side 'starting from the window', a configuration which suggests that, following rebuilding in 1568–69, the books may have been kept in the west range, in rooms retaining their high status, but in a newly and dramatically enhanced space.[12] If Smith's study was one of these new rooms, not only was it enlarged to be some three times wider than the gallery it replaced, its visual importance was further enhanced by cross-lighting from windows to both east and west. Survivals of fine architectural *trompe l'oeil* wall painting to the upper parts of the walls of the rooms in this range have also been found.[13] If these were the spaces where Smith kept his books, and that remains far from certain, they would reinforce the evidence, from the lists and the books themselves, of the status as well as the utility of Smith's book collection in his country house.

But these were not the only books Smith had at Hill Hall. In addition to the lists of books found in his study on 9 April 1576, Smith made a separate inventory of the contents of the stillhouse at Hill Hall on 30 September 1576.[14] This has forty-three entries for printed books, and ten for works in manuscript, as well as the book of the stillhouse accounts. In addition, this inventory lists the equipment used and the products distilled. Further, the letters Smith wrote in 1572 while in France show that what was happening in his stillhouse in Essex was of the greatest personal concern.[15] Taken together, these three sources make it possible to develop further the understanding of books and biography, but also to investigate the relationship between the intellectual and the practical, and between practice and innovation – a relationship which points, in turn, to contemporary questioning of the authority of texts used in practical application.

The inventory of equipment gives an idea of the scale of work in Smith's stillhouse. There were some 138 vessels, from single and double phials, glass and stone bottles, to earthenware pans. In addition, Smith had 31 'bodies', which contained the material being distilled, and over 60 still-heads or 'receivers', as well as 3 glass retorts, 5 stills of pewter and 1 of copper, and a glass 'pellican', an enclosed still which allowed the continuous recirculation of its contents. We can also see from the inventory that the main products of the stillhouse were 'waters of herbs' and 'strong waters', distilled from a variety of substances, from wine-lees to turpentine, as well as from plants.

Smith's letters show that he used these waters as medicines for himself, recommended them to his wife, and sent them to his friends.[16] After a Channel crossing in a December storm, an intensely cold January and February in France spurred Smith's fears for his health, confirmed his anxious reliance on his medicines, and provoked worries about their continued production in his stillhouse at home. As a result, between January and May 1572 Smith wrote a series of letters to his wife and to the local parson, Thurston Shaw, exhorting his wife and instructing Shaw on the overriding importance of the work on the stills.[17] Thurston Shaw, cast by Smith in the role of apothecaries' assistant, but otherwise only known to us as a parson and scholar from Eton at King's College Cambridge – needed instruction, and Smith's letters spelt out what he was to do, and how he was to do it.[18]

First, Shaw was to maintain processes which Smith had already started himself. So in February Smith urged that the *aqua vitae* which 'I left to circulate in the pellican … If you keep in his continual warm heat as I left it fast stopped will be of marvellous operation'.[19] Smith's formulation suggests that he had had a close, even 'hands-on', engagement with the stillhouse before he left for France. He certainly took the view that these were 'medicines which I make for myself',[20] and in a letter to Richard Eden, a former pupil at Cambridge, Smith emphasised his active engagement with the stillhouse work: 'absent nor present I have not ceased from those works since I spoke with you last in England, so desirous am I to see the bottom of it'.[21]

Smith also told Shaw of plans for his return to Hill Hall, for the distillation of plants he had not yet tried, like the celandine, 'whose quintessence and magisterium have marvellous effects'.[22] Writing from Paris in May, Smith's letter also shows that his own researches continued while on official embassy. Shaw, too, was to try new experiments:

> I send you herewith a piece of a book of the *Experiments* of Raymond Lully, the which I do esteem as worth their weight as pure gold. ... I would you should essay both his experiments of tartar, which in English is called argol, and in Dutch winestone. ... How to order the tartar the book I send you tells plainly.[23]

Again Smith's detailed comments suggest a direct engagement with the practicalities. Smith supplemented the processes – the 'ordering' set out in Lull's text – by explaining that when buying the tartar Shaw should choose the sort which 'in the breaking has shining things in it like glass or salt'. Unable to work on the celandine himself, Shaw should also get started, and Smith explained how to identify the plants: 'It grows by the wall's side as you go to the longest pond ... If you pull a leaf ... or break it, it gives out a yellow milk. Put a little of that in your eye it will scour it and you will know the herb ever after'. Direct observation was to supplement the instructions in the text.

This letter brings us to the books and their use as practical texts. Smith's reference to the extract from the *Experiments* attributed to Raymond Lull on the use of tartar – the first two experiments in Lull's book – is carried further in the discussion of the use of celandine, which is set out in Lull's fourth experiment.[24] Lull's texts certainly provided detailed, matter-of-fact, step-by-step instructions. For example: first, pick your celandine in May – hence Smith's instructions to Shaw to get started – and at the time of the full moon, take the whole plant, flowers and roots, but wash the roots carefully to remove soil, dry and then crush the plants, place them in a glass container sealed with wax, and leave to ferment, heated by horse manure, for thirty to forty days, before beginning the distillation itself, for which Lull provided extensive further details.[25] The text itself demands hands-on practicality, based on direct observation, the use of appropriate equipment – a glass container – and a recognition of the needs of sequential processes.

Smith commented in the same letter that Lull's book of *Experiments* 'is the plainest that ever he wrote, and the key, to say the truth, to all his other work, and for anything that I can know, most likely to be true'. Smith's enthusiasm for the alchemical operations attributed to Lull seems to have overcome any implied scepticism. Four years later, in 1576, six of the forty-three entries in the stillhouse booklists referred to works by Lull. Two more entries suggest collections containing works ascribed to Lull, and when identified with available editions these eight entries suggest that Smith had some twenty works attributed to Lull.[26] Some, like the *Liber medicinæ magnæ*, provided lists of the plant and animal material, stone, and metal, from which quintessence could be distilled.[27] Other works placed the practicality of the *Experiments* in a larger explanatory context. For example, Smith listed two, possibly three, editions of the *Books on the Secrets of Nature or the Quintessence*, which drew out the wider medical value and application of the quintessence – and so was of direct relevance to Smith's stillhouse in 1572 – but also discussed its role in transmutation.[28] Smith also listed a copy of the *Testamentum* attributed to Lull, which provided a different approach to that set out in the *Book on the Quintessence*, but also sought the elixir which was the agent of both healing and transmutation, with an explicit concern that empirical working was not enough: natural philosophers should understand the reasons behind their work.[29] This may be reflected in Smith's comment to Shaw that – despite his anxiety that proper care should be taken of the quintessence of 'eyebright' – 'I would not care so much for these as than I would have you learn the fashion, and … the end what they will come to'.[30]

The Hill Hall booklists indicate that Smith's collection of texts attributed to Lull was made in the period after 1569: only one entry in the 1566 lists and its additions refers to a work containing pseudo-Lullian texts, and that is in a larger collection of short alchemical works.[31] But the booklists also show that Smith had possessed other printed books which not only provide a context for his later interest in pseudo-Lull, but also enable us to track parallel experiments through his larger library. For example, methods of preparing celandine were set out in Philipp Ulstadt's *The Philosophers' Universe, or Book of the Secrets of Nature*, first printed in Strasburg in 1526, and first listed by Smith in his gallery in 1566 – listed later in the stillhouse.[32] Ulstadt, who explicitly drew on Lull's work on celandine, supplemented his text with some more or less helpful images of practice – the distilling of celandine, for example.[33] In turn, Ulstadt's text on celandine was used almost verbatim by Conrad Gessner, the distinguished scholarly Zurich physician, in his *Treasury of Secret Remedies*, of 1554, described as 'a book of natural science, of medicine, and partly even of chemistry', and also listed in Smith's gallery in 1566.[34] Gessner also made available Ulstadt's valuation of the quintessence of celandine – an ingredient of 'potable gold' – and of each of the liquors derived from celandine associated with the four elements: for example, the liquor associated with the element of water treated all human diseases, that with air kept the young beautiful, that with fire, as Lull also argued, restored to health men close to death, while the liquor associated with earth, properly treated, was a component of the philosopher's stone.[35] Defining the quintessence and discussing its medical function in preserving health and prolonging life, Gessner privileged Lull as the first to write on the subject, suggesting that he was followed by a contemporary, John of Rupescissa, now recognised as the author of the work on which the *Books on the Secrets of Nature or the Quintessence* attributed to Lull depended.[36] Gessner thus placed pseudo-Lull's work in a historical context which extended to the more recent Ulstadt. Gessner's own work reflected the practice of a contemporary physician, and one informed by humanist study of the antique. For example, Gessner discussed the medical dangers of using metal distillation vessels, recommending the use of glass or glazed earthenware, citing Galen, the Greek physician of second-century Rome, on the damaging effects of using lead pipes in supplying drinking water.[37] Lull's *Experiments* were dated 1330, Gessner's work was that of a contemporary scholar-investigator of the highest repute: Smith's books located the practical procedures in which he was engaged within a wider process of investigation and experimentation recognised as the product of lengthy, sober, human endeavour.

This process was also a continuing one: Smith's use of the *Experiments* attributed to Lull signals an engagement with the latest investigations. Smith sent Shaw an extract from the *Experiments* from Paris in May 1572, the year in which the text was first printed.[38] Another entry in the list of stillhouse books refers to a manuscript copy of Lull's *Experiments* given to Smith by Richard Eden,who was also in France in 1572.[39] The manuscript gift suggests that Eden may have stimulated Smith's interest in pseudo-Lull:[40] the production of a manuscript copy suggests that Eden and Smith were part of a contemporary culture of inquiry to which the printers were responding when they decided to print a text like the *Experiments* for the first time.

And Eden also illuminates Smith's possible links to this culture of inquiry in contemporary France. While at Blois in March 1572, Smith wrote to Eden about their shared interest in the secrets of nature.[41] Thanking Eden for the suggestion that he visit Eden's French patron, Jean de Ferrières, vidame of Chartres, Smith observed that now that the negotiation of the treaty of Blois was reaching completion 'I have some time to play', and that he hoped for 'some long and good communication' on their investigations. De Ferrières, a French Protestant ally of the English, was known personally to Smith, while his own investigative interests were recognised in contemporary comment.[42] On 1 June 1572 Jacques Gohory dedicated his *Book of the Perilous Spring ... containing the hidden code of the secret mysteries of mineral science* to de Ferrières, singling him out from other noblemen for his capability in 'such elevated or profound secrets of nature'.[43] Gohory's work is a commentary on the poem, 'The Perilous Spring', as an alchemical allegory, drawing on a range of authors, including pseudo-Lull, and John de Rupescissa's work on the quintessence.[44] Gohory gave details of his own practical investigations in distillation for medical purposes in his *Guide to the Tobacco Plant*, also dedicated on 1 June 1572, where he described the making of a water, an oil, and a 'salt' from tobacco.[45] Gohory's comments suggest the nature of de Ferrières' investigations, and their interest for Smith. Both letters of dedication were dated at Gohory's 'lyceum San Marcellin', his 'philosophical garden' in the Faubourg Saint Marceau to the south of Paris, where Gohory cultivated special plants, undertook his investigations, and received many 'wise persons from different nations' who had come to his garden for 'conversation on rare and serious studies'.[46] De Ferrières himself had been a visitor, Gohory recalled: often in communication on the most difficult aspects of knowledge, the vidame had first seen Gohory's *The Perilous Spring* on a visit to the garden.[47] Given that the garden was recently acquired, de Ferrières must have visited between February 1572, when he returned to Paris following exile in England and retreat to the country, and 1 June 1572, when Gohory reported his visit.[48] It is even possible that Smith visited Gohory's garden. Smith was in Paris in April and May 1572, the months he hoped for 'some long and good communication' with de Ferrières and Eden on their investigations.[49] These months were a brief moment of reconciliation between Protestants and Roman Catholics, French and English, when inter-communication was eased. Gohory's dedication to de Ferrières – earlier considered a Huguenot traitor[50] – is itself a pointer. Gohory was close to the court: Catherine de'Medicis gave her name to his tobacco products.[51] Hopes for peace were associated with the imminent marriage of her daughter, Marguerite, to the Protestant Henri of Navarre, hopes paralleled, as Catherine herself wrote, in the Anglo-French treaty which Smith had successfully negotiated, and which Gohory himself explicitly saw as ending the hatred of the English for the French.[52] Smith certainly seized another opportunity for direct investigation during these months, when *terra sigillata* – a medicinal clay identified by pseudo-Lull as a material from which quintessence could be made – was found while he was at Blois.[53]

Like investigations at a propitious moment: whether or not Smith visited Gohory in 1572, Smith listed one of his works in the stillhouse at Hill Hall in 1576. Printed under the pseudonym, Leo Suavius, or 'Gentle Lion', Gohory's *Compendium* of Paracelsian philosophy and medicine dated at Paris 1566 points to another major contemporary influence informing the practices of distillation.[54] For example, Gohory discussed the production of a 'salt' by distillation from tobacco with reference to his commentaries attached to the *Compendium*.[55] But Gohory's Paracelsian study also placed such practical application in a larger contemporary medical understanding, which the stillhouse booklist shows Smith actively sought out. His list has seven entries referring to texts by Paracelsus – some twenty-six works[56] – supplemented by Paracelsian studies by Gerard Dorne, Peder Sørensen, and Michael Toxites.[57] Toxites's *Onomasticon*, a sort of dictionary providing German, and some French, Italian, and Spanish equivalents for specialist Latin terms, was only printed in 1574, showing again that Smith's enterprise was informed by the latest works available in print.

Paracelsianism has been characterised as a synthesis between traditional alchemical thought and neo-Platonic ideas: Smith's booklists demonstrate his interest in both.[58] But while Paracelsus might provide an alternative to the humanist focus on Galen, Smith's extensive collection of medical works also included editions of Galen's collected works and of nine individual works – one printed as recently as 1571.[59] Smith also had Johann Guinther von Andernach's latest work, comparing ancient and modern medicine, respecting both Classical medical traditions and elements of Paracelsian theory and practice in a systematic, analytical dialogue – including discussion of distillation – printed in Basel in

1571.[60] At the same time, Smith's books also reflected mid-sixteenth-century opposition to Paracelsus, a fiercely controversial and critical context. Smith listed, for example, a copy of the virulent attacks on Paracelsus – with a focus on his ideas as heretical, dishonest and demonic – by Thomas Erastus from 1571 to 1573, and two copies of Johann Wier's *Five Books on the Deceits of Demons*, which, from 1566, attacked Paracelsus's claims from an ethical standpoint.[61] In terms of practice, Smith's instructions to Shaw on the use of the residue left by distillation – Smith's 'fleam' – suggest that, despite his large collection, Smith did not necessarily follow Paracelsus, who rejected the medical value of residues, as Gohory made clear in 1572.[62] Gohory's own shift against Paracelsian ideas, identified by 1575, suggests the contemporary dynamic of these ideas.[63]

Smith's collection of Paracelsus also suggests a wider role for the stillhouse at Hill Hall. Although smaller than John Dee's exceptional collection dated 1583, Smith's 1576 inventories suggest a collection both earlier in date and larger in scale than the private collections identified hitherto.[64] Gabriel Harvey claimed, in his appeal to Robert Cecil in 1598, that it was from Smith that Harvey had learnt not to condemn 'the true chymique without imposture'.[65] Understandings of such 'effectual practicable knowledge' – as Harvey characterised it – perhaps derived from Smith's stillhouse during visits to Hill Hall in the early 1570s,[66] may have equipped Harvey to recognise, some twenty years later, the expertise of the London Paracelsian, John Hester.[67] We may, then, identify Smith as a precursor to, perhaps one source for, that wider familiarity with the ideas of Paracelsus which Charles Webster has identified in England in the later sixteenth and early seventeenth centuries, with its reflection in the work of writers like John Donne and Ben Jonson.[68]

If the works of Galen and Paracelsus suggest the range of medical texts available to inform Smith's stillhouse work, his booklists indicate an even wider context of practice: the making of medicines and the cultivation of plants. Smith's references in his letters of 1572 to the use of eyebright, angelica, balm, germander, roses and rosemary, as well as celandine, were accompanied by concern for the gardens at Hill Hall. He instructed his wife on manuring the garden, care for the gooseberries, for the apple and pear trees, and the planting of the mustard seed garden.[69] During his earlier French embassy he had sent plants. Writing to William Cecil from Bordeaux in April 1565, he sent:

> certaine rootes of *Hyacynthus* and two or iii *Asphodelus*, because I have not seen them before in England. … It has grieved me many times and specially when I was in the mountains of St Claude, and in Provence and at Avignon, that I had not commodity to send such strange herbs home as we have not in England.[70]

Again, this practical interest in new discoveries can be directly paralleled in books. Smith listed a copy of the *New Note-Book of Plants* by Pierre Pena and Matthias de L'Obel, printed in 1571, which described some 170 species from Provence and 374 from Languedoc, the areas where Smith had seen the 'strange herbs' he had wanted to send home.[71] Pena and L'Obel's work was part of the innovative development of sixteenth-century botany, using direct observation as a supplement to textual study, explicitly based on the foundation of Graeco-Roman botany and medicine.[72] Galen, commenting that botany was better studied from plants than from books, had criticised magical writings on 'holy herbs' while commending the work of Dioscorides, the first-century AD practitioner.[73] Needless to say, Smith listed copies of Dioscorides' *Materia medica*: his entries suggest he owned five editions, one each in Greek and in Latin, and three more in Latin and French with the commentary of Pietro Andrea Mattioli.[74] Later editions of the French version have Mattioli's fierce criticism of the misunderstandings of ignorant alchemists, but also a final, additional section, on the methods of distilling waters from plants.[75]

But Smith's books testify to distillation in an even broader context. Among the books added to his collection between 1566 and 1569, and later kept in the stillhouse, Smith listed Vannoccio Biringuccio's *On the Technology of Fire*.[76] Biringuccio's study ranged from metallurgy and glass-making to fireworks and artillery, including alchemy and distillation.[77] Biringuccio provided working details of distillation, not only of the different vessels used, their purposes and types, but of the construction of furnaces, from those using horse manure, as recommended by pseudo-Lull in the processing of celandine, to those for making oils where the distillation vessel was built-in to the furnace to achieve higher temperatures. Biringuccio praised honest alchemist distillers whose innovations ranged from new medicinal substances to colours and perfumes: it was the origin and foundation of many other arts.[78] But he paralleled his practical details with a ferocious attack on metallurgical alchemists, and a specific attack on their books, 'collections of recipes' incomprehensible except to themselves, and on their reliance on the accounts of witnesses rather than reasoning or demonstrable results. Citing sources like Hermes, Arnold, or Raymond Lull, they demanded a 'respect of faith', 'because of the dignity of these men's philosophical learning or holiness'.[79]

Biringuccio's criticism brings out a tension in the reading of texts for practical application, where verification of meaning is essentially extra-textual. And Smith's booklists help to locate Biringuccio's censure in a wider context of criticism by writers discussing distillation, while also indicating possible responses. One is suggested by the English translation of Biringuccio's text by Richard Eden – Smith's pupil – which simply omitted the whole critical passage.[80] Another may be seen in Georg Agricola's *On Metals* – also listed by Smith – which provides matter-of-fact reports on practice and outcomes, reinforced by images of tools, equipment, the arrangement of the working processes themselves, a representation of results which can be demonstrated, a mediation between texts and direct observation which can, in turn, be checked directly in the workshop.[81]

An explicit response to Biringuccio, Agricola also explained that he took as his model the Roman writer Columella's *On Agriculture* – part of the collection *On Rural Affairs* read by Smith himself, and in the tradition of the solid Roman practical handbook.[82]

Writing to Richard Eden in 1572 to evoke his passion 'to see the unlooked for privities of nature', Smith claimed of their shared investigations that 'there can by that art be made and brought to pass most strange, wondrous and incredible things, both have I had experience myself and I have read much more'.[83] And Smith himself laid specific claim to the use of both books and experimental evidence in a project which paralleled his Hill Hall stillhouse. His letters from France about distillation juxtapose others about the project, undertaken with Lord Burghley, the Earl of Leicester, and Sir Humfrey Gilbert, for making copper out of iron and quicksilver out of antimony and lead, a new art 'discovered after long search by Smith', as claimed in 1571, and confirmed in 1575 as 'through long search in books of divers arts, divers trials in va[i]n assayed'.[84] The stillhouse inventory of 1576 shows that Smith had manuscripts of alchemical works by Roger Bacon, Thomas Norton, and three by George Ripley, as well as *Dialogus inter Hylardum Necromanticum et quendam spiritum*.[85] Smith's letters reveal practical aspects of the experiments: the making of saltpetre, the use of alum and copperas.[86] As the scheme gradually unravelled, Smith remarked to Gilbert that their alchemist 'does as Geber, Ripley and the other alchemists do, that lead a man from this to that and through so many gates that at the last they come through never a one right, and in fine, find nothing'.

Smith's stillhouse at Hill Hall shows us his country house as a centre for investigation, practical experiment, and making, in which Smith himself took a direct, active, part. A centre where he brought together a range of intellectual resources available to him through his ambassadorial travels in France, friends and acquaintances, reinforced by the movements of refugees. A centre to which others, like Eden, might contribute, and from which others, like Gilbert, Harvey and Shaw, might learn. Smith's collection points to the eager exploration of innovation, and also suggests a plurality of engagement, the seeking of opportunities to test new against established knowledge, supported and enabled by the dynamic acquisition of the latest relevant printed book. The stillhouse was part of the economy of a household – from its gardens and plants, to its servants, even the parson – drawn into the intellectual explorations of the 'strange, wondrous and incredible things' of nature. Revealed through books but also through direct observation and hands-on investigation, it was a process of reading, questioning, and testing through practical application, which also explored the utility, credibility and authority of texts.

Notes

1   J[ohn] S[trype], *Life of the Learned Sir Thomas Smith* (London: A. Roper and R. Basset, 1698), Appendix VI, pp. 139–47.

2   Strype's biography of Smith followed that of Cranmer (1694), preceding others like those of John Cheke (1705) and Matthew Parker (1711), and collections of documents, like his *Ecclesiastical Memorials* (1721) and *Annals of the Reformation* (1709–31); see W. D. J. Cargill Thompson, 'John Strype as a source for the study of sixteenth-century English church history', in Derek Baker (ed.), *The Materials, Sources and Methods of Ecclesiastical History*, Studies in Church History, 11 (Oxford: Basil Blackwell for the Ecclesiastical History Society, 1975), 237–47. Strype's work on Smith may also have been stimulated by interest in Smith's constitutional work in the context of the revolution of 1688, see G[uy] M[iège], *The new state of England* (London: H. C. for Jonathan Robinson, 1691), where the letter to the reader states that the work is based on Smith's *De Republica Anglorum*. The analysis of Smith's booklists here relies on my forthcoming study of Smith's library, abbreviated here to *Smith's Booklists*. The categories are: *Theologiae* (*Smith's Booklists*, entries 1–57); *Iuris ciuilis* (64–103); English law (104–22); *Historiographi* (129–231); *Philosophica* (268–342); Mathematics (359–408); Medicine and surgery (431–51); *Grammatica et poetica* (463–524).

3   On his Greek studies, see Smith's letter to Stephen Gardiner, Chancellor of Cambridge University, 12 August 1542, printed as *De recta & emendata linguæ Græcæ pronuntiatione … epistola* (Paris: Robert Estienne, 1568); *Smith's Booklists*, entry 1030.

4   His inaugural lectures on the study of Roman law are at Bodleian Library, MS Top Oxon e 5.

5   For a summary, see Richard Simpson, 'Images and Ethics in Reformation Political Discourse: the Paintings at Sir Thomas Smith's Hill Hall', in Tara Hamling and Richard L. Williams (eds), *Art Re-formed. Re-assessing the Impact of the Reformation on the Visual Arts* (Newcastle: Cambridge Scholars Publishing, 2007), pp. 127 and 137 nn. 2–7.

6   See E. S. Leedham-Green, *Books in Cambridge Inventories* 2 vols (Cambridge: Cambridge University Press, 1986) shows that the libraries of Cambridge scholars in the 1560s and 1570s (inventories 109–41 to 1577), rarely contained over 100 entries (inventories 110, 120, 126, 131, 132, 139), and exceptionally over 160 (inventory 111).

7   A version of the list printed by Strype is at Queens' College Cambridge (hereafter QCC) MS 83 fols 145 ʳ –150 ᵛ: a further copy, with the additions of 1566–69, is at QCC MS 49 fols 70 ʳ –78 ʳ, see *Smith's Booklists*, entries 1–574; the list drawn up on 9 April 1576 is at QCC MS 49 fols 89 ᵗ –99 ᵛ, entries 575–1130.

8   Appointed Chancellor of the Order of the Garter, Smith to Queen Elizabeth, Blois 21 April 1572, *CSP Foreign 1572–74*, no. 280; Principal Secretary, 15 September 1572, *Calendar Patent Rolls Elizabeth 1569–1572*, no. 3153.

9   Richard Simpson, 'The Period 2 Decorative Scheme: Iconographic Choices in the Cupid and Psyche paintings', and 'The Painted Ensemble: Overview and Conclusions', in Paul Drury with Richard Simpson, *Hill Hall a Singular House Devised by a Tudor Intellectual* (London: The Society of Antiquaries, 2009), pp. 206–9, 236–42.

10   Space W1, see Paul Drury, 'Period 2.1: Reconstruction Around the Inner Courtyard, 1557–8', in Drury with Simpson, *Hill Hall*, pp. 46–9 and Fig. 366P.

11   See Drury, 'Documentary Evidence for Chronology and Scope', in Drury with Simpson, *Hill Hall*, p. 39.

12   Perhaps spaces G01 or G02, see Drury, 'Period 2.2: the Rebuilding of the North and West Ranges, 1568–9', in Drury with Simpson, *Hill Hall*, pp. 61–3, 79, and Fig. 367P.

13   Simpson, 'The Period 2 Decorative Scheme: the Wall Paintings', in Drury with Simpson, *Hill Hall*, pp. 199–201, and Fig. 172.

14   QCC MS 49 fol. 119[r–v], *Smith's Booklists*, entries 1131–86 and Appendix 1. The term 'stillhouse' suggests an outbuilding, but currently there is no known evidence for the location of the stillhouse at Hill Hall.

15   The letters are contained in a letter book of Smith's: TNA SP 70/146, *cf. CSP Foreign Series January–June 1583 and Addenda*, nos 413–98.

16   On their importance to his health, see Smith to his wife, Amboise, 9 January 1572, and suggesting that she take some of the infused waters made in the stillhouse for her stomach or coughs and colds, Smith to his wife, Blois, 20 February 1572, TNA SP 70/146 fols 29[r] and 46[v], *CSP Foreign Addenda* nos 415, 435. Smith sent waters to Lord Burghley for his daughter, mentioning others who had appreciated them, see Smith to Lady Burghley, Hampton Court, 7 November 1574, BL Lansdowne MS 19/50 fol. 116[r].

17   Smith to his wife, 9 and 10 January, 20 February, 14 April, 17 and 18 May; see *CSP Foreign Addenda* nos. 415, 419, 435, 462, and 490. Smith to Thurston Shaw ('Mr. Parson') 20 February, 15 April, 17 May (2 letters); see *CSP Foreign Addenda* nos 434, 467, 488 and 489.

18   John Venn and J. A. Venn, *Alumni Cantabrigienses*, Part 1, 4 vols (Cambridge: Cambridge University Press, 1922–27) 1.4, p. 54: from Saffron Walden, matriculated at King's 1557 aged eighteen, ordained 1560, rector at Theydon Mount 1566–88. Smith and his wife were patrons of the living at Theydon Mount.

19   Smith to Shaw, Blois, 20 February 1572, TNA SP 70/146 fol. 46[v], *CSP Foreign Addenda* no. 434.

20   Smith to his wife, Blois, 20 February 1572, TNA SP 70/146 fols 29[r] and 46[v], *CSP Foreign Addenda* nos 415, 435.

21   Smith to Eden, Blois, 9 March 1572, TNA SP 70/146 fol. 55[v], *CSP Foreign Addenda* no. 446. On Smith and Eden, see n. 39 below.

22   Smith to Shaw, Blois, 20 February 1572, TNA SP 70/146 fol. 46[v], *CSP Foreign Addenda* no. 434. 'Magisterium' was a concentrated essence, 'quintessence' a distinct 'fifth-essence' existing in addition to the four elements: both were refined by distillation from corruptible substance.

23   Smith to Shaw, Paris, 17 May 1572, TNA SP 70/146 fol. 76[v], *CSP Foreign Addenda* no. 488. Tartar is dried lees of wine (potassium bitartrate) found in wine barrels.

24   None of the works listed by Smith is genuinely the work of Raymond Lull; they form part of the body of alchemical works attributed to Lull after his death in 1315. I have referred here to the author as Raymond Lull, mainly because that is how they were identified by Smith. I have relied for much of the analysis of the work of pseudo-Lull in this article on Michela Pereira, *The Alchemical Corpus Attributed to Raymond Lull*, *Warburg Institute Surveys and Texts*, XVIII (London: The Warburg Institute, 1989). Lull's *Experiments* were first printed in a collection of works with the title *Libelli aliquot chemici: nunc primum ... in lucem ... editi*, or *Some Short Books of Alchemy now printed for the first time* (Basel: P. Perna, 1572): the *Experiments*, at pp. 193–313, is dated, at the end, 1330, and consists of thirty-four procedures. For Smith's ownership of a copy, see *Smith's Booklists*, entry 1149, and for the work, see Pereira, *The Alchemical Corpus*, Appendix I.21.

25   'Accipe chelidoniam maio mense in plenilunio cum suis radicibus & floribus, sed radices prius expurgentur, & lauentur ab omni sorde terrestri: desiccabis super tabulam nitidam, contunde postea optime, & in vase vitreo contusam tuam chelidoniam pone, & vas cum suo cooperculo sit optime conclusum cum cera gummata: pone in putrefactione sub simo equino per 30 vel 40 dies.' Experiment 4, in Lull's Experiments, in *Libelli aliquot chemici*, 205–8, pp. 205–6.

26   The works, with their entry numbers in *Smith's Booklists* and references in Pereira (n. 24 above) Appendix I, are: *Apertorium*, 1153, 1155, P. I.2; *Ars intellectiva*, 1153, 1155, P. I.5; *Compendium animæ transmutationis metallorum*, 359.(1154), 1145, 1149, 1155, P. I.12; *De tincturis compendium*, or *Vademecum*, 359.(1154), P. I.30; *Conclusio summaria* 1153, 1155, P. I.16; *Elucidatio testamenti* 1149, P. I.19; *Epistola accurtationis lapidis benedicti* 1149, P. I.20; *Epistola sive epitome* 1162; *Experimenta* 1149, P. I.21; *Libellus de mercurio solo* 1155, P. I.25; *Liber artis compendiosæ* 1149, P. I.30; *Liber de intentione alchimistarum* 1155, P. I.33; *Liber lucis mercuriorum* 1149, P. I.47; *Liber medicinæ magnæ* 1149, P. I.17; *Magia naturalis* 1153, 1155, P. I.13; *Mercuriorum liber* 1153, P. I.61d; *De secretis naturæ sive quinta essentia libri II*, 749, 1155, 1163, P. I.39; *Summaria lapidis consideratio*, 1155, P. I.60; *Testamentum universam artem chymicam* [*Testamentum antiquum*], 1145, P. I.61; *Testamentum novissimum*, 1149, P. I.62.

27   *Smith's Booklists*, entry 1149, and see Pereira, *The Alchemical Corpus*, Appendix I.17; the lists in the *Liber medicinae magnae* are in *Libelli aliquot chemici*, pp. 404–10.

28   *De secretis naturæ sive quinta essentia libri II*; Smith's entry 1155 seems only to refer to the Nuremberg, J. Petreius, 1546 edition, in quarto; entry 1163 may refer to other editions, including octavos; entry 749, in the main 'study' list, may be a further copy: see *Smith's Booklists*. The work is mostly by John of Rupescissa; for analysis, see Pereira, *The Alchemical Corpus*, 11–20, pp. 11–13.

29   For this analysis, and the distinction of this book from the work of John of Rupescissa, see Pereira, *The Alchemical Corpus*, 6–11, pp. 6–7.

30   Smith to Shaw, Blois, 20 February 1572, TNA SP 70/146 fol. 46ᵛ.

31   Two works attributed to Lull are included in *De alchimia opuscula complura veterum philosophorum* ([Frankfurt-am-Main: C. Jacobus, 1550]), see *Smith's Booklists*, entry 359. (1154); the *Compendium animæ transmutationis metallorum*, and *De tincturis compendium*, or *Liber artis compendiosae*, or *Vademecum*, Pereira (n. 24 above) Appendix I.12 and 30. Writing to his wife, Blois, 20 February 1572, TNA SP 70/146, Smith reported that he had not known of these distilled medicines when sick in Toulouse during the winter and spring 1564–65.

32   *Cælum philosophorum seu de secretis naturæ liber*, see *Smith's Booklists*, entry 417**.1135.

33   Reference to Lull's work on celandine, Ulstadt, *Cælum philosophorum* (1528), Chapter 13 at fol. 23ᵛ; image at 24ʳ.

34   *Thesaurus Euonymi philiatri de remediis secretis, liber physicus, medicus, et partim etiam chymicus* (Zurich: A. Gessner, 1554) (hereafter Gessner, *Treasury*) see *Smith's Booklist*, entries (297).441.744 and 1147 also for discussion of the original anonymous publication, acknowledged as Gessner's work in 1562.

35   Ulstadt's comment 'quinta essentia … etiam ipsum aurum potabile ingreditur' at his *Cælum philosophorum* (1528) fol. 23ᵛ, other qualities described at fol. 25ʳ⁻ᵛ, quoted by Gessner, *Treasury* (1554) pp. 152, 158–60.

36   In the section headed 'De quinta essentia remediorum', Gessner states, 'De hac primus omnium Raymundus Lullus scripsit … Illum praeter alios sequuti Io. de Rupescissa … ', *Treasury* (1554) p. 131; see also n. 26 above.

37   Gessner, *Treasury* (1554), pp. 82–7 (84).

38   Smith to Shaw, Paris, 17 May 1572, NTA SP 70/146.

39   *Smith's Booklists*, entry 1184 'Experimenta Rai: Lull: ex dono Ric: Eden *written*'. In his English translation of *The arte of nauigation* by Martin Cortes (London: R. Jugge, 1561), see *Smith's Booklists*, entry 404.782, Eden refers to Smith as 'sometyme my Tutor', fol. [5]ᵛ. On Smith and Eden in France, see Smith to Eden, Blois, 9 March 1572, TNA SP 70/146.

40   Smith had not known of distilled medicines in 1564–65 (n. 31 above), but Eden had been engaged in distillation and the production of quintessence, also using pseudo-Lull, by

1549, see C. J. Kitching, 'Alchemy in the Reign of Edward VI: an Episode in the Careers of Richard Whalley and Richard Eden', *Bulletin of the Institute of Historical Research*, 44 (1971), 308–15. Chapter 4 of Cortes' *Arte of Nauigation*, fols v[v]–vi[r], in Eden's translation, is on the quintessence as part of the working universe.

41   Smith to Eden, Blois, 9 March 1572, TNA SP70/146 fol. 55[v].

42   The vidame was a signatory of the treaty of Hampton Court between the English and a group of leaders of the French protestants in 1562, which was critical to Smith's work as ambassador in France from the Anglo-French war of 1562 until his negotiation of the treaty of Troyes in 1564; see [Léon de Bastard d'Estang], *Vie de Jean de Ferrières vidame de Chartres* (Auxerre: Perriquèt and Rouillé, 1858), pp. 68–87. In his letter to Eden of 9 March, TNA SP70/146 fol. 55[v] Smith asked Eden to greet the vidame 'and his bedfellow', on his behalf, a formulation Smith used with his closer friends.

43   'A autre seigneur seroit fort mal adressé, n'en connoissant aucun capable de si haults ou profonds secrets de Nature', *Livre de la fontaine perilleuse … contenant la steganographie des mysteres secret de la science minerale* (Paris: 'pour Iean Ruelle', 1572), Gohory's dedicatory letter at fol. 29[r–v].

44   For Gohory's references to Lull, see fols 39[v], 40[r], and to John of Rupescissa, fol. 43[r]. For the work, and Gohory's analysis, see Didier Kahn, 'Les commentaires alchimiques de textes littéraires', in *Le commentaire entre tradition et innovation: actes du colloque international de l'Institut des traditions textuelles (Paris et Villejuif, 22–25 septembre 1999)*, eds Marie-Odile Goulet-Cazé, Tiziano Dorandi and Richard Goulet (Paris: Librairie philosophique J. Vrin, 2000), 475–80, pp. 478–9.

45   *Instruction sur l'herbe petum* (Paris: Galiot du Pré, 1572); on the discussion of the distillation of a water from the tobacco plant, fol. 7[v]; on the oil, fols 7[v]–9[r]; on the 'salt', fols 9[v]–10[r].

46   On his garden, its plants, and its visitors, see *Instruction*, fols 5[r–v], 3[v]; E.-T. Hamy, 'Un précurseur de Guy de la Brosse. Jacques Gohory et le Lycium Philosophal de Saint-Marceau-lès-Paris (1571–1576)', *Nouvelles Archives du Muséum d'Histoire Naturelle*, 4th series, tom. I (Paris, 1899) pp. 1–26 (18–20); and D. P. Walker, *Spiritual and Demonic Magic from Ficino to Campanella* (Notre Dame, IN and London, 1975), pp. 99–101.

47   'Monseigneur, l'honneur qu'il vous à pleu me faire souvent de votre communication, sur les pluss arduës sciences, m'oblige … à dedier à votre nom illustre … ce livret … lequel un jour vous prinstes plaisir à veoir en mon jardin', *La fontaine perilleuse*, fol. 29[r].

48   [Bastard d'Estang], *Vie de Jean de Ferrières*, pp. 115–16 with n.2.

49   Treaty of Blois initially agreed 19 April, *CSP Foreign 1572–74*, no. 272, Blois, 19 April 1572: Smith to go to Paris 23 April 1572, see Smith to Lord Burghley, Blois, 22 April 1572, *CSP Foreign 1572–74*, no. 281: Smith's letters from Paris during May, *CSP Foreign Addenda*, nos 481–98.

50   [Bastard d'Estang], *Vie de Jean de Ferrières*, pp. 74, 76.

51   *Instruction*, fol. 2[v].

52   For Catherine's welcome for both treaty and marriage, see her letter to Queen Elizabeth, Blois, 22 April 1572, *CSP Foreign 1572–74*, no. 283. For Gohory's reference, see *Instruction*, part 2, p. 15, ll. 3–4, in the context of a comment on the printing of the *New Note-Book of Plants* of Pierre Pena and Matthias L'Obel in London, see p. 3, and below pp. 108–9.

53   On the *terra sigillata* or 'bolus' 'we have found at Blois … which I went to see …' Smith to Dr Wilson, Blois, 11 April 1572, TNA SP 70/146, fol. 55[v], *CSP Foreign Addenda*, no. 460. For pseudo-Lull's reference to *terra sigillata*, see *Libelli quinque*, p. 405.

54   *Philosophiæ et medicinæ, utriusque uniuersæ compendium … cum scholiis*, Smith's *Booklists*, entry 1141.

55 'J'ay traitté trois manieres de faire le sel artificiel … en mes scholies sur Paracelse, imprimez
    à Paris', *Instruction*, fol. 9ᵛ; *Compendium … cum scholiis* (Paris [1567?]), pp. 373–6.

56 Two other entries in the main 1576 list identify three more works. The complete list of
    Paracelsus's works identified, with their entry numbers in *Smith's Booklists*, is: *Apologia*, entry
    1161; *Archidoxorum de secretis naturæ mysteriis libri X*, 1142, 1148; *De cementis metallorum
    [compendiolum]* and *De gradationibus [metallorum]*, 1142; *Chirurgia magna, in duos tomos
    digesta* 721; *Chyrurgia minor*, 721; *Chirurgia minor, in octavo*, 746; *Chirurgia vulnerum*,
    721; *Liber de duplici anatomia*, 1144; *De gradibus, de compositionibus et dosibus receptorum
    ac naturalium libri VII*, with, *scholia*, to the, *De gradibus*, 1144; *De matrice liber*, 1152; *De
    medicamentorum simplicium gradibus et compositionibus, opus nouum*, 1144; *De meteoris liber
    I*, 1152, 1166; *De modo pharmacandi*, 1151; *De morborum physionomia fragmentum*, 1148;
    De natura hominis libri II, 1159; *De natura rerum libri VII*, 1159; *Liber de occulta philosophia*,
    1148; *Liber Paramirum*, 1151; *Philosophiæ magnæ, collectanea*, 1161; *De physionomia
    quantum medico opus est*, 1148; *De præparationibus [libelli II]. Elebori seu veratri præparatio*,
    and, *Tractatus de Porosa Persicariæ præparatio]* 1142; *De thermis [De balneis liber I]* and *[De
    thermarum Favariæ]*, 1151; *Libri de tinctura physicorum*, 1142, 1148; *Appendicula, tincturam
    philosophicarum* in G. Dorn, *Chymisticum artificium naturæ, theoricum et practicum*, 1174;
    De tribus principijs liber tertius, 1152; *De Vrinarum et pulsuum iudiciis libellus*, 1148; *De
    vexationibus alchimistarum [liber]*, 1142; *De vita longa libri IIII*, 1141; *De xeondochio [Liber
    ptochodochii]*, 1151.

57 Gerhard Dorn, *Lapis metaphysicus, aut philosophicus* ([Frankfurt] 1570), *Smith's Booklists*, entry
    1140; Peder Sørensen (Petrus Severinus), *Idea medicinæ philosophicæ, fundamenta continens
    totius doctrinæ Paracelsicæ, Hippocraticæ, & Galenicæ* (Basel, 1571), entry 725; Michael
    Toxites, *Onomastica II* (Strasbourg 1574), entry 1160.

58 Charles Webster, 'Alchemical and Paracelsian Medicine', *Health, Medicine and Mortality
    in the Sixteenth Century*, ed. C. Webster (Cambridge: Cambridge University Press, 1979),
    301–34, p. 316 and *cf.* n. 9 above. On the relationship of Paracelsus's *Archidoxorum libri* to
    the work of John of Rupescissa as elaborated in works attributed to Lull and by Ulstadt,
    see Robert Multhauf, 'The Significance of Distillation in Renaissance Medical Chemistry',
    Bulletin of the History of Medicine, 30 (1956), 329–46, pp. 336–9.

59 Webster, 'Alchemical and Paracelsian Medicine', p. 316; *Smith's Booklists*, entries 284.431.714;
    86.977; 289.436.715; 447.722; <320>.442.736; 737; 743.

60 *De medicina veteri et nova commentarii duo* (Basel: 'ex officina Henricpetrina', 1571) entry
    1187; on distillation of celandine, Part 2, pp. 622–3, following pseudo-Lull; of oils, Part 2,
    pp. 630–80.

61 Thomas Erastus, *Disputationum de medicina nova P. Paracelsi pars prima (-quarta)* (Basel:
    P. Perna, 1573), *Smith's Booklists*, entry 724; Johann Wier, *De præstigiis dæmonum libri* (Basel,
    J. Oporinus, 1563; Basel, J. Oporinus, 1564; Basel, J. Oporinus, 1566; and Basel, 'in off.
    Oporiniana', 1568), entries 343*.794; 356**.

62 Smith on 'fleam' or 'flegma', see his letters to Shaw, Blois, 20 February 1572, TNA SP
    70/146 fol. 46ᵛ, and Paris 17 May 1572, TNA SP 70/146 fol. 76ᵛ. For a comment on 'fecum
    aut phlegmatis', see Toxites, *Onomastica II*, p. 388. The use of residues has been seen as
    distinguishing herbal from alchemical distillers, see Multhauf, 'Significance of Distillation',
    pp. 342–5. Gohory on the residue from the distillation of the 'water' of tobacco, 'iettant les
    FECES dānees, appellees par Paracelse *Caput mortuum*, c'est à dire & entendre, Terre *cui
    nihil tribuit Archeus*', 'The *Caput mortuum*, to which Archeus attributes nothing', *Instruction*,
    fol. 7ᵛ.

63   In Gohory's *Discours responsif* (1575), see Didier Kahn, 'Le paracelsisme de Jacques Gohory', in *Paracelse et les siens (colloque des 15 et 16 décembre 1994 à la Sorbonne)*, ed. Roland Edighoffer, *Aries* 19 (Meudon: 1995), 81–130, p. 81.

64   *John Dee's Library Catalogue*, ed. Julian Roberts and Andrew G. Watson (London: The Bibliographical Society, 1990); Webster, 'Alchemical and Paracelsian Medicine', pp. 320–1.

65   Virginia F. Stern, *Gabriel Harvey. A Study of His Life Marginalia and Library* (Oxford: Oxford University Press, 1979) p. 125; Webster, 'Alchemical and Paracelsian Medicine', p. 307.

66   Lisa Jardine and Anthony Grafton, '"Studied for action": How Gabriel Harvey Read his Livy', *Past & Present*, 129 (November 1990), 30–78, pp. 40–4.

67   Stern, *Harvey*, pp. 84–5; Webster, 'Alchemical and Paracelsian Medicine', p. 327.

68   Webster, 'Alchemical and Paracelsian Medicine', pp. 323, 305–9.

69   Smith to his wife, Amboise, 10 January 1572, TNA SP 70/146 fol. 30^r, *CSP Foreign Addenda*, no. 419.

70   Smith to Cecil, Bordeaux, 16 April 1565, TNA SP 70/77 fol. 132^v.

71   *Stirpium adversaria nova* (London: Thomas Purfoot, 1571); *Smith's Booklists*, entry 717; and A. Louis, *Mathieu de l'Obel 1538–1616, Épisode de l'histoire de la botanique* (Ghent, Louvain: Story-Scientia, 1980), pp. 121–2.

72   Louis, *Mathieu de l'Obel*, pp. 100–40, 487, 491–4.

73   Galen, *De simplicium medicamentorum temperamentis ac facultatibus liber VI, Claudii Galeni Opera Omnia*, ed. Carl Gottlob Kühn (Leipzig, 1821–33) XI, pp. 796–7). For the dominance of citations from Dioscorides over all other authors in Pena and L'Obel's 1571 work, see Louis (n. 71 above), pp. 163–5.

74   *Smith's Booklists*, 288.435.547*.716; 283.434.718; 285.433.1133; 452**; 1190.

75   For the supplemented editions, see *Smith's Booklists* entry 285.433.1133; for Smith's ownership of a French translation, bought in 1572, entry 1191; Mattioli on alchemists' incorrect understanding of the origins of metals, and his favourable references to Agricola (Lyons 1572), pp. 684–5 ; 'De la manière de distiller les eaux', with images, pp. 816–19.

76   *De la pirotechnia*, first printed Venice, 1540; *Smith's Booklists*, entry 454**.1138.

77   Biringuccio, *Pirotechnia* (Venice 1550) 'Dell'arte alchimica' and 'Dell'arte distillatoria', at Book 9, chapters 1–3, fols 123^r–132^r.

78   Biringuccio, *Pirotechnia* (1550) Book 9, Chapter 1, fol. 123^v.

79   Biringuccio, *Pirotechnia* (1550) Book 1, Chapter 1, fol. 5^r.

80   Eden's *Art of Navigation* at fol. 338^v l. 34 after ' ... Italie.' omits Biringuccio, *Pirotechnia* (1550) fols 5^r l. 3–8^v l. 10.

81   *De re metallica libri XII*, dated 1550, first printed Basel, 1556, see *Smith's Booklists*, entry 290.836.

82   Agricola on Columella and Biringuccio (Basel, 1556) sig. α^{r-v}; on the purification of silver and gold using distillation, with images of processes and equipment labelled and described, *De re metallica*, pp. 354–62. For Smith's use of the Roman writers *De re rustica*, see my forthcoming study on Smith's architectural readings.

83   Smith to Eden, Blois, 9 March 1572, TNA SP 70/146 fol. 55^v.

84   Establishment of the 'Society of the new art', 4 December 1571, *Calendar of Patent Rolls, Elizabeth*, vol. 5, pp. 483–5; and 14 February 1575, vol. 6, pp. 509–10.

85   *Smith's Booklists*, entries 1175–83.

86   Smith to Gilbert, [Blois] 8 February [1572], TNA SP 70/146 fol. 39, *CSP Foreign Add.*, no. 428. Under the circumstances, probably blue copperas, a protosulphate of copper.

7

'A most studious searcher after truth': the 9th Earl of Northumberland and *Scientia*

Alison McCann

The 'studious searcher after truth' in my title was not actually Henry Percy, 9th Earl of Northumberland, but Thomas Harriot, the mathematician and astronomer whom the Earl kept in his household. It was the wording on the plaque to Harriot which was on the Bank of England building which stood on the site of St Christopher's church, where Harriot was buried: however, it could serve as a very good description of the Earl. This chapter seeks to give an indication of the Earl's thinking about science, though using that word in its rather wider original meaning – *scientia* – knowledge – and also to give a brief idea of what sources survive among the collections at Petworth House, West Sussex, from which such information can be gleaned.

Henry Percy was born in 1564 in Tynemouth Castle, of which his father was Governor. His father, the 8th Earl, had become Earl of Northumberland in 1572, succeeding his brother who had been executed for his involvement in a plot to free Mary Queen of Scots. The 8th Earl had remained loyal to the Crown during his brother's rebellion in 1569, but was arrested in 1571 and imprisoned in the Tower of London, indicted and fined. He was released in 1573, but was rearrested in 1583 and once more imprisoned in the Tower, where on 21 June 1585 he was found dead in his room. The circumstances of his death were suspicious to say the least. The Government always had concerns about the Percys and it was said that 'the North knows no prince but a Percy': even after they had been forbidden to live in the north on the accession of the 8th Earl in 1572 they remained a powerful family, with extensive northern estates, and a sizeable proportion of Catholic tenants.

The 8th Earl was careful to have his son's initial education provided by the Protestant clergyman, Rev. Thompson, of Egremont on his Cumberland estates.[1] But when Lord Percy was eighteen, he went abroad to continue his education.

It is not surprising that as a young man, enjoying a hedonistic time in Paris, the young Henry Percy was carefully watched by government agents, in case he had any contacts with exiled Catholics. The ambassador in Paris, Sir Henry Cobham, reported to the government his suspicions of Lord Percy's contacts with Sir Charles Paget, who had fled England under suspicion of involvement in the plots for the liberation of Mary Queen of Scots that had led to the 8th Earl's imprisonment.[2] Sir Charles wrote to Secretary Walsingham to explain his conduct: 'My Lord Percy being lodged not far from me, I have haunted his company, because he, not being in a commendable course, either for studies or manners, my poor advice prevailed with him to reform.' Sir Charles added that he had been 'careful not to touch upon matters of religion.'[3]

As the Earl himself said in the advices that he wrote for his son, 'These then were my felicities (because I knew no better) hawks, hounds, horses, dice, cards, apparel, mistresses.'[4] His own serious illness in Paris, and the death of his brother Thomas in 1587, may have been the cause of the Earl abandoning his erratic way of life. His concern in his writings for his son seems to be intended to prevent him from following his father's example. The Earl's *Advice to his Son* (1595), *Discourse which concerneth officers and servants* (1609) and *Advice for the Lord Percy in his travels* (1618) are prime sources for the Earl's views on many things, particularly education and the pursuit of knowledge. These manuscripts are in the Petworth House Archives.[5] They were edited and published in 2002 in the Roxburgh Club volume commissioned by Lord Egremont, the present owner of the Archives.[6] Other sources can be found in the Petworth House Archives, and in Lord Egremont's private library, which contains 379 books definitely identified by Professor Gordon Batho as being from the 9th Earl's time, some with his book mark.[7] More are to be found in the Archives and the library of the Duke of Northumberland at Alnwick. Without going in detail into the descent of the Percy estates, it is necessary to know that in 1750 the estates were split, with the Northumberland estates going to the female heir, Lady Elizabeth Seymour and her husband Sir Hugh Smithson, who changed his name to Percy, and from whom are descended the present Dukes of Northumberland, and the Cumberland, Yorkshire and Sussex estates going to a nephew, Charles Wyndham, who became 2nd Earl of Egremont. Therefore, a considerable amount of the 9th Earl's accounts, and many of his books are in the Duke of Northumberland's archives and library at Alnwick Castle.

In contrast to his own preoccupations in Paris, the Earl recommended to his son that the object of travel was not to indulge in the latest fashions, but 'to gayne the tongues' so that he could read and converse in the languages, 'and soe by comparing the acts of men abroad, with the deeds of them at home, yowr carriage may be made comely, yowr mynde riche, and yowr iudgement wyse to chuse that is best.'[8] In addition to languages, he should make a point of acquiring knowledge of statute and customary law, attending court sessions to hear cases. He should also investigate land tenure, methods of measurement, the value of money, principle commodities, crops and shipping. He should study the inhabitants – the social classes, food, apparel, diseases. He should acquire knowledge of methods of government, geography, fortifications, architecture and weather. He was to take notes on everything, 'for when yow list to take a reweu the leaves of yowr books are easylyer turnd ouer then the leaves of yowr memory'.[9] All this was to fulfil the purpose of education, which the Earl described in *Advices* of 1595, as 'being only to perfect a man … in fower things specially, gracefull mannors, commendable exercyses, true studies, and a well faschioned mynd'.[10]

The Earl did not consider such education necessary for a woman. A woman's role in life did not necessitate 'a well fashioned mind' of the sort that a man could aspire to.

> Marke but womens educations from there cradells, how they are ledde on from one age to another, what there exercises be, what they are taught, the company that is most conversant with them, and then shall wee perceave clearly that there bringings uppe can promise noe deep insight into matters of knowledge, but sutche as are soon got and easely learned, not expecting greater matters of them then sutche as will make them as wyse at fifteen as at fifty.[11]

He also wrote 'that nature itselfe hathe forbid that men should surcharge them with businesses that is not fitting for them'.[12] A weaker woman's body, and the need to preserve their good looks and modesty, meant that their preoccupations had to be different.

It does not seem that the Earl considered that women's brains were naturally inferior to men's. If they were educated sufficiently, they might be able to reach the same intellectual level as a man, but generally their education was limited to what their parents deemed would be suitable for their position in life. Using 'true Ortographie' as an example, he writes, 'for how few of them can doe it, or doeth it; not that it is an impossibilitie for them if they were plyed, but that parents holde it not mutche material for them and therefore they doe not labour them in it.'[13] If a Lady had an aptitude for languages, the Earl thought that she might learn French, Italian, or Spanish, but only to a sufficient level to use literature or poetry to entertain a guest. A particularly pious lady might take an interest in theology. But, 'parents care is spent rather to faschon them modest, neate, gracefull, obedient to draw on the lykings of husbands, whereby fathers may put them of, and provide them fortuns during the rest of there lyfes'.[14]

> Can poore yonge maydes then thirst after great understandings, when nether there parents forces them to it when they are most doceable, or there owen iudgements afterwards tells them, that, that is not the matter must recommend them.[15]

'Will yow be angry then at a poore woman that understands littel?' he asked.[16] He did concede that 'wifes of a poorer sort' might of necessity be given some responsibilities: 'I must needs grant that the managing of somme home causes are to be conferred upon them'. But he certainly did not think that this was necessary in his own class, warning his son against committing 'the managing of yowr estate to the discretion of yowr wyfe'.[17]

The Earl recommended to his son that 'Music, singing, cards, dice, chess and the rest of this nature are but lost labour, being neither profitable to themselves, nor anything else.'[18] In addition to all the information that he could gain in his travels, the Earl recommended to his son the study of

> deeper contemplations, as Arithmetic, Geometry, Logic, grammar universal, metaphysics, the doctrine of motion, Optics, Astronomy, the doctrine of generation and corruption, cosmography, the doctrine de anima, moral, politics, economics, the art nautical and military.[19]

He considered the 'Doctrine de Anima … being the end and scope of all the former speculations … as it is in the end of all speculative meditations, so it is the beginning of all practical directions that are to be well acted and the properest use.'[20] Works on all these subjects can be found in the late seventeenth-century catalogue of the library at Petworth, the *Catalogus Bibliothecae Petworthianae*, which survives in the Archives there.[21] It lists over 2,300 books published before or during the 9th Earl's time, covering a wide range of subjects. It is divided into subjects: History, Theology, Mathematics, Geography, Poetry, Law, Grammar, Tactics, Medicine, Philosophy, Natural History, Picture books, and Miscellaneous.

Some of the books listed there survive at Petworth, including many with the Earl's own annotations. It seems from the annotations that the Earl could read Latin, French and Italian at least, and possibly Spanish. The section on philosophy includes works of Aristotle, which still survive in the private library, together with many commentaries on him. These are heavily annotated by the Earl. But the range of his philosophical reading was wide, and he also annotated Boethius's *The Comfort of Philosophy* and Giordano Bruno's *De gl'heroici furore*. There are also in the Petworth House Archives some manuscript works which echo the subjects found in the library catalogue. These include Edward Johnson's treatise on the soul, which is dedicated to the Earl.[22]

One of the Earl's many interests was alchemy. Its fascination for him seems to have been in the whole philosophical question of the nature of substances, rather than just an attempt to transmute base metals into gold and silver. He stated in *the Advices* that the practice of alchemy was a 'meere mecanicall broiling trade with out this phylosophycal project'.[23] The library lists alchemical works such as Gerard Dorne's translation of *Paracelsus on Alchemy and the Transmutation of Metals* (published in Frankfurt in 1581). The Archives contained ten manuscripts concerning alchemy, including *The Chemical and Artificial Theorick and Practice of Nature* by Gerard Dorne.[24] The still house made for him in the

7.1　A page from *Catalogus Librorum Bibliothecae Petworthianae* listing some of the books about mathematics, c. 1690. Petworth House Archives PHA 5377 f.18v.

Tower in 1606/7, equipped with a furnace, copper vessels and tools may have been wanted for alchemical experiments.[25] It may of course have been used for making usquba – the water of life, i.e. whisky, rather than any experiments in alchemy.

One of the Earl's early interests was military science, and he went to the Low Countries as a soldier in 1600 and 1601. The library catalogue contains several works on military sciences, including Claudio Corte *Il Cavalerizzo* and Salomen de La Broue *Le Cavalerice Francois*, both of which contain the Earl's annotations. Among the manuscripts at Petworth is a translation by Paul Yve of Simon Stevin's *The Building of Fortes*, the translation dedicated to the Earl.[26] There is also Thomas Blondevile's translation of Jacobius Acontius' *Book of Fortifying*.[27] The Earl's library contained Stevin's printed book *La Castramentation*. We know from his accounts that the Earl had 460 model soldiers, and an inlaid table for the practice of the Art Militaire in 1613–1614.[28]

In November 1605, the Earl wrote to the Privy Council:

> Consider, I desire your Lordships, the course of my life; whether it hath not leaned more of late years to private domestical pleasures than to other ambitions. Examine but my humours in buildings, gardenings, and private expenses these last two years.[29]

His interest in architecture and in gardening are reflected in the surviving sources.

The Earl's copy of Palladio's *Y Quattro Libri dell'Archietture* survives in the private library at Petworth, as does Jacques Androuet de Cerceau's *Livre d'Architecture* and both contain his annotations. While he was in the Tower of London, the Earl designed an enormous new house to be built at Petworth.[30] A volume in the Petworth House Archives contains the calculations of the cost of building it, but the Earl's financial problems, caused by his imprisonment and the huge fine demanded of him, meant that the house was never built.[31] He did however have new stables built at Petworth, on a very princely scale.[32] He also made considerable improvements to his house and garden at Syon. The same volume that contains the calculations of the cost of the proposed new house also contains extremely detailed instructions for growing Bon Chretien pears. An entry in the Earl's accounts records a payment for pear grafts from France in 1614–5.[33] The library catalogue lists Thomas Hill's *Of ye Art of Gardening*, as well as Holineus's *Historia Generalis Plantarum*.

The Earl's eyesight was bad – he had eventually to use spectacles; perhaps this explained the presence in his library of Richard Bannister's *Of the diseases of the eyes and eyelids* published in London in 1622, although the library catalogue contains twelve pages of books on the subject of medicine.[34] The library catalogue also lists works on other scientific subjects, including astronomy, and these are complemented by manuscript copies of medieval scientific treatises, including some by Robert Grosseteste, Bishop of Lincoln.[35] In addition to his own reading, the Earl supported three distinguished men in his household, Walter Warner, mathematician and natural philosopher, who entered the Earl's household in 1590, whose duties included the care of the Earl's books and scientific instruments; Robert Hues, mathematician and geographer, who tutored the Earl's sons from 1616 on; and Thomas Harriot, mathematician, expert on navigation, and astronomer.

About a fifth of Harriot's papers are still at Petworth.[36] The rest were given to the British Museum in 1810. Harriot was probably introduced to the Earl by Sir Walter Raleigh, with whom Harriot had been on the expedition to Virginia in 1585, and whose sea captains he instructed in navigation. One of Harriot's two extant publications is the *Briefe and True Report of the New Found Land of Virginia*, published in 1588. Formerly in the Petworth House Archives were a number of manuscripts concerning the early settlements in America.[37] The Earl's brother George Percy was personally involved, being governor of Jamestown in 1611. From 1598, Harriot received an annual pension from the Earl, and had accommodation at the Earl's house at Syon.[38] He has been considered the father of English Algebra, and the other publication of his work was *Ars Analyticae Praxis*, which was put together by his friends after Harriot's death and published in 1631. Mention is made in the book to the intention to publish more of Harriot's work, but nothing came of it.

It is perhaps because he did not publish that Harriot's name was less well known. His friend Sir William Lower pointed out to him in 1608 that others were gaining the glory for scientific work that he had done previously, because he had not published it.[39] But as Harriot had told the Privy Council in 1605, he was 'contented with a private life for the love of learning that I might study freely'.[40] He certainly carried on with his study of navigation, and his manuscript 'Doctrine of nautical Triangles' survives at Petworth.[41] Since 2009 Harriot has perhaps been better known, as that year saw the celebration of the 400th anniversary of his observations of the moon, through a telescope, the earliest of which predated Galileo's by a few months. It may be hard for us now to realise the excitement that the invention of the telescope, probably in the Low Countries in 1608, would have occasioned. Harriot's earliest surviving observation was with a fairly basic telescope of only six times magnification but he was soon using much more powerful ones, up to thirty times magnification.[42] In his will, he left 'perspective trunks' to the Earl 'wherewith I use especially to see Venus horned like the moon, and the spots in the sun'.[43] He also left one each to his executors and the rest to his servant Christopher Tooke, except for two long trunks in sections which were to be left in the Earl's library. He also left the Earl a box of maps, and any of his books that the Earl might want.

Harriot was aware of Galileo's work, even before he acquired a copy of *Siderius Nuncius*, which made Galileo's observations of the moon widely known. Sir William Lower wrote to Harriot enthusiastically in 1610 of 'my diligent

10

from thease greene heads
of good counsaille ~~in them~~ to giue, and my selfe to
take, not being apted as then ~~as a like~~ subiect, out
of want of teaching before; ~~so~~ then were my felicites,
(bycause f knew not better) haukes, hounds, horses, dice,
cards, apparell, mistresses; ~~and~~ all other riot of expence
that follow them, were soe farre a foot and in excesse,
as f knew not where I was, or what f did, till out
of my means of 3000li yearely, f had made shift in
one yeare and a halfe, to be 19000li in debt: Soe as
the burden of my song must still conclude, ignorance ~~&~~
in myne estate, to be the mayne cause; somme may say
good counsells were not strangers to myne eares, for
many discoursed them liberally vpon me, but f must
returne my reply that they were (not), to my iudgemene and
vnderstanding, (though) ~~if not~~ to myne eares, and all bycause my
father had not labored me, in that f was capable of:
ft is most true, that tyme, will teache sonns in long
tyme, otherwyse (read) ~~could~~ experience, without (instructions) ~~teaching~~ of
parents, but fathers comminly are inclined to flatter
them (selues) ~~selues~~, ~~ever~~ soe muche with the longeur of thayr
yeares, as they commit many irrecuerable errors (of deferring) by way
Thus being (then) ~~falen~~ in to creditors clamors, a greater discontent
to me then somme other; my lands being intailed; all our
witts felling a consulting how this burden might (be) passed,
my mynde then being over wearyed with the sutes ~~rumors~~ of
poore people, whose goods f had and could not satisfy;
eache (callinge) for his owne, and youre creaturs (twise) waiting
euery (corner), made me thinke a backe (corner doore) an honest
sally, to escape thayr importunities; a disease that haunteth
an honest mynde and a great debt; will woods weare
concluded the ~~means~~ next means of reliefe, soe as the

axe was put to

7.2   Page from *Advices to his Son* written by Henry 9th Earl of Northumberland. 1609. Petworth House Archives HMC 24/2 f.10.

Galileus' discovery' being 'more important than Magellan discovering the Straits'.[44] Harriot was in correspondence with Kepler in 1608; and he made notes on works by Kepler, Tycho Brahe, and many other scholars whose works we know were in the Earl's library.[45] Also among Harriot's papers are observations of the comets of 1608 and 1618.[46] In the library catalogue is listed the *Description of the Comet that Appeared in 1618* by Dr John Bainbridge, published in 1619. Once the moon and the sun came under observation by telescope, it could be seen that the moon was not a smooth disc, and the sun was not perfect, both of which contradicted the accepted views. And such ideas as Copernican theories of a helio-centric universe, and Giordano Bruno's of the infinity of universes, were regarded with suspicion. (Books by both of these scholars were in the 9th Earl's library.) As the Earl advised his son, 'be not too credulous upon reports of understanding persons who joy more in one hour's belief of a falsehood they desire, than in ten hour's labour to know a truth what is not so pleasing'.[47] To the earl and his circle, ideas were to be tested.

Accusations of atheism had been levied at Raleigh and his circle earlier. Raleigh was in the Tower of London from 1603 until 1616, and in 1605 the Earl of Northumberland was also committed to the Tower, on suspicion of pre-knowledge of the Gunpowder Plot. He was to remain there until 1621. According to his relative, and one of the Gunpowder Plot conspirators, Thomas Percy, as reported by his fellow conspirator, Thomas Winter, 'for matters of religion the Earl troubled not much himself'.[48] But perhaps the difficult reputations of Raleigh and the Earl were the reason that Harriot wrote to Kepler in 1608 'Things are in such a state with us that I am not allowed to philosophise freely. We are stuck in the mud.'[49] During their joint imprisonment, Raleigh, the Earl and their associates could continue their studies and speculation. The Earl's associates and servants could visit him, and his son Algernon came to live with him in 1608, so that his father could supervise his education more closely. The Earl continued to spend money on the purchase of books. The list of books sent to and from Syon and the Tower in 1614[50] includes a large number of books in Italian, so perhaps the Earl was improving his capability in the language, though he did employ Francesco Petrozani as his Italian reader.[51]

The Earl was finally released from the Tower in 1621, on condition that he lived within thirty miles of Petworth, though this was not strictly enforced. He devoted much of his time to improvements to his house and gardens. When he died in 1632, his library at Petworth contained fifty-two chests of books of all sorts, and enough books to fill another twelve small chests, and also seventy-odd books in his closet. He also had over 100 books and pamphlets 'of all sorts' in the closet belonging to his bedchamber. He had a cupboard full of mathematical instruments, and three globes, one of which is still at Petworth.[52]

For the Earl the objective of learning was a well fashioned mind, which would enable a man to play his part in the world. 'If everyone play his part well that is

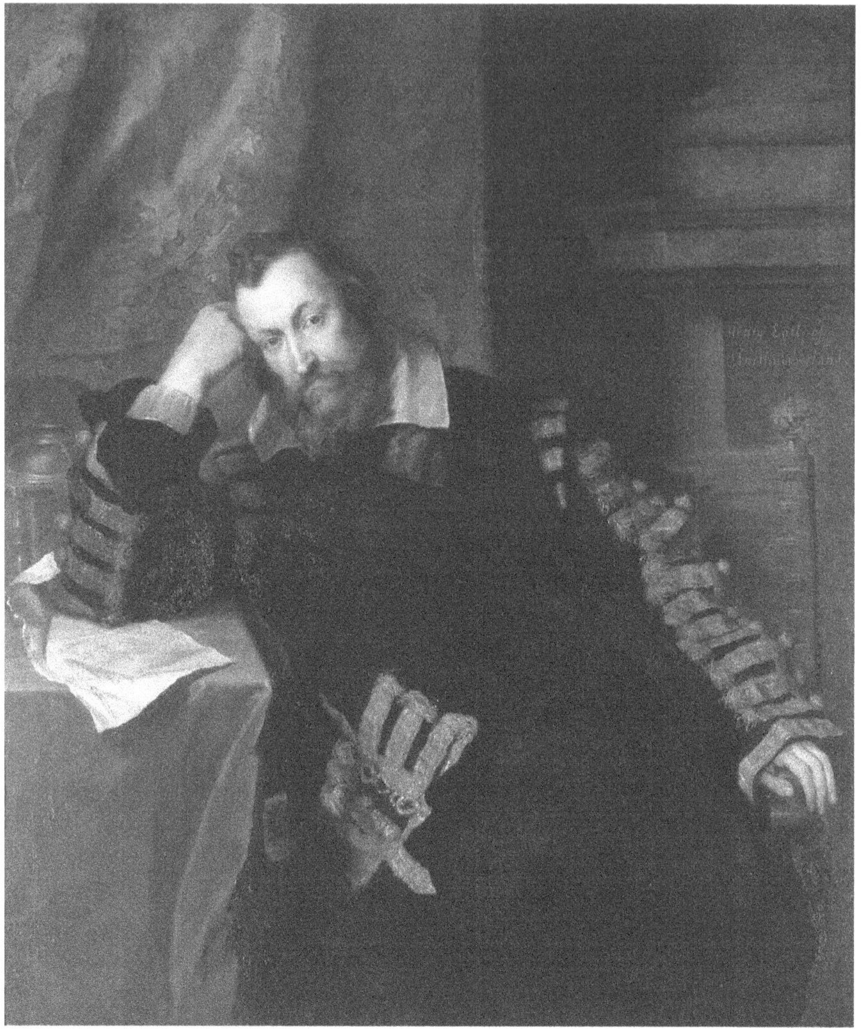

7.3   Posthumous portrait of Henry 9th Earl of Northumberland by Sir Anthony van Dyck.

allotted him, the commonwelth will be happy, if not, then will it be deformed, but whiche is fitte for every one – Quere.'[53] Approaching travel and the education of his son in the same way that he approached the careful and deliberate pursuit of scientific knowledge, the Earl's determination to forge a space of contemplation apart from the public sphere also informed his tastes in building and gardening and the company he chose to keep. Perhaps the Earl was considering his own eventful life when he advised his son that,

There can be but two ways to procure you a happy state in general ... either ... true mindly pleasures, or bodily advantages, as honours and wealth. Contentments, I confess, may be born of either, but especially of knowledge, if it be well apprehended, and that more permanent; the other delightful, but more deceitful and passable.[54]

Notes

1   The Archives of the Duke of Northumberland at Alnwick Castle, Syon House Mss. (hereafter Sy) U.I.1.

2   E. B. De Fonblanque, *Annals of the House of Percy* (Privately published, 1887) vol. II, pp. 178–81.

3   De Fonblanque, *Annals*, Volume II, pp. 178–9.

4   Petworth House Archives (hereafter PHA) Historical Manuscripts Commission (hereafter HMC) 24/2 'Discourse whiche Concerneth Officers and Servants', f. 10; *The Wizard Earl's Advices to his Son*, eds Gordon R. Batho and Stephen Clucas (London: Roxburghe Club, 2002), p. 50.

5   PHA HMC 24/1 'Instructions for the Lord Percy in his Travels'; PHA HMC 24/2: 'The Forlorne State of this Life'; and 'Discourse whiche Concerneth Officers and Servaunts'.

6   I am grateful to Lord Egremont for permission to quote from his archives, and also to cite volumes which are in his private library.

7   G. R. Batho, 'The Library of the "Wizard Earl"; Henry Percy, Ninth Earl of Northumberland (1564–1632)', *Transactions of the Bibliographical Society* (December 1960), 246–61.

8   PHA HMC 24/1, f. 1, *The Wizard Earl's Advices*, eds Batho and Clucas, p. 105.

9   PHA HMC 24/1, f. 6, *The Wizard Earl's Advices*, eds Batho and Clucas, p. 110.

10   PHA HMC 24/2: 'Discourse whiche Concerneth Officers and Servaunts', f. 15; *The Wizard Earl's Advices*, eds Batho and Clucas, p. 20.

11   PHA HMC 24/2: Discourse whiche Concerneth Officers and Servaunts, f. 21; *The Wizard Earl's Advices*, eds Batho and Clucas, p. 61.

12   PHA HMC 24/2: 'Discourse whiche Concerneth Officers and Servaunts', f.19; *The Wizard Earl's Advices*, eds Batho and Clucas, p. 59.

13   PHA HMC 24/2: 'Discourse whiche Concerneth Officers and Servaunts', f. 21v; *The Wizard Earl's Advices*, eds Batho and Clucas, p. 62.

14   PHA HMC 24/2: 'Discourse whiche Concerneth Officers and Servaunts', f. 22; *The Wizard Earl's Advices*, eds Batho and Clucas, p. 63.

15   PHA HMC 24/2: 'Discourse whiche Concerneth Officers and Servaunts', f. 23; *The Wizard Earl's Advices*, eds Batho and Clucas, p. 64.

16   PHA HMC 24/2: 'Discourse whiche Concerneth Officers and Servaunts', f. 25v; Batho and Clucas, 'The Wizard Earl's Advices', p. 69.

17   PHA HMC 24/2: 'Discourse whiche Concerneth Officers and Servaunts', f. 18; *The Wizard Earl's Advices*, eds Batho and Clucas, p. 58.

18   PHA HMC 24/2: 'The Forlorne State', f. 21; *The Wizard Earl's Advices*, eds Batho and Clucas, p. 26.

19   PHA HMC 24/2: 'The Forlorne State', f. 27; *The Wizard Earl's Advices*, eds Batho and Clucas, p. 32.

20   PHA HMC 24/2: 'The Forlorne State', f. 31; *The Wizard Earl's Advices*, eds Batho and Clucas, p. 36.

21   PHA 5377.

22 PHA HMC 107.
23 PHA HMC 24/2: 'The Forlorne State', f.31; *The Wizard Earl's Advices*, eds Batho and Clucas, p. 36.
24 PHA 95 and 96. Other works on alchemy were sold in 1928.
25 Sy: U.I.3/2.
26 PHA HMC 138.
27 PHA HMC 143.
28 Sy: U.I.3/3.
29 State Papers Volume XVI No 77, quoted in De Fonblanque, *Annals*, Volume II, p. 265.
30 PHA 6300, since lost. A draft plan is in Sy: X.11.10. See above, pp. 2–3.
31 PHA 1630. Another copy is PHA 6288.
32 PHA 438.
33 Sy: U.I.3/3.
34 Sy: P.I.3n f.14.
35 PHA HMC 106 and 107. Robert Grosseteste was Bishop of Lincoln from 1235–53.
36 PHA HMC 240 and 241/1–9.
37 PHA HMC 81 and 84, sold in 1928.
38 Sy: U.I.3/5; PHA 429.
39 British Library Add. MS. 6789.
40 Calendar of the Cecil Papers in Hatfield House, vol. XVII, f. 554, ed. M. S. Giuseppi (London, 1938).
41 PHA HMC 241/6b.
42 PHA HMC 241/9.
43 Guildhall Library Ms. 9051/6.
44 British Library Add. MS. 6789.
45 British Library Add. MS. 6789.
46 PHA HMC 241/7 f.9ᵛ.
47 PHA HMC 24/2: 'Discourse whiche Concerneth Officers and Servaunts', f. 45; *The Wizard Earl's Advices*, eds Batho and Clucas, p. 93.
48 Gunpowder Plot book in the National Archives, quoted in De Fonblanque, *Annals*, vol. II, p. 266.
49 *Kepleri Opera Omnia* ed. Christian Frisch, Frankfurt 1859, vol. II, p. 74.
50 Sy: W.II.1.
51 Sy: U.I.3/3.
52 Sy: H.II.16.
53 PHA HMC 24/2: 'Discourse whiche Concerneth Officers and Servaunts', f.47; *The Wizard Earl's Advices*, eds Batho and Clucas, p. 95.
54 PHA HMC 24/2: The forlorne state, f. 1; *The Wizard Earl's Advices*, eds Batho and Clucas, p. 2.

8

Anne Finch and the fallen country house

Nicolle Jordan

Country houses appear with remarkable frequency in the oeuvre of Anne Finch, Countess of Winchilsea (1661–1720), making her an ideal figure through which to investigate the transformation of early modern country house discourse in the wake of epochal events such as the Civil War, the Restoration, and the Glorious Revolution. She belongs to a pantheon of British women writers of the late Stuart era who, since the 1980s, have garnered scholarly attention for their keen insights into the political fault-lines of post-Restoration Britain. Critics point to both the vast range and the aesthetic accomplishment of Finch's verse, and indeed, generic diversity and emotional complexity make her oeuvre legible through both formal and cultural-historical lenses.[1] This chapter explores how Finch's estate poems exemplify the ways in which country house poetry registers changes in the historical and political landscape; at the same time, ecocritical engagement with these works suggests how scholarship on country house literature might profit from an encounter with a methodology that has largely been absent from the critical conversation.[2]

Political instability and personal dislocation converge to a remarkable degree in Finch's life, and this convergence puts into relief the role of country houses as not only the precinct of the powerful but also the resort of the dispossessed in the aftermath of the century's political upheavals. Finch thus offers an intriguing qualification to Mark Girouard's thesis that country houses are 'monuments to power' in a political landscape where monarchical authority is receding before a tide of aristocratic land magnates.[3] Finch's estate poems modify this narrative by giving expression to the experience of a woman whose social status, political orientation, and personal and artistic future are deeply entwined with the factional disputes of the post-Restoration era. Prior to the political crisis of 1688, Finch's poetic talents emerged under the tutelage of James II's wife, Mary of Modena, and Stuart loyalism accordingly permeates much of her poetry.[4] Indeed, Anne, née Kingsmill (Figure 8.1) and Heneage Finch met at Court when the young James was the Duke of York; Anne was a lady in waiting to the future Queen Consort, and Heneage was a groom of the bedchamber to the Duke. They married in 1684. James's exile had tremendous impact on the couple; after losing his position at Court (Anne having resigned hers upon her marriage), Heneage attempted to sail to France to join his king in 1690, but was arrested for Jacobitism, a treasonable offence.[5] Although he was acquitted, the crisis left the Finches disenfranchised and deprived of the opportunity to acquire their own home, given that their resources and the means to acquire them were severely limited by their status as non-jurors. Thus began their quarter-century of peripatetic existence, during which time they relied upon the hospitality of more stable family and friends – a predicament that, as we will see, Finch managed in part by availing herself of country house poetry's hospitality rhetoric in works she addressed to her hosts and hostesses.

The two poems discussed below participate in the discourse of hospitality, the valence of which changes depending upon one's awareness of Finch's personal circumstances. Indeed, knowing both her poetic versatility and her straitened situation attenuates the impression that the poems celebrate artistic rather than natural beauty and thus depart from the Jonsonian country house tradition by embracing rather than disparaging houses 'built for envious show'.[6] The purpose here is not to assert the priority of biographical over other modes of interpretation so much as to scrutinise the conflicting interpretations that arise from readings that do and do not recognise historical context. An awareness of Finch's dependence on the hospitality of others, and her proclivity for non-anthropocentric nature poetry, undermines Kari Boyd McBride's claim that Finch's country house poems 'unashamedly celebrate capital … in its country house manifestation'.[7] This chapter suggests instead that personal circumstance motivates Finch's hyperbolic praise for her hosts' estates more than any proto-capitalist commitment on her part. This approach emphasises the dynamic social and personal contexts that inflect country house literature and thus complicate efforts to identify its ideological orientation.

The first poem under consideration, 'Upon my Lord Winchilsea's Converting the Mount in his Garden to a Terras', describes landscape improvements undertaken at Eastwell, the Finch family seat. The second, 'To the Honorable the Lady Worsley at Long-leate', uses hyperbole to praise the offspring and estate of Sir Thomas Thynne, first Viscount Weymouth, then Lord of Longleat.[8] Both poems feature extensive descriptions of the estates in question, along with other appropriations of country house poetic convention – for example prospect views, allusions to paradise, the conflation of lord and estate, and a preoccupation with lineage. Yet neither poem conforms to convention thoroughly enough to be considered a true country house poem; they are better read as commentaries

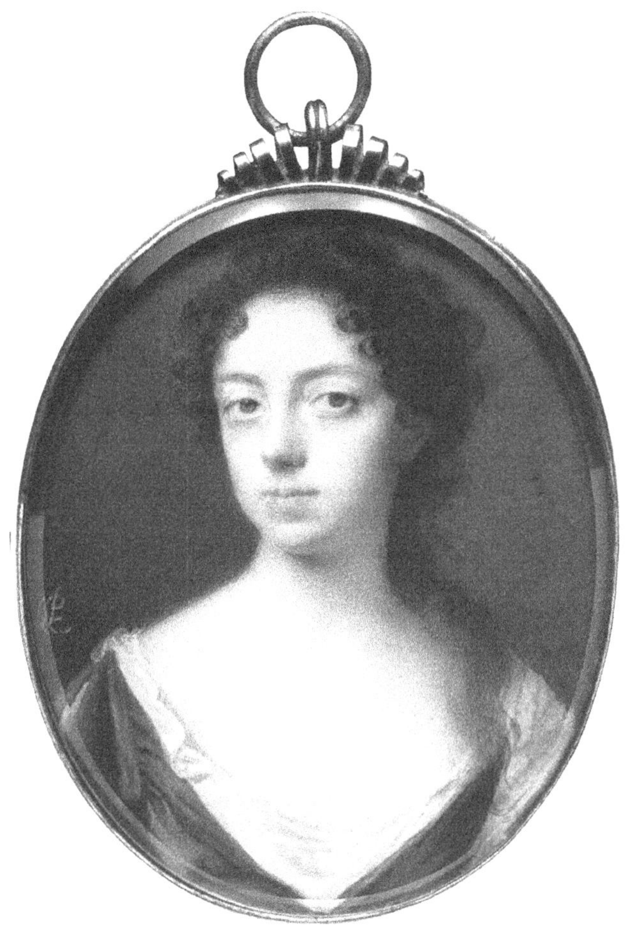

8.1   A miniature of Anne Finch by Peter Cross.

on the genre, texts that delineate how historical contingency alters generic coherence.[9] Nature also figures prominently in both poems, testifying to the virtue of the estate's lord and recalling Lord Sidney in Ben Jonson's 'To Penshurst', whose teeming streams and fruitful orchards are less a matter of nature's bounty than a manifestation of the master's proper estate stewardship. Yet, as occasional poems that name specific acts or people ('Converting the Mount', 'To the Honorable the Lady Worsley'), Finch's texts do not aim for comprehensive assessment of the estates and lords that appear in them. Instead, they intertwine several discursive traditions, with both poems synthesising country house poetry and estate improvement rhetoric. These similarities recede, however, behind

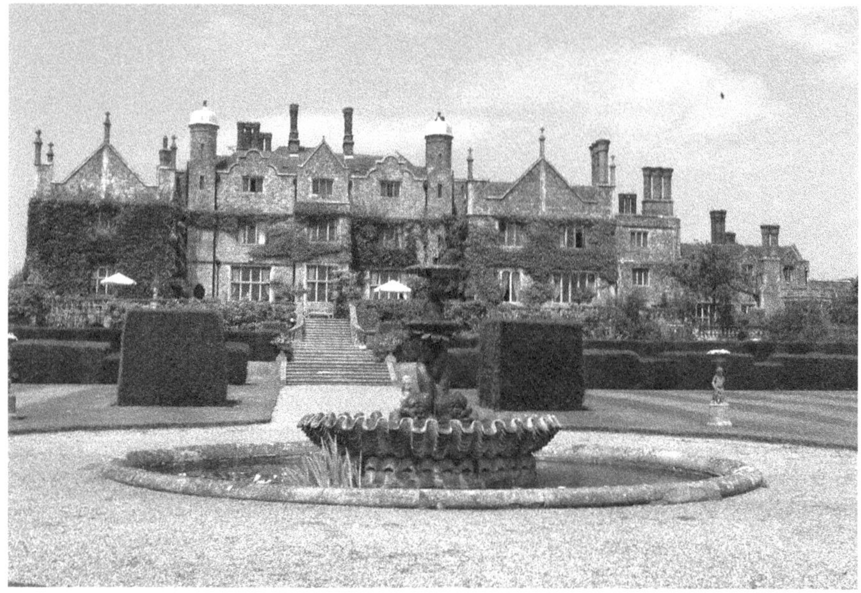

8.2 Eastwell in its current state, though considerably altered from its design when Finch lived there in the early eighteenth century.

the poems' striking differences of tone and topical emphasis. 'Upon my Lord Winchilsea' playfully yet ominously depicts generational conflict, while 'To the Honorable the Lady Worsley' is an disconsolate friendship poem that derives solace from a tableau of father–daughter likenesses. Although biographical interpretation can never be definitive, the circumstances I have sketched and will elaborate further offer a compelling perspective on Finch's rendition of post-Restoration country house culture. The fact that the bucolic serenity of both poems is offset by episodes of violence, in one case, and melancholy, in the other, introduces significant generic dissonance, suggesting how literary convention strains to accommodate a historical situation markedly different from that in which it originated.[10] These readings thus suggest how a writer's personal experience, when filtered through the law of genre, exposes the ideological conflicts encountered by both the writer and the genre.[11]

Improvement rhetoric is apparent in the very title of 'Upon my Lord Winchilsea's Converting the Mount in his Garden to a Terras', which describes the Finch family seat at Eastwell, located about twenty miles south-east of Maidstone in Kent (Figure 8.2). The prominence of improving acts over the estate itself signals how the poem's historical moment differs from canonical predecessors such as Jonson's 'To Penshurst' (1616) or Aemilia Lanyer's 'The Description of Cooke-ham' (1611). Whereas Elizabethan and Jacobean country house poetry expresses the power struggles between monarchy and aristocracy that eventually led to violent (or 'Bloodless') revolution, Finch's post-1688 iteration of the form clearly inhabits a different moment in this centuries-long redistribution of power. The poem offers evidence of both aristocratic ascendancy – in the lord's triumphant accomplishments in estate improvement – and subtextual anxiety about the legacy of absolutism – in his tyrannical ancestor's contrasting estate alterations.[12] Infused with dramatic tension between the benevolent present lord and his fierce predecessor, the poem nevertheless is impossible to interpret as strict political allegory, reminding us of the multiple registers required to appreciate the full resonance of Finch's estate poetry. Moreover, the poem's uneven tone betrays the speaker's ambivalence regarding the situation she is describing. Making sense of this tonal ambiguity requires a return to Finch's biography.

The poem is addressed to her nephew Charles Finch, the current 'Lord Winchilsea' at Eastwell when the poem was written.[13] According to the poet's biographer Barbara McGovern, Charles had invited his aunt and uncle to stay with him around 1690 and, 'For much of the time during the remaining thirty years of her life, Eastwell was to be her home'. When Charles unexpectedly died without heirs in 1712, Heneage Finch acceded to his title and estate and Anne became the Countess of Winchilsea. McGovern asserts that there is little archival evidence that Anne bridled under her dependent condition.[14] However, the fact that the couple relied on their nephew's hospitality for at least twenty years suggests that Anne had ample reason to compose poetry in honour of her kinsman. In light of these considerations, the speaker's veneration and gratitude for the present lord of the poem seem all the more sincere. Yet its construction of a turbulent past versus an idyllic present, while relevant to Finch's personal history, also maps onto the larger historical events that framed – and precipitated – her own story, thus infusing biographical verse with political allegory. The opening lines introduce the comparison between present and past lords which structures the entire poem:

> If we those Gen'rous Sons deserv'dly Praise
> Who o're their Predecessours Marble raise,
> And by Inscriptions, on their Deeds, and Name,
> To Late Posterity, convey their Fame,
> What with more Admiration, shall we write,
> On Him, who takes their Errours from our sight?[15]

A panegyric to the speaker's host, the lines feature the requisite hyperbole, and yet they revise the poetic tradition by praising the removal of errors rather than the commemoration of triumphs. This is our first indication that the poem will revisit a dark aspect of the estate's past, and also our first intimation that the speaker seems torn between present felicity and past adversity.

Before dramatising what turns out to be a rather violent history of 'errour', the next lines celebrate the removal of a mountain 'which long had stood (though threatnd oft in vain), / Concealing all the beautys of the Plaine' (ll. 9–10); they then honour the 'ripen'd Judgment' (l. 13) that has 'hew'n [the mount] from itts rugged height' (l. 17). Already we see the speaker pursuing a delicate balancing act, praising her present lord while criticising his ancestor. Despite subtle suggestions of generational discord, a playful tone initially prevails, as when the speaker treats the landscape improvements in the register of imperial conquest: 'None gone before persu'd the vast design, / Till ripen'd Judgment, joyn'd with Youthfull Flame, / At last but Came, and Saw, and Overcame' (ll. 12–14). Lines such as these give the impression that Finch is wittily honouring her kinsman by comparing his work to that of a legendary conqueror; the speaker seems amused at the incongruity between levelling a mount and vanquishing a kingdom.[16]

Turning to the past precipitates the speaker's shift from light-hearted flattery to wistful censure. While lines 1–22 use the image of levelling in order to praise the man responsible for it, they also prefigure a contrary episode of levelling that occurred in the past, depicted in lines 23–46. After admiring the beautiful view opened by her lord's landscaping improvements, the speaker notices that something is missing from the terrace constructed on the levelled mount. She observes that viewers expect to see a grove of trees nearby and bask in its shelter from rain or sun. They want, the speaker claims,

> To see a sheltring grove the prospect bound,
> Just rising from the same proliffick ground,
> Where late itt stood, the Glory of the Seat,
> Repell'd the Winter blasts, and skreen'd the Somer's heat;
> So prais'd, so loved, that when untimely Fate,
> Sadly prescrib'd itt a too early Date,
> The heavy tidings caused a gen'ral Grief,
> And all combine to bring a swift relief.
>
> (ll. 23–30)

Thus we learn that a grove of trees did at one time bound this prospect, and that it was considered 'the Glory of the Seat' (l. 25). Gloom thus begins to overtake the poem, as the salubrious image of the levelled mounts cedes to a contrasting image of revered trees chopped down at 'a too early date' (l. 28). Consequently, while much of the poem bespeaks gratitude toward the speaker's host, its depiction of his oppressive forebear strains against the fanciful praise of the opening and closing sequences.

The violent episode at the poem's core thus dramatically departs from its opening serenity, introducing politically encoded language that, given the period's extreme factionalism, not to mention Finch's first-hand experience of it, would be foolhardy to overlook:

> Some Plead, some Pray, some Councel, some Dispute,
> Alas in vain, where Pow'r is Absolute.
> Those whom Paternal Awe, forbid to speak,

> Their sorrows, in their secret whispers break,
> Sigh as they passe beneath the sentenc'd Trees
> Which seem to answer in a mournfull Breeze.
>
> (ll. 31–6)

The lines appear after the speaker has lamented the absence of 'the Glory of the seat', moving here into retrospection about a dire incident in the past, when her lord's ancestor felled the trees despite pleas and protests from all quarters. By this point in the text, it is apparent that we have left the realm of country house poetic convention and entered a different rhetorical tradition, reminiscent of the literature of complaint. Indeed, the intrusion of grief at the trees' impending loss (in line 29) exemplifies the difficulty of fixing the poem's ideological commitment. For if one assumes, as is usually the case, that country house discourse endorses principles of benevolent stewardship, then Finch's rendition of that discourse questions the benevolence of some stewards and thereby exposes possible weaknesses in the system. It is indeed hard to fathom a non-ideological interpretation of lines depicting the felling of oak trees, an act whose political resonance is well documented given the long-standing association of the oak with the Stuarts.[17] Indeed, Finch herself wrote a poem – 'Upon an Improbable Undertaking' – that uses two oak trees to allegorise the fall of James II and the withered reign of his usurper, so the rhetoric of the Stuart oak is familiar to her.[18] Arguably lines 31–6 reinforce the poem's subtle yet increasing suspicion of authority and tradition; while a benevolent lord like the speaker's present host is solicitous and attentive to the needs of his guests and dependents, the ancestor who felled the grove is not only derelict of duty but cruel and oppressive as well. Because the poem's first lines establish that the present lord made right what his ancestor did wrong, the text elicits suspicion of tradition and 'Paternal Awe' and calls into question the wisdom of the 'absolute' power referred to in line 32.

This is to suggest that the elaboration of 'errour' in 'Upon My Lord Winchilsea' gives rise to a subtext that works against the speaker's putative admiration for a patriarchal order based upon proper estate stewardship. If at first the speaker suggests that the ancestor's error was his failure to remove the mount, the middle section of the poem discloses the much graver error of wasted resources and abused tenants. The estate's former lord intimidates and silences his dependents, and then magnifies the injury by taking up the axe when they refuse to do so: 'The very Clowns (hir'd by his dayly Pay), / Refuse to strike, nor will their Lord obey, / Till to his speech he adds a leading stroke, / And by Example does their Rage provoke' (ll. 37–40). In taking the 'leading stroke', the lord violates both the natural and the social order. His performance of the labour that he would have his 'clowns' do suggests that destroying the estate's natural resources requires a comparable inversion of the rightful distribution of labour. A tableau of injustice thus seems to have displaced what began as the celebration of a wise and generous lord.

The earlier discussion of political allegory in Finch's biographical verse demands further elaboration, for we cannot assume that allusions to absolute power have an obvious or stable historical referent. The image of an unjust lord could evoke associations with both Charles II and William of Orange (among others), depending upon one's perspective on political illegitimacy. Although it would be stretching the text to treat it as an allegory for the Glorious Revolution, the poem nevertheless hints at how representations of landed estates could encode political affiliations, and indeed, how the wise management of natural resources could likewise become a politicised virtue. Such a tentative reading indicates that the poem's significance changes depending on the historical context in which one places it, and that political resonances accrue to country house poetry even when the text does not sustain an overarching political narrative. When Finch's speaker vilifies her lord's ancestor for mismanaging his estate's trees, readers might recall the similarly mismanaged timber resources that the entire nation faced during the civil wars. Indeed, when we recall that Finch was writing in the wake of a century when deforestation was a grave concern for both Royalists and Parliamentarians, then the poem's violent episode acquires greater political import. Chopping down trees was a dangerous and potentially incendiary act that threatened to incite popular revolt. Richard Grove explains in *Green Imperialism* that the state's timber conservation policy was relatively lax following the civil wars, not because timber was any less precious but because debate during the Long Parliament had revealed that Parliamentarians were as guilty as Royalists for the despoliation of Crown forests and private estates sequestered during the wars:

> The anxiety of the Commonwealth government not to antagonize its important political constituency of common-rights holders prevented any serious commitment to a conservation policy. This set a pattern of policy on the part of post-Restoration governments until as late as the mid eighteenth century. This was despite efforts made by the Royal Society … to ensure future timber supplies for shipbuilding.[19]

Grove's research demonstrates the extent to which timber was a politically volatile topic. Finch's decision, then, to depict tree felling in her poem clearly has political implications. Both Royalist and Republican regimes needed a steady timber supply for the navy, and both had political constituencies that stymied strict forest regulation. The latter scenario deserves consideration for the way in which it exposes the structural similarity between Royal and Republican governments. Common-rights holders impeded forest protection under both King and Protector, suggesting how an increasing commitment to private property motivated both parties in the English Civil War and thereafter. The revocation, despoliation and restitution of Royalist lands play no small part in this aggrandisement of private property, and further suggest why the era's political conflicts occur, literally, over English soil – and also why country house poetry, the *locus classicus* for glorification of the soil and the estates built upon it, would generate figurations of these conflicts.

This foray into the environmental context of political allegory in 'Upon My Lord Winchilsea' demonstrates how far the poem ventures from its roots in country house literature. Not only do the scenes of injustice and cruelty depart from the harmony and reciprocity prescribed by generic convention, but the poem's attention to resource utility and scarcity locates it in the realm of postlapsarian nature rather than the *sponte sua* scenarios that appear in Jonson and Lanyer. Depicting nature giving itself willingly for humanity's use (Penshurst's fish and deer; Cooke-ham's trees, flowers and walks), these scenarios evoke a prelapsarian world that precedes humanity's subjection to labour and scarcity.[20] Finch's poem, while rhapsodising about Eastwell's recently improved beauty and comfort, still occupies a world that requires improvement precisely because nature no longer spontaneously sustains itself or humanity. The case could be made that Penshurst and Cooke-ham also occupy the postlapsarian world but simply banish it to precincts beyond the confines of the estate (or certain ideal but fleeting conditions therein), as seen, for instance, in references to corruption in the form of luxury, toil, and 'difference of degree'.[21] However, the natural world at Eastwell features nothing like the bounty, feasting and fertility of these other estates, a shortfall that seems consonant with the poem's post-Restoration rather than Jacobean provenance. This is not to say that the earlier period pre-dates resource scarcity, of course, but rather that Finch's experience of both historical upheaval and personal deprivation disposes her to depict an idealised but relatively modest retreat, one that is commodious but nevertheless requires maintenance and the requisite resources.[22] Thus, when the speaker shifts from the past to the present after having depicted the chopping down of trees, she hinges the transition on the link between felled timber and building materials for a new addition to the house: 'No longer now, we such Destructions fear, / No longer the resounding Axe we hear, / But in Exchange, behold the Fabrick stand, / Built, and Adorn'd by a supporting hand' (ll. 47–50). The lines reveal an awareness that humanity's comfortable and aesthetically pleasing existence depends upon the exploitation of nature. Moreover, the patent censure of the axe-wielding ancestor for the manner in which he killed the trees implies that nature's exploitation ought to be carefully regulated rather than reckless and autocratic. A few lines later, the speaker further chastises those who fail to value all of nature's 'Elements': 'And though our Ancestors did gravely Plott, / As if one Element they vallu'd nott …' (ll. 55–6). It may be true that the poem honours expensive estate improvements such as the removal of a massive amount of soil to level the mount, but it is also true that the speaker endorses her lord's environmentally sensitive approach to such alteration. A 'shameless' capitalist would not come to the defence of nature's 'Elements', as Finch does, and the admiration for what the trees have made possible – in the form of the modified house – suggests strategic acceptance of folly rather than an assertion that estate improvement necessitates unchecked access to natural resources.[23]

The turn from past folly to present pleasure continues to be channelled through trees when the speaker, positioned inside the newly built room, turns her gaze on the prospect it provides: 'And now we Breath[e] and now the eager View / Through the enlarged Windows take[s] her way, / Does beauteous Fields, and scatter'd Woods survey, / Flyes or'e th' extended Land, and sinks but in the Sea' (ll. 60–3). Here is a speaker who values the aesthetic pleasure provided by trees more than their function as timber. The paradox embedded in such an assertion – since one might argue that the former is impossible without the latter – confronts us with a beguiling problematic in the era's discourse of improvement, as theorised by Robert Markley. In reference to Andrew Marvell's 'Upon Appleton House,' Markley asserts that 'Nature is "corrupt" … because it cannot exist prior to its exploitation.'[24] The formulation offers a compelling way to make sense of the poem's elevation of man-made endeavours over the very materials required for their execution. To put it another way, country house rhetoric necessitates the celebration of nature but at the same time exposes its instrumentalisation in the service of the proto-capitalist economy that the form records.

Turning to the second poem, 'To the Honorable the Lady Worsley at Long-Leate', will offer further insight into the conundrum sketched here.[25] As in the previous case, this poem borrows country house poetic convention but situates itself in a context different from the revelry and friendly communion that typify the genre. The speaker, writing 'from some obscure and lonely recesse' (l. 1), takes up the pen to honor her niece Frances, née Thynne, the daughter of Heneage's sister Frances Thynne, viscountess of Weymouth.[26] The poem declares its biographical orientation in the subtitle: 'Who had most obligingly desired my corresponding with her by Letters.' The speaker's dejection, evident in the first lines, suggests that Finch may have written the poem at a time when her afflictions were particularly acute. Recent scholarship dates the poem to some time between 13 August and 28 November 1690. At this time Heneage Finch was being held in London under suspicion of treason, and Anne was staying at Godmersham, a priory near Eastwell; she thus had ample reason to describe her 'recesse' as 'Fitt only for the Wretch opress'd by Fate' (l. 4).[27] Meanwhile, lines 24–5 ('Utresia in her fresh and smiling bloom / With Joys incompass'd and new Joys to come') likely allude to Frances's recent marriage, Utresia being Finch's name for her.[28] The first section of the poem thus establishes its motive as an expression of gratitude for a kinswoman's commiseration. For the purpose here, the more important feature is the text's synthesis of occasional and country house poetry; what begins as a scenario of despair evolves into a celebration of both Utresia's home – Longleat – and her lord, 'Him […] from whom she sprung'

(l. 20), Thomas Thynne, first Viscount Weymouth, named in line 93. The poem certainly expresses Finch's gratitude to her hosts at Longleat, which she visited frequently over the years; however, her distance from Weymouth compared to her nephew (not to mention present space constraints) leads us to approach the poem primarily through an ecocritical rather than a biographical lens.

The emotional progression of the poem suggests that contemplating the wonders of the famed estate distracts Finch from her distress, thus underscoring the palliative function of post-Restoration country house poetry. Furthermore, like 'Upon my Lord Winchilsea', the poem vacillates between suffering and euphoria, capturing in miniature Finch's struggle between affliction for her political commitments (and their consequences) and fortune for belonging to a milieu that would soften their burden. The poem's middle section, lines 46–75, details the speaker's joy in beholding 'The real splendours of our fam'd Long-leate' (l. 46), and specifically distinguishes Weymouth's estate improvements by depicting how they defy or manipulate the laws of nature. That Finch's conflicted condition should express itself in the form of admiration for man's ability to surpass nature through feats of landscape design further testifies to the vexing status of nature in country house poetry. As we will see, 'To the Honorable the Lady Worsley' exemplifies how a genre originally driven by an impulse to celebrate humanity by aligning it with nature morphs into a form in which humanity supersedes its 'natural' affiliation.

The speaker begins to describe the estate only around line 45, after having honored Utresia at length by comparing her to 'the Sun in her Meridian' (l. 26) and conjuring her as a goddess whose luminous eyes 'Soften our Cares and [we] grow enlighten'd too' (l. 33). Until this point, Utresia is the focus of the poem's natural imagery, but she gradually cedes this role to the estate and its lord once the speaker decides that the best way to pay homage to its eponymous heroine is by depicting the home where she was raised. Though the poem never spells out that Longleat is Utresia's childhood home, references to her father – in line 20 and elsewhere – establish that she is a product of this domain. Such a construction represents a significant revision of country house poetic tradition, which typically portrays the estate as a synecdoche for its lord. If critical consensus considered Aemilia Lanyer as essential as Ben Jonson in the genre's formation, then one might argue instead that Finch continues a female tradition rather than revising a male one. But as scholars from G. R. Hibbard to Hugh Jenkins demonstrate, Jonson more often emerges as its definitive practitioner, in part because of the proliferation of Penshurst-like poems that honour lords by celebrating their estates.[29] Yet the prominence of 'their own Weymouth' (l. 93) in Finch's poem renders such matters moot, for the poem finally celebrates Utresia's father more than Utresia herself.[30] The poem's title, combined with its pervasive figurative language intertwining father and daughter, resists such a conclusion; yet, the poem's attribution of the estate's miraculous beauty to the lord who commanded it ultimately elevates him to a position comparable to that of Penshurst's Sir Robert Sidney. Indeed, the speaker's allusion to John Denham and Abraham Cowley, in which she expresses a desire to write 'Something to Please so moving and so new / As not our Denham or our Cowley knew' (ll. 43–4), establishes her deliberate intervention in country house poetic convention. She embraces their tradition but deigns to surpass them with her 'Transporting Figures n'ere expos'd before' (l. 42).

When the speaker turns her attention to the estate itself, she initiates the description with a conceit that prefigures her elevation of the estate to the preternatural realm. Announcing her plan to 'shew (the harder labour to compleat) / The real splendours of our fam'd Long-leate / Which above Metaphor itts Structure reares' (ll. 45–7), she signals a preoccupation with mimesis that sets her poem in competition with the estate it describes. The pretence that the estate surpasses the language describing it ironically works in the service of the poem itself; as will be suggested later, this conceit anticipates the way in which the poem likewise portrays the estate defying nature's laws. In multiple ways, the speaker manoeuvres by diminishing her poetic ability in words that effectively controvert her modesty. Thus immediately preceding her claim about inadequate metaphor, she declares her poetic ambition to 'raise my Art equal to my desire / Then shou'd my Hand snatch from the Muses store / Transporting Figures n'ere expos'd before' (ll. 40–2). In addition to outshining her poetic forebears Denham and Cowley, then, the speaker casts herself as an interloper who takes from the muses the techniques that will distinguish her. Locating poetry's origins in the natural realm of classical deities, the speaker thus avails herself of a power that the remainder of the poem seems to diminish.

Longleat's landscape follies command the speaker's most extravagant rhetoric, and it is here that readers apprehend an inverted natural order which some would see as evidence of hubris. After several other hyperbolic descriptions ('Long-leate that justly has all praise engross'd / The Strangers wonder and our Nations boast' (ll. 51–2)), the speaker begins to

> Paint her Cascades that spread their sheets so wide
> And emulate th'Italian waters pride
> Her Fountains which so high their streames extend
> Th'amazed Clouds now feel the Rains ascend
> Whilst Phoebus as they tow'rds his Mantion flow
> Graces th'attempt and marks them with his Bow.
>
> (ll. 53–8)

Here the speaker constructs a dynamic tableau in which Weymouth's ingenuity vies with Phoebus's weaponry. Indeed, the fountains' soaring jets interfere with both the meteorological and the divine orders, as the clouds gape at waters rising where they should be falling, a disruption that incites godly interference which presumably misses the mark as the fountains continue to flow and Phoebus's mansion fades before the grandeur of Weymouth's. Thus we see a fanciful production under way whereby the speaker stages a contest of sorts between man and nature, and the former unfathomably wins. But just as previously she belittled her talent in comparison to the muses and the estate itself, so here the speaker uses equivocation simultaneously to diminish and admire that which in fact prevails – poetry and nature. Knowing all along that the speaker surpasses her competitors as we read her poem, so too we appreciate the irony that none of Weymouth's feats would be possible without the materials used to execute them. Nevertheless, as the poem continues to conjure Longleat's wondrous terrain, the speaker intertwines the estate's natural and man-made effects in a way that calls into question the impulse to value the latter over the former.

Introducing her pen as compensation for Phoebus's ineffectual bow, the speaker thus continues:

> Then shou'd my Pen (smooth as their Turf) convey
> Swift Thought o're Terasses that lead the way
> To flow'ry Groves where ev'ning Odours stray
> To Lab'rinths into which, who fondly comes,
> Attracted still and wilder'd with Parfumes,
> Till by acquaintance he their stations knows
> Here twists a Woodbine there a Jasmin grows
> Next springs th' Hesperian Broom and last th' Assyrian Rose,
> Shall endlesse Rove nor tread the way he went
> No Thread to guide his steps, no Clue but ravish'd scent.
>
> (ll. 59–68)

On the one hand, the Terasses, Groves, and Lab'rinths dazzle us as landscape features that organise the visitor's sensory experience. Weymouth subsequently earns credit for these wonders in line 71 ('His Genius who th' original improv'd'). But nature's agency also marks the passage, for the terrace guides the speaker as odours do the visitor, in addition to attracting and bewildering him. However much Weymouth may have orchestrated this sensory delight, nature threatens to outdo him in the same way the poet does; they both perform feats – manipulating sensory perception, crafting 'syllables the most sublimely wrought' (line 76) – that are necessary to appreciate the lord's own work.

The last third of the poem further lionises Weymouth, taking the poem's tribute to new heights of hyperbole. Yet the final tableau engages pre- versus post-lapsarian natural imagery that further entangles the poem in questions about nature's ultimate status. Indeed, the poem's culmination in an allusion to Edenic paradise is all the more significant because it simultaneously suggests that Longleat compares to paradise and that the estate can never regain nature's lost perfection. The penultimate sentence thus begins, 'So Paradice did wond'rous Things disclose / Yet surely not from them itts Name arose' (ll. 99–100). Having denied that paradise is so called because of its landscape and not its inhabitants, the speaker spends the next six lines detailing these purportedly inferior beauties: 'Not from the Trees in their first leaves arraid / Or birds uncurs'd that Warbl'd in their shade / Not from the streams that in new channells rol'd / O're radiant Beds of uncorrupting Gold' (ll. 103–6). The speaker thus delivers a final equivocal coup in listing nature's untrammelled beauty and literal preeminence, marvelling at wonders whose novelty and radiance no one will ever know, except in her rendition of them. Dwelling on prelapsarian nature, the speaker's rhetoric of negation ('Not … or …') has a double meaning, disavowing these features as the source of paradise's name and their very existence in this world. The equivocation extends to the implied comparison between Longleat and paradise, as reiterated in the final couplet: ''Twas Paradice in some expanded Walk / To see her motions and attend his Talk' (ll. 110–11). The image returns us to a similar a irony encountered near the end of 'Upon my Lord Winchilsea' when the speaker supposes she may innocently savour the trees' beauty while sitting in a room made of felled timber. When the speaker of 'To the Honorable the Lady Worsley' invests the ultimate value – whether of paradise or Longleat – in the people who inhabit it, she indirectly (though perhaps ruinously) summons an awareness of humanity's corruption. Walking through Longleat, Weymouth and his daughter may inspire Finch to portray them as the erstwhile Adam and Eve, but doing so leads her, uncannily, to conjure images of lost rather than present perfection.

It is no doubt significant that intimations of corruption appear specifically in both poems' representations of nature. The unsettling scenarios in question – felled timber, streambeds of 'uncorrupting gold' – remind readers of nature's inevitable exploitation and indeed, humanity's implication in its corruption. A similar insinuation of original sin occurs in Jonson's 'To Penshurst' when the speaker claims that its walls were 'reared with no man's ruin, no man's groan' (l. 46). The curse of labour haunts the line despite its fanciful disavowal of toil at Penshurst. Such images suggest that country house poetry inscribes not only a vision of England's ideal society in microcosm but also the damning consequences of an ideal that threatens to exhaust nature's resources. Indeed, Finch's reference to 'birds uncurs'd' reminds us that humanity can only ever know nature in its corrupted form. Written in the wake of a century that witnessed the unsurpassed despoliation of nature, her estate poems extend the tainted dimension of the genre, revealing that in all their glory, country houses are already fallen.

Notes

1   Though the critical bibliography is too large to cite here, Susan Staves and Paula Backscheider are exemplary in distinguishing Finch for both the range and quality of her poetry. See Staves, *A Literary History of Women's Writing in Britain, 1660–1789* (New York:

Cambridge University Press, 2006); Backscheider, *Women Poets and their Poetry: Inventing Agency, Inventing Genre* (Baltimore, MD: Johns Hopkins University Press, 2005).

2　Alastair Fowler considers the term 'estate poem' more appropriate than 'country house poem' to describe the works in question, given that they rarely focus on houses themselves. See Fowler, *The Country House Poem: A Cabinet of Seventeenth-Century Estate Poems and Related Items* (Edinburgh: Edinburgh University Press, 1994), p. 1.

3　The phrase is Kari Boyd McBride's, in *Country House Discourse in Early Modern England* (Burlington: Ashgate, 2001), p. 10. She references Mark Girouard, *Life in the English Country House: A Social and Architectural History* (New Haven, CT: Yale University Press, 1994).

4　For Finch's early poetic career, see Carol Barash, *English Women's Poetry, 1649–1714* (New York: Oxford University Press, 1996), pp. 259–87. For the Finches' experience of the Glorious Revolution, see Barbara McGovern, *Anne Finch and her Poetry* (Athens, GA: University of Georgia Press, 1992), pp. 53–64.

5　McGovern, *Anne Finch*, p. 28.

6　Ben Jonson, *The Poems of Ben Jonson*, ed. George Burke Johnston (Cambridge, MA: Harvard University Press, 1985), 'To Penshurst', line 1. Subsequent citations appear in the text.

7　McBride, *Country House Discourse*, p. 165. Finch's 'Nocturnal Reverie' is perhaps her most famous meditation on nature that deliberately valorises the animal and plant kingdoms in contradistinction to 'tyrant man'. The phrase occurs in line 38. See *The Poems of Anne Finch, Countess of Winchilsea*, ed. Myra Reynolds (Chicago: University of Chicago Press, 1903), pp. 268–70.

8　Both poems have indeterminate composition dates, though it is likely that they were composed in the 1690s. They appear in the Folger folio manuscript 'Miscellany Poems with Two Plays by Ardelia' (Folger Shakespeare Library, N.b.3). Jennifer Keith and Claudia Kairoff, the co-editors of the forthcoming *Works of Anne Finch* date the latest possible transcription of the manuscript to c.1701. However, particular details in the poems – combined with biographical knowledge of their subjects – lead the editors to propose 1693 as the earliest possible composition date for 'Upon my Lord Winchilsea' and 1690 for 'To the Honorable the Lady Worsley'. I am grateful to the editors for generously sharing their expertise in advance of publication. Jennifer Keith (also for Kairoff), personal communication, 19 January 2013.

9　These works are the sole Finch poems in Fowler's *Cabinet*, suggesting their potential inclusion in the genre, depending on how broadly one defines it. See Fowler, *The Country House Poem*, pp. 395–403. William Alexander McClung also distinguishes both works as 'later estate poems' that feature evidence of new tastes in architecture and 'the Restoration conversion to classicism'. See McClung, *The Country House in English Renaissance Poetry* (Berkeley, CA: University of California Press, 1977), p. 175.

10　McClung and McBride analyse the classical precedents for country house discourse; however, early modern British country house poetry is the starting point for my inquiry.

11　Don Wayne sees ideological conflict as the very source of country house poetry; see *Penshurst: The Semiotics of Place and the Poetics of History* (Milwaukee, WI: University of Wisconsin Press, 1984).

12　For detailed analysis of the political inflection of Elizabethan and Jacobean country house poetry, see McBride, *Country House Discourse*, pp. 93–137.

13　McBride misidentifies the addressee as Finch's husband, which makes her blind to the dynamics of indebtedness that would not obtain were Finch honouring her own husband's estate. See McBride, *Country House Discourse*, p. 166.

14　On Charles Finch's death, see McGovern, *Anne Finch*, p. 98. On amicable relations among the Finches, see p. 75. On Eastwell as Charles's aunt's home, see p. 65.

15   The poem appears in Reynolds, *Poems*, pp. 33–6; lines 1–6 are cited here. Subsequent line references appear in the text.

16   The playful quality of Finch's imagery leads me to question Jacqueline Pearson's reading of these lines. A lack of historical precision leads Pearson to align both the allusion to Caesar (above) and the one to Alexander the Great in lines 42–6 with 'the fourth Earl of Winchilsea,' even though the latter lines clearly describe his ancestor and not himself. As I have suggested, recognising the different roles of the poem's two lords requires us to acknowledge its praise for one type of lord and condemnation of another. Thus, while I agree with Pearson that 'the key to Finch's attitude to country estates is ambiguity', I would question her assertion that the poem figures these lords as 'violent and ambiguous embodiments of male power'. Though Finch's proto-feminist orientation inflects the poem, recognising her sincere gratitude to her male relative produces a more historically persuasive interpretation of her experience as a woman. See Pearson, '"An emblem of themselves, in plum or pear": Poetry, the Female Body and the Country House', in Barbara Smith and Ursula Appelt (eds), *Write or Be Written* (Aldershot: Ashgate, 2001), pp. 100, 101.

17   See for example Paul Goetsch, 'The English Oak: the Changing Fortunes of a Political Icon', *Symbolism*, 8 (2008), 279–321.

18   See *The Anne Finch Wellesley Manuscript Poems*, eds Barbara McGovern and Charles H. Hinnant (Athens, GA: University of Georgia Press, 1998), pp. 45–6. *Wither* appears in line 23. See also the critical introduction, p. xxii, on the association between oaks and the Stuarts.

19   Richard Grove, *Green Imperialism: Colonial Expansion, Tropical Island Edens and the Origins of Environmentalism, 1600–1860* (New York: Cambridge University Press, 1995), p. 57.

20   On *sponte sua* tropes, see McBride, *Country House Discourse*, pp. 118–19.

21   The quotation is from Lanyer's 'The description of Cooke-ham', *The Poems of Aemilia Lanyer*, ed. Susanne Woods (New York: Oxford University Press, 1993), pp. 128–36, line 106.

22   Robert Markley's analysis of Andrew Marvell's 'Upon Appleton House' provides the template for my assessment of pre- and postlapsarian nature in Finch's work. See Markley, '"Gulfes, Deserts, Precipices, Stone": Marvell's "Upon Appleton House" and the Contradictions of "Nature"', in Gerald Maclean, Donna Landry and Joseph P. Ward (eds), *The Country and the City Revisited* (New York: Cambridge University Press, 1999), pp. 89–105.

23   Finch of course has important predecessors in what we might call the literature of environmental protest. Michael Drayton's *Poly-Olbion* (1612–22) is perhaps the most important insofar as its resistance to environmental despoliation proceeds, according to Andrew McRae, on aesthetic rather than socio-economic grounds. Scholars debate whether or not Drayton considers nature valuable in its own right (as McRae sees it) or for the myriad uses it has for human beings. See McRae, 'Tree-Felling In Early Modern England: Michael Drayton's Environmentalism', *Review of English Studies*, new series, 63: 260 (2011), 411–30. For a conflicting view, see Sara Trevisan, '"The murmuring woods euen shuddred as with feare": Deforestation in Michael Drayton's *Poly-Olbion*', *The Seventeenth Century*, 26 (2011), 240–63.

24   Markley, 'Gulfes, Deserts', p. 98.

25   Reynolds, *Poems*, pp. 52–5.

26   McGovern, *Anne Finch*, pp. 86, 96.

27   McGovern, *Anne Finch*, p. 61.

28   I am indebted here to Keith and Kairoff's assessment of the quoted lines. Keith (also for Kairoff), personal communication, 19 January 2013.

29   Often cited as the first critic to name the genre, G. R. Hibbard never mentions Lanyer. Writing over forty years later, Hugh Jenkins discusses her in depth but positions her as an outlier, meanwhile using Jonson as the model that others follow. McBride's *Country House*

Discourse grants Lanyer a more central and decisive role. See Hibbard, 'The Country House Poem in the Seventeenth Century', *Journal of the Warburgh and Courtauld Institutes*, XIX (1956), 159–74; Jenkins, *Feigned Commonwealths* (Pittsburgh, PA: Duquesne University Press, 1998); and McBride, *Country House Discourse.*

30 McGovern, *Anne Finch*, p. 86.

9

Elite pageantry as popular news: Elvetham House, John Wolfe and country-house entertainment in print

Elizabeth Zeman Kolkovich

In late September 1591, Elvetham House in Hampshire served as stage and scenery for an elaborate entertainment. After learning that Queen Elizabeth's summer progress would include a visit to this relatively meagre estate, Edward Seymour, the Earl of Hertford ordered quick but extensive renovations and prepared a series of festivities to impress his guests. When the Queen and her train arrived in the late afternoon of Monday 20 September, a group of at least two hundred men met them outside the park and led them to the entrance, where Elizabeth was greeted by a Latin oration, singing and supper. The second day featured a visually stunning water pageant staged in a man-made pond, and the final two days brought more music, tennis playing, fireworks, an exquisite banquet featuring a thousand dishes, a Fairy Queen pageant, and a speech on Elizabeth's departure.[1] Every aspect was characterised by excess as Hertford presented himself as especially eager to please. The occasion offered him the chance to stage a public apology for past transgressions. Hertford had involved himself in intense personal drama with the Queen from the beginning of her reign, when his secret marriage to Catherine Grey, a potential heir to the throne, got him thrown in the Tower and charged with rape.[2] This event haunted him for the rest of the reign as he worked to legitimise his sons who were rendered bastards, to pay off his hefty fine, and to regain favour slowly. Our only known record of the 1591 performance, a printed pamphlet called *The Honorable Entertainement gieuen to the Queenes Maiestie in Progresse, at Eluetham in Hampshire, by the right Honorable the Earle of Hertford* (1591), interprets it as a successful bid for personal favour that carried broader implications about cultural identity.

This entertainment and others staged at aristocratic estates for Elizabeth make especially apparent that early modern country houses were sites for lively intellectual debate. Printed accounts reveal that such events often had lives and influence beyond their ephemeral performances. These texts were not commissioned by the Crown to serve as royal propaganda, but financed in whole or part by publishers who saw their value to existing or emerging audiences.[3] *The Honorable Entertainement* helps us understand why some Elizabethan country house entertainments might have reached print. Published by a stationer whom one book historian calls 'the nearest thing to a news-collecting organization' in Elizabethan England, it reveals that country-house pageants could serve as early sources of printed news, as Lauren Shohet argues of later court masques.[4] Although *The Honorable Entertainement* advances Hertford's interests by claiming that his successful pageantry launched an improved relationship with Elizabeth, the book simultaneously promotes its publisher John Wolfe's agenda by contributing to his career-long project of making political news accessible to a wide audience. It chronicles a recent event in substantial detail and construes its significance as a testament to England's enhanced power on the international stage. The book was popular enough to warrant a second, revised edition, which amplifies its emphasis on nation-building as it transitions from a hurried news report to a longer lasting historical record. In both editions, Wolfe creates and seeks an English national readership varied in class rank and education but united around shared language, religion, monarch and pride in its recent history.

In performance, the Elvetham entertainment would have featured contributions from a collection of writers and performers, but especially in its first edition, the printed record downplays collaboration and focuses on promoting the host's prestige. It features Hertford's name and coat of arms on the title page, and its narrator repeatedly refers to him as 'my Lord', suggesting both deference and intimacy. The narrator even worries at one point about displeasing 'the honorable minded Earle' (sig. B4v). This language indicates that the narrator looked to Hertford as a patron; perhaps Gabriel Heaton is correct in speculating that Hertford subsidised the book to advertise his status and allegiance to the Crown.[5] The text is framed by testaments to Hertford's liberality and loyalty. It begins with a lengthy 'proeme' that describes his careful preparations for the event. This introductory material explains how Hertford hired hundreds of labourers to construct more than twenty new rooms and spaces, including several offices, a large hall, multiple kitchens and sleeping quarters. It describes in detail how he altered the landscape by adding a crescent-shaped pond, a fort and a twenty-foot man-made mountain shaped like a snail. It recounts Hertford's instructions to his servants to please Elizabeth and hopefully to demonstrate his honour, and it describes him leading the charge 'vvith his traine' to greet Elizabeth two miles outside of Elvetham (sig. A4ʳ). In the final paragraph, the narrator once again brings focus to 'my Lord of Hertford', refers to the event as 'his entertainment', and hopes that 'manie, and most happie yeares may her gratious Maiestie continue, to fauor and foster him, and all others which do truly loue and honor her' (sig. E2ᵛ). Here and elsewhere, the first edition of *The Honorable Entertainement* promotes Hertford's interests, and because it identifies no other collaborator except music composer Thomas Morley, the book presents the Elvetham entertainment as Hertford's elaborate personal gift to Elizabeth.

It crafts a reciprocal relationship between the two based on mutual benefit, trust, and adherence to hierarchy. Hertford is 'dutiful', while Elizabeth is 'most gratious' and 'highly pleased' (sigs A2ʳ, A4ᵛ, C1ʳ). It instructs readers to interpret the renovated estate and the event's grandiosity as evidence of Hertford's 'vnfained loue, and loyall duetie to her most gratious highnesse' (sig. A2ʳ). The book insists that Hertford ceded all authority to Elizabeth at the occasion. It never claims that Hertford owns or controls the estate; instead, it prudently identifies Elizabeth as the estate's true owner and refers to Hertford as 'hym, that vnder you doth hold this place' (sig. C3ʳ). The opening speech invites Elizabeth to come inside the house and 'commaund what it containes: / For all is thine: each part obeys thy will; / Did not each part obey, the wholl should perish' (sig. B3ᵛ). As these lines maintain that Hertford is now obedient, they offer Elizabeth uncontested jurisdiction over Elvetham and celebrate her supreme authority. The pageantry's language emphasizes this power by giving Elizabeth a string of active verbs: 'ruleth', 'doth commaund', 'gouerns' and 'wins' (sig. B3ʳ). The opening speech says of her, 'More learned then our selues, shee ruleth vs' (sig. B3ʳ). The book also identifies Elizabeth as witnessing the action from a seated or elevated position to declare her superior station. She watched and listened to performances while seated on her horse, under a canopy, or above the action from her bedroom window. Although Elizabeth often walked and interacted with performers during country house shows, the Elvetham book makes her appear especially powerful by emphasising her distance from others.[6]

All progress hosts desired to please the Queen, but this book places an obsessive emphasis on Elizabeth's positive responses. It is littered with explanations of her 'gratious acceptance' of Hertford's hospitality and delight at the pageantry; twice the narrator claims that the Queen so enjoyed a particular song or performance that she commanded it again (sig. B4ʳ). The entertainment text fashions Elizabeth as poised to offer reward in reciprocation for Hertford's hospitality. It argues that the pageantry has positively affected their relationship; where there was once uncertainty and distance, there is now mutual love and favour. This claim is at least partially a fiction. Hertford's company of players likely performed the pageantry, and their invitation to Court on Twelfth Night in 1592 may have rewarded their performance. But Hertford seems not to have gained any specific reward. He and his sons continued to fight for their legitimacy, and Elizabeth once again imprisoned him in the Tower in late 1595. Although his desired alliance with Elizabeth never quite came to be, the book argues for its value to both of them.

At the same time, Wolfe's interests shape the book as much as Hertford's do. Perhaps best known for his piracy and rebellion against the Stationers Company early in his career, Wolfe consistently endeavoured to publish profitable books that would propagate new and cosmopolitan ideas.[7] His biographers agree that he selected books with care.[8] Even if Hertford solicited a publisher or contributed some finances, Wolfe remained the primary agent behind this publication, and his name stamped on the title-page would have carried meaning for astute readers. In an extended analysis of Wolfe's career, Clifford Chalmers Huffman finds that his books tend to confront political problems, offer flexible strategies or adapt old solutions for new purposes, and value new experiences and tolerant attitudes.[9] When we position *The Honorable Entertainement* alongside Wolfe's other books, we might find appeal in its detailed description of a political performance or its renovation of a long-fractured monarch–subject relationship.

A focus on Wolfe's interests most clearly highlights the book's function as news. By 1591, Wolfe had become one of the most prolific Elizabethan publishers of news, especially foreign political news.[10] He valued news books for their timeliness and therefore published them with great speed. He entered a ballad in the Stationers' Register on 14 November 1588, as *A Joyfull ballad of the Roiall entrance of Quene Elizabeth into her cyty of London the [ ] Day of november 1588.*[11] He left the date blank because he entered it before the event occurred and before he knew the exact date of her arrival. Wolfe prepared to publish the Elvetham book with almost as much speed. He entered it into the Stationers' Register on 1 October 1591, about a week after its performance, and he likely printed it soon after.[12] Its past-tense descriptions and precise dates corroborate the notion that it was printed after the fact to describe a newsworthy event. The narrator refers to it as a 'discourse' (sig. A2ʳ), a term commonly applied to Elizabethan news pamphlets and regularly used in titles of Wolfe's news books.[13] Especially in its first edition, the Elvetham book provides meticulous descriptions of the estate, the host's preparations, the actors' costumes, the fireworks and feasting, and the specific actions and movements during the performance. Its publication shortly after the event was of paramount importance in appealing to readers who desired news of its sights and sounds.

Wolfe's news pamphlets tend to focus on international politics; in 1591 most of his publications offered accounts of the religious wars in France and the Low Countries. Many were newly available in English, and their titles announce the latest and most exciting news, such as *A most excellent exploit perfourmed by monsieur de Diguieres, vpon the popes armie. With a discourse of the ouerthrow of the duke of Sauoyes army* and *Newes lately come on the last day of Februarie 1591 from diuers partes of France, Sauoy, and Tripoli.*[14] They promise a 'true reporte', 'true recital', 'true intelligence', 'discourse', 'discouery', 'articles', or 'aduertisements' about happenings on the continent.[15] Wolfe also nearly cornered the market on pamphlets about the Spanish Armada in the late 1580s and early 1590s, when he had a hand in roughly 60 per cent of the books on the Armada published in London.[16] Although Wolfe's catalogue offers a range of political views, his books are mostly anti-Catholic. When he entered *A Joyfull ballad* about Elizabeth's 1588 civic entry in anticipation of the event, he subtitled the pamphlet *and of the solemnity vsed by her maiestie to the glory of GOD for the wonderful ouerthrowe of the Spaniardes*.[17] Wolfe prematurely interpreted the entry as evidence of England's increased power following the Armada's failure, and the line anticipates his take on the Elvetham entertainment as well.

This context draws attention to the Elvetham entertainment's celebration of England's successful defence against the Armada.[18] Its water pageant features elements that stage naval prowess: a fort surrounded with armed men and a sailing vessel furnished with masts, cables and flags. The book attributes England's achievements to Elizabeth's powerful guidance. It figures her not only as a goddess who rules England, but also as an 'Empresse' who commands a 'hemisphere' and 'the wide Oceans' (sigs C3ʳ–C3ᵛ). It describes India submitting to England at the mere sight of Elizabeth: 'gould-brested India, / Who daunted at your sight, leapt to the shoare, / And sprinkling endlesse treasure on this Ile' (sig. C3ʳ). According to the pageant, the sea gods and ocean are merely Elizabeth's servants, and the waves 'haue swallowd vp your foes, / And to your Realme are walles impregnable' (sig. C3ʳ). When it associates Elizabeth with the ocean by calling her a 'sea-borne Queene' and imagines her controlling the sea ('More rich then seas, shee doth commaund the seas'), it insinuates that she alone stopped the Armada from reaching England (sigs B3ʳ, D1ᵛ). It casts Spain as 'Yon vgly monster creeping from the South, / To spoyle these blessed fields of Albion' (sig. C3ʳ), but the sight of Elizabeth's 'gracious looks' and virtue have transformed the Spanish monster into a harmless snail, represented by the twenty-foot-tall 'Snayl mount' on the side of the pond (sigs A3ʳ, C3ʳ). The book's many references to Elizabeth's wide-reaching power craft England as an emerging empire, and when it vilifies Catholic Spain as a deformed monster, it insinuates that Elizabeth's Protestant rule has made England superior.

The book defines England as centred on Elizabeth and – when read alongside Wolfe's other publications – unlike the continental nations at war. Elizabeth, it claims, has kept England peaceful and affluent. In the entertainment's first pageant, a poet greets her with an olive branch to signify peace, and a pageant on the final day praises her for 'Inducing peace, subduing warres' (sig. E1ᵛ). According to the book, the performance demonstrated aristocratic hospitality on a grand scale. Its descriptions emphasize Hertford's generosity and the opulence of his festivities and embellishments, including banquets of 'plentifull abundance', a lavishly decorated canopy that covered Elizabeth's seat, and a grand display of 'all maner of fireworks' (sigs B4ᵛ, C1ᵛ, D3ᵛ). Through its portrait of a thriving country manor and descriptions of an adored monarch, the Elvetham book indicates that England is more prosperous than ever following the Armada's downfall. It never explicitly argues that Spain's attempt to invade England failed because God has favoured the Protestant nation; instead, it gives credit to Elizabeth. It worships her as a goddess, and all religious language centres on her: she inspires 'holy feare' and is 'blessed' (sigs B3ʳ, C4ᵛ, El ᵛ). The true religion of this text is devotion to Elizabeth. It repeatedly insists that England is defined by and organised around its monarch, who has ushered in a peaceful, prosperous age.

This patriotic rewriting of late Elizabethan England – a place where poverty was fairly widespread and where political power was more dispersed than centralised – may seem unsurprising in an entertainment designed to please the Queen.[19] Yet it is somewhat unusual for this type of regional pageantry. Elizabethan country house shows served as sites for struggles over policy and jurisdictional authority as much as vehicles for flattering the monarch.[20] Opening pageants frequently introduced the estate as owned by its hosts, and Elizabeth tended to interpret such claims to ownership as potential challenges to her power. When a character in the entertainment at Kenilworth Castle (1575) introduced herself as 'the Lady of this pleasant Lake' and told Elizabeth that 'the Lake, the Lodge, the Lord, are yours for to commande', Elizabeth reportedly responded: 'we had thought indeed the Lake had been oours, and doo you call it yourz now?'[21] Accounts of country house performances repeatedly underscore that Elizabeth was a stranger in a new landscape. They describe how lowly shepherds and domestic servants recognised her beauty and importance, but not her identity. Dangerous wild men and other strange characters jumped out from behind trees or appeared suddenly in her path. Most accounts highlight her vulnerability and dependence upon her subjects in these unfamiliar places. In the Ditchley entertainment (1592), a knight led her into a strange grove while explaining, 'this I dare promise you (which is somewhat worth in a strange Country) that so long as I lead you you shall not lose your way'.[22] Even as entertainments praised Elizabeth, they hoped to influence and control her. However, this subtle challenge to the stability of Elizabeth's control over the provinces is relatively absent in *The Honorable Entertainement*, which goes to great lengths to emphasise her centralised power as it illustrates a harmonious relationship between Elizabeth and Hertford, as well as between royal governance and local people.

Besides his specialty in news books, Wolfe's goal of making new perspectives accessible to an English-speaking audience also informs an interpretation of *The Honorable Entertainement*. Although he published several foreign news books in their original languages, his catalogue reveals that he championed the vernacular and regularly financed publications translated from other languages.[23] As many as two-thirds of his publications translated foreign books of news.[24] Several of his texts were printed in two or more languages; for example, a 1589 book includes the same material in English and French in parallel columns.[25] One 1587 title captures Wolfe's approach to political news especially well:

> A briefe discouse of the merueylous victorie gotten by the king of Nauarre, against those of the holy League, on the twentieth of October 1587 Both in English, and in French as it was printed in Fraunce. Whereunto is added as soone as it came to my hand since the first impression, the true copie of a letter sent by the king of Nauarre to his secretary at Rochil, aswel in confirmation of the victorie against the Duke Ioyeuse, as also the ouerthrow that the Switzers gaue to the Duke of Guise.

Its language suggests that Wolfe rushed the material to print as soon as possible; he valued timeliness in this kind of news and expected his readers to do the same. The title also emphasises accessibility. He has extended the book's circulation beyond France, and by printing it in English and French, he can attract cosmopolitan, bilingual readers, as well as those who read only English. Wolfe additionally had an interest in coterie literature and works that enabled popular access to courtly culture, such as ballads about Elizabeth's speech at Tilbury (1588), the third quarto of Spenser's *Shepheardes Calender* (1586), the 1590 *Faerie Queene*, and Thomas Hoby's translation of *The Courtier* (1588).[26] In this group of publications, Wolfe aims not for a class-based audience of elite or common consumers, but for a broad English readership.

Wolfe's prefatory notes to readers often emphasise national benefit. He procured an English translation of a Dutch text about voyages to the East and West Indies in 1598 because a 'learned Gentleman' thought its translation into 'our Language' would be 'very commodious for our *English Nation*'.[27] Wolfe's repeated use of 'our' unites his readers around a shared language and nation. He decided to publish this translation 'to the ende it might bee made common and knowen to euery body' and 'beneficiall to our Countrey and Countrey men'.[28] In a 1588 preface, Wolfe writes that the book 'will not onely be pleasant, but also verie profitable to our English nation'.[29] Another of Wolfe's publications, a Spanish grammar book, includes a note from the translator, who observed that the original book in Spanish and French limited its audience: 'none could reape any benefit by reading of it, but such as were acquainted with both the foresayd languages'. In response and 'mooued with loue and affection toward my country men', he decided to translate it into English so 'that any English man may vse it to his profite'.[30] One of Wolfe's books begins with a table of authors divided into 'Foraine writers' and 'Brittaine writers'.[31] As these examples demonstrate, Wolfe specialised in books that resonated with the interests of a broad English audience. These books do not all advance a kind of Crown-centred patriotism as the Elvetham one does; instead, they together envision a national community of readers united by shared language and history. Wolfe selected books he could market as 'profitable' or 'commodious' for the creation and advancement of this community.

Wolfe likewise marketed the Elvetham entertainment toward a wide national audience. As *The Honorable Entertainement* writes England as a flourishing nation with a strong monarch and international reach, it seeks and fashions an English readership. The text emphasises its accessibility to all English readers when it provides a Latin speech from the performance along with an English translation and adds: 'Because all our Countrey-men are not Latinists, I thinke it not amisse to set this dovvne in English, that all may bee indifferently partakers of the Poets meaning' (sig. B2ᵛ). Like Wolfe's prefatory notes to other books, this aside imagines a unified national community of readers. The book does not translate all Latin – it includes one four-line Latin verse that had been written on a shield during the performance – but the translation of a three-page speech into the vernacular makes it much more accessible to a non-elite literate public. Because this particular speech establishes Hertford's position as a loyal subject and submissive host, Hertford would have favoured its reaching a wide audience, but the desire to include 'all our Countrey-men' shows Wolfe's influence and contributes to a central goal of his career: making political news accessible to an educated and cosmopolitan English readership.

The Elvetham pamphlet must have sold well in its first edition. Before the year was out, Wolfe published a revised version once he gathered more specific and accurate information.[32] The expanded edition, which announces itself 'Newlie corrected and amended' on its title-page, continues to function as news and to interpret the event as a personal success for Hertford, but its several revisions alter the book's meaning in subtle and crucial ways. Some changes simply clarify or correct errors. Whereas the first quarto claims that Hertford employed 300 laborers, the corrected version changes the number to 'two hundred or thereabouts,' and offices identified as 'new builded' in the earlier quarto are now described as 'newlie converted' (sigs A2ʳ–A2ᵛ). The second edition cuts certain details, such as the distance the Queen travelled, a brief description of the 'Yellow and Black feathers' that Hertford's retinue wore in their hats, and a list of the dishes served at a banquet. Instead, the revised version focuses more intensely on the dramatic shows. It inserts more descriptive song titles that allow a reader to visualise the pageantry more fully. Instead of 'The Sea nymphes Dittie' and 'The Plovvmans Song,' we get 'The song presented by Nereus on the water, sung dialogue wise, euerie fourth verse answered with two Ecchoes' and 'The three mens song sung the third morning, vnder hir Maiesties Gallerie window.'[33] These expansions enrich the reader's experience of the dramatic part of the entertainment, as the second quarto appears interested in creating a play text that will last beyond the immediate aftermath.

Whereas the first quarto crafts a personal relationship between Elizabeth and a country gentleman, the second quarto describes the occasion more as a communal event centred on a loving and beloved monarch whose presence unifies men and women of all ranks. It places more emphasis on Elizabeth's joyful interactions with performers and spectators as it situates her even more firmly at the centre of the entertainment. It adds five song verses that praise 'hir sacred name'; reiterate the way her presence 'doeth so increase our Climes delight' and benefits 'Our happie Soile'; and celebrate her fame beyond compare (sigs C2ᵛ–C3ʳ). A spectacle that Elizabeth 'desired to see and hear it twise ouer' in the earlier version (sig. E1ᵛ) becomes one that 'she commanded to heare it sung and to be danced three times ouer, and called for diuers Lords and Ladies to behold it' (sig. D3ʳ). This description makes especially clear Elizabeth's powerful position. She controls the performance and the audience. She does not simply desire; she commands. Nature 'yeeldes' to her in the Virgins' song in the second quarto (sig. B3ᵛ), whereas it simply 'giues' in the first (sig. B4ʳ). The second quarto's added descriptions of her reactions make her seem even more satisfied with the entertainment. A new marginal note says of the Fairy Queen's song: 'It was a most extreame rain and yet it pleased hir Maiestie with great patience to behold and heare the whole action' (sig. D3ᵛ). Another marginal note declares of the final song at her departure: 'As this song was sung, hir Maiestie nothwithstanding the great raine, staied hir Coach, and pulled off hir mask giuing great tha[n]ks' (sig. D4ᵛ). Although this obsession with Elizabeth's enjoyment might increase the book's celebration of Hertford's success, it actually moves the focus somewhat away from Hertford as it adopts a more formal tone and heightens its Crown-centred patriotism. It changes all insistences of 'my Lord' to 'the Earl', and it adds descriptions of others who attended and participated in the performance.

One of the most striking changes involves Hertford's wife, Frances Howard Seymour. Frances was a well-connected former maid of honour, and the couple had received Elizabeth's consent to marry in 1585.³⁴ When they welcomed Elizabeth to their estate for the first time as a couple in 1591, they displayed their marriage as a public one sanctioned by her. They presented Hertford not as a troublemaker or marginal figure, but as a social and political insider whose recent marriage had the potential to improve his standing with the Queen. Although the first quarto does not mention Frances as it creates the impression of an intimate interaction between Hertford and Elizabeth, the second quarto makes apparent her crucial roles as co-host and intermediary. It includes a longer account of Elizabeth's entrance into Elvetham that highlights Frances's welcome: 'hir maiesty alighted from horsbacke at the hall dore, the Countesse of Hertford, accompanied with diuers honourable Ladies and Gentlewomen, moste humbly on hir knees welcomed hir highnesse to that place: who most graciously imbracing hir, tooke hir vp, and kissed hir, vsing manie comfortable and princely speeches, as wel to hir, as to the Earle of Hertford standing hard by, to the great reioysing of manie beholders' (sig. B3ᵛ). This description represents the two women as intimate friends. Elizabeth had watched the opening pageantry from an elevated position on her horse, but to greet Frances, she stepped off the horse and interacted more familiarly with her former companion. In a public performance of their alliance, Frances played the role of hospitable host and humble servant as she kneeled before the Queen, and Elizabeth acted in accordance with her high position by delivering 'princely speeches'. When the book describes Elizabeth lifting up Frances so that the two women stand on equal footing, it has Elizabeth symbolically accept Frances's new role as mistress of Elvetham.

The second quarto also inserts new descriptions of the commoners in attendance, which again directs attention slightly away from Hertford and toward Wolfe's emphasis on nation-building. It adds a line about Elizabeth's entrance into the park: 'where (to her Maiesties great liking) were by estimat, neer tenne thousand people, from sundrie places' lined up to catch a glimpse of her arrival (sig. A4^r). In the narrative about the second day's entertainment, these new lines appear: 'And as hir maiestie sate at dinner, there was a dore set wide open for ayer, whereby the people might (to their great comfort) behold hir Maiesties presence in open view' (sig. B4^v). These passages, and especially their parenthetical statements, fashion Elizabeth as affectionate toward and adored by the masses. These added pieces of narration, which represent Elizabeth's common subjects as excited simply to view her, bolster the pageantry's claim that the whole region revels in Elizabeth's arrival and mourns at her departure. William Leahy cautions us not to assume that royal progresses were as successful as some texts claim, and he suggests that the Queen's visits often prompted 'mutual suspicion' and fear rather than delight.[35] The Elvetham second quarto, however, insists that all audience members were united in their devotion to Elizabeth and awe at the event. This claim serves the interests of both Hertford and Wolfe.

Yet some of its additions expose the fiction within its idealism. Its added song lyrics amplify its praise of Elizabeth but undercut its celebration of her unchallenged power over unified subjects in subtle ways. It states that Elizabeth 'neuer feares approching night' (sig. C2^v), a foreboding line that implies that worst times are ahead. When it wishes that she will never experience 'dismall daies or deadly teene' (sig. C3^r), it casts her reign as an idyllic 'Golden Age', but it again draws attention to the possibility of darker times. Although the second quarto insists that the thousands of spectators worship Elizabeth as the centre of a unified England, it reveals that they are divided by class rank. It includes this description: '*Siluanus*, being so vgly, and running toward the Bower at the ende of the pond, affrighted a number of the countrey people, that they ran from him for feare, & thereby moued great laughter' (sig. C4^r). According to the book, the country people are simple and easily frightened, and those of higher rank laugh at them. As the second quarto exposes class division, it heightens the representation of Elizabeth as a goddess who sits above and apart from her people. It reveals that she heard the final verses from within her coach, illustrating that she kept her distance from the performers. At the end of the first edition, the narrator says that the Queen so enjoyed Hertford's entertainment that 'hereafter hee should finde the rewarde thereof in her especiall fauour' (sig. E2[v]). In the second version, that phrase becomes 'shee would not forget the same' (sig. D4[v]). The revised edition underscores that Elizabeth is in control of their relationship; it promises nothing specific and suggests that she might withhold favour. The first quarto crafts a close personal relationship between Elizabeth and Hertford that fashions Elizabeth as generous and Hertford as deserving in a bid for favour. The revised edition, however, moves focus away from Hertford and places even more emphasis on Elizabeth as the powerful leader of an emerging empire.

Both editions of the Elvetham entertainment reveal how printed accounts of pageantry could serve as political news for readers both popular and elite. Although revisions to the second edition help transition it from current news to historical account, later readers may have collected both versions as historical record. Some time between 1605 and 1610, Richard Bancroft, the Archbishop of Canterbury, bound his copy of the Elvetham entertainment with nine other pamphlets, including Elizabeth's coronation pageantry, a mayoral speech to Elizabeth, and late Elizabethan foreign political and military news books.[36] In the middle of the seventeenth century, public notary Humphrey Dyson bound his copy with one news pamphlet and twenty-one other Elizabethan and Jacobean pageants and masques.[37] Dyson's library reveals his desire to preserve texts that record important events in English history, and he identified the Elvetham entertainment as one such event.[38] *The Honorable Entertainement* is only one of several country house entertainments printed in small pamphlets, poetry anthologies, and authorial collections. Flexible and widely appealing, these texts served a variety of functions for a wide audience, and they deserve more attention. When we shift focus from writers and hosts to publishers, we can consider the broader influence of printed entertainments on the intellectual cultural of Elizabethan England.

Notes

1   *The Honorable Entertainement Gieuen to the Queenes Maiestie in Progresse, at Eluetham in Hampshire, by the Right Honorable the Earle of Hertford. 1591* (London, 1591). All quotations come from this text, the first edition, unless otherwise noted.

2   For a reading of the entertainment focused on this context, see Curtis Breight, 'Realpolitik and Elizabethan Ceremony: The Earl of Hertford's Entertainment of Elizabeth at Elvetham, 1591', *Renaissance Quarterly*, 45 (1992), 20–48.

3   Although Elizabethans did not typically use the modern term 'publisher', the anachronism usefully designates the agent behind a publication, or the stationer who is financially and conceptually responsible for a book's publishing. On the distinction between publishers and other stationers, see Peter Blayney, 'The Publication of Playbooks', in John D. Cox and David Scott Kastan, *A New History of Early English Drama* (New York: Columbia University

Press, 1997), pp. 389–92. Helen Watanabe-O'Kelly identifies continental festival books as commissioned by the government, and several scholars have assumed the same is true in England. See Watanabe-O'Kelly, 'The Early Modern Festival Book: Function and Form', J. R. Mulryne, Helen Watanabe-O'Kelly and Margaret Shrewing (eds), *Europa Triumphans: Court and Civic Festival in Early Modern Europe* (Aldershot: Ashgate, 2004), p. 9; Axel Stahler, 'Imagining the Illusive/Elusive? Printed Accounts of Elizabethan Festivals', in Christa Jansohn (ed.), *Queen Elizabeth I: Past and Present* (Munster: Lit Verlag, 2004), pp. 61–88, esp. 65–67; and Jean Wilson, *Entertainments for Elizabeth I* (Woodbridge: Boydell, 1980), p. 10. In a preface to *The Princelye Pleasures, at the Courte at Kenelwoorth* (1576), publisher Richard Jones explains that he gathered texts of the Kenilworth pageantry (1575) and financed their printing because he identified an existing readership. This book is now lost, but a transcription of the Preface is included in *Kenilworth Illustrated; or, The History of the Castle, Priory, and Church of Kenilworth* (Chiswick, 1821), p. 52.

4   Matthias A. Shaaber, *Some Forerunners of the Newspaper in England 1476–1622* (Philadelphia: University of Pennsylvania Press, 1929), p. 288; Lauren Shohet, *Reading Masques: The English Masque and Public Culture in the Seventeenth Century* (Oxford: Oxford University Press, 2010), pp. 150–88.

5   Gabriel Heaton, *Writing and Reading Royal Entertainments From George Gascoigne to Ben Jonson* (Oxford: Oxford University Press, 2010), p. 98.

6   For an example of the interactive nature of progress pageantry, see the entertainment at Wanstead (better known as 'The Lady of May') in Philip Sidney, *The Covntesse of Pembrokes Arcadia* (London, 1598). The performance began when the Queen walked through the gardens and an actor 'apparelled like an honest mans wife' appeared 'svddenly' in her path (sig. Bbb3v). As the Queen stood among the performers, the entertainment presented a singing debate between two shepherds and asked her to choose a victor.

7   For more on Wolfe's piracy, see Joseph Loewenstein, 'For a History of Literary Property: John Wolfe's Reformation', *English Literary Renaissance*, 18: 3 (1988), 389–412. For general discussions of Wolfe's biography, see Harry R. Hoppe, 'John Wolfe, Printer and Publisher, 1579–1601', *The Library*, 4th series, 14:3 (1933), 241–88; and Ian Gadd, 'Hunting Down John Wolfe for the New DNB', in Robin Myers, Michael Harris and Giles Mandelbrote (eds), *Lives in Print: Biography and the Book Trade From the Middle Ages to the 21st Century* (New Castle, DE: Oak Knoll Press, 2002), pp. 193–201. For analysis of Wolfe's motivations, see Harry Sellers, 'Italian Books Printed in England Before 1640', *The Library*, 4th series, 5:2 (1924), 108; and Matthias A. Shaaber, *Some Forerunners of the Newspaper in England 1476–1622* (Philadelphia: University of Pennsylvania Press, 1929), pp. 286–8.

8   In addition to the works cited in the previous note, see Clifford Chalmers Huffman, *Elizabethan Impressions: John Wolfe and His Press* (New York: AMS Press, 1988), pp. 1–121.

9   Huffman, *Elizabethan Impressions*, esp. pp. 11–19, 83.

10   Shaaber, *Some Forerunners*, pp. 286–8; Huffman, *Elizabethan Impressions*, pp. 69–98.

11   Edward Arber (ed.), *Stationers Register: A Transcript of the Registers of the Company of Stationers of London; 1554–1640 A.D.* ([1875] New York: Peter Smith, 1950) vol. 2, p. 506.

12   Arber, *Stationers Register*, vol. 2: p. 596.

13   For lists of Wolfe's publications, see Huffman, *Elizabethan Impressions*, pp. 133–61 and *A Short-Title Catalogue of Books Printed in England, Scotland, and Ireland and of English Books Printed Abroad, 1475–1640*, eds A. W. Pollard, G. R. Redgrave, W. A. Jackson et al., 2nd edn (London: Bibliographical Society, 1976–91) vol. 3, p. 186.

14   *A Most Excellent Exploit* (London, 1591) and *Newes Lately Come* (London, 1591).

15   Examples include *Aduertisements from Britany, and from the Low Countries* (London, 1591); *A Discourse Vppon a Question of the Estate of this time* (London, 1591); *A Discouery of the*

Great Subtiltie and wonderful wisedome of the Italians (London, 1591); *A True Recital of the armie leuied by the princes of Germanie* (London, 1591); *Articles concerning the Yeelding of Grenoble* (London, 1591); *True Intelligence Sent … Concerning the estate of the English forces now in France* (London, 1591); *The True Reporte of the Seruice in Britanie* (London, 1591).

16   Shaaber, *Some Forerunners*, p. 285.

17   Arber, ed., *Stationers Register*, vol. 2: p. 506.

18   See Harry H. Boyle, 'Elizabethan Entertainment at Elvetham', *Studies in Philology*, 68 (1971), 146–66. Boyle identifies several allusions to Anglo-Spanish relations and interprets them as a personal tribute to Charles Howard, Hertford's brother-in-law and commander of the English Navy. However, these references make a broader political statement, especially when printed. The entertainment places Elizabeth, not Howard, firmly at the centre of England's military success.

19   For more on political power and poverty in Elizabethan England, see especially David Loades, *Power in Tudor England* (New York: St. Martin's, 1997), pp. 4–16; and Jim Sharpe, 'Social Strain and Social Dislocation, 1585–1603', in John Guy (ed.), *The Reign of Elizabeth I: Court and Culture in the Last Decade* (Cambridge: Cambridge University Press, 1995), pp. 192–211.

20   Breight, 'Realpolitik', pp. 20–48; Breight, 'Caressing the Great: Viscount Montague's Entertainment of Elizabeth at Cowdray, 1591', *Sussex Archaeological Collections*, 127 (1989), 147–66; and Michael Leslie, '"Something nasty in the wilderness": Entertaining Queen Elizabeth on Her Progresses', *Medieval and Renaissance Drama in England*, 10 (1998), 47–72.

21   George Gascoigne, 'The Princely Pleasures at Kenilworth', in John W. Cunliffe (ed.), *The Complete Works of George Gascoigne* (New York: Greenwood, 1969) vol. 2: 93–4; Robert Laneham, *A Letter*, ed. R. J. P. Kuin (Leiden: Brill, 1983), pp. 10–11.

22   The Ditchley entertainment is preserved in manuscript at the British Library, Add. 41499A. I quote from the transcription in E. K. Chambers, *Sir Henry Lee: An Elizabethan Portrait* (Oxford: Clarendon Press, 1936), pp. 276–97.

23   For more on Wolfe's specialities in Italian books and French news pamphlets, see Huffman, *Elizabethan Impressions*, pp. 1–47 and 69–98.

24   Shaaber, *Some Forerunners*, p. 287.

25   *A Discourse Vpon the Declaration, published by the Lord de la Noue. Discours sur la declaration faicte par le Sieur de la Noue* (London, 1589).

26   Thomas Deloney, *The Queenes Visiting of the Campe at Tilsburie with her entertainment there to the tune of Wilsons wilde* (London, 1588); T. I., *A Ioyful Song of the Royall Receiuing of the Queenes most excellent Maiestie into her highnesse campe at Tilsburie in Essex: on Thursday and Fryday the eight and ninth of August. 1588 To the tune of Triumph and ioy* (London, 1588); Spenser, *The Shepheardes Calender* (London, 1586); Spenser, *The Faerie Queene* (London, 1590); Castiglione, *The Courtier*, trans. Thomas Hoby (London, 1588).

27   Iohn Huighen van Linschoten, *His Discours of Voyages into ye Easte & West Indies Deuided into foure bookes* (London, 1598), sig. A1ᵛ.

28   John Hughen van Linschoten, *His Discours of Voyages*, sigs A1ᵛ–A2ʳ.

29   Juan Gonzalez de Mendoza, *The Historie of the Great and Mightie Kingdome of China* (London, 1588), sig. *4ᵛ.

30   *The Spanish Grammer vvith Certeine Rules teaching both the Spanish and French tongues. By which they that haue some knowledge in the French tongue, may the easier attaine to the Spanish; and the likewise they that haue the Spanish, with more facilitie learne the French: and they that are acquainted with neither of them, learne either or both. Made in Spanish, by M. Anthonie de Corro. With a dictionarie adioyned vnto it, of all the Spanish wordes cited in this booke: and other*

more wordes most necessarie for all such as desire the knowledge of the same tongue (London, 1590), sigs A3ʳ–A3ᵛ.

31   *A Learned and True Assertion of the original, life, actes, and death of the most noble, valiant, and renoumed Prince Arthure* (London, 1582), sig. B2ᵛ.

32   *The Honorable Entertainment geuen to the Queenes Maiestie in Progresse, at Eluetham in Hampshire, by the right Honorable the Earle of Hertford* (1591). A copy of this edition, which has not been assigned an STC number, can be found in the Royal Collection at Windsor Castle, RCIN 1024755. Wolfe issued at least three versions of the entertainment: a first quarto, a slightly corrected issue of that quarto, and an expanded version. Compared to the first edition, the many spelling and spacing variants of the second quarto reveal that its type was completely reset. To publish this copy, Wolfe must have sold out of the earlier runs and expected enough demand to print it anew.

33   In the first quarto, see sig. C3ᵛ, D3ʳ; in the second quarto, see sig. C2ᵛ, D1ʳ.

34   Longleat House, Archives of the Marquis at Bath, Seymour MS, vol. 5 (microfilm, reel 4, Institute of Historical Research), ff. 164–9.

35   William Leahy, *Elizabethan Triumphal Processions* (Aldershot: Ashgate, 2005), pp. 81–91.

36   London, Lambeth Palace Library, shelfmark (ZZ)1593.29.07. This is a copy of the first quarto.

37   London, British Library, shelfmark C33e7. This is also the first quarto.

38   Heaton, *Writing*, p. 254.

III

The country house library and its intellectual significance

10

Country houses and the beginnings of bibliomania

James Raven

Collecting books became increasingly, and, for some, alarmingly common in early modern British country houses, even though the dimensions and origins of this passion are imprecise. In the words of David Pearson: 'the English private library in the seventeenth century is an area where there is scope both to increase our knowledge of the facts and also thereby our understanding of book ownership in the society of the time'.[1] Gaps in our understanding are obvious despite the apparent abundance of studies of individual early modern libraries and book collections. 'Private library' is an accepted term but also a problematic one; an exploration of the enthusiasm to collect books within the compass of the country house is both a helpful modification to the terminology of 'private' and 'library' and a further contribution to the social history of early modern book ownership.

Bibliophily, a relative rarity for gentlemen in Britain in 1500, was more widely recognised (and feigned) by the mid-seventeenth century, although the difference between owning and collecting books is moot. Book love might be found in examples throughout the period, but in many respects the collecting of books also began to resemble the 'bibliomania' identified and so labelled in the eighteenth century and widely applied in the nineteenth century to the book-buying disease of numerous Georgian collectors.[2] Different ways of hoarding or displaying tests our use of the word 'private' for these activities; different spaces to contain and consult books makes the word 'library' problematic; and, just as in the later, more celebrated period of book lust, the place of the book collection or collections within houses or moving between houses, forces us to think more widely about the relationship between books, their owners and their households.

In Elizabethan England, the greatest private book and print collections eclipsed important institutional libraries and archiepiscopal libraries. Notable were the libraries of John Dee in 1583 (some 3,000 printed books and 500 manuscripts) and Andrew Perne in 1589 (some 2,900, mostly printed, volumes). As has been observed,[3] where institutional libraries recovered, it was often as a result of private bequest – Perne's to Peterhouse, Cambridge being a case in point. By about 1640, however, still more private libraries began to exceed the size of institutional ones, with most private – and certainly country house – libraries accumulating many more printed volumes than manuscripts (as was not necessarily the case in the late sixteenth century). Indeed, several college and cathedral libraries faced a bleak century ahead. Significantly, the obsession by propertied individuals for books and for keeping their collection together continued to benefit institutional library development. Some of the greatest late seventeenth-century book collectors such as Christopher Codrington and John Moore, Bishop of Ely bequeathed their libraries to All Souls (12,000 volumes) and Cambridge University Library (c.30,000 volumes) respectively.[4] Most of Bishop Moore's books however, had been kept in Ely House, Holborn; there is an important issue here about the way in which country house collections accumulated in situ over generations of house owners.

What, then, was the motive for collecting on this scale and how important was the country house to it? For some collectors among the gentry and aristocracy, desire exceeded love: a madness that was as much disease as it was wholesome; and one that by the early eighteenth century seemed to some based far more on collecting for collecting's sake than on any appreciation of literature or of ideas between covers. The bibliomania of the seventeenth century, however, was linked to the intellectual culture of the country house. That association was the more obvious given the malaise in much institutional collecting, even though little agreement prevailed about collecting objectives.

Country house and private libraries contributed to the increase in the proportion of vernacular books shelved by the end of the seventeenth century. The grander cognoscenti acquired a passion for fine bindings and luxury books such as those of grand travel excursions, topography or genealogy. For some collectors notable trophies included ancient manuscripts, whose rarity and historic and aesthetic interest appealed to a relatively limited group of antiquarians and scholars. Others, and certainly the most studious of Protestant households, developed an equally fervid devotion to English favourites, such as Foxe's *Book of Martyrs*, Bishop Lewis Bayly's *The Practise of Piety*, the collected works of Bishop Joseph Hall and the sermons of Edward Stillingfleet.[5]

Passions for acquiring new publications and increased purchase of vernacular texts and of modern rather than classical authors should not obscure the enhanced market in antiquarian books. Historical study of early modern enthusiasms for old volumes has been overshadowed by renewed appreciation of the burgeoning market for incunables and rare first editions in the late eighteenth and early nineteenth centuries.[6] The scale of the later revolution in the valuation and passion for early print and rare books dwarfs the bibliophilia of the seventeenth century, but this earlier period of collecting must also be measured in the context of relatively small levels of book production (and accumulated production), a more limited economy and comparatively modest disposable incomes. It makes for some spectacular book hoarding, enjoyment and sharing, all from the country estate. Hence Sir William Boothby (1637–1707) despatched desperate letters from his seat of Ashbourne Hall, Derbyshire, to his bookseller in London, Richard Chiswell, demanding booksellers' term catalogues so that he could select and order new publications. To his more local Lichfield bookseller, Michael Johnson, Boothby requested 'all the printed pamphlets sermons and discourses which come out'. His library of some 6,000 volumes (praised on his memorial in the local church) was 'the true pleasure of my life, all else is but vanity & noyse'. The library was his joy, a pleasure demonstrated by the care with which he arranged and displayed his books, created stamps of his coat of arms and his crest to apply to the uniform bindings, and his readiness to loan volumes to a local country house network of fellow bibliophiles and men of letters.[7] The library at Ashbourne Hall was known to and helped serve a circle of Boothby's fellow book enthusiasts at Renishaw Hall, Chatsworth, Hardwick Hall and Beresford Hall and the nearby market town of Chesterfield. At least two booksellers traded in Chesterfield by the late seventeenth century and, according to probate inventories, several 'libraries' (some, very modest collections of books) were owned by local gentlemen.[8]

The Derbyshire and Yorkshire country house libraries, like most others in Britain, advanced with the financial prospects of their owners. The general economic growth of the seventeenth century, and especially of the final third of the century, stabilised prices and increased disposable income to strengthen the market for books and other luxuries. This was most noticeable in London and proximate counties but a ripple of new prosperity (and of certain wealth redistribution advantageous to the propertied) radiated to the further provinces, and in Scotland certainly included lowland and border estates. The development of the book trade, domestically and internationally, and especially including book auctions from the 1670s, contributed to a widespread seventeenth-century country house passion for the library. There were scores of country house owners as enthusiastic as Boothby. According to his friend Anthony Wood, Ralph Sheldon (1603–84), gentleman and antiquary of Worcestershire, 'spard not any mony to set up a standing library in his house at Weston'.[9] Many of these collections were also household collections, not simply private or indeed just personal. Collections treasured by the head of the household and owner of the house and estate, were also often influenced by the choices and advice of family, friends and advisers.[10]

Financial investment and a sense that a book collection might be a marketable commodity were not motives in the building of country house libraries. Early modern probate or resale values of books are generally less than their original purchase price, even though the surviving evidence is variable and apparently often dependent upon lost assumptions about value.[11] This financial realism, or put another way, the library as indulgence and pleasure rather than economic investment, offers further illumination of the tension between the materialities of collecting, the impulse to own fine luxury objects, and the expense of intellectual pursuits by propertied men and women. This extends discussion of practical versus intellectual, where the passion for books began to verge on the impractical.

The motivation, then, for collection was many faceted. The pursuit of book ownership was one in which intellectual enquiry, specific interest, an urge to improvement, practical problem solving and entertainment subtly combined with prestige, status, family pride and the concern to bequeath a collection, whether to kin or to a favoured institution or community.[12] The spectrum ranged from the presentational fussiness of a Boothby or indeed Pepys to Gabriel Naudé's advice, translated by John Evelyn in 1661, that it was absurd and uninformed to judge books by their covers. Nonetheless, many copies of Evelyn's Naudé are today found sumptuously bound in house libraries alongside volumes of uniform quality. Fine binding did not preclude avid reading (at least, that seems a reasonable assertion in the absence of serious research on such a question for this period). A safer conclusion is that the collector's choice of texts *and* of their material forms widened with the deepening of book production and trade.

A rudimentary summary of the first three hundred years of the *ancien regime* of printing in Britain (that is, of the manual printing press and the response of scribal publication to it) is that between about 1470 and 1650 domestic production was overshadowed by the importation of books from the continent, that the reliance on manuscripts continued to be appreciable, and that domestic printing often operated at under-capacity. The first published considerations by Richard Atkyns, *The Original and Growth of Printing* in 1664, gave natural prominence to the arrival of the printing press. The advance of the general market for printed books, however, together with the destruction and redistribution of ancient collections after the dissolution of the monasteries in England and the religious wars in continental Europe, also generated a new age for the collection of the manuscript and the antiquarian book. After the mid-seventeenth century, and especially following the Restoration, a certain self-reflection and criticism typified by Naudé and Atkyns accompanied the expansion of domestic demand for books and print. Innovations in both book trade and form ranged from the book auction to the serial and newssheet, while pride in book ownership and collection was expressed in the creation of the book-plate. Most towns in England boasted engravers and book-plate makers by 1700, and the greatest

London workshop, that of William Jackson, employed several engravers and produced more than 600 book-plates between 1695 and 1715.[13]

Historians of British libraries of this period, however, habitually lament the unknowns, failings, and muddle in the history of private collections,[14] and proposals for new library provenance studies recording copy-specific details to build up a directory of early modern libraries are much to be welcomed.[15] The general landscape is at least well described. The *Cambridge History of Libraries* calls library-building part of 'the profession of a gentleman'.[16] The propertied, nobility and gentry, built using newly acquired lands and wealth, with many building in new style, some with long galleries to display their newly acquired pictures and a library room to display their newly purchased books and 'cabinets of curiosities'. With new emphasis on education, both at home and from travel abroad, a country house aristocracy and gentry now often comprised scholars, collectors and connoisseurs.

In Elizabethan and Jacobean England, four collectors are frequently cited as revered book lovers: the gentleman scholar, Sir Richard Worsley (d. 1621) of Appledurcombe House in the Isle of Wight ('wonderful studious … [who] whollie spent his tyme when he wase alone att his booke'),[17] Sir Thomas Lucy III (d. 1640), the judge Sir Henry Yelverton (d. 1630), and Lady Anne Clifford (d. 1676). Sir Thomas Lucy's favourite authors were carved on his funerary monument at Charlecote Church, Warwickshire, while Sir Henry Yelverton and his wife are memorialised at Easton Maudit, Northamptonshire, half-reclining on their elbows before shelves of books from their library, fore-edges of the volumes to the front. A triptych commissioned by Lady Anne Clifford herself (and now at Abbot Hall, Kendal), celebrates her bibliophilia as she poses (retrospectively) aged fifteen in the left-hand panel below shelves of her books, bound spines outwards.[18]

Even so, evidence survives for more than a hundred gentry libraries during the period 1560–1640, even if library historians understandably fret about the gaps in our knowledge about the number, size and content of early modern book collections. The pioneering work of Sears Jayne in identifying catalogues, inventories, donations and household account books and booksellers' records has been extended by the ongoing Private Libraries in Renaissance England Project (PLRE). Yet the base for such a scholarship remains relatively slight, especially as many book collections were lost by fire and accident. Many apparently important collections were dispersed during the Civil War, and notably those from Raglan, Brampton and Wardour castles.[19]

For the eighty years between 1560 and 1640, surviving collections and additional evidence from some 123 country houses in England provides basic statistical information. In addition, there survive twelve country house libraries of this period from Scotland, and four from Wales. Of these British collections, some fifty have been, or are in the course of being, edited and about thirty more described in varying detail. All of them suffer from difficulties of incompleteness, problematic provenance, and questions about where they were kept. Many large collections, like those of Longleat, were divided (and indeed moved at different times) between properties, including between a family's country and its London house, or divided, like the Cecil collection, between heirs to different properties. As Hannah DeGroff demonstrates in her study of Naworth (Chapter 12 in this volume) different collections were also often kept in different parts of a house, and these themselves moved; numerous individual collections, numerous encounters.

It is at least clear that from the late sixteenth to the mid-seventeenth century there is a great increase in the size of what counts as a significant collection or 'library' of books. Some 200 or so books counted as a comparatively large private collection in the 1560s, while before 1600 half a dozen recorded country house libraries contained more than 600 books. This is slighter therefore than several important institutional libraries and archiepiscopal libraries, but by 1640 the size of private libraries begins to exceed institutional ones. By 1650 many private country house libraries boasted more than 1,000 books: those of Thomas Howard at Arundel and that of the Sidney family at Penshurst, both included some 4,500 books. The *Cambridge History of Libraries* lists some eight country house collections of more than 2,000 books before mid-century, namely those of Branthwaite, Percy, 9th earl of Northumberland, Paget, Knyvett, Drummond, the Cecil library at Salisbury House, Coke and Herbert, baron of Cherbury. The continuing database edited by David Pearson currently includes about 1,200 names of seventeenth-century English book owners.[20] The size of a minority of these collections is also known and form this we can compute that the average number of volumes in these private libraries stood at about 1,400 in the 1600s and 1620s, and somewhere between 3,000 and 3,500 between 1650 and 1700.[21]

The importance of imported books, quite as much as the arrival of monastic loot or antiquarian collecting, becomes very obvious also. Thomas Smith's 1566 gallery, explored by Richard Simpson in Chapter 6, plainly illustrates this dependence on the foreign. Imprints from Strasbourg, Nuremberg, Augsburg and Cologne among others dominate Smith's gallery book lists. If this is a bibliomania it is one where foreign purchase and acquisition is paramount. Baron Stafford, at the beginning of the period (1563) left a library in which all his law books were continental printings, and English-language books comprised only thirty-two of the total of 300 items. Latin books were often predominate and these also predominately of continental origin. In Lord Lumley's library, the low number of vernacular items was especially striking, amounting to about 12 per cent of the entire collection (including 187 English books, sixty-eight Italian, fifty-eight French), Sir Thomas Knyvett's much larger and more comprehensive library lies somewhere between that of Lumley's and the Cecils': nearly 74 per cent of the collection is in Latin, 11 per cent in English, 7 per cent in French; and just under 15 per cent of the books were printed in England.

In his introduction to Nicolas Barker's *Treasures from the Libraries of National Trust Country Houses*, Simon Jervis has emphasised the importance of little 'studies' as the genesis of private libraries from Henry VIII to Stafford. The journey from study to library is mediated the 1622 advice of Henry Peacham in *The Compleat Gentleman*: 'To auoide the inconuenience of the moathes and moldiness, let your studie be placed, and your windows vellum-bound if it may be, towards the East rather than to the south or west, and them not to lie neglected'.[22]

As Susie West notices in Chapter 10, much has been made of the closets, the small rooms within the private apartments of a gentry family. The 1618 inventory of Sir William Ingleby's books, for example, shows that he kept his books at Ripley Hall, Yorkshire in the new study, the old study and the dining parlour. Many other owners of country houses kept their books and papers in closets, chests, trunks and studies.[23] Closets were frequently used both to store and to read books, and yet their lineal relationship to the panelled room of the libraries of the early seventeenth century is often underestimated. The design for a closet by the English architect Richard Smythson in about 1600 shows four elevations newly fitted out with shelves divided into compartments and with four built-in desks. The inventory drawn up on the death of Henry Percy, the 'wizard earl' in 1632 shows both chests and closets still being used for books. By then, Percy owned a library with fifty-two chests of books and books to fill twelve small chests besides. His example is one of many that question the idea of the importance of a separate library room. Its role for the display of books on shelves took hold only gradually even among the wealthier gentry, as J. T. Cliffe emphasised in his *World of the Country House in Seventeenth-Century England*.

An inventory for a closet drawn up on the death of Sir Edward Zouch describes a room in 1634 with four elevations for a library containing 250 books. It was not, however, until the end of the seventeenth century that the libraries of English and some Scottish country houses became the ornately decorated room, lined with books in uniform bindings and celebrated in iconic eighteenth-century prints.[24] We also need care in considering certain overlapping categories, and especially the advancing libraries of clerics. Substantial book collections were accumulated by dozens of country priests at the end of the seventeenth century, many of them epitomising the 'squarson' cross between squire and parson. Many clerical gentlemen inhabited grand parish-gentry style houses and built up splendid libraries. They included Revd William Burkitt of Dedham, whose vanished library has been reconstructed from his catalogues and correspondence,[25] and yet we know almost nothing of how the library was arranged. Nor, as with so many gentlemen's lost libraries before 1700, do we have the books themselves.

Such libraries notably contributed to the increase in the proportion of vernacular books at the end of the seventeenth century. A clash of country house worlds also developed. The grander cognoscenti maintained a passion for fine bindings and luxury books such as those of impressive travel excursions, topography or genealogy (a passion that sometimes bordered on a mania), and the equally enthusiastic textual devotion to English favourites like Foxe, Stillingfleet, Bayly, Hall and, later, John Tillotson. Many vernacular books on duelling, husbandry and planting, architecture and gardening similarly vied with collections, many in classical languages that served to celebrate the gentleman as an English connoisseur or virtuoso. Such gentlemen were actually often noblemen, or at least led by an aristocratic model: the library of what was to be known as the 'stately home' rather than the country house. Thomas Howard, earl of Arundel, 'the father of virtu' according to Horace Walpole later in the eighteenth century, championed the fascination with all things Italian, Rather differently, Lord Burghley's 'private passions' included genealogy and cartography.

What does link these types of private library, whatever the size and type of house, is what might be called a passion of interestedness. Simon Jervis quotes, as do many, from Evelyn Waugh's *Vile Bodies*, with its description of a country house library lined with 'bookcases of superbly unreadable books'.[26] By and large this is not the case in the seventeenth century, whatever was to happen in the book market explosion of the eighteenth century. Cliffe rightly alludes to seventeenth-century literary figures who came of gentry stock. He also stresses the importance of country house library cataloguing in diverse forms in the second half of the seventeenth century. Such cataloguing was taken even to the point of a certain priggishness. In the early eighteenth century, Thomas Coke, writing from his Grand Tour stopover in Turin, at the age of seventeen, assured his father that 'most certainly one of the greatest ornaments of a gentleman or his family is a fine library'.[27] Before we apply such comments too broadly, however, we should note absences. Celia Fiennes, touring the country on horseback in the 1680s, does not mention a single private library in her travelogue.

Nevertheless, activity in the book world markedly quickened. The increase in the number of individual obsessive country house book collectors is suggested by the history of auctions, salesrooms and sale days from the late seventeenth century. Anthony Wood acquired ninety London book auction catalogues issued by London auctioneers from 1676 until his death in 1695. An auction catalogue often rapidly followed the death of a country house library owner. Catalogues of the recently deceased included Robert Bruce Earl of Aylesbury, Ralph Button, Richard Davis, John Maynard, Thankful Owen, Thomas Parkhurst, Robert Wallis and John Warner. Books were often listed in the catalogues according to size but also subject: foreign books, 'Bibliotheca Gallica, Italica, Hispanica', 'English books', medicine and history. Catalogues by booksellers including John Bullord, Richard Chiswell, William Cooper, Edward

Millington and Benjamin Walford were also distributed gratis by booksellers in London, Cambridge and Oxford. Book sale catalogues, similar to the auction catalogues and issued by London and Oxford booksellers such as William Cooper, William Crook, Richard Davis, William London, Humphrey Moseley, Henry Playford and Philemon Stephens, included libraries of deceased persons such as William Ducie the viscount Downe, Henry Howard the Duke of Norfolk, John Maitland the Duke of Lauderdale, and Henry Parker. Sections of such library sale catalogues also offered new priorities: headings by author such as Robert Boyle, John Gauden, Thomas Hobbes, John Ley, John Owen, or William Prynne, headings by general category such as Frankfurt fair catalogues (indispensable for the collector of early print); and specialist headings such as divinity, drama, heraldry, law, the popish plot and manuscripts.

This activity further highlights the distinction between the bibliomania of new publication – the torrent of new books – and the enhanced market in antiquarian books. Book collection proceeded against a rash of warnings in Britain and across mainland Europe against indiscriminate purchase and reading. Stern voices offered vivid testimony to the escalating obsession with book collecting. Very soon after the increase in sales and production of books in the second half of the seventeenth century, pronouncements about an avalanche of publication circulated in British, French and German news-sheets, journal and letters. The strain to household purses became familiar enough and featured in numerous early modern jeremiads about domestic extravagance and luxury. Leibniz typified mid-seventeenth-century concern about the over-abundance of books. He deplored a manufactured flood that was further swollen by increasing imports of antiquarian and scholarly books. Famously, in 1680 Leibniz proposed that in order to contain the 'horrible mass of books', bad books should be banned before even they were printed and that Louis XIV should prescribe a set of canonical texts as recommended by appointed specialists.[28]

English comments seem more direct. As early as 1632, the poet and pamphleteer George Wither proclaimed: 'Good God! how many dungboats full of fruitless works do they yearly foist on his Majesty's subjects; how many hundred reams of foolish, profane, and senseless ballads do they quarterly disperse abroad'. In 1653, Margaret Cavendish, Duchess of Newcastle, mused that, 'Besides the World hath already such a weight / Of uselesse Bookes, as it is over fraught'.[29]

Such English expostulations appear not to invoke the word 'bibliomania' until the beginning of the eighteenth century. The earliest use in English – or rather of 'bibliomanie' -apparently dates from 1719 when Myles Davies reported in his newssheet, *Athenae britannicae*, that a Mr Menschen, then editing writings by the Library Keeper to the King of Denmark 'declared against those who are troubl'd with Bibliomanie, of having too many Books: that is, who will neither read them themselves nor let any Bode else'. The origins of that penchant for 'the bookcases of superbly unreadable books' are found hereabouts and their association is with collection, with the assemblage of books in one place. A hundred years later, in 1766, Jacques Lacombe invoked the mania in his history of Queen Christina of Sweden (who reigned 1632–54 and died in 1689) when he wrote of 'the great disorder in her finances for the gratification of this *Bibliomania*'.[30]

Of course, many country house bibliophiles found genuine correspondence between books as conveyers of thought and books as adored material objects. Nevertheless, questions of materiality do dominate the glorification of books, as well, as their commercialisation and their wider social distribution from the early seventeenth century. Mania for books, however much the specific interest for some in the antique and the rare, was closely related to the changing history of book *production* – and, in the view of many – of their overproduction. As T. F. Dibdin, author of *The Bibliomania; or, Book-madness*, was later to write, focusing not on the maniac collector but on the historical advance of the disease, ' ... during this [seventeenth] century ... like the fumes of tobacco, which drive the concealed and clotted insects from the interior to the extremity of the leaves, the infectious particles of the Bibliomania set a thousand busy brains a thinking, and produced ten thousand capricious works'.[31]

This mania was a mania not just for collecting but a mania that reflected the unprecedented availability of a material good. Comparative perspectives are illuminating. Numerous other consumer goods besides books advanced as a result of the increased strength of disposable incomes. As the money economy deepened and prices stabilised, foodstuffs became relatively cheaper. Increased disposable income boosted the demand for non-essential and luxury goods.[32] The book, pamphlet, broadside, print, newspaper and magazine reside full square in the consumer and innovation revolution that filled the homes and work and lounging places of the early modern propertied, along with painted, printed and embroidered cottons, silverware, porcelain and fine pottery, tobacco, tea and teapots, quality shoes, caps and ready-made clothes, sugar, coffee and chocolate.[33]

The consequences of the overwhelming number of domestic print products were debated in parallel with a moral debate about new luxuries. For some, the debate led to a confusion of values and became the key to subtly changing definitions of bibliomania. Many publishing booksellers, including the infamous John Dunton in the late seventeenth century, were to promote larger and cheaper editions in a manner that courted charges of literary devaluation and vulgar commercialism, despite the appeal of price and swift production. The progressive distancing of refinement from commodification proved a later feature of the consumerism that often seemed to engulf publishing and bookselling. Crudely put, men and women of property regarded books as vehicles of enlightenment and instruction, but also, in consequence, as instruments of social and cultural assertiveness. From the mid-seventeenth century at least, many collectors perceived valued books – new as well as antiquarian – as quite different entities to chapbooks – increasingly objectified as popular literature – and to increasingly commercialised, gadfly ephemeral literature. John Evelyn remarked that 'most of the trifling books' in a library 'should be weeded out to give place to better till it were thro'ly purged'.[34] The contents of most country house libraries reflected such discrimination, although the appeal of the chapbook and miscellany remained for some, if with a certain guilty acknowledgement.

There were also variant anxieties. Within the private library, much early bibliomania was destructive of rare and precious books. The great early collector John Bagford, as Dibdin was obviously but not critically aware, was an obsessive mutilator of rare books and broadsides. Joseph Ames also established his 'museum of [torn out] title pages' (now in the British Library). It was an act that *was* later denounced as that of a 'biblioclast' by William Blades in his 1896 *The Enemies of Books*. Recent scholarship on the production history of sammelbande is much detained by debates about what was split and rejoined in the age of incunabula and in the early sixteenth century and what was put together and destroyed as a result of collecting manias from the late sixteenth century.[35]

Such action claims a distinguished history of commentary that linked criticism of the use or non-use of books with destruction, indifference and misplaced valuation that went back to the mid-sixteenth century. René Wellek long ago acknowledged the literary and bibliographical achievements of John Bale when accompanying John Leland as he toured the emptying monasteries of England in the 1540s. Bale's 1548 *Illustrium Majoris Britanniae scriptorium summarium* and 1549 'A Regystre of the Names of English Wryters' were catalogues that created virtual libraries. In bibliography Bale found salvation – and Leland and Bale, if only by repute, were celebrated figures to many of the country house book collectors already described. Leland was also liable to be identified as the first bibliomaniac, after Bale's assertion in his 1549 annotated edition of *The Laboryouse Journey & Serche … for Englandes Antiquitees* that Leland had suddenly fallen mad some three years previously. Bale condemned the monkish avarice that kept books 'tyde up in chanes, and hidden undre dust in the monkes and fryers libraryes' and so, as the *Laboryouse Journey*, concludes, 'avarice … hath made an ende both of our lybraryes and bokes'.[36] Again, it was Bale in his conclusion to the *Laboryouse Journey* who attacked the destroyers of monasteries for seeing only books as 'commodytees'.[37] Bale reflected, even then, upon an idea of the market value of books that reduced their cultural worth: 'We sende to other nacyons to have their commodytees … we drynke the wynes of other landes, we bye up their frutes & spyces, yea, we consume in aparell their sylkes & their velvets. But alas our own noble monumentes and precyouse Antyquytees, which are the great bewtie of our lande, we as lyttle regarde as parynges of our nayles'. The reduction of books to the status of consumables resulted from their destruction rather than the changing methods of production and publication.[38]

In the early modern country house, therefore, at least two 'bibliomanias' were operating, one working off the other. The one is of passionate, maniacal collecting, disdainful of the common and the incurious; the other the rude deluge of books, or rather the rude deluged by books in which taste and reason was overwhelmed. The book craze that impelled and deluded individual collectors reflected a much wider bibliomania, and one rooted in changing economic and social circumstances and the redistribution of wealth that assisted the country house collectors. For wealthy bibliophiles, the hiring of book dealers and agents became indispensable. An increasingly active and organised second-hand market is evident by the end of the seventeenth century. Second-hand book and library auctions, which appear to have been uncommon before about 1650, rapidly increased in size and frequency. Few early auctioneers bought their stock of books; instead, most were selling on behalf of others. Relatively generous credit arrangements also seem to have eased the trade, many auctioneers allowing up to a month to pay and accepting the return of any books found to be imperfect. Auctions quickened the dispersal of gentlemen's' libraries, and as one auction catalogue declared, it was now to 'be more easie for any Person of Quality, Gentlemen, or others, to Depute any one to Buy such Books for them as they shall desire.'[39] Judging by the circumstances mentioned in some of these catalogues, remarkable personal fortunes were both lost and gained at this period. Not all sales were post-mortem, and the buoyant book market was a sign of wealth reallocation as well as accumulation. A few of the book agents might also have been among the losers. Most famously, Gabriel Rogers, agent to Sir Edward Leighton of Wattlesborough Hall in Shropshire, waited for more than twenty-five years for final settlement of his bill in 1702.[40]

A key issue was the extent to which booksellers, like all businessmen, were able to stimulate demand and tempt the propertied and the library builders. The structural concentration of business in London helped to focus on the recognition (not only confined to the book trades) that if a market was limited, profit margins could never be high. For booksellers especially, encouragement of demand was largely dependent upon good, country-wide printed advertising. This developed from the early promotional use of title-pages to the early issue of London printed catalogues. From the late sixteenth century, inland and coastal transport developments were essential extensions to the importation of books as well as to domestic production, enabling what Richard Simpson called in Chapter 6 'the dynamic acquisition of the latest printed book'.

As important for country house bibliophilia, if not mania, increased custom from the propertied classes was mainly responsible for this remodelling of the book trade. Provincial sales outlets were extended and London booksellers launched new titles of both religious and 'entertaining and instructive' literature with no advanced assured custom. For the majority of metropolitan booksellers, the sales of open market publications became the basis for survival. The rise of a consumer society, like the rise of the middle class, has become a cliché of historical analysis, transferable between several centuries, but the effect of new consumerism upon the book trade is certainly evident from the late sixteenth century, and particularly in the decades following the Restoration. The key to the growth of consumption was not simply the seventeenth-century recovery from the price inflation, but redistribution within the economy, a process enlivened by pointed contemporary reports. Under the earlier inflationary regime many landowners had benefited by marketing food surpluses in a rising market in which most of the poor and dispossessed became the real losers. The near doubling of population between 1550 and 1700 was set against a six-fold increase in the price of grain, in which the gentry and some yeomanry were the real gainers, most notably following the improvement of newly acquired land in the second half of the sixteenth century.[41]

The growing seventeenth-century book market was to be sited in a landscape of sturdy farmhouses and coaching inns, new town houses and confident city and country gentlemen, burghers and tradesmen. The popularity of the book-plate from the 1680s followed several decades' increase in armigerous gentry, the unprecedented building of funerary monuments in churches, and the bogus claims to gentility much reported in print. This was, with obvious regional variation, an increasingly prosperous and redistributive economy in which the aggregate incomes of a rising, propertied group contributed to the development of a luxury market, and of the creation of country house libraries on a new scale, with new purpose, new tensions and new passion.

Notes

1   David Pearson, 'The English Private Library in the Seventeenth Century', *The Library*, 7th series, 13:4 (December 2012), 379–99, p. 379. I am most grateful to David Pearson, David McKitterick and Andrew Foster for advice on various sections of this chapter.

2   See James Raven, 'Debating Bibliomania and the Collection of Books in the Eighteenth Century', *Information and Library History* (February 2013), 196–209.

3   Elisabeth Leedham-Green and Teresa Webber, 'Introduction', in Elisabeth Leedham-Green and Teresa Webber (eds), *The Cambridge History of Libraries in Britain and Ireland Volume I, to 1640* (Cambridge: Cambridge University Press, 2006), 1–10, pp. 4–5.

4   Edmund Craster, *The History of All Souls College Library* (London: Faber and Faber, 1971), pp. 66–81; David McKitterick, *Cambridge University Library: A History* (Cambridge: Cambridge University Press, 1986), pp. 47–152.

5   The broader and multiple contestation between ancient and moderns is set out in Joseph M. Levin, 'Ancients and Moderns: Cross-Currents in Early Modern Intellectual Life', in Giles Mandelbrote and K. A. Manley (eds), *The Cambridge History of Libraries in Britain and Ireland: Volume II, 1640–1850* (Cambridge: Cambridge University Press, 2006), pp. 9–22.

6   See in particular the excellent reappraisals of Arnold Hunt, 'Private Libraries in the Age of Bibliomania', in Mandelbrote and Manley (eds), *Cambridge History of Libraries*, 438–58; and Kristian Jensen, *Revolution and the Antiquarian Book: Reshaping the Past, 1780–1815* (Cambridge: Cambridge University Press, 2011); see also Philip Connell, 'Bibliomania: Book Collecting, Cultural Politics, and the Rise Of Literary Heritage in Romantic Britain', *Representations*, 71 (2000), 24–47.

7   Peter Beal, '"My books are the great joy of my life": Sir William Boothby, Seventeenth-Century Bibliophile', *The Book Collector*, 46 (1997), 350–78; Giles Mandelbrote. 'Personal Owners of Books', in Mandelbrote and Manley (eds), *Cambridge History of Libraries*, 173–89, pp. 173–7.

8   R. Milward, 'Books and Booksellers in late 17th-Century Chesterfield', *Derbyshire Miscellany*, 10 (1985), 119–45.

9   Cited in J. T. Cliffe, *The World of the Country House in Seventeenth-Century England* (New Haven, CT: Yale University Press, 1999), p. 163.

10   See Pamela Selwyn and David Selwyn, '"The Profession of a Gentleman": Books for the Gentry and the Nobility', in Leedham-Green and Webber (eds), *Cambridge History of Libraries, Volume I*, 489–519, esp. p. 495.

11   Pearson, 'The English Private Library in the Seventeenth Century', pp. 381–2.

12   For various explorations of these, see Raymond Irwin, *The Origins of the English Library* (London, 1958); William Sherman, *Used Books* (Philadelphia: University of Pennsylvania Press, 2008); David Pearson, 'Patterns of Book Ownership in Late Seventeenth-Century England', *The Library*, 7:11 (2010), 139–67; and James Raven, 'Liberality and Librolarceny: Archbishops and their Public Libraries in the Seventeenth Century', *Lambeth Palace Library Annual Review 2010* (London, 2011), pp. 58–76.

13   See especially (with excellent illustrations) Brian North Lee, 'Gentlemen and their Book-Plates', in Robin Myers and Michael Harris (eds), *Property of a Gentleman: The Formation, Organisation and Dispersal of the Private Library, 1620–1920* (Winchester: Oak Knoll, 1991), pp. 42–76; and Brian North Lee, *British Bookplates* (London: Scolar Press, 1979). Jackson's pattern book survives in the British Library.

14   See, for example Selwyn and Selwyn, '"Profession of a Gentleman"', p. 499; and Felicity Heal and Clive Holmes, *The Gentry in England and Wales, 1500–1700* (Basingstoke: Palgrave, 1994), p. 278.

15   See Pearson, 'English Private Library in the Seventeenth Century', pp. 389–92.

16   Selwyn and Selwyn, '"Profession of a Gentleman"'.

17   The verdict of his neighbour, Sir John Oglander, cited in Cliffe, *World of the Country House*, p. 168.

18   J. H. Baker, 'Common Lawyers and the Inns of Court', in Leedham-Green and Webber (eds), *Cambridge History of Libraries, Volume I*, 448–60, p. 454; and Selwyn and Selwyn, '"Profession of a Gentleman"', pp. 490, 492.

19   Selwyn and Selwyn, '"Profession of a Gentleman"', p. 500.

20   www.bibsoc.org.uk/content/english-book-owners-seventeenth-century, accessed 15 January 2015.

21   A fuller synopsis is given in Pearson, 'English Private Library in the Seventeenth Century', p. 381, fig. 1.

22   Henry Peacham, *The Compleat Gentleman* (London, 1622), 54f; see also A. Hughes, 'Sussex Clergy Inventories 1600–1750', *Sussex Record Society*, 91 (2009).

23   Further examples given in Selwyn and Selwyn, '"Profession of a Gentleman"', pp. 505–7.

24   Outstanding survivals are described by Nicolas Barker and Simon Jervis in Nicolas Barker, *Treasures from the Libraries of National Trust Country Houses* (New York: Royal Oak

Foundation and the Grolier Club, 1999); and Simon Jervis, 'The English Country House Library: an Architectural History', *Library History*, 18 (2002), 175–90.

25 Gerard G. Moate, 'The Lost Library of William Burkitt, 1650–1703', *The Library*, 12:2 (June 2011), 119–41.

26 Jervis, 'Introduction: The English Country House Library', in Barker, *Treasures from the Libraries*, pp. 13–33.

27 Charles Warburton James, *Chief Justice Coke: His Family and Descendants at Holkham* (London: Scribners, 1929), p. 190.

28 Richard Yeo, *Encyclopaedic Visions: Scientific Dictionaries and Enlightenment Culture* (Cambridge: Cambridge University Press, 2001), p. 94.

29 Margaret Cavendish, *The Poetresses Hasty Resolution* (London, 1653).

30 J L [Jacques Lacombe], *The History of Christina, Queen of Sweden* (London, 1766), p. 95.

31 Thomas Frognall Dibdin, *The Bibliomania; or, Book-madness; Containing Some Account of the History, Symptoms and Cure of this Fatal Disease. In an Epistle to Richard Heber,* 2 vols (London, 1809), vol. I, 22.

32 See E. A. Wrigley, *People, Cities and Wealth: the Transformation of Traditional Society* (Oxford and New York: Oxford University Press, 1987), Chapters 1, 7, 9; and Sara Pennell, 'Consumption and Consumerism in Early Modern England', *Historical Journal*, 42 (1999), 549–64.

33 See John Styles, 'Product Innovation in Early Modern London', *Past and Present*, 168 (2000), 124–69.

34 Giles Mandelbrote, 'John Evelyn and His Books', in F. Harris and M. Hunter (eds), *John Evelyn and His Milieu* (London: The British Library, 2003), 71–94, p. 73.

35 Alexandra Gillespie, 'Poets, Printers, and Early English Sammelbände', *Huntington Library Quarterly*, 67:2 (2004), 189–214; Alexandra Gillespie, *Print Culture and the Medieval Author: Chaucer, Lydgate, and Their Books 1473–1557* (Oxford: Oxford University Press, 2006); Jeffrey Todd Knight, *Bound to Read* (Philadelphia: University of Pennsylvania Press, 2013).

36 *Laboryouse Journey and Serche of Johan Leylande for Englandes Antiquities,* sigs Cv[r–v], cited in Jennifer Summit, *Memory's Library: Medieval Books in Early Modern England* (Chicago: Chicago University Press, 2008), p. 141.

37 *Laboryouse Journey,* sig. Giii[r].

38 Discussed in Summit, *Memory's Library*, p. 142.

39 William Cooper, 'Note to the Reader', cited in Anthony Hobson, 'Foreword', in A. N. Munby and Leonore Coral, *British Book Sale Catalogues, 1676–1800: A Union List* (London: Mansell, 1977).

40 Estimate derived from Cliffe, *World of the Country House*, p. 167.

41 Some historians have suggested that almost all the population enjoyed trickle-down benefits; see, for example, Eric Kerridge, *The Farmers of Old England* (London: Allen & Unwin, 1973), pp. 160–3.

11

Looking back from 1700: problems in locating the country house library

Susie West

Studies and Cabinets … not being much known, or visited, remain buried in perpetual silence.[1]

'The care of books' was how J. W. Clark memorably gathered together his research on historical libraries 'and their fittings', as his title page proclaims.[2] This chapter carries on looking at the care of books, by early modern private owners, a group who rose in succession to Clark's dominant medieval ecclesiastical keepers of books. Taking care of books suggests a degree of thought in their arrangement, a level of investment in their housing, and perhaps a degree of anticipation for their future lives, as heirlooms carefully catalogued. As the examples from the Norfolk gentry discussed here show, not all heirlooms were cared for, nor were their resting places preserved, but enough care was passed down through a number of families to demonstrate widespread practices in living with books. Specifically, the owners of early modern country houses invested in making book rooms to house their collections; the failure of these rooms to survive is the result of the success of the idea of a library in the country house. The early rooms, relatively modest in scale and assigned unobtrusive spaces within the domestic plan, were successively remodelled and repositioned around the house to become, by the late eighteenth century, part of the public suite of reception rooms and an essential component of the nineteenth-century entertainment for house parties. This chapter looks back from the viewpoint of 1700, a point when private libraries in England are still elusive to architectural historians compared to the rapid increase in known examples from the 1720s, and considers the nature of their invisibility and how it might be investigated.

Research on the practices of keeping and using books, gathered together as the history of reading, investigates how readers stored, processed and made use of the content of their books. This is a flourishing field, with the past decade of research producing rich accounts of individuals and networks of readers and writers. Print culture provides the material and intellectual basis for historians interested in the early modern history of ideas, of reformed religion, of the emergence of science, of literature and political debate. In England, the seventeenth century and its political and religious fractures have proved particularly fruitful contexts.[3] The circulation of new forms of print, such as the first news sheets, were consumed in now-familiar locations such as urban coffee houses and, after the Restoration, in the emerging clubs and societies.[4] These spaces for the consumption of print, and for ensuing debate, have been characterised as spaces for male, civic discourses.[5] More recent scholarship has begun to attend to how the same forms of print reached the country house, keeping the household in touch with metropolitan news. This work brings a welcome dynamic to our sense of what was read regularly in the homes of the landed classes.

However, the material conditions of keeping a book collection, as a library, within the early modern country house have received less attention.[6] This is partly a problem of evidence, in that pre-1700 library rooms and their intact collections are almost invisible, and partly a division of labour between modern disciplines. Working with the current state of the history of reading scholarship and with a detailed survey of a county network of book owners, some of the gaps in our understanding of the early modern country house as a space for books can be addressed.

This chapter addresses some of the challenges for scholars investigating aspects of the consumption of print within the early modern country house; it offers new case studies for the physical presence of book collections and extends the understanding of how the pre-1700 book room in English country houses can be made visible. The following discussion draws attention to the chronological problems attendant on largely archive-based research.

The three chronologies

A county survey, based on Norfolk, offers an insight into the 'three chronologies' of houses, their library rooms and their book collections.[7] The combined resources of surviving country houses, lost houses and their archives, architectural and bibliographical scholarship were assembled to produce a table of when the country houses were built, when the first reference to a book room was dated and when the first reference to a book collection could be established. The evidence was gathered for the date range 1660–1830, although earlier evidence was noted. From this survey, sixteen houses were identified with evidence for book collections before 1700, and four with presumed ownership of books.

Table 11.1 The three chronologies

House and date	Date of first evidence for book ownership	Date of first evidence for pre-1700 book room
Raynham Hall 1620s	1500	Nil
Old Holkham Hall (demolished) ? sixteenth century or earlier	1543	Nil
Channons (renamed Shadwell) (demolished) later sixteenth century	1620s	Nil
Old Houghton Hall (demolished) sixteenth century or earlier	Mid-seventeenth century, valued 1663	1588 study; nil thereafter
Oxburgh Hall c.1483	Mid-seventeenth century	1684 closet
Oxnead (demolished) late sixteenth century	Assumed mid-seventeenth century, sold 1732	Nil
Quidenham Hall early seventeenth century	Mid-seventeenth century, sold 1729	Nil
Hockwold Hall late sixteenth century	Mid-seventeenth century, brought to Norfolk after 1670, sold 1709	Nil but book cases noted in 1709
Old Kimberley Hall (demolished) seventeenth century or earlier	Assumed mid-seventeenth century from eighteenth-century evidence	Nil
Old Hillington Hall 1627	Assumed later seventeenth century from eighteenth-century evidence	Nil
Costessey Hall 1564	Assumed late seventeenth century from eighteenth-century evidence	Nil
Narford Hall mid-sixteenth century rebuilt 1702	Assumed late seventeenth century from eighteenth-century evidence	Nil
Felbrigg Hall 1620s	1665	1670s wing
Ryston Hall 1668	1668	1668
Hunstanton Hall 1500	1676	seventeenth century
Heydon Hall 1581	1671	1671
Stow Bardolph Hall (demolished) 1589	1672	1672
Blickling Hall 1619	1676	1676
Melton Constable Hall 1664–87	1680s	1687
Rougham Hall (demolished) 1694	1694	1694

Table 11.1 summarises the Norfolk families and their houses discussed in this chapter, according to their place within the 'three chronologies'. The first eight houses are discussed as short case studies for their evidence for book ownership. The four houses with assumed book ownership are briefly mentioned in connection with the problem of the lack of direct evidence. The remaining eight houses are not discussed here (their evidence for book rooms has been given priority elsewhere) but need to be included as part of the total picture available for Norfolk country house book ownership before 1700.[8] Table 11.1 suggests that the date of the house does not have a direct relationship to the survival of evidence for book ownership or for a book room; houses were periodically remodelled and updated internally to incorporate new uses for rooms. Knowing that families had books in the seventeenth century is also unrelated to the availability of evidence for how they kept them. The most useful class of evidence for the book room chronology is the survival of early inventories; this table is really a commentary on the nature of the family archives.

Before considering some of the problems of working with these results, it is worth emphasising that the sample includes families and their landed estates from across the socio-economic layers of the resident peerage and county gentry. The eight Norfolk houses who form the case studies of this discussion span social layers of the landed classes. The resident nobility by the end of the seventeenth century were the recently ennobled Viscounts Townshend of Raynham Hall, and the Pastons, Earls of Yarmouth at Oxnead Hall. The knight baronets (KB) were (including the Townshend family, KB 1617) Bedingfeld (KB 1661) of Oxburgh Hall and Holland (KB 1629) of Quidenham Hall. Jacobean wealth from the law raised the Cokes of Godwick to larger landholdings and the purchase of old Holkham in 1612; in contrast, the Walpoles of old Houghton Hall had not yet acquired the fortune of the future Sir Robert Walpole. Old Holkham and old Houghton would be spectacularly rebuilt in the eighteenth century while retaining their foundation collection of family books. The smallest landowner was the Buxton family at Channons and the newest was Sir Cyril Wyche, former Secretary of State for Ireland.

Sixteen houses (47 per cent) of the thirty-four that were possible to investigate in detail had evidence for book collections before 1700, the earliest dating back to 1500. This sample divides into eight houses that also had evidence for library rooms: a mere eight examples, clustering from 1660 to 1700, although the earliest reference to a study was in 1588. This sample of sixteen book collections yielding evidence for eight book rooms is a 50 per cent success rate for the historian, i.e. it informs our understanding of the evidential problems to a greater degree than it advances an understanding of the country house library. However, we cannot conclude that it represents anything like a reality of only eight book rooms in the county of Norfolk before 1700. Overall, deriving only eight book rooms from the original thirty-four houses (owned by established county families, regardless of how many times they rebuilt their homes) leaves a 23 per cent possibility that a pre-1700 library room can be identified from any archive sources. So in any detailed investigation of a number of family archives before 1830, one in two may reveal a book collection but only one in four may produce what the architectural historian is searching for.

This rapid reduction in the sample size as the research question moves from books to rooms is a clear indication that the results should not be interpreted at face value. This is to return to my opening point, that by 1700 the culture of the book (in print and in manuscript circulation) was woven in to the culture of the landed classes. The landowners of Norfolk before 1700 were undoubtedly readers and owners of books; it is also worth noting that the county families shared a tradition of sending their sons to the University of Cambridge. Here, the students would encounter the 'care of books' in college libraries, mainly first-floor gallery spaces set up with the stall system, of which Wren's Trinity College library (1675) was the latest and most elegant example. There were plenty of visual models for housing a book collection.

The evidence for book ownership, reduced as it is, provides the reason for questioning the low results for library rooms. Eight Norfolk houses with good evidence for book ownership before 1700, have left no evidence at all as to how or where they housed their books. These largely unremarked houses and their families represent a group of book owners rarely seen in the published scholarly literature on libraries or reading. This is partly because they do not provide substantial catalogues with an individual collector as a historical focus for analysis and also that there are few surviving personal records of the experience of reading. Instead, inventories, accounts, sale catalogues and the occasional legal dispute dominate the range of sources and provide some contexts for provenanced books and the 'lost rooms' in surviving houses. The following account summarises these eight examples of pre-1700 libraries that have lost their rooms. They are grouped into the pre-1600 collections and the seventeenth-century collections.

The pre-1600 library collections

Two early collections from Norfolk country houses emerged from the survey of thirty-four family archives: the well-known origins of the library of the Coke family of Holkham and the less well-known foundation of the library of the Townshend family of Raynham Hall. Both these families have continuously owned their landed estates since at least the dates of the book evidence, and both houses have been rebuilt but survive today. Raynham Hall offers the best example of the frustration of working with good evidence for long-term book ownership and collecting, but with a visual source that denies the existence of a book room.

Raynham Hall is the present house of the Townshend family, Viscounts Townshend, and it is the successor seat to East Raynham Old Hall, the family's late medieval house. Sir Roger Townshend (d. 1493) owned over forty manuscripts and printed books, of which more than half were legal volumes.[9] The books were mainly kept in 'large chests in the vault at Raynham', a room with a chimney which should therefore be thought of as one with a vaulted (stone) ceiling.[10] Continuity of ownership is demonstrated with his son who listed twenty-six of the volumes in an early sixteenth-century memorandum book, with five further volumes.[11] The founder's great-great grandson, the builder of the present hall, was the first baronet, Sir Roger Townshend (1588–1637). He inherited some of the books of his maternal grandfather, Sir Nathaniel Bacon (1549–1622) of Stiffkey Hall, Norfolk. Sir Nathaniel's will divided his 286 books amongst his family: the English texts to his wife and daughters, the French law books to his grandson Roger Townshend, and his Latin books to his grandson Henry Gawdy. Sir Roger bought three books about architecture in 1619 when designing the present Raynham Hall, however his will and the 1637 post-mortem inventory omit any reference to books.[12] Later, the collection was something worth showing to the gentleman architect Sir Roger Pratt. Pratt wrote to Horatio, Baron Townshend (1630–87), referring to 'the unexhausted literature of your Ldshps numerous great volumes of the elder & later English authors, & Spanish & French authors' and to Townshend's grandfather's 'many Italian and French books of architecture', lightheartedly asking to be Townshend's library keeper at Raynham.[13] Pratt was clearly impressed by the quality and range of books he saw at Raynham. However, architectural floor plans made for the royal progress around Norfolk in 1671 name every room but do not name a library or study.[14] It is not until c.1729 that the 'old library' is mentioned, on the occasion of moving its contents into the newly created (and present) library room on the ground floor. It is impossible to deduce where this old library was within the house or when it was created, but it is mostly likely to have been when the interiors of the 1619 house were finished from 1659–62.

The great library collection at the eighteenth-century Holkham Hall is probably best known as the result of a precocious Grand Tour collecting campaign by Thomas Coke, later 1st Earl of Leicester, undertaken before he rebuilt old Holkham from 1734. Aside from this burst of activity, Holkham's multiple libraries contain generations of family books, demonstrating the personal interests of their purchasers. Indeed, the present Long Library in the eighteenth-century house was designed to hold the inherited collections, while Thomas Coke's Grand Tour acquisitions remained in his London house. The old hall had been the home of the Coke family since 1612, although the Norfolk-born Chief Justice Edward Coke (1552–1634) had already begun to build up estates in the parish. The family books begin with 'Wenefred Coke, widow' after 1543, Sir Edward's mother, and his mother-in-law Anne Arrowsmith's prayer book. Sir Edward himself was eulogised on his tombstone as a living library and he bequeathed his books as heirlooms. By 1679 there were books valued at £60 (if a shilling per volume is a rough valuation, this suggests 1,200 volumes). Thomas's parents, Edward and Carey, were both keen book buyers but spent beyond their means, both dying young in 1707. Trustees reserved books to the value of £193 for Thomas's inheritance, a considerable increase in numbers to shelve at the old hall. Nothing is known of the library room before 1707, although the antiquarian Peter Le Neve saw Sir Edward Coke's books there and the trustees intended to commission a catalogue in 1708 (not known today).[15]

The post-1600 libraries

The minor gentry Buxton family lived at Channons Hall, near Tibenham, in Norfolk. John Buxton I (1608–60) and his wife Margaret (d. 1687) built up a collection together, although the scale is unknown. John's will directed that some of the book's were his wife's property to keep for her own use and the rest were to be held in trust for whichever of their sons began a professional career (as opposed to running the family estates). The Buxton books are known from personal accounts from 1627, purchases made in London, and some provenanced surviving books, which passed to the later family house at Shadwell. Nothing survives of Channons except one image, and there is no indication of how John and Margaret housed their books. They bought books they wanted to use, read or enjoy with neighbours, from standard law books to about fifty play texts, in English or translation into English and recently published: a household resource.[16]

The Buxton's library is the earliest of the seventeenth-century group that has been analysed, but a much older collection has yet to be investigated fully. The old house at Houghton, home of the Walpole family who had owned the estate from 1307, had a study by 1588. With continuity of family ownership of the old house, it is reasonable to assume that the Elizabethan study contents also survived into the seventeenth century but there is no known evidence that illuminates the nature of the study or the collection until 1663, when the books were valued at only £3.[17] Subsequent accounts and surviving books with family signatures suggest that each generation added to the collection. Sir Robert's mother, Mary Burwell, brought some of her father's books with her, and added hers; Sir Robert's father, Colonel Robert Walpole, was cited by Roger North for 'study and learning extraordinary'.[18] The old house survived while the present Houghton Hall was built (from 1720); by 1721 Walpole's steward was complaining that the study in the old house was overrun by destructive mice. This collection was catalogued shortly after 1717, listing 850 titles.[19] A preliminary review of dated titles in the present collection suggests that a later seventeenth-century collection survives, with contributions from several generations of Walpoles and their relatives.[20]

The survival of a late medieval house as well as continuity of family ownership does not guarantee early visibility of a book room. Oxburgh Hall, built by the 1480s and still in the occupation of the original family of Bedingfeld, had, until a sale in 1951, a large collection probably assembled in the mid- to late seventeenth century, ranging across classifications and intended for household use rather than a single collector.[21] Yet there is no evidence for the presence of a study or library room until a plan of 1774 naming a library. This room was on the ground floor corner of the entrance front and west range, which had other family rooms. The house was modernised from 1775, with the regrettable loss of the medieval great hall. It is unlikely that the 1774 room was the seventeenth-century library. In turn, it has been superseded by the present library room, fitted out after 1830.[22] The material witness of the books points to the need for a book room before the eighteenth-century arrangement, and after the house was restored from the Civil War depredations it experienced. The man who repaired it, benefiting from a hard-won baronetcy for his royalist loyalty but little else, died in 1684, leaving 'the Madona [*sic*] in my closet' to the Earl of Yarmouth.[23] A seventeenth-century closet could contain a library of books, but a house on the scale of Oxburgh could easily accommodate a separate study.

Oxnead Hall, Brampton, was the great Elizabethan home of the Pastons, later earls of Yarmouth. The second largest house in Norfolk by the time of the 1664 Hearth Tax, it may be the county's most romantic example of hubris followed by nemesis. By the time the 2nd Earl of Yarmouth died without sons and massively in debt, the celebrated treasures of the collections within the house had already begun to be sold and the house would lie in ruins by 1744. The greatest days of the early modern Pastons were in the decades before the Civil War, when Oxnead was lived in by William Paston, 1st Baronet (d. 1663) and his wife Lady Katherine Bertie (d. 1637). William was an early virtuoso, collecting everything rare and curious, and travelling beyond the usual Grand Tour routes into Egypt and Jerusalem. His cousin summed up the collections: 'I might spend another week and not see all the rarityes.'[24] As a patron, he was noted for being 'a great receiver of dedications' particularly during his Commonwealth exile.[25] His son and heir Robert (1631–83) was one of the first Fellows of the newly founded Royal Society, known for his interest in alchemy; he also hosted Charles II on the royal visit to Norfolk in 1671.[26] Created Earl of Yarmouth in 1679, he was heavily mortgaged and his son and heir William, 2nd Earl, maintained the family spending habits. The Yarmouth library collection is recorded in the great sale of 1734, of 1,513 lots, usually of one title each.[27] If multiple volumes are allowed for, this might mean up to 4,500 volumes requiring to be housed. The principal modern historian of the Pastons, R. W. Ketton-Cremer, was unable to give any examples of surviving Oxnead printed books.

The ill-luck of the Pastons at Oxnead extended to the two surviving daughters of the family. Lady Rebecca married Sir John Holland of Quidenham in 1698 but their son William, 3rd Baronet, died without a male heir in 1729. The Holland books from the substantial Jacobean house (surviving but much altered) were sold off: 1,591 titles (so a very similar scale to the Oxnead collection), mostly from the second half of the seventeenth century, including printed library catalogues.[28] In the absence of archives for the house, the location of the presumed library room is unknown.

The final house in this group of seventeenth-century collections is Hockwold Hall, home to Sir Cyril Wyche's collection, after his retirement from London law in the 1670s. This collection is known because it was sold by auction in 1710. The books are dated from the sixteenth century to the 1690s. The sale catalogue of *Bibliotheica Wichianii* was compiled from Sir Cyril's own manuscript catalogue of his books, with shelfmarks 'the whole appearing exactly as they stood in the library'. It is therefore possible to link the scale of the collection with the shelving required, for an estimated 2,400 titles housed in eleven cases of twelve shelves each and three cases of one, two and three shelves respectively (B, O and P). Shelf B was the last to be added, for an overflow of fourteen titles dated after 1699. This outline record of the disposition of cases around a large room provides the best view within this group of a lost library environment.

Lost books and lost rooms

There are a few other Norfolk country houses that must have held a reasonable collection of books by 1700; in the absence of evidence the presumption must be on the side of book ownership, and four are suggested in Table 11.1. Commissioning a book-plate suggests multiples of books to justify the expense of a personalised copperplate engraving. For example, Martin Folkes (1640–1705) (father of Sir Martin Folkes, President of the Society of Antiquaries), was a wealthy lawyer who married Dorothy Hovell of Hillington Hall, co-heir of her father. Hillington Hall became the Folkes estate and Folkes senior died in possession of a book-plate but that is all that is known about the Hillington books before the later eighteenth century; Dorothy's male forebears were scholars at Gonville and Caius College, Cambridge and should have been readers at Hillington. Other eighteenth-century libraries lack a prehistory: the Catholic Jerningham family, courtiers to Mary I, arrived at Costessey Hall in 1555 and rebuilt it in 1564. Eighteenth-century accounts show the family to be regular purchasers of books, and Sir George Jerningham (1680–1774) commissioned a book-plate, but nothing is known of earlier ownership. Right at the end of the period under discussion, the Wodehouses of Kimberley rebuilt their house in c.1700. Prior to that, the seventeenth-century baronets earned a reputation for gentlemanly accomplishments, hailed by Thomas Peacham 'as not only learned but accomplished in what ever may lend lustre to worth and true Gentilitie'. Sir Philip Wodehouse wrote of his father, 'His home-delights were musiq and a book': Sir Philip had inherited his father's manuscript music collection and would go on to name music books as heirlooms in his own will.[29]

Finally, the great friend and adviser on virtuoso matters to Viscount Townshend and the Earl of Leicester, Sir Andrew Fountaine (1676–1753), added a large library room by 1718 to his father's house, Narford Hall, constructed c.1702. Andrew Fountaine senior had made a Grand Tour with John Coke of Holkham, but there is currently no evidence for a preceding study or book collection, in the absence of provenance research on the surviving books.

On their own, these few examples are fragmentary hints, but taken with the previous examples of known collections, all of these families need to be understood as members of a county network, who intermarried, travelled on Grand Tours together and acted as trustees and executors for the children of their neighbours. The families who can be positioned within two of the three chronologies, for houses and for collections, can be joined by the families who can be represented in all three chronologies: build dates, book collections and the elusive pre-1700 library room evidence. These families, and there are eight of them (see Table 11.1) living at Hunstanton, Felbrigg, Ryston, Heydon, Stow Bardolph, Blickling, Melton Constable and Rougham Halls, point towards emerging patterns in gentry provision for book rooms within their houses.[30] *In toto*, all of these families suggest a great undercurrent of ownership and 'care of books'. The differential survival of early modern books and their rooms is primarily a problem of evidence for the modern historian, and not a guide to the realities of intensive household use of books in the daily life of a country house during the seventeenth century.

An interdisciplinary approach to the pre-1700 library

The shared project of reconstituting the intellectual culture of the early modern country house unifies many of the overarching questions, and source categories, across these chapters, but it also encourages reflection on where the evidence is found and how it is treated, methodologically and philosophically. This chapter is the product of a diametrically opposite training to the text-based disciplines, rather, it originates from the material culture methods and philosophies of archaeology and architectural history, and is written from within a university department of art history. It takes the book as an object, and treats the book room as social space: both objects and spaces are cultural projects subject to human interventions observed across cultures by anthropologists, as material manifestations of the ideational structures of daily life. This approach meets text-based disciplines within the field of the history of the book.[31]

The history of the book, framed as a total approach to the social, economic and cultural production and impact of the written word, was drawn together by the pioneering French historians Lucien Febvre and Henri-Jean Martin.[32] Their work emerged from over a century of European scholarship on the material conditions of production, circulation and to a more limited extent, consumption of the word, both in print and in manuscript form. The sea change was for greater attention to the social uses of books and for much of the evidence to be gathered from the material traces of books that have been repeatedly read, annotated, sold and repurchased. The total approach contrasted with specialist literary fields of textual analysis, concerned with tracing the relationship of texts (words as signs) rather than the relationship of objects (words as material marks). The former has been noted as the Anglo-American tradition, paying close attention to what has been published and to edition histories, but reluctant to investigate the wider contexts.[33]

Decades on from the first publication of *L'Apparition du Livre* in 1958, the social life of books underpins research projects of great breadth, in national 'histories of the book' as well as a steady flow of case studies of individual readers and digitised archives, notably the online resource Early English Books Online.[34] The consequences of a call for a total history approach to the written word have been noted as running to a potential for 'interdisciplinarity run riot'; in practice, divisions between work on book trades, reading and writing remain distinctive.[35] Chapter 10 represents the fruit of research that does take up the challenge of investigating how prospective readers interacted with the book trade; some country house owners interacted with riotous enthusiasm, even before the historical high point of bibliomania. Interdisciplinary rioting has, perhaps thanks to the contributions of the many research-active librarians in the book history community, been hushed in tone.

Interdisciplinarity is often a *de facto* series of practices for higher research in the humanities, although academic allegiances are usually expressed by traditional disciplines. Book historians tend to emerge from English departments to follow the infiltration of texts into social life, both historic and contemporary. More recent decades have produced cross-fertilisations, between literary historians who engage with political and wider cultural history (after the New Historicism), and social historians who take up the challenge of integrating visual and material sources into historical narrative. The 'material turn', as the latter shift has been called, has quite reasonably tended to produce research on aspects of undocumented lives of the urban middling and lower socio-economic classes.[36] The English country house as a field of material culture has remained largely the remit for the disciplines founded on an engagement with the aesthetic, namely art and architectural history.

An immediate challenge to this equation of the country house with aesthetics comes from the increasing amount of work produced by book historians investigating country house libraries, created from generations of their owners' interaction with the book trades discussed in Chapter 10. This work has been led in England by the National Trust's willingness to recognise the historical specificity of each of the libraries in the houses it holds in trust.[37] The scale of their surviving private library holdings has been until recently the dominant obstacle in producing the base-line bibliographical research (cataloguing as a term denies the complexity of bibliographic identification and description required for historic books) necessary for in-depth understanding of the process of acquisition, accumulation and use. New research is emerging; this volume is sustained by exactly this commitment to relating collections to their past readers, and to wider spatial and visual identities.

The absence of pre-1700 library rooms

The impact on the senses of a well-furnished country house is inevitable, thanks to the rich layering of visual and material textures and the iconographic and metatextual allusions available to the viewer, discussed throughout this book. Out of this richness, each of the present authors probably enters a historic house with a different research question in mind. Mine is invariably 'where was the first library?' Not, 'where is the library?', enjoyable though a surviving room full of books may be, but to ask what came before that room, making a private bet with the guidebook that the first library is either a 'known unknown' or not discussed. The pace of architectural remodelling or change of interior schemes is usually such that the nineteenth-century presentation of the library room bears little relation to the room for books used by seventeenth-century or earlier owners.

One of the earliest surviving library rooms in England, albeit one that lacks any fittings, is at Stoke Bruerne, Northamptonshire. Sir Francis Crane (1579–1636) commissioned a house, attributed to the first architect of the Palladian revival in England, Inigo Jones. The house, now gone, has two surviving pavilions attached to it by passages, one for the library and one for the chapel.[38] This is the library as architectural statement, something of a contrast with the other survivors. For the period up to 1700, it is the Duke of Lauderdale's tiny wood-lined book room in Ham House, Surrey, set up in 1674 and accessed from the upper floor gallery, that is inevitably held up as the sole survivor of its time.[39] Other surviving aristocratic library rooms include the attic library of Thomas Ken, Bishop of Bath and Wells (1637–1711), at Longleat. Sir Thomas Thynne, Viscount Weymouth, was the patron of Bishop Ken, who lived in the house after

1691 and who left his personal library there (housed in the attic storey). The ducal palace of Petworth, Sussex, displays a nineteenth-century library room on the ground floor, a location unknown to the Proud Duke who remodelled the house in the 1680s and whose old library survives over the medieval chapel. A surviving but little known (in private ownership) gentry library at Denham Place, Buckinghamshire, was fitted out in the 1690s. It is large enough to be lit by two windows, and is beautifully panelled so that bookshelves and decorative panelling are completely integrated. It is on the ground floor looking out from the original entrance façade.

The research problem, then, is not about whether there were book collections in early modern country houses (although there are pockets of empirical resistance to this collective conclusion) but there are still questions about the nature of these collections, their expected readers and how far the accumulation of library collections went down the stratified layers of the landed classes. How much would a country house owner wish to invest not only in books but in the 'care of books' within the house? Henry Peacham warned his early seventeenth-century readers of the dangers of displaying books without internalising the knowledge they contained: 'to be stored with bookes, and have well furnished Libraries, yet keep their heads empty of knowledge.'[40] Peacham seems to be drawing attention both to the practice of keeping numbers of books and of displaying them in library rooms. In the general absence of pre-1700 book rooms that can be visited, the library collections that have been examined have inevitably been discussed without a sense of the space that housed them. The few extant rooms make it extremely difficult to relate collections back convincingly to any detailed conclusions about their surroundings. This absence of a sense of the material environment matters if the 'material turn' is to make a difference to a historically situated understanding of the conditions of early modern lives. Collections need physical contexts, as well as intellectual arenas. An anthropologically informed approach suggests that objects and spaces act back on the viewer or user; shaped by human actors, the inanimate world acquires some animation in producing effects back on its creators.

Rooms are not just spaces for display, but environments that guide and prompt behaviours, or sometimes provoke dissenting actions such as iconoclasm. The occasional discovery of a tiny book secreted behind panelling or under floorboards may represent dissent from the household order of properly housed and diligently studied books. Samuel Pepys exerted his influence over disorderly books. While reordering his books he felt dissatisfied by the visual disorder resulting from slight variations in height; he corrected this by inserting wooden blocks to remedy the departure from the ideal. He commissioned portable book cases to his own design to hold his collection and selected portraits of friends to hang above them. Pepys created a very specific combination of visual and material elements to produce his own sense of order; exceptionally, books, cases, drawings of the interior scheme and Pepys's own written account of his activities survive.[41] It seems fair to assume that the finished scheme continued to 'give' pleasure back to Pepys each time he contemplated what he had achieved: 'giving' used here in the sense that objects can have agency.

What we know about Pepys's last library room is exceptional, and it is unclear how representative it is as the product of a metropolitan lifestyle. If he initiated a distinctive style for free-standing bookcases, there is little evidence for their adoption beyond survivors at Dyrham Park, Gloucestershire. For the lost country houses, replaced by their wealthy owners or demolished by their impoverished heirs, rooms for books seem to leave few sources.

The 'three chronologies' proposed here for the relationship between the build date of the house, the evidence for books and the evidence for a book room will probably never be brought into alignment. However, clarifying the existence of these three threads of development should be useful for the disciplines who meet at the country house as a locus for intellectual history. Such a history is not disembodied, and the physical environment of the early modern country house remains a fruitful research area for questions about social practices as the expressions of interior lives.

Notes

1   G. Naudé, *Instructions Concerning Erecting of a Library*, trans. J. Evelyn (London: G. Bedle, T. Collins, J. Crook, 1661), p. 14.

2   J. W. Clark, *The Care of Books* (Bristol and Tokyo: Thoemmes and Kinokuniya, 1997).

3   H. M. Weber, *Paper Bullets: Print and Kingship under Charles II* by (Lexington, KY: University Press of Kentucky, 1996 [1902]); J. M. Lander, *Inventing Polemic: Religion, Print, and Literary Culture in Early Modern England* (Cambridge: Cambridge University Press, 2006); L. Knight. *Of Books and Botany in Early Modern England: Sixteenth-Century Plants and Print Culture* (Aldershot: Ashgate, 2009); J. A. Knapp, *Illustrating the Past in Early Modern England: The Representation of History in Printed Books* (Aldershot: Ashgate, 2003).

4   K. Sharpe, 'The King's Writ: Royal Authors and Royal Authority in Early Modern England', in K. Sharpe, *Remapping Early Modern England, the Culture of Seventeenth Century Politics* (Cambridge: Cambridge University Press, 2000), pp. 127–50; J. Raymond, 'Irrational, Impracticable and Unprofitable: Reading the News in Seventeenth-Century Britain', in K. Sharpe and S. Zwicker (eds), *Reading, Society and Politics in Early Modern England* (Cambridge: Cambridge University Press, 2003), pp. 185–212; B. Cowan, *The Social Life of Coffee: the Emergence of the British Coffeehouse* (New Haven, CT and London: Yale University Press, 2005); J. Broadway, 'No historie so meete', *Gentry Culture and the Development of Local History in Elizabethan and Early Stuart England* (Manchester: Manchester University Press, 2006); M. Mendle, 'Preserving the Ephemeral: Reading, Collecting and the Pamphlet Culture of Seventeenth-Century England', in J. Anderson and E. Sauer (eds), *Books and Readers in Early Modern England* (Philadelphia: University of Pennsylvania Press, 2002), pp. 201–16.

5   E. J. Clery, *The Feminisation Debate in Eighteenth-Century England* (London: Palgrave Macmillan, 2004), see particularly Chapter 1.

6   Although Harold Love drew attention to the role of the country house in his *Scribal Publication in Seventeenth-Century England* (Oxford: Clarendon Press, 1993), pp. 197–202.

7   The data has been drawn from my wider survey, S. West, 'The Origins and Development of the Private Library in Norfolk Country Houses, 1660–1830' (PhD dissertation, University of East Anglia, 2001).

8   The latter eight houses are discussed as part of the presentation of evidence for book rooms in the date range 1660–1720 as the basis for an architectural typology in S. West 'An Architectural Typology for the Early Modern Country House, 1660–1720', *The Library*, 14:4 (2013), 441–64.

9   C. E. Moreton, 'The "Library" of a Late-Fifteenth-Century Lawyer', *The Library*, 6th series, 13 (1991), 338–46, citing Norwich Record Office (hereafter NRO) MS1503, 1D2.

10   Chest is a debatable term, referring to permanent fittings in the studies of Renaissance Italy: D. Thornton, *The Scholar in His Study: Ownership and Experience in Renaissance Italy* (New Haven, CT and London: Yale University Press, 1997), pp. 68–9; S. West, 'Studies and Status: Spaces for Books in Sixteenth-Century Penshurst Place, Kent', *Transactions of the Cambridge Bibliographical Society*, 12 (2002), 271–2.

11   Moreton, '"Library" of a Lawyer', p. 339 citing British Library (hereafter BL) Add. Mss 41, 139, fol. 23.

12   L. Campbell, 'Documentary Evidence for the Building of Raynham Hall', *Architectural History*, 32 (1989), 52–67 citing Raynham Hall archive, Bickerton's Account Book; H. Bradfer-Lawrence, 'The Building of Raynham Hall', *Norfolk Archaeology*, 23 (1929), 93–146.

13   R. T. Gunther (ed.), *The Architecture of Sir Roger Pratt* (New York, 1979 [1928]), pp. 132–3 citing Ryston Hall archive, Folio f.2.

14   R. Blomfield, 'Raynham Hall, Norfolk', *Journal of the Royal Institute of British Architects*, 3rd series, 33:18 (1926), 527–9; Bradfer-Lawrence 'Raynham Hall', pp. 141–3.

15   See C. W. James, *Chief Justice Coke, His Family and Descendants at Holkham* (London: Country Life, 1929) and A. M. W. Stirling, *Coke of Norfolk and His Friends* (London: John Lane, 1912), particularly James, pp. 2, 4; W. O. Hassall, *The Holkham Library, Illuminations and Illustrations in the Manuscript Library of the Earl of Leicester* (Oxford: Roxburghe Club, 1970), p. 5; Holkham Hall (hereafter HH), Norfolk, ms F/TC1 'Minutes of T. Coke's Guardians, 1707–14', p. 60, 14 April 1708; HH MS F/TC1, 'Minutes', p. 39 18 December 1707; Hassall, *Holkham Library*, p. 10 citing Bodleian Library, Oxford, Ms Rawl. D888, Fol. 15; HH MS F/TC1, 'Minutes', p. 77, 14 May 1708.

16   D. McKitterick, '"Ovid with a Littleton": the Cost of English Books in the Early Seventeenth Century', *Transactions of the Cambridge Bibliographical Society*, 11 (1997), 184–234.

17   The house with the 1588 study probably survived (extended) until 1721, although J. Harris suggests post-1660 renewal: 'The Architecture of the House', in A. Moore (ed.), *Houghton Hall, the Prime Minister, the Empress and the Heritage* (Norwich and London, Norfolk Museums Service/Philip Wilson, 1996), p. 20.

18   Burwell of Rougham Hall, Suffolk, provenance in Sotheby, *December 6, 1955, Books from the Library of Sir Robert Walpole at Houghton Hall, Norfolk* (London: Sotheby, 1955), lots 396–413; J. H. Plumb, *Sir Robert Walpole, the Making of a Statesman* (London: Cresset Press, 1956), pp. 81–2, citing Roger North.

19   Plumb, *Walpole*, pp. 82–3; Houghton Hall archive, RB 1/51 inventory, Robert Walpole May 1, 1663; Houghton Hall archive, Library, L.8a.1 MS library catalogue, 1717.

20   By kind permission of the Marquess of Cholmondeley; 'Interim Catalogue of the Library at Houghton Hall', December 1998 (unpublished); dated titles examined from 1500–1810, showing clusters of over 40 titles each decade for the later seventeenth century; for 1720–40 and for 1780.

21 Now owned by the National Trust; some of the book lots were bought back, sale catalogue retained by the National Trust: Charles Hawkins and Sons of King's Lynn, *Oxborough Hall, 31 October, 1 November 1951*.

22 J. Britton, *The Architectural Antiquities of Great Britain*, 5 vols (London: Longman, 1807–35), vol. II (1809), p. 87.

23 J. H. Pollen, 'Bedingfeld Papers', Catholic Record Society, Miscellanea 6, vol. 7 (1909), pp. 1–92. NRO, MF/RO 235/11 Norwich Consistory Court, 'Will Sir Henry Bedingfeld, March 1684'.

24 R. W. Ketton-Cremer, *Norfolk Assembly* (London: Faber, 1957), p. 26.

25 Ketton-Cremer, *Assembly*, p. 36.

26 D. R. Dickson, 'Thomas Henshaw and Sir Robert Paston's Pursuit of the Red Elixir: an Early Collaboration between Fellows of the Royal Society', *Notes and Records of The Royal Society*, 51 (1997), 57–76. (MLA International Bibliography, EBSCO host accessed 6 February 2013).

27 O. Payne, *A Catalogue of the Library of the Right Honourable the Earl of Yarmouth* (London, 1734); discussed in Ketton-Cremer, *Assembly*, p. 200.

28 H. Cross-grove, *Bibliotheca Hollandiana, sive Catalogus Librorum In quaris Facultate Insignium A Viro Honorabili ac Erudito Domino Johanne Holland Baronetto, De Quidenham in Comitatu Norfolciae* (Norwich, 1729).

29 H. Peacham, *The Compleat Gentleman*, 2nd impression (London: Francis Constable 1634), p. 192; F. Blomefield, *An Essay towards a Topographical History of the County of Norfolk*, 11 vols. (London, 1805), vol. 2, p. 539; J. Wodehouse, Earl of Kimberley, *The Wodehouses of Kimberley* (privately printed, 1887) p. 49; R. W. Ketton-Cremer, 'The Rhyming Wodehouses', *Norfolk Archaeology*, 33 (1962), 35–42.

30 These houses and the evidence for considering the book rooms are discussed in West, 'Architectural Typology'.

31 The turn to materiality can be seen in L. Price, 'From *The History of a Book* to a "History of the Book"', *Representations*, 108:1 (2009), 120–38; T. Hamling and C. Richardson (eds), *Everyday objects: Medieval and Early Modern Material Culture and its Meanings* (Farnham: Ashgate, 2010); S. Frye, *Pens and Needles: Women's Textualities in Early Modern England* (Philadelphia and Oxford: University of Pennsylvania Press, 2010).

32 L. Febvre and H. Martin, *L'Apparition du Livre* (Paris: Editions Albin Michel, 1958); trans. D. Gerard as *The Coming of the Book: the Impact of Printing 1450–1800* (London: NLB, 1976).

33 J. Feather, 'Cross-Channel Current: Historical Bibliography and l'histoire du livre', *The Library*, 6th series, 2:1 (1980), 1–16.

34 For example, the multi-volume *Cambridge History of the Book in Britain*, 6 vols (Cambridge: Cambridge University Press, 1999–2011).

35 A scholar in the French tradition, Robert Darnton hoped for creative interdisciplinary work, cited in a useful overview of the field by E. Jacobs, 'Buying into Classes: the Practice of Book Selection in Eighteenth-Century Britain', *Eighteenth-Century Studies*, 33 (1999), 43–64, p. 43.

36 L. Cowan Orlin (ed.), *Material London c.1600* (Philadelphia and Oxford: University of Pennsylvania Press, 2000).

37 The exhibition and accompanying catalogue marked a shift in approach, N. Barker ed., *Treasures from the Libraries of National Trust Country Houses* (New York: The Royal Oak Foundation and The Grolier Club, 1999).

38 G. Worsley, *Inigo Jones and the European Classicist Tradition* (New Haven, CT and London: The Paul Mellon Centre for Studies in British Art, Yale University Press, 2007), p. 112;

A. Gomme and A. Maguire, *Design and Plan in the Country House, from Castle Donjons to Palladian Boxes* (New Haven, CT and London: Yale University Press, 2008), p. 275, plan 218.

39 C. Rowell, *Ham House: Four Hundred Years of Collecting and Patronage* (New Haven, CT and London: Paul Mellon Centre for Studies in British Art, Yale University Press, 2013).

40 Peacham, *Compleat Gentleman*, p. 54.

41 Margaret Willes, *Reading Matters: Five Centuries of Discovering Books* (New Haven, CT and London: Yale University Press, 2011), Chapter 2, pp. 51–4.

12

'My Laydes Bookes att Noward …': book use and book storage at Naworth Castle in the late seventeenth century

Hannah DeGroff

A plainly bound, folio copy of Monsieur de Vaumoriere's *The Grand Scipio: An Excellent New Romance* (London, 1660) which once belonged to Elizabeth, 2nd Countess of Carlisle (1646–96) can be found today at Castle Howard, the Yorkshire country house that became the Howard family's main country seat at the beginning of the eighteenth century. Fifteen hand-drawn profiles appear out of the folds from the opening pages of this volume. The swept-back hairstyles date their creation to the decades that immediately followed the book's publication (Figure 12.1). Neither the artist nor the sitter(s) are known. The name 'E: Morpeth' written alongside these sketches is the only indication of their origin. Following her marriage in 1668 to Edward Howard, 2nd Earl of Carlisle (1646–92), Elizabeth adopted her husband's courtesy title, Morpeth, as her last name.

Prior to the eighteenth century, Naworth Castle in Cumbria had been the primary country seat of the Earls of Carlisle. Situated fifteen miles north-east of the city of Carlisle, it is perhaps best known today as the home of the antiquarian Lord William Howard (1563–1640). In the second half of the seventeenth century, this rural residence, which had been castellated in 1335, housed a number of individual book collections including Howard's celebrated library of incunabula and rare manuscripts.[1] A booklist dated 1693 also records the presence of the personal library of the 2nd Countess of Carlisle, the wife of Howard's great-great grandson. Offering insight into one aristocratic woman's engagement with books in rural Cumbria, what follows adds to our growing knowledge of women's reading practices in the early modern period. Focusing attention on Morpeth's collection, this chapter examines the role that books played at Naworth in the final decades of the seventeenth century. It will consider where the Countess's books might have been stored as well as the significance of

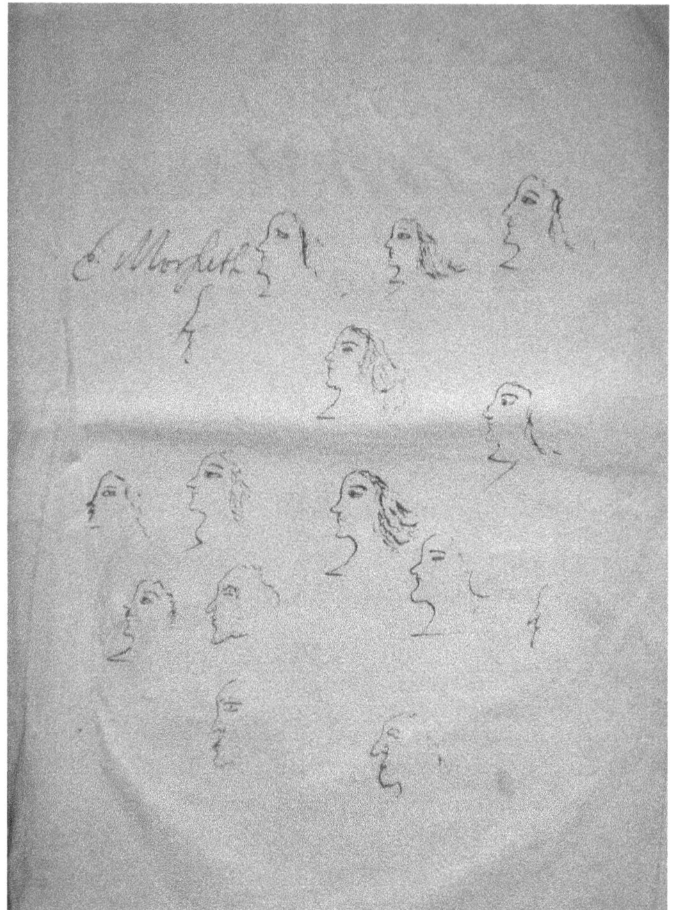

12.1   Detail from Monsieur de Vaumoriere's *The Grand Scipio* (1660).

the fact that her collection was kept apart from Howard's, and also demonstrate the ways in which other figures in the household, including the Countess's young children, made use of her library. Emphasising the domestic nature of reading and book use, it also contributes to the current volume's exploration of country houses as sites of textual and intellectual engagement.

Morpeth was born in the midst of the English Civil War to Sir William Uvedale of Wickham in Hampshire and his wife, Victoria Cary. Little is known of her first husband, Sir William Berkeley, whom she married at a young age. After his death at sea she entered into one of northern England's leading aristocratic families through marriage to the 2nd Earl of Carlisle. The couple had four sons but only the first survived into adulthood. Two daughters, Mary and Ann, also died young. In 1696, at the age of fifty, the Countess died and

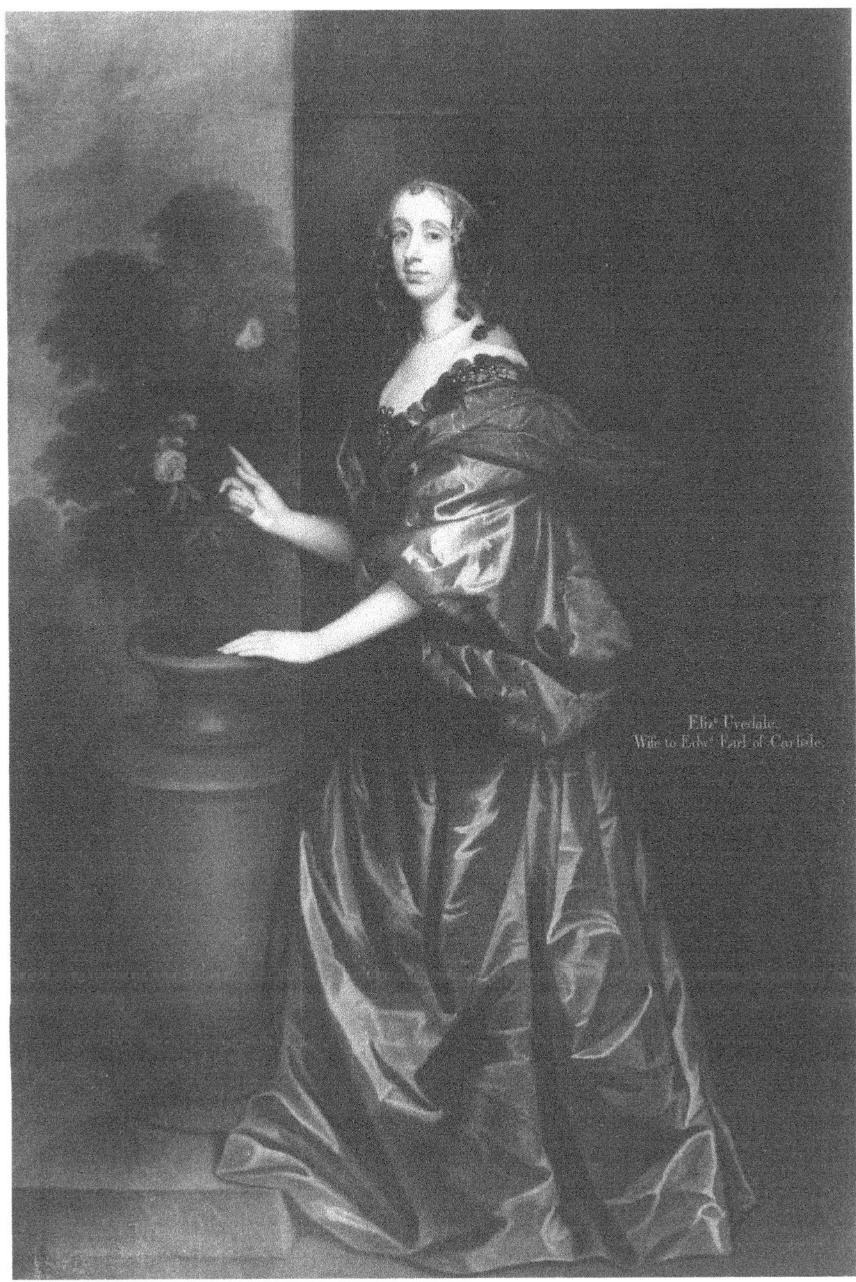

12.2 Elizabeth Uvedale, 2nd Countess of Carlisle, Peter Lely, date unknown.

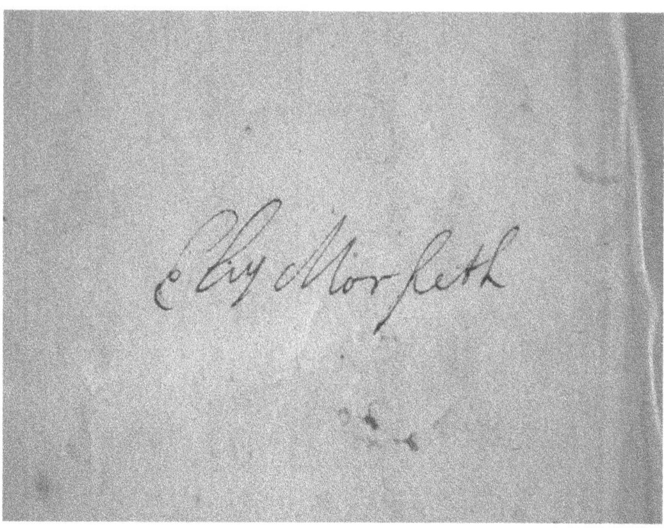

12.3   'Eliz Morpeth', in Madame de Scudéry's *The Grand Cyrus*, vol. 4 (1655).

was subsequently buried alongside her husband and father in the parish church in Wickham. A Restoration portrait by the artist Sir Peter Lely highlights her membership of London's fashionable society (Figure 12.2, date unknown). Little more is known, however, about her life, either in London or at Naworth Castle.[2] The discovery of the 1693 booklist, therefore, as well as marginalia in several extant books from the Countess's collection, not only enables the reconstruction of the intellectual world in which she participated in Cumbria but assists in our understanding of her social and cultural life at Naworth Castle.[3]

Inscriptions in six more volumes now at Castle Howard confirm Morpeth's ownership of multiple books. These ownership markings reflect her shifting social identity, for at various times she signs herself Elisabeth Morpeth (Figure 12.3), The Right Honourable The Lady Morpeth (Figure 12.4), and the Countess of Carlisle (Figure 12.5). In one instance, at the bottom of an end-paper in Joseph Beaumont's *Psyche: Or, love's mystery* (London, 1648) we also find her monogram 'EM'. As the images reveal, these inscriptions were written by two distinct hands. The first, apparent in Figures 12.3 and 12.5, was that of the Countess. The identity of the second, seen in Figure 12.4, is unknown. As the style of this second hand is more formally constructed, hinting at some kind of writing instruction, this second writer might have been her husband, a learned companion, or household secretary.

Leaving aside the simple pleasure that comes from inscribing one's name in a newly acquired book, there are a number of reasons why the Countess might have placed her name within these volumes.[4] Her membership of a community

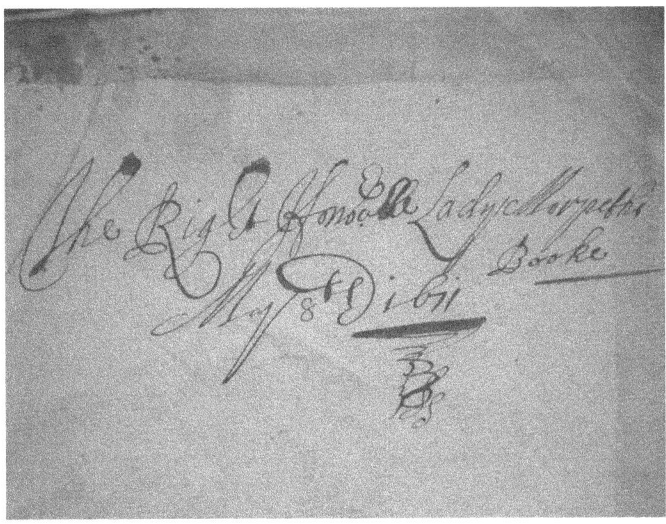

12.4 'The Right Honourable The Lady Morpeth', in Monsieur de Vaumoriere's *The Grand Scipio* (1660).

in which books were lent out to friends and acquaintances is suggested by a faint inscription in the fourth volume of another of her books, Madame de Scudéry's *Artamènes : Or, the Grand Cyrus* (London, 1653–55). It reads 'Thomas Ingram/ But not his Book/ 1667'. This type of marking leads us to believe that the exchange of books was not uncommon across the social networks in which the Countess participated.[5] One Sarah Downing has tentatively inscribed her name above that of the Countess in the third volume of de Scudéry's heroic novel, signalling what Sara Mendelson has identified as 'the dynamic quality of [early modern] female activities, the continual transformation of objects from one form to another, the constant circulation of possessions and commodities from one woman or household to another'.[6] These signatures indicate that at various times people outside of the Howard family utilised books from the Countess's library.

A second possible reason why the Countess placed ownership markings in her books is that she needed to distinguish volumes from others within her own household. Tradition has it that during the first half of the seventeenth century, when Lord William Howard and his wife were resident, the castle and its surrounding estate were over-run with their children, children's spouses, and their grandchildren (a total of fifty-two at one point).[7] This type of domestic set-up continued at Naworth in the late seventeenth century when the 2nd Countess resided there. In the 1680s and 1690s her eldest son, the future 3rd Earl of Carlisle, also lived at Naworth with his wife and young family. It was during these years in Cumbria that he began to amass his own personal book collection

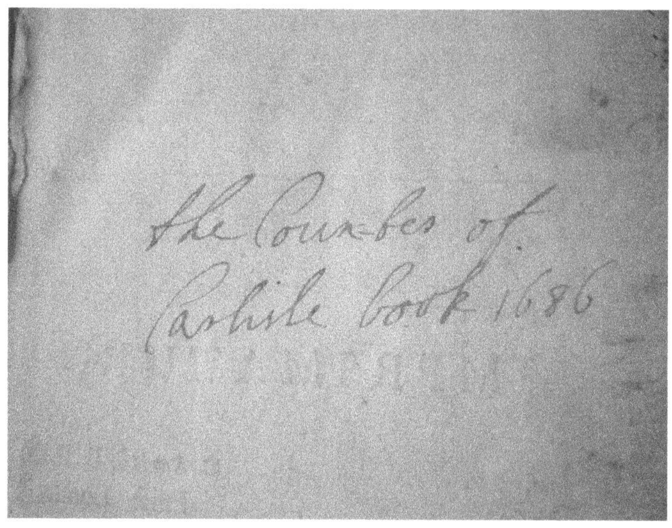

12.5   'Countess of Carlisle', in Thomas Comber's *Companion to the Altar* (1678).

which would eventually go on to form the basis of the Castle Howard library.[8] His wife, Anne Capel, Lady Carlisle (1674–1752), also had a book collection.[9] There is every chance that she brought to Naworth some of the same books that were in her mother-in-law's library. De Scudéry's *Artamènes* , for instance, was a highly popular work throughout the seventeenth century. It appeared in many an elite woman's library including that of Elizabeth Pepys, the wife of the famed diarist.[10] Fifty years after the work's initial publication, it also featured in an account of a lady's library in *The Spectator*, an appearance which suggests it remained popular even at the end of the century.[11]

The type of domestic arrangement found at Naworth in the seventeenth century was not unusual in the early modern period yet it is one that is all too often overlooked when book use in country houses is examined. Such a large household would have engendered a variety of textual encounters for all sorts of people with all kinds of texts. Recognising the possibility that multiple book collections belonging to different family members often existed concurrently in an early modern country house is important for a number of reasons. Not only does it mean that we can start identifying the different types of textual interactions that occurred in large and complex households, but it also allows us to understand more fully the palimpsest-like mode through which aristocratic book collections were formed. Furthermore, it brings to light the possibility that both individual *and* collective libraries were present under one roof. The identification of the presence of such collections within a country house demands an evaluation of how these different types of libraries were utilised alongside each other. Details of Morpeth's personal library are found in a booklist entitled

My Laydes Bookes att Noward Augt. 31: 1693 (Figures 12.6 and 12.7).[12] The survival of this document means that the Countess joins a handful of early modern aristocratic women whose book collections can be reconstructed.[13] *My Laydes Bookes att Noward* bears similarities to another aristocratic woman's booklist from the seventeenth century: that which details the library of Frances Egerton, Countess of Bridgewater (1585–1636).[14] *A Catalogue of my Ladies Bookes at London*, a title that recalls that of Morpeth's booklist, lists 241 books by size and then by subject and author. A number of texts, including sixteenth-century editions of Cervante's *Don Quixote*, Matthew Hale's *Contemplations Moral and Divine*, a collection of Shakespeare's plays, a biography of Elizabeth I, and volumes of Balzac's letters and Bacon's essays, appear in both booklists. In her research on Egerton's book collection, Heidi Brayman Hackel notes that, because they often had more than one home (in town and in the country, for example), aristocratic women were likely to have multiple book collections.[15] This possibility could explain the duplication of some books, including Jeremy Taylor's *The Worthy Communicant* (first published in London in 1660) in the 2nd Countess of Carlisle's booklist.

In total, 143 books are recorded in Morpeth's booklist. They are divided into two categories but, unlike Egerton's list, there does not appear to be any categorisation within these sections. It is unclear whether the booklist reflects how the volumes were organised at Naworth, on open shelves, in trunks, or possibly in cupboards. The first section contains texts of practical divinity and other religious works, including, for example, 'a Large New Testimt', 'Direccions to praye', 'method for meditacons' and 'A Guid to divotion'.[16] Milton's *Paradise Lost* (first published in 1667) appears in this section indicating that in Morpeth's household at least it was conceived as a textual aid to practical devotion.[17] The second part of the list is headed 'History Books' though this does not fully encompass the variety of subjects that it encompasses. Along with a handful of books which detailed British and world history, for instance 'The life & Raigne of Henry 8th', 'The Life of queen Eliz:', 'The History of Barbadoes', and 'A discourse of Jamica', we find works of poetry such as 'Wallers Poems', 'Sr Jo Sucklings fragmts', and 'Cleavlands poems'. 'Shakspeares history & Comedyes' would have sat alongside works of classical literature, including 'Homers odysses' and 'The History of Thucydides'. The Countess also owned books of epigrams and songs; one work in this second part is listed simply as 'Mr Brooms songes'.

As far as I can determine, all the works recorded in Morpeth's booklist were published in English. Translations enabled access to foreign-language texts and her library included, for instance, English editions of Balzac's letters, Lucian's *Dialogues*, and the Duc de Rohan's memoirs.[18] One entry that reads 'Memoryes dutchs mazaraine' signifies Morpeth's ownership of the memoirs of Hortense Mancini, Duchess of Mazarin, the niece of Cardinal Mazarin. Notably, these memoirs include details of Mancini's scandalous time as Charles II's mistress.[19]

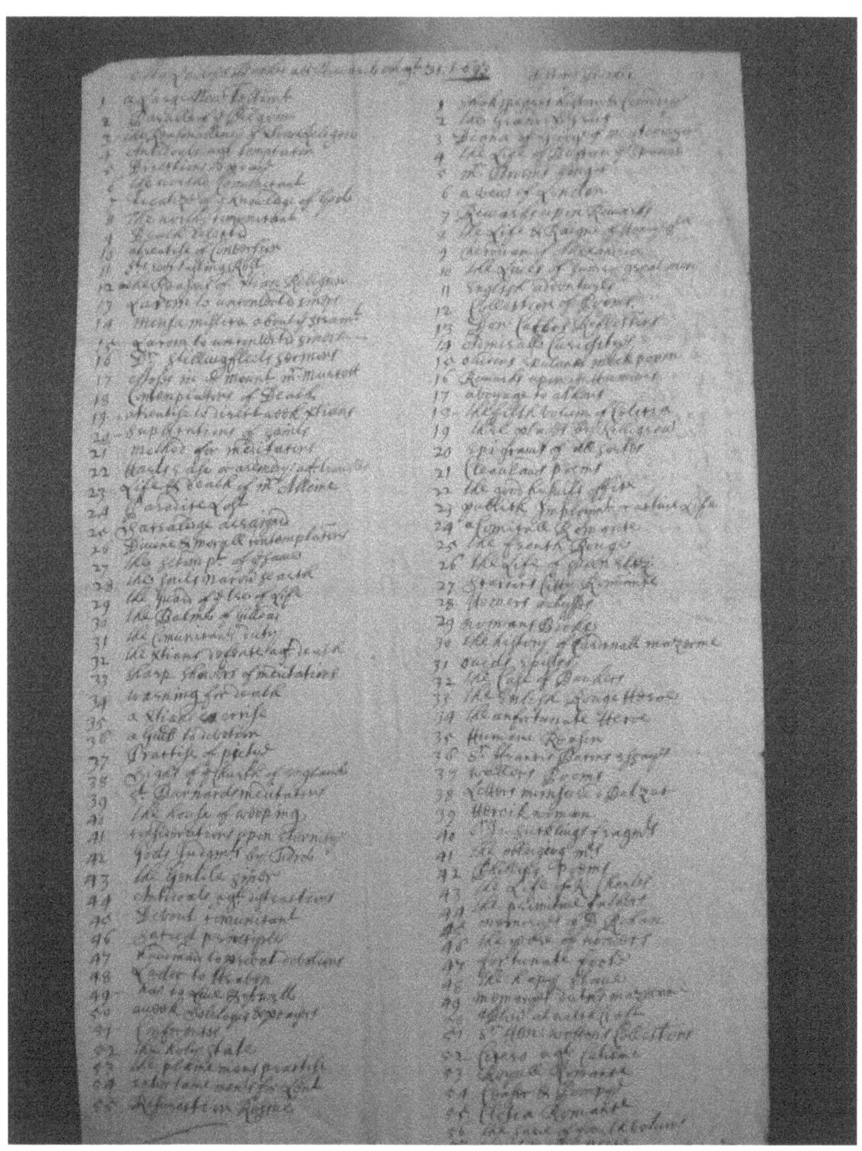

12.6   *My Laydes Bookes att Noward Augt. 31: 1693* (front) Castle Howard Archive, H/2/3/6.

The Countess's interest in other (in)famous female figures is attested by the inclusion in her collection of a work recorded on the booklist as 'Heroik woman'. Though works detailing the lives of learned and celebrated women were numerous in the seventeenth century, the translation of *The Gallery of Heroick*

12.7 *My Laydes Bookes att Noward Augt. 31: 1693* (back) Castle Howard Archive, H/2/3/6.

Women by the Marquess of Winchester published in London by Henry Seile in 1652 seems the most likely volume for Morpeth to have owned.[20]

The separation of the Countess's religious works from her secular books in *My Laydes Bookes att Noward* highlights the division which characterised female reading habits in the early modern period. As one book historian has pointed out, women (and in particular wealthy women) could choose whether they wanted to be devoted or diverted.[21] Whilst Morpeth's dedication to devotional reading is apparent in the many works of practical divinity that appear in the first section of her booklist, the appearance of numerous romances and other types of light-hearted literature (both of English and continental origin) in the second part of the list suggests that she was equally willing to be diverted. We have already encountered two of these works, de Vaumoriere's *Grand Scipio* and de Scudéry's *Artamènes*, but many others were present, including 'Love Letters from a nun', 'A Comicall Romance', 'Royall Romances' and 'Scarrens Citty Romances'. The Countess also had two copies each of Gabriello Faerno's *The French Rogue being a Pleasant History of his life and fortune, adorned with variety of other adventures of no less rarity ...* (London, 1672) and Richard Head's *The English Rogue Described, in the life of Meriton Latroon, a witty extravagant. Being a compleat discovery of the most eminent cheats of both sexes*, first published in London in 1665.

The presence of such recreational works in the Countess of Carlisle's collection highlights how the social and cultural restrictions which had limited women's reading in earlier centuries were, by the seventeenth century, on the whole overcome.[22] In fact, from as far back as the sixteenth century authors like Robert Greene and John Lyly had been targeting female audiences with their romantic prose fiction. At the same time, however, the increasing ability by women to collect and read romances also provoked anxiety about what constituted suitable reading material for them.[23] Indeed, by the last decades of the seventeenth century, women's reading of romances was seen as symptomatic of the fact that figures like Morpeth had the requisite leisure time to buy recreational texts.[24] This reasoning, in turn, contributed to the negative assumption that aristocratic women, particularly when resident in the countryside, lived idle existences, reading books of no practical value.[25]

Other texts that feature in Morpeth's booklist reveal, however, that at the end of the seventeenth century aristocratic women remained very much involved in the management of England's country houses. A number of books signal a clear domestic element to the Countess's reading habits and the inclusion of John Evelyn's *Public Employment and an Active Life* (London, 1667) suggests that she was at least aware of contemporary defences against idle, solitary living. 'The female reader', Amanda Vickery has observed, 'could study sermons preaching domesticity in one mood and philosophies praising active citizenship in another.'[26]

At certain times within an early modern household, then, reading was, as Naomi Tadmor has argued, 'connected not to idleness, listlessness or frivolity but to a routine of work'.[27] Alongside a publication which was recorded in the booklist as 'The good huswifs office', two books offering medical advice

('The skilfull phisian' and 'A mannuell of Phisick') suggest that the Countess was actively involved in running her household, a role which often included the making and administering of medicinal remedies and treatments for both family and servants.[28] One work, recorded in the booklist as 'Womans Booke', encourages us to think about how women utilised practical manuals within an aristocratic household.[29] This entry probably refers to a seventeenth-century edition of the popular sixteenth-century medical treatise *The Birth of Mankind: Otherwise Named, the Woman's Book*.[30] *The Woman's Book*, the contents of which had been gathered together by a number of practitioners over the course of almost two centuries, was an important guide to female and reproductive health used by generations of women in the early modern period. The inclusion of Andreas Vesalius's anatomical diagrams from the 1545 edition onwards meant that both literate and illiterate women could engage with the fundamentals of conception, pregnancy and childbirth. Such a possibility was of particular necessity in more rural areas (like north-east Cumbria) where speedy access to a trained physician would have been difficult and female household members and neighbours would have been important local practitioners.[31] As Morpeth's copy of *The Woman's Book* does not survive, we have no evidence of whether other women at Naworth read her edition. Yet the indispensable content of this large and unwieldy text certainly suggests that it would have engendered communal reading within a household. Indeed, its English editor and contributor, Thomas Reynalde, specified in his introduction that the information it provided 'is now so plainly set forth, that the simplest midwife which can read, may both understand for her better instruction, and also other women that have need of her help.'[32]

The recording of the 2nd Countess of Carlisle's library as separate from other book collections at Naworth Castle prompts us to revisit critical assumptions regarding book organisation in rural, aristocratic houses in the early modern period. It is unclear who compiled Morpeth's booklist or why; it is also hard to tell whether its creation was motivated by financial or bibliographical concerns. The running numbers alongside each of the book titles in conjunction with the omission of pressmarks suggests that it was an inventory rather than a catalogue or index. While written in a regular, neat style, inaccuracies and inconsistencies in spelling indicate that whoever compiled the list was not copying directly from the title-pages of the Countess's books. Though not proven, the handwriting bears similarities to the second, more formal hand which inscribed Morpeth's name in a number of her books.

The death of the 2nd Earl of Carlisle sixteen months before the list was written is likely to be a significant factor in its compilation. The accession of the couple's eldest son to the earldom in 1692, and his subsequent inheritance of the family's properties (including Naworth), would have prompted a need to establish the ownership of various personal belongings in these households. Fold marks across the piece of paper signal that at some point the list was likely enclosed within a letter, possibly sent to someone for inspection or record purposes.[33] Distinguishing the Countess's books from those belonging to other members of her family, its creation could indicate the relocation of Morpeth and her personal effects to her family home in Wickham, freeing up Naworth for the new Earl and his young family.

While we can learn much about Morpeth's reading habits from assessing individual entries in her booklist, locating where the collection was stored at Naworth and how it was used within a physical space broadens our understanding of aristocratic female book use in the early modern period. The traditional layout of medieval and early renaissance English country houses, including Naworth, was highly social. Built around an inner courtyard, and often lacking separate entranceways and private staircases, interaction between family members, visitors, and servants was inevitable in such a structured space.[34] The sociability engendered by this type of architectural design affected both book use and book storage in the early modern period.

Marginalia found in Morpeth's four volumes of de Scudéry's *Artamènes* indicates that the book culture which was present at Naworth in the late seventeenth century was highly sociable. While no annotations appear alongside the text itself, the end papers and flyleaves of the four volumes are the site of much scribbling. Though the markings in question reveal little about the Countess's engagement with de Scudéry's work, they do convey the social and textual interactions that occurred between Morpeth, her children, her books, and other members of the household at Naworth. At the front of the fourth volume we find an early attempt by the future 3rd Earl of Carlisle at writing his name alongside a drawing of what was perhaps intended to be the hind legs of a dog (Figure 12.8). In the third volume we see that, with the adolescent flourish of a young girl taking pleasure in the act of inscribing her name, his sister, Mary, had written her name just below that of their mother's (Figure 12.9). These markings indicate the presence of children in the same spaces where books were read at Naworth. Playful spiral scratch marks on the leather bindings of some of the volumes further support this proposal.[35] They also suggest that either Morpeth did not consider her books to be precious objects or that her young children managed, at some point, to gain unsupervised access to the collection. Early modern reading was, according to Robert A. Gross, 'a shared pastime' that 'became a valued site for the cultivation of more informal, mutual, affectionate relations.'[36] In this particular instance, however, it was not the act of reading that cultivated familial relations but rather the book as object which became a key site for the development of mother-child bonds.

Other handwriting in these volumes of *Artamènes* gives the impression that Morpeth was happy for her books to be utilised as practical objects. The

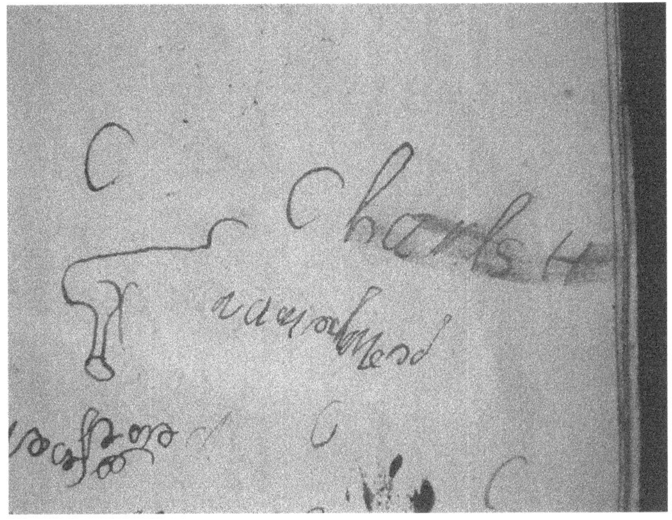

12.8 Detail from Madame de Scudéry's *The Grand Cyrus*, vol. 4 (1655).

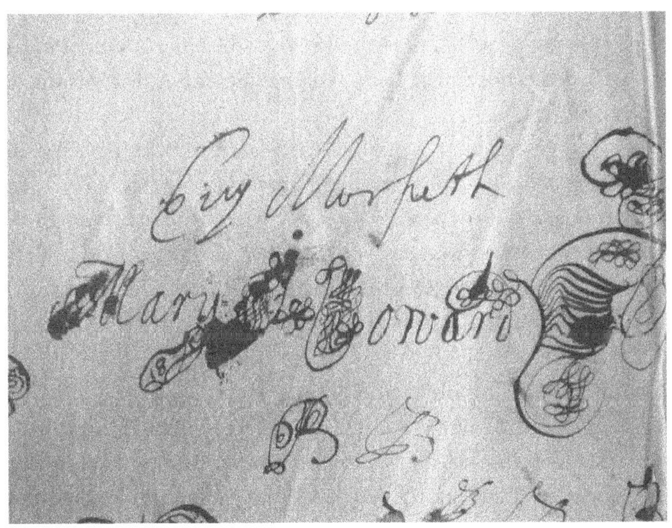

12.9 'Mary Howard', in Madame de Scudéry's *The Grand Cyrus*, vol. 3 (1654).

discovery of 'Thee Cotess of Carlliules Buters Byle' in the third volume further highlights the active, domestic setting in which the book was used (Figure 12.10). The bill records that Morpeth was to pay just over 40s for a shoulder and leg of mutton and 30s 60d for a turkey. Was this information recorded on one of the front pages of de Scudéry's novel by a servant?[37] Or was it relayed by

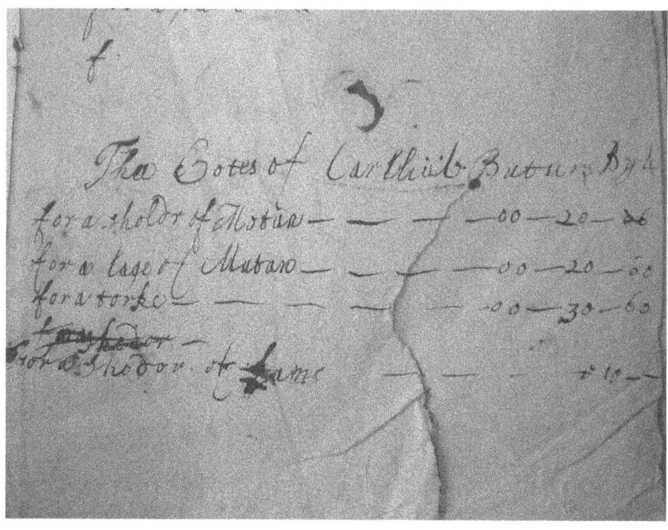

12.10 'Thee Cotess of Carlliules Buters Byle', in Madame de Scudéry's *The Grand Cyrus*, vol. 3 (1655).

one and quickly jotted down by someone else, the Countess's young daughter perhaps? The logging of what meat the Howard family ordered and how much it cost shows that the boundary between intellectual and domestic spheres at Naworth was permeable.[38]

It has been suggested that women in the early modern period dealt with the cultural segregation of the sexes by creating 'their own culture, in part, by demarcating and controlling their own space'.[39] Can we see such an appropriation of space and material goods in the way that the 2nd Countess and other members of the household, in particular her children and staff, used her books at Naworth? In order to answer this question we must consider Morpeth's collection in light of Lord William Howard's library which was present in the house while the Countess and her young family resided there.

Howard had, in the first decades of the seventeenth century, gathered together an impressive collection of manuscripts, books, and incunabula via his extensive social and antiquarian connections.[40] Though he died in 1640, his antiquarian library remained *in situ* until the twentieth century in the castle's south-east tower, guarded by a heavy iron door and accessed by a single-width stone staircase.[41] All in all, it is not surprising that individuals, whether male or female, kept their books separate from other collections at Naworth. On a practical level, the cramped, medieval structure would have certainly restricted the storage of books on a large scale, unlike those libraries which began to appear in the country houses of the early eighteenth century. The separation between Morpeth's and Howard's books plausibly reflects a symbolic division between different types of books, between antiquarian and scholarly works and reading material that had an 'everyday' purpose. Morpeth's booklist may even suggest that it is precisely because women often conducted their reading in what might be termed 'unscholarly' settings (i.e. in domestically active spaces rather than in solitary towers behind closed doors) that they have, for so long, been assumed to have occupied confined intellectual spheres. The physical settings of reading, and the types of records kept, appear to have influenced our evaluation of early modern male and female reading practices. Scholars have perhaps assumed too readily, and sometimes against their own experience, that no fulfilling engagement with books could occur in spaces where children and servants were present and active. Our limited understanding of female aristocratic book use in country houses, indeed our limited understanding of how spaces were used by all members of the household within these great residences, has served to limit our understanding of the intellectual worlds that these women inhabited.

Notes

1   Howard counted Robert Cotton and William Camden amongst his circle of scholarly friends. For more information on Howard and his antiquarian circle, see Richard Ovendon, 'The Libraries of the Antiquaries (c.1580–1640) and the Idea of a National Collection', in Elisabeth Leedham-Green and Teresa Webber (eds), *The Cambridge History of Libraries in Britain and Ireland*, vol. I [to 1640] (Cambridge: Cambridge University Press, 2006), pp. 527–61. See also Howard S. Reinmuth Jr., 'Lord William Howard (1563–1640) and his Catholic Associations', *Recusant History*, 12 (1973–74), 226–34, and Michael A. R. Graves, 'Howard, Thomas, Fourth Duke of Norfolk (1538–1572)', *Oxford Dictionary National Biography*, online edition, January 2008, www.oxforddnb.com.ezproxy.york.ac.uk/view/article/13941, accessed 8 October 2012.

2   The portrait was likely to have been completed at some point between the couple's marriage in 1668 and Lely's death in 1680. No archives connected to the Countess of a personal nature (e.g. letters) survive in the Castle Howard archives. There are, however, a small number of financial documents (see J/7/1–2).

3   As Robert A. Gross acknowledges that within 'the history of books and reading lie important clues for social history'. Robert A. Gross, 'Reading Outside the Frame' in Heidi Brayman Hackel and Catherine Kelly (eds), *Reading Women: Literacy, Authorship, and Culture in the Atlantic World, 1500–1800* (Philadelphia: University of Pennsylvania Press, 2007), 247–54, p. 252.

4   Jason Scott-Warren, 'Reading Graffiti in the Early Modern Book', *Huntington Library Quarterly*, 73.3 (2010), 363–81.

5   'Reading involved social transactions and was also part of sociability', Naomi Tadmor observes. She continues that 'purchasing, lending and borrowing of books were closely connected with other social networks'. N. Tadmor, '"In the even my wife read to me": Women, Reading and Household life in the Eighteenth Century', in J. Raven, H. Small, and N. Tadmor (eds), *The Practice and Representation of Reading in England* (Cambridge: Cambridge University Press, 1996), pp. 165–6.

6   S. H. Mendelson and P. Crawford, *Women in Early Modern England* (Oxford: Clarendon Press, 1998), p. 221.

7　　Anon., *A Week at Gilsland, with Visits to Naworth Castle and Lanercost Priory, and a Descriptive Ride by Rail, from Carlisle to Newcastle* (Newcastle upon Tyne: Robert Ward, [1851]), p. 30.

8　　For information about Morpeth's son, the 3rd Earl of Carlisle, who built Castle Howard at the turn of the eighteenth century see Charles Saumarez Smith, *The Building of Castle Howard* (London: Pimlico, 1997); Quentin Wilson, 'Revelation, Religion and Reason: Some Manuscript Remains of Charles Howard, 3rd Earl of Carlisle', unpublished MA thesis, Centre for Eighteenth-Century Studies, The University of York, 2004; Quentin Wilson, 'The Literary Remains of Charles Howard, 3rd Earl of Carlisle (1669–1738): A Critical Edition with Introduction and Notes', unpublished PhD thesis, The Department of English and Related Literature, The University of York, 2006; and Hannah DeGroff, 'Textual Networks and the Country House: The 3rd Earl of Carlisle at Castle Howard', unpublished PhD thesis, The Department of English and Related Literature, The University of York, 2012.

9　　On 24 April 1698, £2 1s 6d was 'payd for 5 bookes covered with green vellum and gilt for my Lady Carlisle'. Castle Howard Archives, H/1/1/3.

10　*Artamènes: Or, the Grand Cyrus* appears on three occasions in Pepys' diary, on 7 December 1660, 12 May 1666, and 21 May 1667. See *The Diary of Samuel Pepys: A New and Complete Transcription*, eds Robert Latham and William Matthews, 16 vols (Berkeley, CA and Los Angeles: Harper Collins and University of California, 2000), vol. 1, p. 312 for 1660 entry; vol. 7, p. 122 for 1666 entry; and vol. 8, p. 225 for 1667 entry.

11　*The Spectator*, 37 (12 April 1711). Printed in Joseph Addison, *The Spectator*, ed. with an introduction and notes by Donald F. Bond, 5 vols (Oxford: Clarendon Press, 1965), vol. 1, pp. 153–7. Despite (or because of) its popularity amongst women, both Addison and Samuel Pepys were dismissive of the work.

12　Castle Howard, H/2/3/6. For a printed version of this list see DeGroff, 'Textual Networks and the Country House', Appendix A.

13　While research in this area faces inherent challenges, not least because of the restricted property rights of women in the early modern period, some important advances have been made in the identification of individual women's book collections from the sixteenth to the eighteenth centuries. See, for example, Stephen Orgel, 'Reading Lady Anne Clifford's "A Mirovr for Magistrates"', in Karen Hearn and Lynn Hulse (eds), *Lady Anne Clifford: Culture, Patronage and Gender in Seventeenth-Century Britain*. Yorkshire Archaeological Society Occasional Paper, 7 (2009), 109–16; Mary Ellen Lamb, 'The Agency of the Split Subject: Lady Anne Clifford and the Uses of Reading', *English Literary Renaissance*, 22 (1992), 347–68; and Heidi Brayman Hackel, 'Turning to her "Best Companion[s]": Lady Anne Clifford as Reader, Annotator and Book Collector', in Hearn and Hulse (eds), *Lady Anne Clifford*, pp. 99–108. For work on other early modern women see Paul Morgan, 'Frances Wolfreston and "Her Bouks": A Seventeenth-Century Woman Book-Collector', *The Library*, 6th series, xi.3 (1989), 197–219 and David McKitterick, 'Women and their Books in Seventeenth-Century England: The Case of Elizabeth Puckering', *The Library*, 7th series, I (2000), 359–80. Moving into the eighteenth century, see Isobel Grundy, 'Books and the Woman: An Eighteenth-Century Owner and Her Libraries', *English Studies in Canada*, 20.1 (1994), 1–22.

14　Heidi Brayman Hackel, 'The Countess of Bridgewater's London Library' in Jennifer Anderson and Elizabeth Sauer (eds), *Books and Readers in Early Modern England* (Philadelphia: University of Pennsylvania Press, 2002), pp. 138–59. Egerton's booklist was compiled at various stages between 1627 to 1633.

15　Hackel suggests that different collections would contain books that were 'appropriate to … local needs and activities', Hackel, 'The Countess of Bridgewater's London Library', p. 144.

16 According to Hackel and Kelly, around '40% of the increase in book production around 1600 was made up of Bibles and devotional texts'. They continue, '[w]omen's self-defining through book consumption extended … to the rewards of piety, promising the possibility of allowing women to entertain spiritual questions previously reserved for men and to elevate themselves above the commodification of gentlewomen readers at leisure', Hackel and Kelly (eds), *Reading Women*, p. 13. Mary Ellen Lamb observes that, as more religious works appeared on the market, 'women could participate within a spirituality previously reserved for those "set apart": for nuns in a convent and for saints in a desert'. Mary Ellen Lamb, 'Inventing the Early Modern Woman Reader through the World of Goods: Lyly's Gentlewoman Reader and Katherine Stubbs', in Hackel and Kelly (eds), *Reading Women*, p. 28. See also Suzanne Hull, *Chaste, Silent, and Obedient: English Books for Women, 1475–1640* (San Marino, CA: Huntington Library, 1982).

17 See Chapter 4 in David Ainsworth's *Milton and the Spiritual Reader: Reading and Religion in Seventeenth-Century England* (Abingdon: Routledge, 2008).

18 It is not known which edition of Balzac's letters or Lucian's *Dialogues* the Countess kept in her library. As it was the only edition, however, we can be certain that she owned *The Memoires of the Duke of Rohan: or, A faithful relation of the most remarkable occurrences in France … Written originally in French, by the Duke of Rohan and now Englished by George Bridges of Lincolns-Inne, Esq.* (London, 1660).

19 Hortense Mancini, Duchesse de Mazarin. *The Memoires of the Dutchess Mazarine written in French by her own hand, and done into English by P. Porter, Esq; together with the reasons of her coming into England. Likewise, a letter containing a true character of her person and conversation* (London, 1676).

20 My thanks go to Helen Smith for suggesting various possibilities as to the identity of this work.

21 Heidi Brayman Hackel, *Reading Material in Early Modern England: Print, Gender, and Literacy* (Cambridge: Cambridge University Press, 2005), p. 209.

22 Jacqueline Pearson, 'Women Reading, Reading Women', in Helen Wilcox (ed.), *Women and Literature in Britain, 1500–1700* (Cambridge: Cambridge University Press, 1996), p. 81–2.

23 See, for example, Helen Hackett, *Women and Romance Fiction in the English Renaissance* (Cambridge University Press, 2000), pp. 9–12. For a further introduction to romance fiction in the early modern period see Lori Humphrey Newcomb, *Reading Popular Romance in Early Modern England* (New York: Columbia University Press, 2002).

24 In truth, men were equally voracious readers of these types of recreational texts. The most extensive collections of romances belonged to men. The collections of Sir Robert Gordon of Gordonstoun (d. 1656) and Edward, 2nd Viscount Conway (d. 1655) are particularly noteworthy. See Sasha Roberts, 'Engendering the Female Reader: Women's Recreational Reading of Shakespeare in Early Modern England' in Hackel and Kelly (eds), *Reading Women*, p. 37. See also Lori Humphrey Newcomb, 'Gendering Prose Romance in Renaissance England', in Corinne Saunders (ed.), *A Companion to Romance: From Classical to Contemporary* (Malden, MA: Blackwell, 2004), pp. 121–39.

25 Lamb, 'Inventing the Early Modern Woman Reader', in Hackel and Kelly (eds), *Reading Women*, p. 15. The view has been challenged by scholars including H. Barker and E. Chalus, 'Introduction', in H. Barker and E. Chalus (eds), *Gender in Eighteenth-Century England: Roles, Representations and Responsibilities* (London & New York: Longman, 1997), pp. 1–28; and Amanda Vickery in *The Gentleman's Daughter: Women's Lives in Georgian England* (London and New Haven, CT: Yale University Press, 1999).

26 Vickery, *The Gentleman's Daughter*, p. 7.

27 Tadmor, '"In the even my wife read to me"', p. 165.

28   'The good huswifs office' could refer to the third essay in Gervase Markham's *A Way to Get Wealth, by approued rules of practice in good husbandry and huswifrie …* (London, 1625) which is entitled 'The office of the English housewife in physicke, surgerie, extraction of oyles …' For information about domestic practices and the use of household manuals see Wendy Wall, 'Literacy and the Domestic Arts', *Huntington Library Quarterly*, 73 (2010), 383–412. 'The skilfull phisian' probably refers to *The Skilful Physician Containing Directions for the preservation of a healthful condition, and approved remedies for all diseases and infirmities (outward or inward) incident to the body of man …* (London, 1656). *A choice manual of rare and select secrets in physick and chyrurgery collected and practised by the Right Honorable, the Countesse of Kent, late deceased; as also most exquisite ways of preserving, conserving, candying …* (London, 1653) by Elizabeth Grey, Countess of Kent, was probably the work recorded as 'A mannuell of Phisick'. For an introduction to the use of medical texts by women in the early modern period see Mary E. Fissell, 'Introduction: Women, Health, and Healing in Early Modern Europe', *Bulletin of the History of Medicine*, 82.1 (2008), 1–17.

29   Elaine Leong draws connections between the medical information that was regularly gathered together by aristocratic women in the early modern period and the role that this information played within their households. Elaine Leong, 'Making Medicines in the Early Modern Household', *Bulletin of the History of Medicine*, 82.1 (2008), 145–68.

30   Thomas Reynalde, *The Birth of Mankind: Otherwise Named, The Woman's Book …* ed. and with introduction by Elaine Hobby (Farnham: Ashgate, 2009). See p. xxxix for details of seventeenth-century editions. See also Mary E. Fissell's *Vernacular Bodies: The Politics of Reproduction in Early Modern England* (Oxford: Oxford University Press, 2004), particularly pp. 14, 29–35, 150–1 and 186. The last edition of this text was printed in London in 1654. My thanks go again to Helen Smith for helping me identify the work.

31   Hackel notes that the absence of medical texts in the urban libraries of aristocratic women may signify their close proximity to qualified physicians and pharmacists. Hackel, 'The Countess of Bridgewater's London Library', p. 144.

32   Reynalde, *The Birth of Mankind*, ed. Hobby, p. 3.

33   My thanks go to Professor Neil Harris for pointing out the relevance of the fold marks on this document.

34   Maurice Howard, *The Early Tudor Country House: Architecture and Politics, 1490–1550* (London: George Philip, 1987), particularly the chapter, 'The Courtyard and the Household', pp. 59–106.

35   See Scott-Warren, 'Reading Graffiti in the Early Modern Book'.

36   Gross, 'Reading Outside the Frame', p. 251.

37   It is well documented that Lady Anne Clifford shared her books with her household staff. See Hackel, 'Turning to her "Best Companion[s]"', p. 103.

38   Domestic spaces in the English country house which have often been thought of as personal, private, or intimate (e.g. the closet) often functioned in communal ways. As Hackel observes, 'the variety of uses of early modern domestic spaces complicates any easy equation of space and practice, of habitat and habit'. Hackel, *Reading Material*, p. 35.

39   Mendelson and Crawford, *Women in Early Modern England*, p. 205.

40   Howard's books have received little attention in comparison to the manuscripts that he owned (see n. 1). An account of Naworth in 1838 includes a reference to a booklist 'among the leaves of an old black letter folio, clasped, and bound in oak' entitled *A Catalogue of my Lord's books in the shelves next to the fire*. On the reverse is *A Catalogue of my books at Naward*. His collection was primarily made up of works from the sixteenth century, many of which were in Latin. See Samuel Jefferson, *The History and Antiquities of Carlisle: With an Account*

of the Castles, Gentlemen's Seats, and Antiquities, in the Vicinity; and Biographical Memoirs of Eminent Men Connected with the Locality (Carlisle, 1838), pp. 366–8.

41 A detailed physical description of Howard's library-room was recorded in the nineteenth century. Jefferson, *History and Antiquities of Carlisle*, p. 365. Much of his library remained *in situ* until the twentieth century. Over 200 volumes (plus five commonplace books) were purchased by Durham University in 1992. According to the sale catalogue almost half of the books that were sold were of a religious or theological nature. Other subjects included history (approximately seventy-five volumes), classics, reference works, poetry, science, and law. It also reveals that the majority of those books that were still extant were published on the continent, with only thirty-two printed in England. See entry for Lot 171 in Sotheby's auction catalogue, sale date 14–15 December 1992.

IV

Case study: Wilton House

13

Wilton House, theatre and power

Marta Straznicky

Isaac de Caus's published engravings for the new garden built at Wilton in the 1630s include a design for a cypress grove laid out to resemble an amphitheatre.[1] The focal point of the engraving is a curved double staircase, with one concave and one convex flight of steps meeting at a platform that evidently 'reads' as a stage. The staircase gives access to three tree-lined terraces excavated out of the hillside, bounded at the outer reaches by woods and at the innermost arc by a retaining wall enclosing a grotto, which itself opens onto a flat, geometrically landscaped area. The amphitheatre is thus both at the centre of the engraving and physically located on a central axis that has a strong kinetic force, inviting and orchestrating a transition from the walled garden below to the open agricultural estates beyond. De Caus's aerial view of the whole garden positions the amphitheatre at the furthest end of the great walk leading from Wilton House – that is, outside the garden walls, but still clearly within the grounds being controlled by the plan.[2] We have no evidence that the amphitheatre was used for performances, nor do we know whether the structure was ever built. But its very presence in this celebrated re-design of the garden suggests a rich interplay between architecture, landscape and the theatrical arts at Wilton, renowned as the site of one of Renaissance England's most distinctive intellectual traditions, Arcadianism.

This chapter focuses on the role of theatre and theatricality at three formative stages in the development of Wilton's Arcadian identity: Sir Philip Sidney's deliberate setting of the composition of *The Countess of Pembroke's Arcadia* at Wilton; the Countess's own writing and patronage of drama in the 1590s; and the rebuilt garden of the 1630s as a performance space within which Wilton's legacy is re-enacted and its political identity redefined. An important context for this study is the family's extensive history of theatrical activities, activities

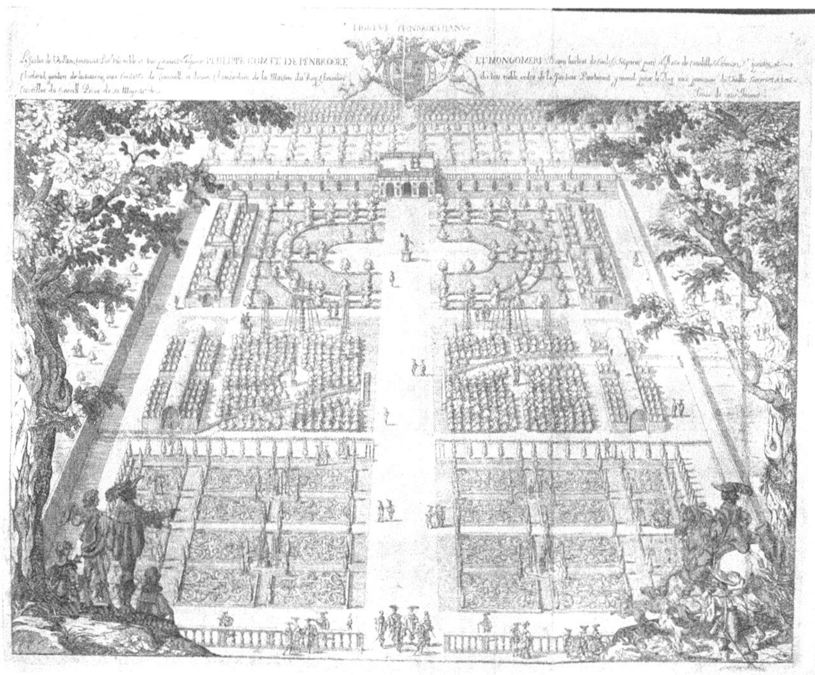

13.1   Isaac de Caus, *Wilton Garden*, 1645, unnumbered plate, showing an aerial view of the garden looking out from the house.

that include and cross freely among an almost indiscriminate range of practices, settings and social and occupational categories: they wrote, sponsored, and performed in shows, masques, plays, and dances; they were patrons of both private and public stages; they include among their coterie amateur as well as professional, and male as well as female, dramatists and performers; and they engaged in all the principal modes of circulation for drama in this period, including performance, manuscript and print. William Herbert, the 1st Earl, hosted Queen Elizabeth at the family's London home of Baynards Castle on at least two occasions that included masques and other forms of display.[3] He also had in his service William Hunnis, Master of the Chapel Children from 1566 to 1597, who was directly responsible for six known court performances and was involved in the company's earliest commercial acting ventures at the Blackfriars.[4] The double wedding of Herbert's son and daughter at Baynards Castle in 1563 was celebrated with 'gret mummers and masks'.[5] The 2nd Earl, Henry Herbert, who married Mary Sidney in 1577, was patron of a professional acting company, the Lord Pembroke's Men, active in the 1590s in London and the provinces and having in their repertory historical plays by Marlowe and Shakespeare. He hosted the Queen on progress at Wilton in 1574, and at Ramsbury in 1592,

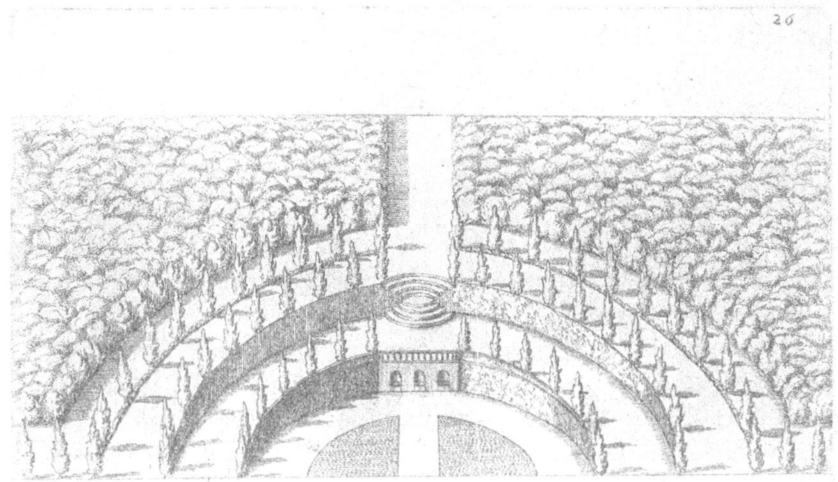

13.2   Isaac de Caus, *Wilton Garden*, 1645, Plate 26, showing a detail of the amphitheatre.

and attended the performance of an academic drama at Oxford in 1582.[6] This play was also attended by Philip Sidney, himself a regular performer in tilts and jousts at Court, one of four principal actors in the entertainment 'Four Foster Children of Desire', and author of 'The Lady of May', a pastoral show performed for the Queen at Wanstead.[7] Most famous of the Sidney-Herberts' theatrical contacts is probably the dedication of Shakespeare's First Folio in 1623 to William and Philip Herbert, Mary Sidney's sons, renowned dancers of masques, tiltyard champions, and leading cultural patrons, including among their protégés Ben Jonson, Inigo Jones, George Chapman and Philip Massinger.[8] William and Philip both in turn held the office of Lord Chamberlain, and were in this capacity directly responsible for court revels. Philip even employed his household servants in the presentation of William Habington's *The Queen of Aragon* before the Court in 1640.[9] Sir Robert Sidney, uncle to William and Philip Herbert, was also closely tied to theatrical culture: he entertained Queen Elizabeth at Baynards on at least one occasion, and as Chamberlain to Queen Anna's household, he had jurisdiction over the Queen's Men, reputedly the most downmarket of the professional companies;[10] his daughter Mary Sidney Wroth was the only woman to whom a professional play was dedicated (Jonson's *Alchemist*, in 1610) as well as being a regular dancer in masques at Court and the author of *Loves Victorie*, an original pastoral drama.[11] One would be hard-pressed to think of another family with so extensive and ongoing an engagement with theatrical culture. But why, of all their properties – which include at least three other houses for which we have records of theatrical entertainments

(Baynards Castle, Ramsbury, and Penshurst) – was Wilton the place where these traditions intersected so fruitfully?

Here we turn inevitably to Sir Philip Sidney and the contingencies that brought him to Wilton in the late 1570s. The most definitive of these was the marriage of his sister Mary to Henry Herbert, 2nd Earl of Pembroke, in 1577, through which Wilton became available to the Sidneys for their intellectual and political pursuits. Needless to say, Wilton had a rich history of its own before the Sidneys' arrival, extending back to the tenth century when a priory of nuns was located there. This was succeeded in the thirteenth century by a Benedictine Abbey for high-born women, which in turn was surrendered to the Crown at the Dissolution and granted in various stages to William Herbert, who by marriage to Anne Parr had become brother-in-law to Henry VIII and thereafter one of the wealthiest and most powerful of Tudor courtiers.[12] Herbert was fully in possession of the house by 1544, created Knight of the Garter in 1548, and 1st Earl of Pembroke in 1551. The house he left to his son Henry at his death in 1570 had been rebuilt over a period of twenty years at tremendous expense into 'a large & high built square of hewen stone', with a well-supplied armoury, a stable for eighty horses, a walled forecourt and gatehouse displaying the Herbert arms, and a massive stone porch featuring portrait busts of William and Anne being among the features that transformed Wilton from a medieval abbey to a monument of Herbert's status.[13] The surrounding estate was reshaped in this same image: gardens with extensive walks and new hunting parks were made, one of which obliterated the entire village of Washern, formerly across the Nadder to the south of Wilton. Intriguingly, Herbert built a platform within the park from which he could survey the estate, a prospect to be taken 'pro placito suo', confirming through the display of landscape and architecture his wealth and power as a Tudor magnate.[14] Such was Wilton House as Sidney knew it, militarism harmonised with pleasure park, politics with leisure. Overlaid with a classically derived pastoralism, it would serve uniquely well to localise the stance of the disempowered Elizabethan courtier.

Sidney first came to Wilton in the summer of 1577, several months after Mary's wedding, at the time of which he had been on embassy in Europe. Immediately on his return he had gone to Greenwich, but within a few weeks raised Elizabeth's suspicions for having made contacts among the more radical of continental Protestants. There are no records suggesting he was sent down to Wilton to 'chill', as we might say, but he did arrive there already at odds with the Queen. Joining him at Wilton in August were his uncles the Earls of Leicester and Warwick, both of whom had also visited in June. One of Sidney's presumed earliest pastoral pieces, 'A Dialogue Between Two Shepherds, Utter'd in a Pastoral Show, at Wilton', may have been written at this time; certainly the conjunction of its locale and pastoral rhetoric captures the affect of an Elizabethan courtier in disfavour.[15] Read outside its setting, Sidney's brief dialogue between Dick and

Will concerning Dick's enslavement to a cruel mistress 'Whose wages makes me beg the more, who feeds me till I starve' does little more than articulate a familiar Petrarchan paradox and pastoral conceit as it was deployed by innumerable Elizabethan writers. But by explicitly situating the performance at Wilton, mere months after receiving the first of several rebukes from the Queen, Sidney gives the piece considerably more political edge. Whether it was indeed acted at Wilton is perhaps less important than that it was imagined (and eventually proclaimed in print) as having been performed there, its mildly oppositional tone 'utter'd' – a term of some importance here, meaning 'to put into circulation', or 'to make public' – in a fictional landscape as yet defined more by its ironic stance than by any particular geography. If we accept 1577 as the date of Sidney's pastoral show, it is all the more fitting that he appeared in that year's Accession Day Tilts as 'Philisides, the shepherd good and true'.[16] About a month later, Sidney was back at Wilton, where he was again joined by Leicester and Warwick for 'revels' with the Herberts. While his uncles returned to Court, Sidney sought permission to stay at Wilton for the Christmas festivities, returning only at New Year's Day, when he rather audaciously presented the Queen with a pastoral garment, a 'smock of camerick', as his gift for 1578.[17] Elizabeth may have been attuned to the potential threat emerging in Wiltshire. Less than two years later, Walsingham wrote to Henry Sidney conveying the Queen's disapproval of his repeated visits to Wilton House.[18] Inconclusive as these records are, there does seem to be something taking shape here: Wilton is becoming the base for the Leicester-Sidney-Herbert families, its spatial, geographic and political identities aligning almost effortlessly with the rhetorical and performative stance of pastoral, to which the brilliant creative mind of Philip Sidney begins to give a distinct and lasting expression.

Against this background, Sidney's setting of the composition of *The Countess of Pembroke's Arcadia* at Wilton seems overdetermined, but we should nevertheless consider its significance and impact.[19] Wilton is not named in Sidney's dedication of *The Arcadia* to his sister, but he creates there an association between the easeful writing of the romance, her presence, and the place where 'most' of it was composed that proved remarkably durable: 'Your dear self', he writes, 'can best witness the manner, being done in loose sheets of paper, most of it in your presence, the rest by sheets sent unto you as fast as they were done'.[20] Mary Sidney's whereabouts in the years around 1580, when the writing of *The Arcadia* was likely in progress, include brief stays at Penshurst, Baynards Castle, Richmond and possibly Ramsbury, but she was throughout this time primarily at Wilton.[21] Sidney, by his own account, was only periodically at Wilton: we have records locating him at Court, Baynards Castle, Leicester House, Oxford, at Dover and Gravesend, at Flushing and Antwerp. His last recorded visit to Wilton was for the christening of Mary's second son, Philip, in October of 1584. If 'most' of the *Arcadia* was written at Wilton, 'the rest' was written at any of the above or other locations. But Sidney chooses to associate 'this idle work of mine' with Wilton alone, the place, perhaps, where his idleness was most acutely felt, as a condition both resented and yet pleasingly hospitable to writing.[22] Baynards Castle, by contrast, was the site of the decisive meeting of the Dudley-Sidney-Herbert alliance in August 1579 where Philip is thought to have agreed to write his letter against the Anjou match which, ironically, landed him back at Wilton for several months in 1580.[23] In other respects, Baynards Castle was a known Protestant stronghold at this time, and could equally well have served as the imaginative stage for a literary project that embodied an ethos of chivalry and civility, but it must have lacked for Sidney the kind of resonance that Wilton had acquired: that much closer to Court, that much more the domain of Henry Herbert than Mary Sidney, that much less given to the fantasy of idleness. Wilton thus appears *by design* in *The Arcadia*, occluding other sites at which the work was undoubtedly composed; and it appears in a guise that is very much the invention of Sidney himself – its repose, its harmony with creative genius, and most especially its feminised passivity inherently opposed to the militaristic Wilton fashioned by William Herbert.

It is one of Sidney's unacknowledged achievements that the pastoral Wilton came to dominate the English imagination, but the strong association between Wilton and elite literary culture is attributable more properly to Mary Sidney, as Philip himself may have hinted by naming his romance *The Countess of Pembroke's Arcadia*. Interestingly, the famous dedication is absent from both the *Old* and *New Arcadia* manuscripts, our only substantive text being the first printed edition of 1590.[24] Henry Woudhuysen suggests that the dedication may have existed uniquely in the Countess's manuscript of the *Old Arcadia* and that it was she who sent it to Greville when he was preparing copy for the 1590 edition.[25] In any event, the presence of the dedication in print confirmed Wilton as the 'imaginative ground-plot' of Sidney's immensely popular romance, positioning Mary Sidney as a partner in its genesis and preparing the way for her creation of Renaissance England's most influential literary network, the Wilton circle.[26] When it is described as the seat of Mary Sidney's extensive coterie, Wilton is imagined as pleasing to both body and mind, 'Wholsome' and 'dilicious' for its setting in the Wiltshire downs, the 'best Schoole', a 'college', perhaps less rousingly 'a kind of little court'.[27] This latter epithet recalls Philip Sidney's much-remarked belittling of *The Arcadia* as his 'toyfull book',[28] 'a trifle, and that triflingly handled', 'stuff' no better than the 'glasses or feathers' found in a haberdasher's shop,[29] signalling something key about the perception of Mary Sidney's Wilton: for all its brilliance as a centre for the learned arts, it is not in fact at the centre of academic nor political culture. If this is indeed faint praise, it could be explained by the anomaly of a woman presiding over the Wilton academy. But its rhetorical echo of Philip Sidney's ironic detachment from his own creative labour suggests that the feminisation of Wilton more likely played to Mary Sidney's strengths – just as it did, albeit differently, to her brother's – enabling her to cultivate one of the most extensive patronage networks in Renaissance England, to promote through a vigorous publishing programme her family's religious and intellectual values, and to realise her own creative ambition.

The writing, reading and performance of drama at Wilton was a significant part of these endeavours. Sidney herself translated Robert Garnier's classical tragedy *Marc Antoine* and published it in 1592 with her translation of Philippe de Mornay's *Discours de la vie et de la mort*. This latter work was finished 'at Wilton' on 13 May 1590, and *Antonius* 'at Ramsbury' on 26 November, but it is likely Sidney worked on both titles simultaneously, since, read against one another, as they are apparently meant to be, they convey the shared moral and political philosophy of the two Protestant source writers.[30] Sidney's *Antonius* quickly gave rise, both directly and indirectly, to a suite of Senecan plays on the theme of tyranny: Samuel Daniel's *Cleopatra* (1594), Thomas Kyd's *Cornelia* (1594), and Samuel Brandon's *Octavia* (1598). In the midst of this publishing activity, Sidney had her own translation reprinted in 1595, without the de Mornay text. Some of these plays were read widely enough to be quoted in anthologies and commonplace books, and the 'myth' of a dramatic circle based at Wilton quickly took hold.[31] Samuel Daniel explicitly states that *Cleopatra* was commissioned by Mary Sidney as a companion piece to *Antonie*, but all of the neo-classical plays written in the wake of Sidney's translation offer probing critiques of monarchic power and in this respect share the political stance of the 'little court' she cultivated at Wilton.[32]

When Mary Sidney prepared to welcome the monarch in person, however, she reached back to a different dramatic tradition, one Elizabeth may well have expected to encounter at the Wiltshire estate. In the 'Dialogue betweene two shepherds, Thenot and Piers', written for a planned visit of the Queen to Wilton in 1599, her two speakers debate the very possibility of praising 'the divine Astrea', setting in motion a brilliant rhetorical interplay that allows Sidney to articulate Elizabeth's virtues in the most extravagant terms and yet never fully affirm them: 'Words from conceit do only rise, Above conceit her honour flies; But silence, nought can praise her.'[33] This is praise and not-praise at once, asserting in one move the Queen's godlike attributes and Sidney's subtle mastery of the discourse in which Elizabeth was accustomed to being described and addressed. Some twenty years earlier, in a performance of Philip Sidney's pastoral entertainment *The Lady of May*, written for the Queen's visit to the Earl of Leicester's hunting-lodge at Wanstead in 1578, it was Elizabeth who took control of the discourse, thwarting Sidney's creative design by favouring the argument for contemplation and retreat over action and commitment.[34] However, when the entertainment came to be printed under Mary Sidney's auspices in the 1598 edition of *The Countess of Pembrokes Arcadia*, the Queen's reasons were deliberately excluded:

'what words, what reasons she used for it, this paper, which carieth so base names, is not worthy to containe.'[35] In her own pastoral dialogue for the Queen's visit, where the monarch is similarly un-represented, Mary Sidney can be said to redeploy a genre and imaginative landscape that at some level renews Wilton's claim to her family's literary authority.

Had the Queen actually come to Wilton she would surely have remembered her first visit in September of 1574.[36] Entertained on that occasion by Henry Herbert and his second wife, Catherine Talbot, Elizabeth was greeted a full five miles away from the house by the Earl 'accompanyed with many of his honourable and worshipfull friends, on a fayre, large, and playne hill ... having a good band of men in all their livery coates.'[37] An elaborately choreographed display of Herbert's followers and attendants, 'well horsed, [and] placed in a ranke of order', framed the Queen's procession to Wilton House. There she rode through the Tudor gateway into the outer courtyard, where another assembly of the Earl's men, 'as thicke as could be, standing one by another', formed a corridor through which she passed. Finally, at the inner gate, she was greeted by the then-Countess of Pembroke, 'with divers ladyes and gentlewomen, [who] meekly received her highnesse'. Although the entertainment is devised for the Queen, who was reportedly 'merry and pleasant' throughout her stay, it couldn't be more conspicuously about Herbert – the size of his retinue, the expanse of his estate, the virtue of his wife. The differences between this and Mary Sidney's planned entertainment for Elizabeth's visit in 1599 are striking: hers foregrounding intellectual rather than military prowess, a Sidney rather than a Herbert pedigree, feminine rather than masculine command. In this light, there is also a significant difference in the role played by the landscape and architecture of Wilton itself: in Herbert's entertainment, the grounds and house are a kind of environmental stage on which his status is displayed; in Sidney's entertainment, the setting is vague to the point of obscurity, and yet a decidedly Arcadian pastoral landscape is evoked by the verse. Following as this occasion did on the carefully orchestrated publication of Philip's and her own works throughout the 1590s, that landscape was considerably more expressive of Wilton's intellectual climate in 1599 than it had been at any time since.

There is a third historical moment when landscape, architecture and the theatrical arts intersected conspicuously at Wilton, the rebuilding of the house and garden in the 1630s by Mary Sidney's younger son Philip, 4th Earl of Pembroke.[38] As Adam Nicolson has suggested, the new design for Wilton can be understood as the culmination of the Herbert brothers' successful political careers at the courts of James and Charles, a radical departure from the cautiously oppositional politics played by the Sidney-Herbert families throughout Elizabeth's reign.[39] In this changed context, Wilton became a favourite retreat of the Court. In the very first year of his reign, prevented by an outbreak of plague from settling at Whitehall, James was based periodically at Wilton where he was entertained, famously, by the premier London acting troupe that would soon come under his direct patronage.[40] Other visits by James are recorded in 1615 and 1618, the latter of which related to the King's creation of Robert Sidney as Earl of Leicester at nearby Bishop's Palace in Salisbury.[41] In 1620 James was again at Wilton and from there commissioned Inigo Jones to prepare an antiquarian account of Stonehenge.[42] A planned visit to Wilton on 6 August 1623 has not been documented, but John Taylor records having seen rooms at Wilton some few days later, still 'richly adorned with Costly and sumptuous hangings' from the King having 'dined there with most magnificent Entertainment'.[43] Six months after James's death in 1625, the new king and queen were expected to arrive, ushering in the period of Wilton's greatest prominence as an English country house. According to Aubrey, Charles 'did love Wilton above all places, and came thither every summer'.[44] It was reportedly he who set Philip Herbert the enormously expensive task of rebuilding both house and garden.

Roy Strong has written that this Wilton effectively became 'the King's Arcadia', an ironic appropriation of Sidney's counter-court aesthetic to be sure, but one that might also be understood as a synthesis of the 1st Earl of Pembroke's chivalric Wilton and the pastoral retreat allegorised in *The Arcadia*.[45] The hinge between these two imaginative landscapes is the Stuart court masque, a singularly important formative influence, as Strong has also noted, on the design of the new garden. As successive Lords Chamberlain, frequent masque performers themselves, and fantastically wealthy patrons of both empirical and creative arts, William and Philip Herbert were ideally positioned to leverage the foremost political aesthetic of the time into a physical expression of their power and cultural dominance. This expression can be traced at Wilton in the earlier landscape designs of Adrian Gilbert, William Herbert's gardener from about 1610 to 1628.[46] As Louise Noble writes in Chapter 14, the elaborate geometric and symbolic design of Gilbert's garden both represented and sustained the various intellectual and scientific interests of the Herberts, including chemistry, entomology, mathematics, and horticulture. Described in 1623 by John Taylor as playing the part of 'a true *Adamist*, continually toyling and tilling', Gilbert created at Wilton a magnificent garden of arbours, walks, hedges, and fruit trees, 'planting and placing them in such admirable Artlike fashions, resembling both divine and morrall remembrances'.[47] When Taylor visited Wilton again in 1649, while the house was under repair after the disastrous fire of 1647, he found an even more breathtaking landscape:

> the Springs, and Fishponds, the Garden, the Walkes, the rare Artificiall Rocks and Fountaines, the Ponds with fish on the house top, the strange figures and fashions of the water workes, the numerous, innumerable varieties of fruits and flowers; yea all, and every thing that may make an earthly Paradice, is there to be seene, felt, heard, or understood.[48]

Intervening between these two accounts is Isaac de Caus's redesign of the garden in 1632–35, famed for the very features that distinguish Taylor's description of 1649 from that of 1623, the ingenious water-works and the synesthetic experience produced by these and other of the garden's various marvels.

The language of affect in Taylor's later description is richly suggestive of the theatrical potential of de Caus's garden. While William Herbert's garden was also 'pleasing and ravishing to the sense', what impressed most about it was the workmanship, chiefly the 'paines and industrie' of Adrian Gilbert: Taylor's breathless succession of gerunds foregrounds the labour of the ingenious gardener, his 'intricate Setting, Grafting, Planting, inocculating, Rayling, hedging, plashing, turning, winding, and returning', his designs being 'every way curiously and chargeably conceited', his Walkes 'made most rarely round and spacious.' The work to Taylor's mind 'seemes endlesse', and Gilbert 'so industrious and ingenious a Gentleman' that he is deserving at the very least of a bespoke anagram.[49] Conversely, in 1649 Taylor's praise of the 'most exceeding good work and workmen' at Wilton is by his own admission unequal to the many 'rare' and 'strange' artifices he has experienced but is unable to understand.[50] A Lieutenant Hammond, visiting Wilton garden just after its completion in 1635, was similarly awe-struck by the water-works and took note, as had Taylor, of the tremendous expense incurred by Herbert in their construction:

> … that rare Water-worke now making, and continuing by this outlandish Engineer, for the singing, and chirping of Birdes, and other strange rarities, onely by that Element, the finishing which rare peece of Skill, with satisfaction to the engenious Artist will cost (they say) a great Summe of Money.[51]

The industrious gardener toiling in a horticultural paradise of his own making is here replaced by the 'outlandish Engineer' who skilfully manipulates the elements and physical forces of nature to create 'strange rarities' that captivate the garden's visitors. It is not much of a stretch from the experience described here to the multi-media extravagance of court masque, designed as both environments are to produce wonder in the spectator. Thomas Heywood's address to the reader of *Love's Mistress: or the Queen's Masque*, performed at Denmark House in 1634 in honour of the King's birthday, provides similar testimony, crediting Inigo Jones's 'excellent Invention' for giving every scene 'an extraordinary Luster; upon every occasion changing the stage, to the admiration of all the Spectators: that, as I must Ingeniously confesse, It was above my apprehension to conceive, so to their sacred Majesties, and the rest of the Auditory'.[52]

In this light, the involvement of Inigo Jones in the 1630s redesign of Wilton is intriguing, even if he seems to have acted more as a consultant than principal architect. Among Jones's designs for masque settings is at least one perspective that has been thought to resonate with Wilton, the garden scene for *The Shepherd's Paradise*, performed by the Queen and her ladies at Somerset House in 1633,[53] but there is a more general interplay between Wilton garden and masque form that suggests a deliberate theatricality might lie behind de Caus's design. One of the most renowned features of the garden is its grotto, visible in de Caus's aerial view at the southernmost end of the great walk. Engravings of the grotto interior show a strange combination of geometric order and an almost grotesque use of natural elements, its walls a riot of shells and unusual rock formations set within a symmetrical spatial design framing reliefs of mythological figures.[54] Entered through a triple-arched arcade, the grotto was divided into several alcoves, each of which featured the famous water-works that might spray visitors, suspend an object on a jet of water, or make statues weep. The song of nightingales could be heard in one of the side rooms, and among the 'other rarities' reported by Lieutenant Hammond was a machine that could produce a triple rainbow. The overall effect of surprise and wonder was enhanced for being triggered by one's movement through the illusion: architecture becomes theatre, the very space of the grotto transformed into a show of wonders as the visitor moves from room to room. The grotto itself, however, is located within a larger landscape representing the triumph of order, something which is clearly visible in both the floor plan and the panorama of the garden.[55] Similar kinds of architectural and scenic ingenuity are found in many court masques, of course, and there, too, they introduce spontaneity and excitement to an otherwise ceremonial art form.

A second example of the theatrical dimension of Wilton garden is the wilderness area situated between the formal parterres closest to the house and the furthest section, the oval grove in front of the grotto at the centre of which is a statue of a gladiator by Hubert le Sueur.[56] The wilderness is described by de Caus as 'two Groves or woods cutt with diverse walkes and through those Groves passeth the river Nadder'.[57] There is a bridge over the river where it flows across the path of the great walk, and at the centre of each grove is a marble statue eight feet high, of Bacchus on one side and Flora on the other. The unrestrained flow of the Nadder through this section of the garden is perhaps its most unusual feature. De Caus was one of the leading hydraulic engineers of his time and presumably could have diverted the river in keeping with the otherwise symmetrical order of the garden. That the Nadder was left uncontrolled must speak of a deliberate decision, a decision that has two significant effects: to draw the visitor's attention to the river as a natural element of Wilton's landscape, and to arrest movement where the walks unexpectedly end at the riverbank. This second effect is best seen in the plan for the three main sections of the garden.[58] The river dominates the middle section, visually, aesthetically and kinetically; it also creates a sense of contrast with surrounding areas which reveal their marvels in orderly progression. Thematically, the wilderness is nature opposed to art, passion to reason, violence to civility, the very same antitheses found in many court masques; in theatrical terms, it is the antimasque to the garden's magnificent display of harmony and order.[59] Politically, however, it does something more reminiscent of the pastoral entertainments of Philip Herbert's predecessors: transforming landscape into theatre, it creates a contrast among different kinds of power; physically, it might be read (and experienced) as an assertion of Pembroke's ownership of the estate in which the King takes his pleasure.

If Wilton garden has much the same theatrical and political dimension as court masque, it nevertheless continues the tradition of self-fashioning revels at Wilton extending back at least to the 1570s. Interestingly, while the gardens of Adrian Gilbert and Isaac de Caus are both troped by John Taylor as paradise, it is the latter iteration of Wilton that is imagined as 'a Pallace for the greatest King in Christendome',[60] a designation with which Henry Herbert would heartily have agreed. Other elements of Wilton garden could be interpreted in these terms, for instance the various stairs and terraces that provide an ongoing transformation of perspective on the garden, the house, and the agricultural lands outside the scope of formal display. In the garden design, there is a pronounced orchestration of prospects and views conducting the eye towards the garden itself, but also outwards from its various platforms – up into the estates beyond, or back down across the garden and to the house.[61] In this context, the amphitheatre with which this chapter opened might take on a deeper significance. Situated above and beyond the walls of the garden, the most important theatrical function of this structure may not be staging after all: for the visitor who ascends the stairs and turns around to take in the view, as is reasonable to assume was intended, it offers a prospect on the garden and house that transforms Wilton itself into a richly allusive spectacle, a spectacle representing order, wealth, and power at the height of the family's political influence. This is a long way indeed from Philip Sidney's short pastoral dialogue; in many respects, it recalls more the performative use of the grounds and house made by Philip Herbert's grandfather to signal his wealth and eminence at the Court of Henry VIII. He, too, had built a platform within a newly planted park from which to enjoy the prospect of his estate.[62] But there is a significant difference there, too, at least on the level of aesthetics: Philip Herbert's Wilton is shaped to a large extent by continental influences, not only in landscape architecture, but also in literature. The literary influence is particularly important at Wilton, for the garden includes not only a programme of references to Ovid, as might be expected of its Italianate design, but, at the end of the alley leading through the woods from the amphitheatre, a cascade dominated by a statue of Pegasus.[63] This allusion to the springs of Helicon is brilliantly apt in the early 1630s, its very placement suggesting that the poetic imagination is ultimately the source of Wilton's grandeur. Intentionally or not, it materialises a setting from Sidney's *Old Arcadia* that, presciently, bridges nearly a century of intellectual and political culture at Wilton:

Round about the meadow, as if it had been to enclose a theatre, grew all sorts of trees as either excellency of fruit, stateliness of growth, continual greenness, or poetical fancies have made at any time famous.[64]

Notes

1   Isaac de Caus, *Wilton Garden* (New York: Garland Publishing Inc., 1982 [1645]), p. 26.
2   *Wilton Garden*, unnumbered plate titled HORTVS PENBROCHIANVS.
3   E. K. Chambers, *The Elizabethan Stage*, 4 vols (Oxford: Clarendon Press, 1923), vol. IV, pp. 77, 80, 81, 82. See also Adam Nicolson, *Arcadia: The Dream of Perfection in Renaissance England* (London: Harper Perrennial, 2008), p. 79.
4   Chambers, *The Elizabethan Stage*, vol. III, pp. 79–80.
5   Chambers, *The Elizabethan Stage*, vol. III, p. 160.
6   Chambers, *The Elizabethan Stage*, vol. IV, pp. 90, 107; III: 318.
7   Chambers, *The Elizabethan Stage*, vol. I, p. 144; III: p. 492. 'The Lady of May' was first published as one of the 'new additions' appended to the third edition of *The Countesse of Pembrokes Arcadia* (London: Richard Field for William Ponsonby, 1598).
8   On the patronage network of the Herberts, see Michael G. Brennan, *Literary Patronage in the English Renaissance: The Pembroke Family* (New York: Routledge, 1988).
9   G. E. Bentley, *Jacobean and Caroline Stage*, 7 vols (Oxford: Clarendon Press, 1941), vol. I, p. 62.
10 Chambers, *The Elizabethan Stage*, vol. I, p. 121; vol. IV, p. 113; vol. II, p. 237.
11 Chambers, *The Elizabethan Stage*, vol. III, pp. 371, 375; Bentley, *Jacobean and Caroline Stage*, vol. IV, p. 620. See also Margaret P. Hannay, *Mary Sidney, Lady Wroth* (Burlington, VT: Ashgate, 2010), *passim*. Wroth's play *Loves Victorie* survives in two manuscripts: a privately owned copy is at Penshurst Place (edited by Michael G. Brennan for the Roxburghe Club in 1988); a substantively different manuscript is at the Huntington Library (HM 600). My edition of the Huntington manuscript is in preparation for The Other Voice in Early Modern Europe series.
12 For an outline of Wilton's early history see John Bold, *Wilton House and English Palladianism* (London: HMSO, 1988), p. 25. The social and political contexts surrounding transfer of the property to William Herbert is fully described in Nicolson, *Arcadia*, pp. 46–58. Interestingly, the earliest dramatic entertainment connected with Wilton is a *Visitatio Sepulchri*, dating from c. 1250 to 1350 when the estate was a Benedictine Abbey. See Susan K. Rankin, 'A New English Source of the *Visitatio Sepulchri*', *The Journal of Plainsong and Medieval Music Society* 4 (1981), 1–11, and Alison Findlay, *Playing Spaces in Early Women's Drama* (Cambridge: Cambridge University Press, 2006), pp. 148–9.
13 Bold, *Wilton House*, pp. 31–3.
14 Nicolson, *Arcadia*, pp. 60–1.
15 The dialogue was first published with the *Arcadia* in 1613; its authorship by Sidney has not been independently verified, but it appears to have been accepted as genuine by Mary Sidney, Robert Sidney, and Fulke Greville, all of whom were alive when this edition was published. The dialogue appears in all subsequent editions of *Arcadia*. See William A. Ringler (ed.), *The Poems of Sir Philip Sidney* (Oxford: Clarendon Press, 1962), pp. 343–44, 517. See also Chambers, *The Elizabethan Stage*, vol. III, p. 492.
16 Alan Stewart, *Philip Sidney: A Double Life* (London: Chatto & Windus, 2000), p. 233.

17   John Nichols, *The Progresses and Public Processions of Queen Elizabeth*, 2nd edn, 3 vols (New York: B. Franklin, 1965), vol. II, p. 77.

18   Stewart, *Philip Sidney*, p. 229.

19   Stewart, *Philip Sidney*, p. 226.

20   Jean Robertson (ed.), *The Countesse of Pembroke's Arcadia (The Old Arcadia)* (Oxford: Clarendon Press, 1973), p. 3.

21   Margaret P. Hannay, *Philip's Phoenix: Mary Sidney, Countess of Pembroke* (Oxford: Oxford University Press, 1990), pp. 38–58, *passim*.

22   Robertson (ed.), *Arcadia*, p. 3.

23   Stewart, *Philip Sidney*, p. 218.

24   Robertson (ed.), *Arcadia*, p. 418.

25   H. R. Woudhuysen, *Sir Philip Sidney and the Circulation of Manuscripts, 1558–1640* (Oxford: Clarendon Press, 1996), p. 306.

26   'Imaginative ground-plot' is Sidney's suggestive term in *A Defence of Poetry* for the fictional base upon which the 'profitable invention' of allegory is built. See *Miscellaneous Prose of Sir Philip Sidney*, eds Katherine Duncan-Jones and Jan Van Dorsten (Oxford: Clarendon Press, 1973), p. 103. On Mary Sidney's coterie see Mary Ellen Lamb, *Gender and Authorship in the Sidney Circle* (Madison, WI: University of Wisconsin Press, 1990).

27   John Taylor, *A New Discovery by Sea* (1623), sig. C2; Samuel Daniel, *The Complete Works in Verse and Prose of Samuel Daniel*, ed. Rev. Alexander B. Grosart, vol. 4 (New York: Russell & Russell, 1963), pp. 35–6; John Aubrey, *Brief Lives*, ed. Oliver Lawrence Dick (London: Secker & Warburg, 1958), p. 139; Nicholas Breton, *The Works in Verse and Prose of Nicholas Breton*, ed. Rev. Alexander B. Grosart, vol. 2 (New York: AMS Press, 1966), p. 19.

28   Woudhuysen, *Sir Philip Sidney*, p. 305. Letter to Robert Sidney, October 1580.

29   Robertson (ed.), *Arcadia*, p. 3.

30   Marta Straznicky, *Privacy, Playreading, and Women's Closet Drama, 1550–1700* (Cambridge: Cambridge University Press, 2004), pp. 51–2.

31   See Mary Ellen Lamb, 'The Myth of the Countess of Pembroke: The Dramatic Circle', *The Yearbook of English Studies* 11 (1981), 194–202.

32   Samuel Daniel, *Certaine Small Workes* (1611), sigs E3–E3ᵛ.

33   *The Collected Works of Mary Sidney Herbert, Countess of Pembroke: Poems, Translations, and Correspondence*, eds Margaret P. Hannay, Noel J. Kinnamon and Michael G. Brennan (Oxford: Clarendon Press, 1998), p. 91.

34   A lively account of the politics of this occasion is given by Stewart, *Philip Sidney*, pp. 205–6.

35   *The Countesse of Pembrokes Arcadia* (1598), p. 576. On Mary Sidney's part in the invention and transmission of Philip's literary legacy, see Margaret P. Hannay, '"Bearing the livery of your name": The Countess of Pembroke's Agency in Print and Scribal Publication', *Sidney Journal*, 18 (2000), 7–42.

36   The occasion for the dialogue has been presumed to be the Queen's planned visit to Wilton in 1599, but, as Chambers notes, 'there was no progress in 1599, and progresses planned to Wiltshire in 1600, 1601, and 1602 were abandoned' (Chambers, *Elizabethan Stage*, vol. III. p. 337).

37   John Nichols, *Progresses and Public Processions*, p. 77.

38   The garden is fully described in Roy Strong, *The Renaissance Garden in England* (London: Thames and Hudson, 1979), pp. 147–65.

39   Nicolson, *Arcadia*, pp. 198–9.

40   Nichols, *Progresses and Public Processions*, vol. 1, p. 250; Chambers, *The Elizabethan Stage*, vol. IV, p. 168.

41   Hannay, 'Bearing the livery of your name', p. 203.

42   Bold, *Wilton House*, p. 33.

43   Taylor, *A New Discovery*, sig. C2.

44   John Aubrey, *The Natural History of Wiltshire*, ed. John Britton (Salisbury: Wiltshire Topographical Society, 1847), p. 83; quoted in Strong, *The Renaissance Garden*, p. 149.

45   Strong, *The Renaissance Garden*, pp. 161–4.

46   Cristina Malcolmson, 'William Herbert's Gardener: Adrian Gilbert', in Christopher Hodgkins (ed.), *George Herbert's Pastoral: New Essays on the Poet and Priest of Bemerton*, (Newark, DE: University of Delaware Press, 2010), pp. 113–33.

47   Taylor, *A New Discovery*, sig. C2[v].

48   *John Taylors Wandering, to See the Wonders of the West* (1649), p. 20.

49   Taylor, *A New Discovery*, sigs C2[v]–C3.

50   *John Taylors Wandering*, p. 20.

51   *Relation of a Short Survey of the Western Counties*, Camden Miscellany, Third Series, vol. XVI (London: Camden Society, 1936), p. 66.

52   Thomas Heywood, *Loves Maistresse: Or, The Queens Masque* (1636), sigs A2–A2[v].

53   Nicolson, *Arcadia*, pp. 200–1. For the design, see Stephen Orgel and Roy Strong, *Inigo Jones: The Theatre of the Stuart Court*, vol. 2 (Berkeley, CA: University of California Press, 1973), p. 519, Plate 252.

54   De Caus, *Wilton Garden*, Plate 23, Plate 24.

55   The grotto floor plan is shown in de Caus, *Wilton Garden*, Plate 22.

56   Strong, *The Renaissance Garden*, p. 153.

57   De Caus, *Wilton Garden*, Plate 2.

58   De Caus, *Wilton Garden*, unnumbered Plate.

59   On the wilderness as a garden space, see Kristina Taylor, 'The Earliest Wildernesses: Their Meanings and Developments', *Studies in the History of Gardens and Designed Landscapes* 28 (2008), pp. 237–51. Taylor attributes the wilderness section of Wilton Garden to Lady Anne Clifford who had married Philip Herbert in 1630 and lived at Wilton throughout the time of the garden's reconstruction (p. 243).

60   *John Taylors Wandering*, p. 20.

61   Strong, *The Renaissance Garden*, p. 156.

62   Nicolson, *Arcadia*, p. 61.

63   Strong, *The Renaissance Garden*, p. 158. On the relationship between gardens and theatres in Renaissance Italy, see John Dixon Hunt, *Garden and Grove: The Italian Renaissance Garden in the English Imagination: 1600–1750* (London: J. M. Dent & Sons, 1986), pp. 59–72. Dixon Hunt discusses the influence of these designs on Wilton on pp. 139–42, where he links the double staircase in Wilton Garden to a similar structure at the Vatican Belvedere.

64   Robertson (ed.), *Arcadia*, p. 46.

14

Wilton House and the art of floating meadows

Louise Noble

I propose to raise a golden world (for commonwealth) in the Golden Vale in Herefordshire,' writes Rowland Vaughan in his dedication to a distant cousin, William Herbert, the Third Earl of Pembroke. The dedication, which appears in his 1610 treatise, *Most Approved and Long Experienced Water-workes*, is an appeal to Pembroke for financial support for Vaughan's vision to create an ideal Commonwealth on his Welsh estate (see Figure 14.1).[1] Central to Vaughan's bold plan is the establishment of sophisticated irrigation technology in the form of floated water meadows. The general scholarly consensus is that William, and his brother Philip, paid little heed to Vaughan's work.[2] However, Vaughan's treatise suggests a meeting of minds with his cousins and the renowned intellectual culture of Wilton House.[3] The organic utopian vision and scientific empiricism expressed in *Water-workes* resonate deeply with the intellectual preoccupations of the Wilton Circle: a group of thinkers and writers championed by Pembroke's mother, Mary Sidney, and later by Pembroke himself, and which included in its mélange his close friend, Francis Bacon. The Pembrokes strongly encouraged the development of water meadows on the expansive Wilton estates, which spread over 50,000 acres, and there were obvious pragmatic reasons for doing so. Yet Vaughan's agrarian ideal, in which social utility is a direct outcome of observation and experiment, is consistent with Bacon's theory of 'historia mechanica' and in fact in many ways anticipates by fourteen years Bacon's *New Atlantis*.[4] Significantly, in a land on the hinge of the medieval and the modern, Vaughan's imagined 'golden world' registers the paradox of the Arcadian ideal of England's past, and Bacon's vision of a new 'golden age', which Wilton came to signify.

MOST APPROVED,

And

Long experienced VVater-VVorkes.

Containing,

The manner of *Winter* and *Summer*- drowning of *Medow* and *Pasture*, by the aduantage of the leaft, *Riuer*, *Brooke*, *Fount*, or *Water-prill* adiacent; there-by to make thofe *grounds* (*especially if they be drye*) more Fertile *Ten* for *One.*

As alfo a demonftration of a *Proiect*, for the great benefit of the *Common-wealth* generally, but of *Hereford-fhire* efpecially.

Iudicium *in melius perplexus cuncta referto,* *Vera* rei, *donec fit manifefta* fides.

By ROWLAND VAVGHAN, Efquire.

Imprinted at London by GEORGE ELD. **1610.**

14.1   Title page of Rowland Vaughan's *Most Approved and Long Experienced Water-workes.* London: 1610. STC (2nd edn).

Much has been written about Wilton House as a gathering place for writers, thinkers and scientists who shared creative and intellectual interests and Protestant convictions, and about Mary Sidney, whose hospitality, encouragement and patronage they enjoyed.[5] With its rich and eclectic intellectual culture, Wilton House was the seat of one of the most important literary groups of the age, frequently referred to as the Wilton Circle, or Sidney Circle.[6] Mary was the sister of Philip Sidney, who wrote a good part of his *Arcadia* during extended visits to Wilton and for several years was a central figure in this influential group. For more than a decade after his death in 1586, Mary was considered to be 'the primary female patron of Protestant letters'.[7] An intellectual and respected writer in her own right, she was an enthusiastic supporter of science and literature and frequently hosted and encouraged such writers as Edmund Spenser, Samuel Daniel, Michael Drayton, Abraham Fraunce, Fulke Greville, Nicholas Breton, Thomas Nashe, and a distant relative John Davies of Hereford who, for a period, was secretary to the family.[8] Indeed her commitment to writing and education at Wilton was notable enough for Thomas Churchyard to mention in 1593 that 'she enjoys, the wise *Minervaes* wit, / And sets to schoole, our Poets ev'ry where,' and for Aubrey to identify this collection of 'so many learned and ingeniose persons' as a 'College'.[9] Further, William's tutor at Wilton, Samuel Daniel, in his dedication to William in *A Defence of Ryme* appears genuinely appreciative of Mary for her support: 'Having beene first incourag'd and fram'd thereunto by your most worthy and honourable Mother, and received the first notion for the formall ordering of those compositions at *Wilton*, which I must ever acknowledge to have beene my best schoole, and therof always am to holde a feeling and gratefull memorie'.[10] Consistent with her patronage of the arts, Mary also amassed an extensive library at Wilton, described by John Aubrey as 'the noble librarie of bookes, choicely collected in the time of Mary Countesse of Pembroke'.[11]

This atmosphere of intellectual advocacy and creative endeavours, and exposure to new ideas and aspirations influenced William in his love of poetry and his aesthetic and intellectual interests.[12] On taking up his duties as earl in 1601, Pembroke continued and expanded his mother's function as a literary champion – he was patron to John Donne, Ben Jonson, Inigo Jones, William Shakespeare, and to his kinsman George Herbert – to become, 'the most important patron of the arts of the period'.[13] Brian O'Farrell describes William as 'an improving landlord, a powerful industrial entrepreneur, and an indefatigable promoter of colonial enterprises'.[14] He also forged his own strong academic links: he was Chancellor of the University of Oxford, founded Pembroke College with King James, and played a pivotal role in the establishment of the Bodleian Library.

For Vaughan, of crucial importance to a sympathetic reception of his *Most Approved and Long Experienced Water-workes* was the deep interest in science and chemical experiment at Wilton. Aubrey writes of Mary Sidney that 'She was a great chymist and spent yearly a great deale in that study.'[15] To this end, Mary established, and William continued, a chemistry laboratory at Wilton, which was run for a time by Walter Raleigh's half-brother, the chemist and surveyor, Adrian Gilbert, who resided at Wilton from 1610–28.[16] This scientific curiosity broadened the intellectual milieu of Wilton to also include such thinkers as John Dee, Francis Bacon, and the physician and esteemed entomologist – at one stage the family physician at Wilton – Dr Thomas Moffet (also Muffet, Moufet or Mouffet) who, like Bacon, was a strong advocate of observation and experiment as the foundation of science.[17] Significantly, Adrian Gilbert designed the Wilton garden prior to the elaborate 1630s design of Isaac de Caus, discussed by Marta Straznicky in Chapter 13. Roy Strong describes Gilbert's creation as 'a famous Jacobean garden at Wilton of a heavily geometric and symbolic nature.'[18] Gilbert brought to his task many of the creative and scientific interests dear to the family of Wilton House – gardening, chemistry, mathematics, navigation and alchemy – to painstakingly produce a garden of intricate plantings and a complex, spherical walk of concentric circles.[19] Thus the Pembrokes fostered a strong culture of creative and intellectual inquiry, and participated in the early empirical experiments of modern science in England; these activities permeated and informed every aspect of Wilton: the house, the gardens and the estates. Further, what constituted an advancement of collaborative learning at Wilton House chimed well with Bacon's mandate that 'there is not any more worthie, then the further endowement of the world with sound and fruitfull knowledge', and was a blueprint of sorts for Bacon's grand design for collaborative research and laboratories in Salomon's House in his *New Atlantis*.[20]

The circulation of knowledge gleaned from observation and experiment is identified by Vaughan as a major purpose for the production of his work. 'You shall,' he tells the reader, 'have all I know to the uttermost.'[21] The scientific empiricism of his hydrological innovation and the practical and social benefits which are the direct outcomes of its success have much in common with Bacon's theories as well as the activities and preoccupations of Wilton. It comes as no surprise then that Vaughan would appeal to William Pembroke, a man with the progressive interests and learning to appreciate his vision, who was not only his cousin but also a person of wide-reaching influence, or that he would invoke another of his cousins, John Davies of Hereford, a poet and writing-master who was also an insider in the Wilton group, to write an introduction to the work. Vaughan's dedication to William opens with the declaration that 'I have out of my lives experience, prepared a Watry workemanshipp.'[22] This attempt at wry humour is belied by the earnestness of his claim that the irrigation system he describes is founded on details observed through experience. This is entirely consistent with Bacon's concept of social utility. Indeed Frederick O. Waage proposes that 'Bacon's most "visionary" scientific writing actually contains his most viable, proven, empirical assumption: that the authority of experiment leads directly to successful practical application.'[23] The pioneering and experimental atmosphere of Wilton with which Bacon was closely associated was ripe for agricultural and hydrological innovations such as the irrigated water meadows on which Vaughan's rural utopia depends. In addition, the complex design and economic and social benefits of Vaughan's meadow irrigation project fits well with what Adam Nicolson describes as the 'conceptual geography' and 'organic integrity' of Wilton House, its gardens and estates.[24] By dedicating his work to William Pembroke, Vaughan consciously inserts his text not only into the rarefied air of Wilton but also into the arena of the most significant agricultural advancement of the age.

The art of floating meadows has a long and significant history in rural England. An innovative form of artificial irrigation, water meadows presented an elegant yet practical solution for managing and distributing rural water, and for several centuries had a major impact on the productivity of English agriculture. While there is evidence in the historical landscape of catchwork meadow irrigation since the Middle Ages, with some evidence pointing as far back as Roman Britain, the more complex bedwork system was advanced and adopted primarily in the sixteenth and seventeenth centuries, and was enthusiastically developed and embraced in the wave of agrarian reform of the eighteenth and nineteenth centuries.[25] In 1849, the editor of the *Journal of the Royal Agricultural Society*, Philip Pusey, heralds water meadows as,

> The triumph of agricultural art: changing as it does, the very seasons … .a slight film of water trickling over the surface rouses the sleeping grass, tinges it with living green amidst snows or frosts, and brings forth a luxuriant crop in early spring, just when it is most wanted while other meadows are bare and brown. It is a cheerful sight to see the wild birds haunting these green spots among the hoar-frost at Christmas; or the lambs, with their mothers, folded on them in March.[26]

Pusey's rhetoric here reveals not only the long-term significance of water meadows for agricultural production but also, with their ability to manipulate the seasons, their evocative power for a cultural imagination deeply invested in the ideal of a perfect green world. The mirror-glazed appearance created by the surface irrigation of meadows – usually referred to as 'floating' or 'drowning' – is indelibly imprinted on much of the historic English physical and cultural landscape. Two hundred and fifty years earlier than Pusey in his Panegyrick introduction to Vaughan's work, John Davies similarly describes the magical quality of a water meadow landscape: 'Such is this Water-glasse, wherein these Times / Do see how to adorne their Meades in Greene.'[27] And Andrew Marvell is inspired to paint the meadows at Appleton House as 'polished grass / A landscape drawn in looking glass' which 'seem' like the ocean until 'Denton sets ope' its cataracts,' flooding the meadows so that they 'truly be … a sea.'[28] Such figuring reflects the startling effectiveness of this technology to produce green

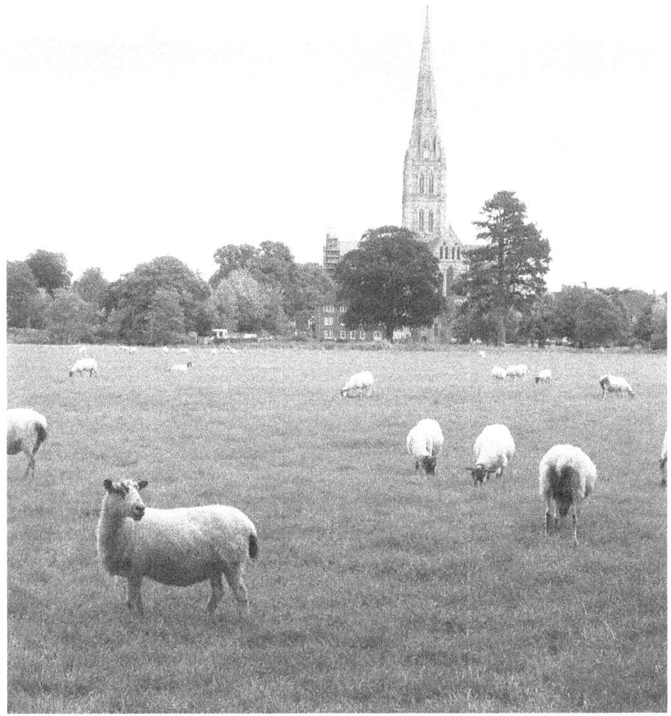

14.2　The Harnham water meadows near Wilton, Wiltshire. A number of individual meadows were part of the Wilton estate.

pasture from nutrient deficient and browned winter fields and is reinforced in Vaughan's witty imperative: 'Let all men drowne before they Mowe, and after Mowing, your grasse will not bee yellow, but as greene as a Leake.'[29]

While meadow irrigation was carried out in almost all of Britain – Vaughan developed his water meadows in Herefordshire – the practice is most characteristic of the mineral-rich chalklands of Dorset, Hampshire and Wiltshire: a landscape within which Wilton House and its estates are deeply embedded (see Figures 14.2 and 14.3).[30] An efficient and ecologically sustainable system of channels, carriers, weirs, hatches and drains were deployed to control rivers and streams by carrying water onto fields, keeping it gently moving, and draining it off again. Joseph Bettey explains that this controlled watering solved

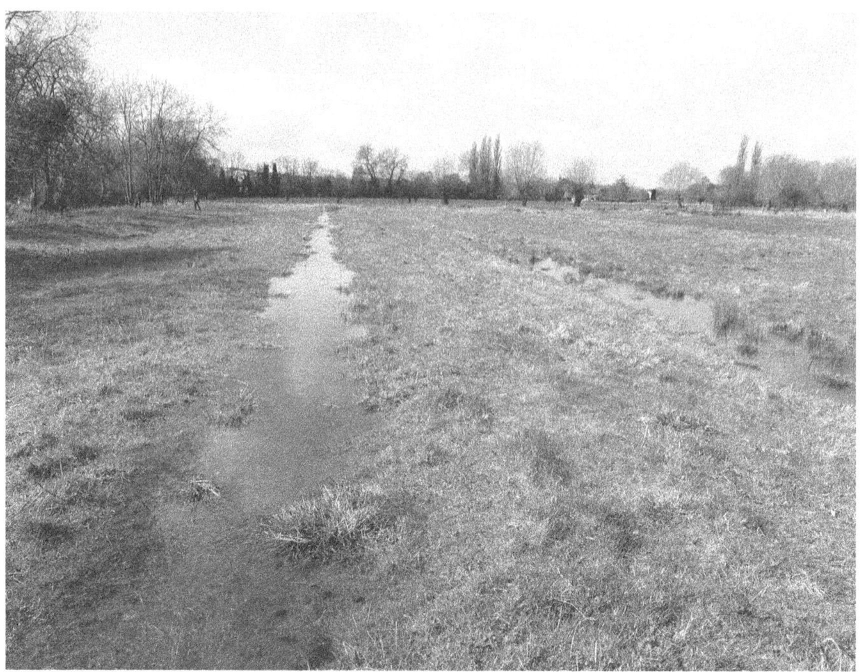

14.3   Drowning of the lower Seven Acres on the Harnham water meadows near Wilton, Wiltshire. A number of individual meadows were part of the Wilton estate.

an age-old problem of lack of feed during March and April by pre-empting spring growth by several weeks.[31] The more complex bedworks required the services of a specialist drowner to carefully control the irrigation times and flow rates of water across the surface. Further, once the system was established it was important to ensure the fair distribution of water to all users.[32] Briefly, the major benefit of water meadows was enhanced agricultural efficiency achieved by producing early grass for grazing and a later crop that could be cut for hay, richly fertilised by valuable nutrients from the water and dung from intensive sheep folding; furthermore, water meadows substantially improved the value of rural land.[33] Davies highlights this when he writes that, 'in His Drownings … [Vaughan] … makes Lands arise, / In grace and goodnesse to the highest pitch; / And Meades and Pastures price he multiples.'[34] For these reasons, the more sophisticated forms of floated meadows had many proponents amongst agricultural innovators such as Rowland Vaughan and his Pembroke cousins.

In 1610, Vaughan dedicates *Water-workes* to William Pembroke in an effort to secure funds for his dream of transforming his Hereford estate into a self-contained commonwealth of social well-being and high productivity. Here his neighbours, referred to as 'my Mechanicals', some 'five hundred poore habitations:

whose greatest meanes consist of spinning Flaxe, Hempe, and Hurdes' will be gainfully employed in their respective crafts and in his mills; thus the poverty, hunger, sickness and idleness created by winter and unreliable seasons of crop failure will be alleviated.[35] *Water-workes* is a heartfelt expression of concern for the physical and moral well-being of the unemployed labourers and craftspeople in the Golden Valley of Hereford and an inspired welfare solution. Vaughan, it seems, will be an exacting but benevolent and fair master whose mechanicals 'shall never loose an houres time to provide for such meanes as backe or belly requires: bread, beefe, butter and cheese of my own provision, shall attend their appointed hours, without their trouble or losse of labor'.[36] Crucial to the success of this 'golden world' is the installation of water meadows – in fact, all improvements and guaranteed employment and production will flow from this effective and environmentally enriching water technology (see Figure 14.4). By extending the growing season and thus increasing productivity, Vaughan will provide reliable employment and sustenance for the poverty-stricken workers in his district. In the fashion of a true empiricist, Vaughan's brainwave comes from his observations of the riverside habits of moles on his estate and his curiosity about what he perceives as the irrigation benefits of their behaviour:

> I happened to find a Mole or Wants nest, raised on the brim of the Brooke like a great hillocke; from which nest or hillocke, there issued a little streame of water (drawne by the working of the wante) downe a shelving or descending ground, one pace broad, and some twenty in length. The running of which little Streame, did (at that time) wonderfully content me, seeing it pleasing Greene; and that other on both sides full of Mosse, and Hide-bound for want of water. This was the first cause I under-tooke the drowning of grounds.[37]

From this observation Vaughan extrapolates and puts into practice the principles and methods of controlled meadow irrigation. He is keenly perceptive and practical and his treatise represents the creative application of his close study. While the utopian socialist propositions of the text are somewhat visionary, the description of meadow irrigation technology is not. The water meadow project on Vaughan's estate was fully operational for some twenty years before his text was published. His vision, therefore, is firmly underpinned by his knowledge of the practical outcome of direct observation and experiment.

Moreover, Vaughan believes his prototype to be not only unique but also crucial to the intelligent management of water nationally. 'Since the first Time I undertooke the drowning of my groundes,' he writes,

> I … sought to better my understanding by other mens labours: yet in the whole Kingdom I never found, nor heard of a work worthy of observation: Having so many Rivers, Brooks, Fountaines and Springs, which run idely unto the Sea: without Weare, Sluce, Stay, Stanke or dam, to turne some part of them upon grounds that need them.[38]

By way of encouragement, Vaughan urges his reader to 'pry into every Fallow-field, Dung hil, and Water-course in your neighbourhood' to gauge the quantity

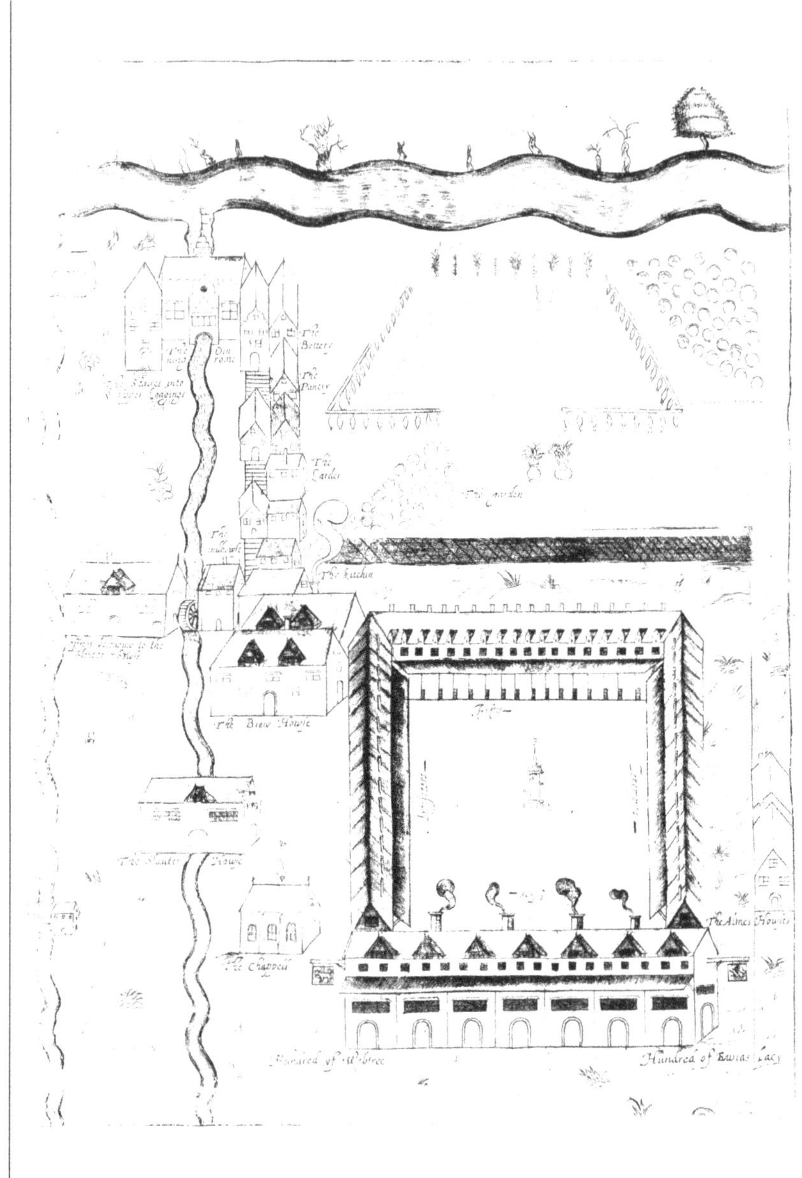

14.4   Vaughan's imagined commonwealth. *Most Approved and Long Experienced Water-workes*. London: 1610. STC (2nd edn) from the Henry E. Huntington Library and Art Gallery.

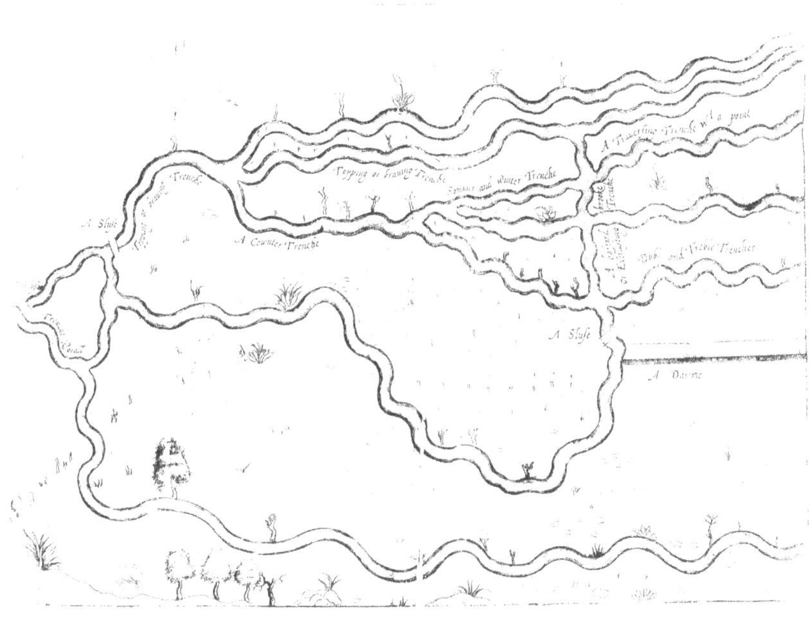

14.5　Vaughan's water meadow irrigation system. *Most Approved and Long Experienced Water-workes*. London: 1610. STC (2ⁿᵈ edn) from the Henry E. Huntington Library and Art Gallery.

and quality of water to be diverted. Then, he continues, 'plant your weare or scluce in height levell with the bank … and carry your Trench-Royall … so farre as your ground extends … levell'. This enables the flow of water from the weir to the end of the trench and back again 'over your scluce into the River or brooke'. This affords a 'full command forward and backward to drowne at your pleasure' (see Figure 14.5).[39] Clearly evident in his text is an already tested and perfected – Vaughan is, after all, in 'full command' – hydrological model, the proven benefits of which inspire his model commonwealth where all will reap the profits. Thus *Water-workes* represents a genuine effort to disseminate the practical outcomes of his experiment and their relevance and advantages for daily life. His aim is 'to put a foote the Mistery of Winter and Sommer-drownings, to the comfort of the Countrey and present profit of the present Inhabitants.'[40] Here we recognise the spirit of Bacon's imperative of the importance of the mechanical arts as sources of empirical knowledge and the application of this knowledge to the restoration of society as expressed by one of the Fathers of Salomon's House in *New Atlantis*: 'The End of our Foundation is the knowledge of Causes, and secret motions of things; and the enlarging of the bounds of Human Empire, to the effecting of all things possible.'[41] In fact, although written fourteen years earlier, there are several other important aspects of Vaughan's utopia that are recognisable in Bacon's text. For example, the wide range of trades and crafts that appears in the comprehensive catalogue of the skills of the Golden Valley community closely resemble those of the inhabitants of Salomon's House who are 'in function craftsmen'.[42] In addition, Vaughan's model of surface irrigation to accelerate spring growth is a utilitarian art that functions to 'Helpe Nature in her Workes, that workes for you.'[43] A similar process of manipulating natural cycles to enhance production is practiced in Salomon's House, where they 'make (by art) in ... orchards and gardens, trees and flowers to come to earlier or later than their seasons; and to come up and bear more speedily than by their natural course they do.'[44]

Hence as a student and synthesiser of natural phenomenon, Vaughan is a true natural philosopher. *Water-workes* fits into the category of what Waage calls 'a vernacular literature of empirical scientific investigation'.[45] The explication of the 'Mistery of winter and summer drownings' and the expression of benevolence surrounding the application of this technology strongly reflect Bacon's theory of 'historia mechanica', as set out in *The Advancement of Learning*, which is

> ... of all others the most radicall and fundamentall towards Naturall Philosophie, such Natural Philosophie, as shall not vanish in the fume of subtile, sublime, or delectable speculation, but such as shall bee operative to the endowment, and benefit of Mans life: for it will not onely minister and suggest for the present, Many ingenious practises in all trades, by connexion and transferring of the observations of one Arte, to the use of another, when the experiences of severall misteries shall fall under the consideration of one mans mind.[46]

Bacon's mandate for 'the benefit of Mans life' echoes Vaughan's humanitarian vision; indeed, Vaughan himself represents Bacon's ideal man of science for whom compassion is invariably the true mark. This is embodied in the figure of the Father of Salomon's House who appears in *New Atlantis* and whose defining quality has to do with compassion: 'He was a man of middle stature and age, comely of person, and had an aspect as if he pitied men.'[47] Certainly *Water-workes* can be seen as a serious attempt to establish a duty of care for the struggling workers of Vaughan's Hereford vale.

The philosophy of commonwealth that underpins Vaughan's image of a 'golden world' hovers between two worlds: one holding on cautiously to the customs of the past, and one reaching out eagerly for the challenges of modernity. While this vision has much in common with Bacon's futuristic imagining of a new 'golden age', in its organic utopianism, where a fine balance exists between the landscape, the estate and the people, it also registers the holistic nature of the traditional rural systems that managed the ideal 'golden world' of the past. Wilton House came to embody both of these worlds: in its rural seclusion the appearance of idyllic social order for the Pembroke estates and all of its inhabitants depended on an ancient hierarchical system of checks and balances that maintained the equilibrium between landscape and people. The English stream, described by Nicholson as 'one of the lingering afterglows of feudalism' is the lynch pin for this socio-ecological balance.[48] At Wilton the expression of such organic perfection can be found in the sparkling chalk streams, the Wylye, Nadder and Ebble that have converged through the centuries in the region dominated by the Pembroke estates. But as Bettey points out, these streams, 'with their constant temperature, valuable nutrients and calcareous nature were ideally suited for watering meadows and for encouraging an early and abundant growth of grasses'.[49] For the inhabitants of Wilton these streams also represented an opportunity to move into a new age underwritten by empirical science.

As England moved into the seventeenth century, the Pembrokes were poised, both practically and intellectually, for the development of floated water meadows on their Wiltshire estates. The earliest records of these innovations occur in the Wilton manorial surveys, which show that from 1605 onwards water meadows were enthusiastically developed along the Wylye, Nadder and Ebble. The 1620s records of the Earl's manors of Chalke, Chilmark and Netherhampton make reference to meadows as 'water mead', 'water close', and 'wett mead', suggesting that this form of irrigation was already well established by this date.[50] A detailed description of the communal process for the adoption of a major irrigation scheme can be found in the 1632 Court Rolls of the Manor of Wylye, with 'An Order for the Flotting and Watering of the Meadowes'. The record states:

> It is ordered, concluded and agreed at this courte betweene Sir Gyles Mompesson, knight, and Guy Everley, freeholders within this mannor, and others the tenantes of the residue of the freeholders, and the customary tenants and others of this mannor now present, and by and with the consent and approbacion of the said William Kent, steward of this mannor, of thone parte, and John Knight of Stockton in the County of Wiltes, for and concerninge the wateringe and flotting of the groundes within this mannor called the Marshe, Nettlemeade and the Moores, for the better improvement of them in yerely value.[51]

This agreement represents a comprehensive community engagement process in which all stakeholders agreed on the development and future management of water meadows for mutual benefit. In this document, all aspects of water meadow management are settled: the construction and maintenance of the meadows; the sharing of costs, labour and benefits; the number and times of drownings per season; and the penalties for misappropriating water. All parties agree to 'performe this agreement upon paynes and penalties to be therein expressed, being a business conceived to be very behoofefull and beneficiall to all the inhabitants of this mannor'.[52] Here we see an example of the old custom of communal decision-making rubbing up against the introduction of the new technologies of agrarian reform, which were rapidly being adopted.

Evidence suggests that the pragmatic and progressive Pembrokes quickly introduced the new technology, which reached its 'earliest perfection' in the Salisbury Plain region at the beginning of the seventeenth century;[53] however, it is reasonable to assume that water meadows were developed well before this date on the Wilton estates, coinciding with their earlier implementation on Vaughan's Hereford estate. In Sidney's *New Arcadia*, written during his visits to Wilton, Zelmane, who is watching Philoclea bathing in the River Ladon, addresses the river to bewail those 'unjust niggards [who] make weirs to spoil thy beauty.'[54] This attack on greedy users who hoard water for their own use suggests the development of floated water meadows on the Wilton estates some time before Sidney's death in 1586, and registers the frequent conflicts over water rights and distribution that these innovations provoked. Certainly the description of the waters of Arcadia's River Ladon, which 'run upon so fine and delicate a ground as one could not easily judge whether the river did more wash the gravel, or the gravel did purify the river', evokes the clear, chalk-filtered purity of the rivers he and the Pembrokes would have enjoyed at Wilton.[55] And elsewhere in *Arcadia* we are introduced to ' … these fresh and delightful brooks, how slowly they slide away, as loath to leave the company of so many things united in perfection! And with how sweet a murmur they lament their forced departure!'[56] In Sidney's celebration of the perfection of the Wilton streams, and his lament for the potential of irrigation technology to spoil such perfection, we see a world at odds with itself: momentarily lost in the transition between old and new, between a world that idealised the human relationship with nature and a world that grasped the human potential to manipulate nature for its own ends.

Similarly, Vaughan's *Water-workes* also hovers in this transitional space. Davies declares that with Vaughan's invention, 'The Golden-age is now return'd again.'[57] Yet the text is not attempting to recall a lost ideal: with its forward-thinking hydrological scheme and its utopian vision that so clearly anticipates Bacon's *New Atlantis*, its trajectory is firmly futuristic. The Earl of Pembroke may very well have been indifferent to Vaughan's work, as others have argued. However, the positive impact of hydrological innovation for the future economic and social stability of the community on Vaughan's own estate is convincing. With its appeal to his cousin for support, its scientific empiricism and social utopianism, which so closely resembles the thinking of one of William's closest friends, *Water-workes* circulated in a complex system of the advancement of knowledge and new science that defined the Wilton Circle. Thus there is a compelling connection to be made between Vaughan's text, the intellectual culture of Wilton House, and the establishment of water meadows on the Pembroke estates.

Acknowledgements

I wish to thank the Folger Shakespeare Library for awarding me a Short-Term Research Fellowship in 2009, which enabled me to conduct much of the research presented in this chapter.

Notes

1   Rowland Vaughan, *Most Approved and Long Experienced Water-workes* (London: 1610) sig. E2[r]. This work is the first known published, detailed description of how to plan, develop and manage floated water meadows. The Pembrokes had close historical family ties with the Vaughans and with Herefordshire.

2   For example Frederick O. Waage writes that Pembroke was indifferent to Vaughan's work, although no evidence is supplied to support this, in 'Touching the Compass: Empiricism in Popular Scientific Writing of Bacon's Time', *Huntington Library Quarterly*, 41: 3 (1978), 206.

3   My thinking here is consistent with that of Joseph Bettey who notes that it is plausible that this family connection facilitated the introduction of water meadows to the southern chalklands; see 'The Development of Water Meadows in the Southern Counties', in Hadrian Cook and Tom Williamson (eds), *Water Management in the English Landscape: Field, Marsh and Meadow*, (Edinburgh: Edinburgh University Press, 1999), p. 180.

4   Waage also identifies the relationship between Vaughan's text and Bacon's work in 'Touching the Compass: Empricism in Popular Scientific Writing of Bacon's Time', *Huntington Library Quarterly*, 41:3 (1978), 201–16.

5   See for example Francis Berkeley Young, *Mary Sidney, Countess of Pembroke* (London: D. Nutt, 1912); Tresham Lever, *The Herberts of Wilton* (London: John Murray, 1967); Margaret P. Hannay, *Philip's Phoenix: Mary Sidney, Countess of Pembroke* (Oxford: Oxford University Press, 1990); Mary Ellen Lamb, *Gender and Authorship in the Sidney Circle* (Madison, WI: University of Wisconsin Press, 1990); Adam Nicolson, *Arcadia: The Dream of Perfection in Renaissance England* (London: Harper Perennial, 2008).

6   I am mindful here of Mary Ellen Lamb's caution that the terms 'circle' and 'influence' can be misleading and should be used carefully when referring to intellectual and literary alliances in the age. See 'The Myth of the Countess of Pembroke: the Dramatic Circle', *The Yearbook of English Studies* 11 (1981), 202.

7   Hannay, *Philip's Phoenix*, p. 79.

8   It is difficult to ascertain exactly who circulated at different times within the Wilton ambit, but the names of these particular writers occur frequently in the scholarship.

9   John Aubrey, *Brief Lives*, ed. Andrew Clark (Oxford: Clarendon Press, 1898), p. 311. Original emphasis. Thomas Churchyard, *A Pleasant Conceite Penned in Verse* (London, 1593) sig. B[r].

10   Samuel Daniel, *The Complete Works in Verse and Prose of Samuel Daniel*, ed. Rev. Alexander B. Grosart, vol. 4 (New York: Russell & Russell, 1963), pp. 35–6. Original emphasis.

11   John Aubrey, *The Natural History of Wiltshire*, ed. John Britton (1847), *Project Gutenberg*, January 2004. www.gutenberg.org.cache/epub/4934/pg4934.html, accessed 13 January 2013, p. 78.

12   Brian O'Farrell, *Shakespeare's Patron: William Herbert, Third Earl of Pembroke, 1580:1630: Politics, Patronage and Power* (London: Continuum International Publishing Group, 2011), p. 5.

13   O'Farrell, *Shakespeare's Patron*, p. vii.

14   O'Farrell, *Shakespeare's Patron*, p. vii.

15   Aubrey, *Brief Lives*, p. 311.

16   Christina Malcolmson, 'William Herbert's Gardener: Adrian Gilbert', *George Herbert's Pastoral: New Essays on the Poet and Priest of Bemerton* (Newark, DE: University of Delaware Press, 2010), p. 113.

17   Janice Neri, *The Insect and the Image: Visualizing Nature in Early Modern Europe, 1500–1700* (Minneapolis: The University of Minnesota Press, 2011), p. 30.

18   Roy Strong, *The Renaissance Garden in England* (London: Thames and Hudson, 1979), p. 123.

19   Malcolmson, 'William Herbert's Gardener', p. 121.

20   Francis Bacon, *The Advancement of Learning*, ed. Michael Kiernan (Oxford: Clarendon Press, 2000).

21   Vaughan, *Most Approved and Long Experienced*, sig. M2[v].

22   Vaughan, *Most Approved and Long Experienced*, sig. D4[r].

23   Waage, 'Touching the Compass', p. 206.

24   Nicolson, *Arcadia*, pp. 25, 29.

25   For explanations of these different forms of meadow irrigation systems, and the earliest instances of irrigated water meadows in England see Christopher Taylor, 'The Archaeology of Water Meadows', pp. 22–34, and Tom Williamson, '"Floating" in Context: Meadows in the Long Term', pp. 35–51, in Hadrian Cook and Tom Williamson (eds), *Water Meadows: History, Ecology and Conservation* (Windgather Press, 2007). See also Hadrian Cook, Kathy Stearne and Tom Williamson, 'The Origins of Water Meadows in England', *British Agricultural History Review*, 51.2 (2003), 155–62.

26   Philip Pusey, 'On the Theory and Practice of Water-Meadows', *The Journal of the Royal Agricultural Society of England*, 10.2 (1849), 462.

27   Vaughan, *Most Approved and Long Experienced*, sig. B2[v].

28   Andrew Marvell, *Upon Appleton House*, *The Norton Anthology of English Literature: The Sixteenth Century / The Early Seventeenth Century*, ed. Stephen Greenblatt, 8th edition, vol. B (New York: W.W. Norton, 2006), pp. 457–68.

29   Vaughan, *Most Approved and Long Experienced*, sig. R2.

30   Cook and Williamson, *Water Meadows*, note that while water meadows were developed in other regions they did not have the long-term central role in agricultural production as they did in the counties of Wiltshire, Dorset and Hampshire, p. 5.

31   Joseph Bettey, 'The Floated Water Meadows of Wessex: A Triumph of English Agriculture', in Cook and Williamson (eds), *Water Meadows*, p. 8.

32   Joseph Bettey (ed.), *Wiltshire Farming in the Seventeenth Century*, Wiltshire Record Society (Salisbury: Salisbury Printing Company, 2005), p. 238.

33   Bettey, 'The Floated Water Meadows', pp. 185–7.

34   Vaughan, *Most Approved and Long Experienced*, sig. B[v].

35   Vaughan, *Most Approved and Long Experienced*, sigs E2[v], E3[r].

36   Vaughan, *Most Approved and Long Experienced*, sig. E4[v].

37   Vaughan, *Most Approved and Long Experienced*, sig. L[v].

38   Vaughan, *Most Approved and Long Experienced*, sig. M[v].

39   Vaughan, *Most Approved and Long Experienced*, sig. M2[v]. Also quoted in Waage, 'Touching the Compass', p. 208.

40   Vaughan, *Most Approved and Long Experienced*, sig. H4[v].

41   Francis Bacon, *New Atlantis and The Great Instauration*, ed. Jerry Weinberger (Wheeling: Harlan Davidson, Inc., 1989), p. 71.

42   Vaughan, *Most Approved and Long Experienced*, sig. E4[r]. Waage, 'Touching the Compass', p. 205.

43　Vaughan, *Most Approved and Long Experienced*, sig. B3[r].

44　Bacon, *New Atlantis*, 74.

45　Waage, 'Touching the Compass', p. 202.

46　Bacon, *The Advancement of Learning*, 65.

47　Bacon, *New Atlantis*, 69.

48　Nicolson, *Arcadia*, p. 2.

49　Bettey, 'The Floated Water Meadows', p. 179.

50　Bettey, 'The Floated Water Meadows', p. 180.

51　Eric Kerridge, *Surveys of the Manors of Philip, First Earl of Pebroke and Montgomery, 1631–2* (London: Headley Brothers, 1953), p. 138.

52　Kerridge, *Surveys*, p. 139.

53　Eric Kerridge, 'The Sheepfold in Wiltshire and the Floating of the Watermeadows', *The Economic History Review*, new series, 6:3 (1954), 282.

54　Philip Sidney, *The Countess of Pembroke's Arcadia*, ed. Victor Skretkowicz (Oxford: Oxford University Press, 1985), p. 190.

55　Sidney, *The Countess of Pembroke's Arcadia*, p. 188.

56　Sidney, *The Countess of Pembroke's Arcadia*, p. 45.

57　Vaughan, *Most Approved and Long Experienced*, sig. B3[v].

15

Wilton House and seventeenth-century country house literature

Anne M. Myers

In 1774, George Richardson published *Aedes Pembrochianae, Or a Critical Account of the Statues, Bustos, Relievos, Paintings, Medals, and Other Antiquities and Curiosities at Wilton-House*. Here, claims the title page, 'The ancient poets and artists [are] made mutually to explain and illustrate each other.' Also advertised as part of the volume's content are 'An Extract of the Rules to Judge of the Goodness of a Picture' and 'The Science of a Connoisseur in Painting'.[1] These descriptions of the volume's content reflect two distinct approaches to interpreting Wilton House and its collections. The first is grounded in the methodology of early modern antiquarianism: it is concerned not only with objects but with their histories as understood through the corroboration of textual with non-textual remains. Indeed, the Preface to the *Critical Account* frames the work as 'the antiquary's *Vade Mecum*'[2] and notes that the contemporary house-steward had 'supplied the Editors with the books and manuscripts that related to the collection, and with every other material in his power that could throw light on the undertaking'.[3] In fact, the author suggests that the guidebook might 'be in great measure amusing and interesting' even to those who would not have the opportunity actually to visit Wilton in person.[4] Thus, he imagines that the antiquities and curiosities of Wilton House might be experienced through reading a text containing 'many historical and classical remarks', rather than through direct visual experience or aesthetic response.[5] In addition, Richardson's tour through the house includes not only the names of the artists to whom he attributes works of art and architecture, but the names, histories and characters of socially prominent individuals connected with the site. For instance, he writes, 'Henry VIII. on the dissolution of the monasteries, bestowed on Sir William Herbert, first earl of Pembroke, the house and site of Wilton-abbey, and the lands belonging to it. This monarch was fond of pomp and magnificence; and his nobility having imbibed his expensive taste, the spoils of the church enabled them to imitate his example.'[6]

Richardson's second approach to the interpretation of Wilton House, though, has less to do with classical texts or human history. Instead, it has precisely to do with the direct visual experience and aesthetic response that could not be gained by reading a text about the house. 'Painting', he says in 'The Science of a Connoisseur in Painting', 'affords us a great variety of this kind of pleasure in the delicate or bold management of the pencil; in the mixture of its colours, in the skilful contrivance of the several parts of the picture, and infinite variety of the tincts, so as to produce beauty and harmony.'[7]

This chapter begins with Richardson's eighteenth-century guidebook to Wilton House because its two distinct approaches – the historical and textual on the one hand, and the visual and aesthetic on the other – succinctly illustrate two ways in which the architecture and contents of Wilton House have been interpreted and written about since at least the early seventeenth century. That is to say, the house has become the object of two modes of architectural literacy. Further, this chapter will demonstrate that in its reflection of these two different and sometimes competing modes, writing about Wilton House participates in a broader trend, which is visible in other seventeenth-century writing about the English country house. Here, this broader context is represented with analysis of passages from two well-known country house poems of the period, Ben Jonson's 'To Penshurst' (c.1612) and Thomas Carew's 'To My Friend G.N., from Wrest' (1639). Taken together with these other works, writing about Wilton House reveals the sixteenth- and seventeenth-century roots of two forms of architectural interpretation that coexist, in many cases, to the present day.

Wilton House's status as both a converted monastery and an early masterpiece of English Palladian style has made it particularly susceptible to the emphases of both antiquarian and aesthetic modes of architectural literacy. The monastic grounds and buildings were handed over to William Herbert, soon to be Earl of Pembroke, between 1542 and 1544, shortly after the dissolution.[8] Early modifications to the house seem to have consisted of a piecemeal adaptation of parts of the old monastery.[9] Because of its medieval history, it appealed to the concerns of the antiquarian chorographer William Camden, who dedicated a long paragraph to Wilton (monastery, town and house) in the first English edition of the *Britannia* (1610). Judging by the space Camden allots to various portions of his account, the most noteworthy features of Wilton were found in its antiquity, and Camden gleans the early history of the building by consulting historical documents, exemplifying an approach to architectural interpretation which is more textual than it is either visually descriptive or archaeological. He quotes from two documents at some length: a 'Charter of [King] *Eadgar* himselfe, bearing date, *An.* 874', and 'the life of Saint Edward the Confessor', from which Camden takes the following description: 'Whiles S. Edward went in hand with the building of the Monasterie of S. Peter in Westminster, Editha his wife began at Wilton (where she was brought up) a Monastery princely built of stone, in lieue of the Church, made of timber, following the Kings good affection with the like devotion of her own.' Of the seventeenth-century house, Camden has much less to say, noting only that Wilton, the 'small Village' has 'in it a passing fine house of the Earles of *Pembroks*, raised out of the ruines of the old religious house.'[10] Camden's narration is typical of the antiquarian and chorographic perspectives of the *Britannia* in two ways: first, its methodology is based partly on the inspection of written documentary evidence (some approximation of library research). Camden's only vaguely aesthetic judgment of the building is that in its reconstructed form it is 'passing fine.'

Second, there is a marked interest in the building's human history, in the social identities and even the characters of prominent individuals associated with the place. We might see, in Camden's mention of Editha's 'like devotion', manifested in the construction of the monastery, a foreshadowing of Richardson's interest in the qualities and penchants of past historical figures. Despite the different historical periods to which they refer, both the medieval documents Camden draws from and his own, post-Reformation, description of the house share an emphasis on these human connections, on the way buildings could be made to speak about people. In antiquarian chorography, it is difficult to speak about the 'architecture' of Wilton House because architecture, landscape and patron or landowner each form a strand of the integrated text.

In addition to its antiquarian appeal, Wilton House has been the object of considerable aesthetic and architectural study since the early part of the seventeenth century, only a decade or two after the publication of the English *Britannia*. Known as an example of early English Palladianism, and, slightly later, as the site of a fine collection of sculpture and painting, Wilton House has attracted sustained attention as a work of visual interest and an example of a particular aesthetic style.[11] These critical lenses may feel more familiar to the modern reader of architectural history than Camden's antiquarian approach because, as Dana Arnold has shown, they characterise the way architectural history is often studied and departmentalised in the modern academy. The tendency to locate architectural history in art history departments, Arnold writes, has made it the 'institutional preserve' of a discipline 'whose primary concern is properly with aesthetics.'[12] In *Wilton House and English Palladianism: Some Wiltshire Houses* (1988), John Bold and John Reeves offer a useful description of the features and architectural developments that come sharply into focus when Wilton House is viewed from the perspective of its aesthetic features and stylistic allegiances. It is worth pausing to consider their modern account of these features as a context for understanding early modern accounts. A survey of Pembroke's lands made in 1565 illustrates a new gatehouse and east entrance range, which Bold and Reeves characterise in terms of aesthetic period and style as having an 'air of early Renaissance endeavor'.[13] The main surviving vestige of the Tudor house is the Holbein Porch, so called because its design is traditionally assigned to Hans Holbein, although, as Bold and Reeves point out, the attribution is chronologically impossible, since Holbein died in 1543, and the heraldic panels on the porch make a date earlier than 1548 impossible. The authors interpret this feature through a comparison to the standards of classical aesthetics, noting that we encounter an unusually advanced 'understanding for the proportions and relationships of its superimposed Orders'.[14]

During the seventeenth century, Wilton House underwent further, more famous modifications. It was during the 1630s that work on the renowned south front began.[15] This portion of the house lends itself well to what Arnold identifies as another preoccupation of some modern architectural historiography: identification with the career of a particular architect.[16] The south front is often noted not only for its early reference to Palladian style, but for its indirect association with Inigo Jones, who, according to John Aubrey, gave his 'advice and approbation' to the design.[17] Aubrey attributes the design to Solomon de Caus, but Howard Colvin has since shown the designer to have been de Caus's son or nephew, Isaac, who had worked under Jones at both the Whitehall Banqueting House and Covent Garden.[18] De Caus's original design was, in Bold and Reeves's estimation, 'nothing short of palatial', and the version that was actually realised, and that remains partly intact today, was significantly scaled down.[19] A fire in 1647 led to Wilton's association with another, perhaps better known, student of Jones, as reconstructions were carried out under the direction of John Webb.[20] While it might be argued that Camden did not mention these aesthetic innovations because they had not yet been completed at the time he wrote, his concern with documentary evidence, human history and aristocratic association is characteristic of the *Britannia* as a whole. Only once, in more than 800 folio pages, does he identify any architecture with Italian aesthetic style, and his description of the house as 'passing fine' is an accurate representation of his rather blunt verbal tools for describing architectural appearances.[21]

There is no seventeenth-century account of Wilton House that displays anything like Bold and Reeves's finely tuned vocabulary for the description of architectural style and aesthetic influence. In 1635, however, a Lieutenant Hammond visited the house and recorded his reactions in his *Relation of a Short Survey of the Western Counties*. And Hammond, while not equipped with the architectural connoisseurship of a modern architectural historian, nevertheless testifies to the incipient development of a strain of architectural appreciation based on visual experience, rather than on a purely historical or antiquarian sensibility. Hammond writes that he visited Wilton to see a 'stately, and Princelike House; the Roomes, Chambers, and other delights within, and the pleasant Gardens, Orchards, and walkes without, such as renders it indeed, the onely Grace and Glorie of the Towne, where I had curteous admittance'.[22] Hammond does not mention the exterior of the house; he may either have found it unremarkable, since the main works there do not seem to have begun until the year following his visit, or he may simply have had little interest or education in evaluating the façades of houses. Having entered the house, however, Hammond's description is generated by intense visual stimulation. The description also gives a sense of the house's spatial arrangement, since he describes his tour room by room. First, he was shown

> the Gallery, richly hung, and adorn'd with stately and faire Pictures; next through a near withdrawing Roome into the Earles Bed-Chamber, which was most richly hang'd. The chamber next the Garden, call'd the King's Chamber, the Hangings therein being Cloth of Gold, and on over the Chimney Peece is the statue of King Henry 8th. Richly cut, and gilded over. Next was I shew'd the King's withdrawing Roome, and the Billiard table Chamber, next the Chapell, both richly hung. The great Dyning Chamber, very richly hang'd; in it is a most curious Chimney Peece, of Alabaster, Touch-Stone, and Marble, cut with severall statues, the Kings, and his Lordships owne Armes, richly sett out: All the rest of the Chimney Peeces, are very rich, and faire.[23]

Unlike Camden, Hammond does not even name the owner of the house, who, in 1635, would have been Philip Herbert, the fourth earl of Pembroke (1584–1650). He might, however, have assumed the identification was too obvious to be necessary, and he does recognise 'his Lordships owne Armes'.

It is true that Hammond displays a rather imprecise and limited vocabulary for describing visual effects: 'rich[ness]' is certainly his favorite attribute, although this term is sporadically supplemented with 'stately', 'curious', and 'faire'. He neither systematically evaluates proportion nor articulates an aesthetic standard or framework (such as classicism or Palladianism) upon which his judgment is based. While Hammond is a long way from Bold and Reeves's modern art-historical analysis, though, his approach is very different from Camden's historical and chorographic treatment of the house. We are assaulted with objects and materials – 'Cloth of Gold', 'Alabaster', 'Touch-Stone', and 'Marble' – rather than with stories about people, and the narrative is arranged according to spatial movement, rather than diachronic historical progression. Prominent people associated with the house are mentioned in the phrases 'the Earles Bed-Chamber' and 'the King's Chamber', but markers of noble and royal identity become inscriptive: they refer to particular rooms, as much as to particular people.

In fact, Hammond's reaction to the house as a collection of discrete ornamental objects, rather than a unified work of architecture, shows a characteristic early modern interest in the decorative arts that has been richly documented by scholars such as Anthony Wells-Cole and David Evett. What their studies show is that Hammond's visual response to the ornamental elements of the house is an engagement with classical and continental influences, whether or not Hammond himself recognised them as such. While the rich hangings, elaborate woodwork, and sculpted chimney pieces of late sixteenth- and early seventeenth-century English houses might not have shown a unified or systematic appropriation of classical style, they often bore the marks of foreign aesthetic trends nonetheless. Wells-Cole has meticulously traced the impact of pattern books and prints from Italy, France, Germany and the Netherlands on England's decorative arts between 1558 and 1625.[24] The dissemination of the Italian architect-author Sebastiano Serlio's (1475–c.1555) work provides an instructive example of England's piecemeal consumption of Renaissance architectural forms. Serlio's five-book treatise on architecture, which was published in stages in Venice and Paris between 1537 and 1547, appeared posthumously in 1584 as *Tutte l'opere d'architettura*. Although the treatise was not translated into English (as *The Five Books of Architecture*) until 1611, ornament drawn from Serlio's illustrated treatise is discernible in English masonry and woodwork from at least the 1560s onward, and its use does not seem to have been confined to foreign workmen. Wells-Cole argues that the treatise had little evident impact on the spatial arrangement or construction of buildings, but 'it had an irreversible impact on architectural decoration'.[25] The scope and illustrations of the treatise extend far beyond the requirements of a pattern book, but this seems to have been the selective way in which Serlio's work was used by English consumers.[26] Evett has described the decorative arts of this period as fragmented refractions of the continental Renaissance, as English craftsmen and patrons selected the elements of classical architecture that most readily served their purposes. Columns and pilasters, for instance, 'were readily adaptable to English structures … in fact, they could be broken away from their original structural function and applied in a totally decorative way'.[27] Hammond's failure to recognise these classical aesthetic affinities is unsurprising: for anyone unaccustomed to seeing a column or pilaster fulfilling its 'original structural function' these ornamental elements would not appear to have been 'broken away' from anything at all. Despite his lack of access to the broader aesthetic frameworks that would later enable art and architectural historians to draw comparisons between English architecture and that of the continental Renaissance, Hammond demonstrates the beginnings of a mode of architectural description that is invested in aesthetic and visual response.

While neither Hammond's *Short Survey* nor the *Britannia* is generally allotted a place in the literary canon, the juxtaposition of visual and antiquarian forms of architectural literacy evinces important tensions that are registered in some of the seventeenth century's most famous country house poems. An examination of these poems shows that writing about Wilton House is indicative of larger cultural perceptions concerning the interpretation of architecture. The examples discussed here – Jonson's 'To Penshurst' and Carew's 'To My Friend G.N., from Wrest' – are dismissive of both visual impressions and of architectural design more broadly. That is to say, they demonstrate an awareness of the concerns that structure an account like Hammond's, but they regard those concerns with a degree of suspicion. In fact, they go so far as to suggest that these preoccupations are inimical to a correct understanding of the connections among history, land and landowner that the country house poem, like antiquarian chorography, articulates.

Each of these poems offers its own lesson in architectural connoisseurship. But these lessons do not, as we might expect, point out physical or spectacular features for the visitor to admire. Rather each poem conveys the message that looking is not the right way to understand the country house at all. 'To Penshurst', for instance, famously begins not by describing the house, but by comparing it, in negative terms, to some unnamed competitor:

> Thou art not, Penshurst, built to envious show
>> Of touch, or marble, nor canst boast a row
> Of polished pillars, or a roof of gold:
>> Thou hast no lantern, whereof tales are told,
> Or stair, or courts; but standst and ancient pile,
>> And these grudged at, art reverenced the while.[28]

Notably, this comparison is not aimed at helping the reader to understand the physical appearance of Penshurst. Instead, we are pointedly given a list of features that Penshurst does not have. Already, Jonson's assertion that the house is not 'built to envious show' suggests his distrust of or resistance to the kind of visually inspired admiration that Hammond recorded on his visit to Wilton House. The only positive quality of Penshurst Jonson provides in these lines is the fact that the house is 'ancient', a descriptor that has more to do with history than with appearance. The word is an accurate index of Jonson's emphases in the poem: history, it turns out, is one of his most central concerns. The poem does not offer us architectural history in the modern sense, however, but a history that resembles Camden's description of Wilton House, insofar as both are comprised of stories about specific people associated with the place. As Jonson's gaze turns outward to the grounds of the estate, we are introduced to the 'taller tree, which of a nut was set' at the 'great birth' of Sir Philip Sidney and whose 'writhèd bark' is now 'cut' with 'the names/ Of many a sylvan taken with his flames' (ll. 13–14; 15–16). Soon after, we encounter 'thy lady's oak' and a 'copse, too, named of Gamage' (ll. 18, 19). Barbara Gamage was Robert Sidney's wife, who was said to have been taken with labor pains under the oak mentioned here and to have enjoyed feeding deer in the copse. Later, Jonson mentions the unannounced visit of King James and Prince Henry who 'when hunting late this way … saw thy fires/ Shine bright on every hearth' (ll. 76, 77–8).

Jonson evidently felt such human histories were crucial to the celebratory aims of his poem, for the sense of historical depth he creates seems deliberately manufactured in this case. In fact, while Penshurst was indeed an old estate, the Sidney family was newly enriched by the spoils of Reformation politics, and they had actually owned Penshurst only since 1552, when Robert's grandfather, William Sidney, had been rewarded for his service to Edward VI.[29] After moving outward to the grounds of the estate, 'To Penshurst' does come to centre on the rooms of the house itself, but not to praise its symmetrical disposition or well-proportioned floor plan. Instead, Jonson uses his tour of the house as a way of praising the noble qualities of its owners and the exceptional hospitality he receives there. The house memorialises character.

Neatly framing the poem, Jonson's closing lines return readers to the exercise of comparing houses to one another. We are made suddenly aware that the poem provides a lesson for performing this sort of comparison, one which changes the criteria readers take into account. Prepared by the stories of human history and virtue that fill 'To Penshurst', we are at last ready to look beyond the negative description of the opening lines of the poem, and judge Penshurst on the basis of what it is, rather than what it is not:

> Now, Penshurst, they that will proportion thee
>   With other edifices, when they see
> Those proud, ambitious heaps, and nothing else,
>   May say, their lords have built, but thy lord dwells.
>
> (ll. 99–102)

Having read the poem ('Now'), the reader sees architectural 'proportion' differently; no longer attached to visual symmetries or physical size, the term is redefined as the reader is engaged in an act of deliberation that relies on a different kind of 'see[ing]'. While the 'proud, ambitious heaps' attract visual interest, they are judged empty and wanting, not because there is nothing to see there, but because there is *only* something to see and 'nothing else'. By contrast, the reader judges Penshurst by incommensurate standards, through the perception of virtues less tangible or aesthetic than moral, historical, and narrative. The tense shift of the final line (from 'have built' to 'dwells') insists that the house be compared or 'proportion[ed]' historically, rather than being measured by its physical dimensions. Gauged temporally, the house outstrips its competitors as its vitality and interest extend to the present moment, rather than being limited to the past by Jonson's use of the perfect tense.

In 'To My Friend, G.N., from Wrest', Thomas Carew presents a more direct denunciation of visual and aesthetic experience as a means of judging architectural value. He seems pointedly opposed to the kind of visually stunning richness that so struck Hammond on his visit to Wilton House. In fact, the virtues of Wrest are evident precisely to the degree that the house fails to invite such attention at all. According to Carew, the house is

> Devoid of art; for here the architect
> Did not with curious skill a pile erect
> Of carvèd marble, touch, or porphyry,
> But built a house for hospitality.[30]

The ideal architect, strangely, is not one whose name is known and celebrated as a creator of magnificent designs, but one who does not use 'curious skill' or exercise 'art'. For the professional architect described in Italian Renaissance treatises by authors such as Leon Battista Alberti or Andrea Palladio, the goal of an architect's 'curious skill' would be to integrate the artful and the useful, not to separate them from each other. But for Carew, the visual seems necessarily to counteract the functional, rather than to harmonise with it. As the poem continues:

> No sumptuous chimney-piece of shining stone
> Invites the stranger's eye to gaze upon,
> And coldly entertains the sight, but clear
> And cheerful flames cherish and warm him here.

(ll. 25–8)

We might be reminded here of Hammond's admiration for the dining chamber at Wilton House, wherein he discovered 'a most curious Chimney Peece, of Alabaster, Touch-Stone, and Marble, cut with severall statues', and indeed, it seems that many English patrons of the period commissioned elaborate chimney pieces, which were frequently based on designs drawn from foreign pattern books.[31] In *The Elements of Architecture* (1624), an early English treatise on the building and evaluation of the country house, Henry Wotton included a section about chimney pieces that makes impressive fireplaces a point of national identity. 'Italians,' he observes, 'who make very frugall fires, are perchance not the best Counsellers'; nonetheless, one might learn from them 'how to raise faire *Mantels* within the roomes'.[32] With the *Elements*, Wotton tried to introduce to England a version of the classical or Italian architectural treatise, and the 'faire' Italianate mantel in no way interferes with the practical purposes of the English fireplace. For Carew, however, the opposite is true. He judges modes of perception, not fireplaces. The deliberate emphasis on the irrelevance of visual perception is evident in the words 'shining', 'eye', 'gaze', and 'sight'. The sight even seems to blunt the perception of the other senses, along with the perception of less visually-oriented virtues, as Carew places the phrase 'coldly entertains' in opposition to the words 'clear', 'cheerful' and 'warm'.

   Just as he indicates his awareness of the fashion for spectacular chimney pieces only to reject such embellishments, Carew also demonstrates his familiarity with the components of classical and Renaissance architecture, even though he proudly claims that Wrest does not have them:

> No Doric, nor Corinthian pillars grace
> With imagery this structure's naked face:
> The lord and lady of this place delight
> Rather to be in act, than seem in sight.

(ll. 29–32)

Carew knows the architectural orders (or types of columns), it would seem, but these elements of aesthetic decorum are dismissed, with the word 'imagery', as unnecessary and insubstantial concessions to the 'sight'. In concert with Carew's general precept that sight is a means of delusion, rather than accurate perception, 'act[ing]' in this case is stripped of its theatrical connotations. Rather than mere performance, it is 'to be' instead of to 'seem'.

In these poems, then, we see a marked antagonism between the sort of antiquarian architectural interpretation exemplified by Camden and the kind of visual enthrallment reflected in Hammond's description. In a later and more extensive description of Wilton House, John Aubrey would attempt a reconciliation – or at least a combination – of these strands of country house description. In *The Natural History of Wiltshire*, completed between the years 1656 and 1691, the biographical and the historical are freely mixed with the aesthetic and visual. Aubrey's account begins

> [t]he old building of the Earl of Pembroke's house at WILTON was designed by an architect (Hans Holbein) in King Edward the Sixth's time. The new building which faced the garden was designed by Monsieur Solomon de Caus... But this was burnt by accident and rebuilt in 1648, with Mr. Webb then being surveyor.[33]

Incorrect though Aubrey's attributions to Solomon de Caus and Hans Holbein might be, the prominence of architects' names alongside the name and title of the earl himself is striking. Aside from Wotton, none of the seventeenth-century sources discussed so far – from Camden to Carew – identifies an architect; such attributions are more characteristic of modern architectural historiography. In Hammond's case, this omission might be due to a lack of interest or knowledge, but in the poems of Jonson and Carew, the intrusion of such a figure would pose a threat to the celebration of the houses' patrons and of the idealised connections among architecture, ancestry and aristocrat. To emphasise the role of architect as designer or creator of a house, then, would be to displace the concerns of a different kind of architectural narrative that commemorated socially prominent individuals, and, as a result, better served the social priorities of most country house poets.

At the same time, however, Aubrey's detailed and appreciative description of the house's interior and exterior – too extensive to quote in full – is freely intermixed with the names of Wilton's socially important connections. 'The house is great and august, built all of freestone, lined with brick', Aubrey writes, 'which was erected by Henry Earle of Pembroke. Mr Inigo Jones told Philip ... Earle of Pembroke, that the porch in the square court was as good architecture as any was in England.' According to Aubrey, it was King Charles I who

> did love Wilton above all places, and came thither every summer ... that did put Philip ... Earle of Pembroke upon making this magnificent garden and grotto, and new build that side of the garden that fronts the house, with two stately pavilions at each end, all *al Italiano*.[34]

On the one hand, the name of Inigo Jones will surely pique the interest of architectural historians. On the other, Aubrey's remark about King Charles I's affection for Wilton might remind of us Jonson's anecdote about James I's spontaneous visit to Penshurst. Here, though, the king is described as an enthusiast of magnificent garden landscapes and Italianate architectural style, rather than an admirer of remarkable husbandry, hospitality, and household economy. Aubrey also combines architectural history with a kind of royal name-dropping in his description of Wilton's famous double cube 'dining roome, or roome of state; which is a magnificent, stately roome; and his Majesty King Charles the Second was wont to say 'twas the best proportioned roome that ever he saw'.[35]

As he inventories the treasures of Wilton's 'noble library of bookes, choicely collected in the time of Mary Countesse of Pembroke', Aubrey reminds us of Wilton's more literary historical associations. According to Aubrey, the contents of the library had once included '[a] translation of the whole book of Psalmes, in English verse, by Sir Philip Sydney, writt curiously, and bound in crimson velvet and gilt; it is now lost'.[36] In the subsequent chapter, he elaborates evocatively on these impressive literary connections. 'In the former Chapter,' he writes, 'I endeavoured to adumbrate Wilton House as to its architecture. We are now to consider it within, where it will appeare to have been an academie as well as palace … The apiarie to which men that were excellent in armes and arts did resort and were caress't.'[37] Aubrey's determination to 'consider' Wilton 'within' reflects the ways in which human and architectural histories freely intersect with and diverge from one another in his account. '[W]ithin' here cannot literally mean 'inside the house', because he has already observed several interior rooms in his 'adumbrat[ion]' of the 'architecture'. Instead, he seems to view the house as a container or repository of stories and memories that record significant people and their activities. Mirroring the values of the country house poem, he writes 'The hospitality here was very great.'[38] Even more tantalising to literary scholars is likely to be his memorialisation of 'the illustrious Lady Mary, Countesse of Pembroke, whom her brother had eternised by his Arcadia; but many or most of the verses in the Arcadia were made by her Honour, and they seem to have been writt by a woman'. Aubrey claims that Philip Sidney himself 'spent much, if not most part of his time here; and at Ivychurch, near Salisbury … when he was in England'. Furthermore, he adds, 'I cannot imagine that Mr. Edmund Spenser could be a stranger here.'[39] He notes, as well, that the playwright Philip Massinger was a servant to Philip, the fourth Earl, although his patron 'did not delight in books or poetry, but exceedingly loved painting and building in which he had a singular judgment, and had the best collection of any peer in England'.[40]

While Aubrey here takes a step towards the interests of a modern art or architectural historian, he retains the eclecticism so characteristic of antiquarian historiography, as this notice regarding the earl's patronage of the fine arts is immediately followed by the intriguing detail, 'He had a wonderful sagacity in the understanding of men, and could discover whether an ambassadour's message was reall or feigned; and his Majesty King James made great use of this talent of his.'[41] Aubrey thus writes fluently in two modes of architectural historiography without allowing one to supplant or supersede the other. And these antiquarian and aesthetic strands have continued to coexist, intersecting at times, since Aubrey's day. Bold and Reeves's thorough account of the house's development has already been offered as a modern example of visual and stylistic analysis, but later attempts to establish networks among prominent historical figures, texts and the Wilton estate attest that the logic of the country house poem persists, as well. Aubrey's assertions, along with the documented presence of Mary Sidney, have led many literary scholars to assume that at least some of the *Arcadia* was written at Wilton, and in 1851, James Smith quoted extensively from Sidney's prose romance with the following introduction: 'Among the descriptive passages in the Arcadia the reader who is familiar with the park and pleasure grounds at Wilton will have no difficulty in recognizing the accuracy of the following, – landscape paintings, evidently sketched on the spot.'[42] Further, Smith speculates

> that the scenery of [Wilton] Park may have been reproduced in the pages of the Faery Queen … If it be a delusion to suppose that some the picturesque descriptions of landscape scenery (conveyed in a language that is absolutely music) that occur in the 2nd and 4th books of this great poem were inspired by the natural objects which would meet the poet's eye in Wilton Park, it is a delusion we do not care to have dispelled.[43]

Smith's musings may indeed be delusions, but they are worth including because the connections they forge between human history, text, and the country estate demonstrate the author's awareness of the social, historical and textual networks that characterise the country house poem. Rather than writing a poem about Wilton House, however, Smith makes existing works of literature – the *Arcadia* and *The Fairy Queen* – into specimens of the genre. For Smith, the landscape of Wilton estate is not merely visually beautiful; he experiences it, as well, through his knowledge of history and his reading of texts. In this way, he examines and describes the estate through the application of an antiquarian lens.

Much more recently, in an essay of 2011, Hester Lees-Jeffries constructed a similar network of text, architecture and landscape by exploring possible relationships among the architecture of Wilton House, its gardens, and the garden settings of Lady Mary Wroth's *Countess of Montgomery's Urania* (1621).[44] Wroth's connection to Wilton seems less firmly established than those of Mary and Philip Sidney, but Lees-Jeffries hypothesises that Wroth's landscape descriptions are influenced by a copy of a French translation, the *Songe de Poliphile* (Paris, 1564) of the fifteenth-century Italian romance *Hypnerotomachia Poliphili* (Venice, 1499), held in the library of Wilton House, although its presence there is apparently undocumented. Drawing on Marion Wynne-Davies's idea that both Penshurst and Wilton provided "'safe houses" which gave the Sidney women in particular rooms of their own', Lees-Jeffries suggests that Wroth had access to the *Songe*, and that this book influenced both Wroth's *Urania* and the gardens at Wilton, which in turn might have influenced each other.[45] The thesis is intriguing, but we are less interested in the veracity of Lees-Jeffries's claim than in the complicated way her reading interweaves architecture (Wilton's library and Wynne Davies's 'safe houses'), texts (the *Urania* and the *Songe*), important literary figures (Wroth), and the physical landscape of Wilton estate. Although Lees-Jeffries's article is a far cry from Camden's *Britannia*, this very recent study appears to adapt part of its approach from one principle underlying antiquarian chorography and espoused by seventeenth-century country house poems: the architecture and landscape of the country estate is explicated in part through the reading of texts and the consideration of human histories attached to it. Thus, while Hammond's emphasis on visual impression might be seen as the sign of a slow progression towards the concerns of Bold and Reeves's modern architectural history, Aubrey, Smith and Lees-Jeffries equally demonstrate that one mode of architectural literacy has not superseded the other. Instead, both modes persist, intersecting at times, and both retain their appeal and critical utility.

Keeping these examples drawn from the seventeenth through the twenty-first century in mind, we can perhaps view the advertisements of Richardson's eighteenth-century guidebook to Wilton House, the *Aedes Pembrochianae*, in a new light. Rather than appearing merely eclectic, Richardson's antiquarian and aesthetic concerns are manifestations of a particular intellectual inheritance that included two ways of interpreting Wilton House, and of responding to architecture more generally. Richardson's desire to provide the 'antiquary's *Vade Mecum*', his use of texts, and his interest in human history reflect the methodology of post-Reformation English antiquarians such as Camden. His investment in systemising perceptions of the house and its contents as a means to effective aesthetic judgment, however, demonstrates his simultaneous attention to visual experience. Seventeenth-century writing about Wilton and other country houses shows us the emergence of these dual strands of architectural literacy, as well as the ways the two might contend or intersect with one another. Although architecture is often classified as a 'visual' art, the authors discussed here remind us that there are more ways of interpreting a building than may initially meet the eye.

Notes

1   George Richardson, *Aedes Pembrochianae, Or a Critical Account of the Statues, Bustos, Relievos, Paintings, Medals, and Other Antiquities and Curiosities at Wilton-House* (London, 1774), title page.

2   Richardson, *Aedes Pembrochianae*, Preface, p. 4.

3   Richardson, *Aedes Pembrochianae*, Preface, p. 3.

4   Richardson, *Aedes Pembrochianae*, Preface, p. 4.

5   Richardson, *Aedes Pembrochianae*, Preface, p. 4.

6   Richardson, *Aedes Pembrochianae*, p. 2.

7   Richardson, *Aedes Pembrochianae*, p. x*.

8   John Bold with John Reeves, *Wilton House and English Palladianism: Some Wiltshire Houses* (London: Her Majesty's Stationery Office, 1988), p. 25.

9   Bold with Reeves, *Wilton House*, p. 31.

10   William Camden, *Britannia*, trans. Philemon Holland (London, 1610), p. 246.

11   Bold and Reeves offer an excellent example of this approach, as I will go on to discuss. For the development of the sculpture collection, see Malcolm Baker, '"For Pembroke Statues, Dirty Gods and Coins": The Collecting, Display, and Uses of Sculpture at Wilton House', in Nicholas Penny and Eike D. Schmidt (eds), *Collecting Sculpture in Early Modern Europe* (New Haven, CT: Yale University Press, 2008), pp. 379–98.

12   Dana Arnold, 'Introduction', in Dana Arnold, Elvan Altan Ergut, and Belgin Turan Özkaya (eds), *Rethinking Architectural Historiography* (New York: Routledge, 2006), p. xvii.

13   Bold with Reeves, *Wilton House*, p. 32.

14   Bold with Reeves, *Wilton House*, p. 32.

15   Bold with Reeves, *Wilton House*, p. 33.

16   Dana Arnold, *Reading Architectural History* (New York: Routledge, 2002), p. 42.

17   John Aubrey, *Aubrey's Natural History of Wiltshire* (New York: Augustus M. Kelley, 1969), p. 84.

18   Howard Colvin, 'The South Front of Wilton House', in Colvin, *Essays in English Architectural History* (New Haven, CT: Yale University Press, 1999), p. 138.

19   Bold with Reeves, *Wilton House*, p. 34.

20   Bold with Reeves, *Wilton House*, p. 41–4.

21   In his description of Shropshire, Camden describes the house of Robert Corbet, 'who, carried away with the affectionate delight of Architecture, began to build in a barraine place a most gorgeous and stately house, after the Italians modell' (Camden, *Britannia*, p. 594).

22   Lieutenant Hammond, *Relation of a Short Survey of the Western Counties*, ed. L. G. Wickham Legg. *Camden Miscellany*, 16 (1936), 66.

23   Hammond, *Relation*, p. 66.

24   Anthony Wells-Cole, *Art and Decoration in Elizabethan and Jacobean England: The Influence of Continental Prints, 1558–1625* (New Haven, CT: Yale University Press, 1995).

25   Wells-Cole, *Art and Decoration*, pp. 11, 15–16.

26   Sebastiano Serlio, *The Five Books of Architecture* (New York: Dover, 1982 [1611]).

27   David Evett, *Literature and the Visual Arts in Tudor England* (Athens, GA: University of Georgia Press, 1990), p. 57.

28   Ben Jonson, 'To Penshurst', in *The Oxford Authors: Ben Jonson*, ed. Ian Donaldson (Oxford: Oxford University Press, 1985), lines 1–6. Subsequent quotations from the poem are cited by line number in the text.

29   Alastair Fowler, *The Country House Poem* (Edinburgh: Edinburgh University Press, 1994), p. 57.

30   Thomas Carew, 'To My Friend G.N., from Wrest', in Fowler, *The Country House Poem*, lines 21–4. Subsequent quotations from this poem are cited by line number in the text.

31   Fowler, *The Country House Poem*, p. 93; Christy Anderson, 'Learning to Read Architecture in the English Renaissance', in Lucy Gent (ed.), *Albion's Classicism: The Visual Arts in Britain, 1550–1660* (New Haven, CT: Yale University Press, 1995), pp. 239–42; Wells-Cole offers

many examples of chimney pieces. See, for example, his illustration of the overmantel at Castle Ashby, Northamptonshire, dated 1599 (p. 57).

32 Henry Wotton, *The Elements of Architecture* (London, 1624), pp. 59–60.
33 Aubrey, *Aubrey's Natural History*, p. 83.
34 Aubrey, *Aubrey's Natural History*, p. 83.
35 Aubrey, *Aubrey's Natural History*, p. 85.
36 Aubrey, *Aubrey's Natural History*, p. 86.
37 Aubrey, *Aubrey's Natural History*, p. 89.
38 Aubrey, *Aubrey's Natural History*, p. 89.
39 Aubrey, *Aubrey's Natural History*, p. 89.
40 Aubrey, *Aubrey's Natural History*, p. 91.
41 Aubrey, *Aubrey's Natural History*, p. 91.
42 James Smith, *Wilton and Its Associations* (London: J. B. Nichols and Son, 1851), p. 70.
43 Smith, *Wilton*, p. 59.
44 Hester Lees-Jeffries, 'Pictures, Places, and Spaces: Sidney, Wroth, Wilton House and the *Songe de Poliphile*', in Helen Smith and Louise Wilson (eds), *Renaissance Paratexts* (Cambridge: Cambridge University Press, 2011), pp. 185–203.
45 Lees-Jeffries, 'Pictures, Places, and Spaces', p. 186. The phrase 'safe houses' is quoted from Marion Wynne-Davies, '"For Worth, Not Weakness, Makes in Use but One": Literary Dialogues in an English Renaissance Family', in Danielle Clarke and Elizabeth Clarke (eds), *This Double Voice: Gendered Writing in Early Modern England* (London: Macmillan, 2000), p. 164.

Afterword

Andrew Loukes, Mark Purcell and Nicholas Pickwoad

Re-presenting the intellectual culture of the country house
Andrew Loukes

Petworth, West Sussex (National Trust) has seen a tradition of unbroken occupancy by branches of the same family since the 1150s.[1] Yet, despite this notable dimension of continuity, Petworth's cultural legacy – its architecture, landscape and collections – has been shaped by a particularly complex history, briefly outlined here. Although perhaps an extreme example in this respect, Petworth brings into focus how encounters with country houses today can be informed by many years of organic development. The curatorial issues of display and interpretation raised by this broadly common circumstance are pertinent, to varying degrees, for all country houses open to the public. Inevitably, related questions frequently involve more than scholarly considerations, but the approach of each house to repackaging its distinctive inheritance collectively represents, for better or worse, a significant contribution of our own age to the intellectual culture of the country house.

Architecturally, Petworth House principally reflects its major baroque rebuild of the 1690s. Yet this scheme underwent significant alterations and additions – both externally and internally – in the eighteenth, nineteenth and twentieth centuries, while previously standing on the site were a succession of manor houses and associated buildings which had increasingly expanded from the mid-twelfth to mid-seventeenth centuries; these included the fourteenth-century chapel which was both consumed and transformed by the baroque house, within which it is still experienced today. Petworth Park, now frequently regarded as an early masterpiece by Lancelot 'Capability' Brown, shares a similarly involved past. Brown's landscape replaced George London's extensive baroque garden of arguably greater significance, which itself necessitated the demolition and resurfacing of the last and most ambitious developments of the sprawling medieval-Tudor-Stuart site. Even Brown's park was largely given its defining shape in the later eighteenth and early nineteenth centuries, and was necessarily replanted with thousands of new trees following the great storm of 1987.

Petworth's collections, often trumpeted as the most important in the care of the National Trust, also reflect the shifting tastes of successive generations. The 10th Earl of Northumberland was a great collector of old masters, and among the leading patrons of Van Dyck. The 6th Duke of Somerset, whose marriage into the Percy dynasty brought about the rebuilding of Petworth in the late seventeenth century, commissioned many of the leading craftsmen of the day – notably the master-carver Grinling Gibbons. The 2nd Earl of Egremont in the mid-eighteenth century was an archetypical Grand Tourist, amassing European paintings and ancient marbles. His son, the 3rd Earl, was perhaps the most important of all, supporting contemporary British art in the early nineteenth century not only by buying and commissioning major works by artists such as J. M. W. Turner but also through entertaining them to such a degree that the house gained significance as an unofficial academy during the period.

In its range of dynastic names and titles, this extremely brief overview of Petworth's key collectors also gives some indication of the intricacies of the family line itself. All of these owners – and referenced above are just four of the most significant – disposed of objects as well as acquired them, and all owned major houses other than Petworth – including large London homes – ensuring that today's residual collection was at various times often widely dispersed. Making sense of the convoluted historical basis of the collection is today compounded by the fact that within the twelve state rooms open to the public in the house (there are over 100 rooms in total) are objects belonging to the National Trust alongside many which are still owned by the resident donor family and the twenty paintings by Turner which are the property of Tate. There are also a great number of objects, mainly still privately owned but some in the ownership of the National Trust, which are not on display. Despite these complexities, the collection at Petworth is actually among the most authentically indigenous of those found in major country houses open to the public.

Even the truncated summary of Petworth's built and collected legacy above immediately raises questions of priorities. Which aspects and objects are most deserving of conservation, presentation and interpretation? Which period or owner should be given greatest emphasis? And what are the criteria for making such decisions? In general terms, the National Trust's approach to the way in which it considers its presentation of historic interiors and collections, at least, is defined by Christopher Rowell in the organisation's extensive *Manual of Housekeeping*. Primarily regarding the conservation of objects, Rowell explains a preferred difference in methodology between historic interiors and museum displays as principally that in the former there should be a high degree of sensitivity to setting: 'all the elements are indivisible from the whole'.[2] Beyond this, the National Trust seeks to foster individuality at its properties by developing each one according to its own unique spirit of place.

In terms of priorities for a house such as Petworth, decisions founded on these basic principles are guided largely by its surviving legacy. At Petworth, this has largely meant an on-going policy since the 1990s to achieve, as far as possible, a recreation of the appearance and atmosphere of the house as it was in the early nineteenth century – the time of the 3rd Earl of Egremont and Turner, which arguably represents not only its most significant period but actually is that which lends itself most readily to representation by virtue of what survives. As well as refining Brown's park into its distinctive components, the 3rd Earl remodelled many of the interiors of the house and redefined the collection by selling off some 200 of his father's European paintings, preferring instead to focus on contemporary British art. In this regard, as one of the great collectors from the golden age of British art, the 3rd Earl's retentions become as significant as his acquisitions. Although there were some significant architectural alterations to the house in the later nineteenth century – principally by the Victorian architect Anthony Salvin – there was little in terms of cultural impact following the 3rd Earl's death in 1837, and much of Salvin's work was confined to the south end of the house, still occupied by Petworth's donor family and lying outside of the main state rooms now open to the public.[3]

Yet, when the National Trust took ownership of the house and park in 1947 it was certainly not pickled in Regency aspic. Naturally, there had been some significant sales and alterations, and in advance of opening to the public in 1953 the Trust itself invited Anthony Blunt, then Surveyor of the Queen's Pictures, to re-hang the public rooms. In doing so he unwittingly unpicked many of the picture arrangements which had been in situ for over 100 years; something he later regretted and which the National Trust, in collaboration with the present Lord and Lady Egremont, has attempted to redress over the last thirty years.

This programme has ensured some notable reinstatements within several key interiors to bring back the essence of their early nineteenth-century arrangements. The Red Room, for example, has been largely returned to its eponymous 1820s scheme, having been reconfigured in the 1950s as 'The Turner Room' by Blunt to showcase the majority of the artist's paintings, hung on new yellow silk hangings. Also, the Beauty Room – once a key space in the baroque house but much altered subsequently – has had the 3rd Earl's quirky shrine to the Napoleonic Wars reinstated, with its paintings and sculpture returned to the room on loan from the Egremont family.

Some rooms, however, present more of a challenge in terms of returning them to their early nineteenth-century heyday. The Carved Room, with its magnificent baroque carvings by Grinling Gibbons and others – substantially altered in the 1790s, regained much of its atmosphere of the 3rd Earl's room following an intensive restoration programme completed in 2002. This saw the return of many of the carvings which had been removed in the later nineteenth century, and – critically – the reinstatement of four landscape paintings by Turner, commissioned specifically for the room in the late 1820s. Yet, despite these great steps towards recovering this period, the room today is still quite different to that which originally received the Turners: the 3rd Earl's room featured whitewashed panelling and a magnificent long dining table – two key elements which are now missing. While calls to reinstate Gibbons's original scheme of the 1690s can be countered by the fact that this was irrecoverably altered on an architectural level in the late eighteenth century, the National Trust has stopped short of a wholesale recovery of the later Regency scheme for reasons of conservation, aesthetic considerations and the practical constraints of limiting the public's view of internationally important paintings and carvings.[4]

Petworth's Carved Room reflects some typical challenges of balance which distinctively affect the presentation of historic interiors as opposed to the more straightforward display of objects in a museum. In their specifics, these differences go beyond the general will to maintain an overarching spirit of place at each property. Regarding conservation, measures need to be in place to ensure the long-term survival of objects situated on open display in spaces never intended for long periods of exposure and heavy footfall. This has involved developing different means of striving for optimum standards regarding light control and environmental conditions than those employed by a modern museum, and opening hours and freedom of movement are often necessarily more curtailed. These considerations alone affect the visitor experience to a country house, but in terms of interpretation there are further determining factors resulting from the desire to maintain historical context.

To avoid compromising the overall integrity of spaces in historic houses and parkland, written interpretation cannot readily follow the standard museum pattern of introductory panels and individual object captions. Neither can audio-visual screens and interactive devices be easily integrated. Instead, interpretation needs to be achieved by more subtle means. At Petworth, this is delivered by a range of different techniques: folders of information introduce each room and identify objects, providing further details about key exhibits. There is also a menu of 10-minute talks, delivered by volunteer guides to give insights into specific aspects of the house, its history and collections. For a small fee, visitors can also opt for a handheld multimedia tour of the house, providing an overview of its history with the facility to explore many aspects of the collection in focus. Finally, a range of guidebooks are on sale.

Despite necessarily different approaches to display and interpretation, country houses share similar commercial pressures to public museums and face the same subsequent demand to grow and sustain visitor numbers. In order to help achieve this, and to strive towards meeting organisational targets for visitor satisfaction, houses have become increasingly creative in their attempts to engage with a wider audience. Petworth, for example, has in recent years introduced – with a considerable degree of success, based on feedback from family visitors – a number of children's trails and activities.

In terms of addressing the hidden and complex elements of its history, Petworth has also adopted a number of initiatives. While principally guided by the early nineteenth century in the presentation of its main showrooms, the earlier and later periods of the house are not ignored. A number of recent projects demonstrate this, such as: extensive conservation work on the Victorian 'Tijou' gates;[5] archaeological excavations to uncover the footprint of the 9th Earl of Northumberland's demolished north wing; and ongoing doctoral research – in partnership with the University of Sussex – into an important group of sixteenth- and seventeenth-century play quartos, not normally on public display. In addition, a new temporary exhibitions programme, featuring major loans, addresses selected themes related to the cultural history of the house which are otherwise not apparent through the permanent displays.[6] Finally, tours of 'behind the scenes' areas such as the attics, stables and basement are increasingly offered to the public.

While there remain fundamental differences between historic houses and conventional museums, there are enough similarities to ensure that some 150 of the National Trust's country houses – including Petworth – are formally designated as accredited museums.[7] In terms of dealing with their often complex stories, closely concerned with the history and context of place as well as objects, the future for country houses open to the public perhaps lies in an approach which both respects legacy and maximises its potential through the tested museum line of celebrating significance. Although this might most obviously focus on the most apparent components or periods – for example, the early nineteenth century at Petworth – a layered approach can ensure a wealth of hidden histories may also be explored.

The strange disappearance of the country house library
Mark Purcell

Shortly after I took over as Libraries Curator to the National Trust I was invited to join a bevy of National Trust staff for a private tour of one of England's grandest country houses. The house in question was Houghton, the great Norfolk mansion built for Sir Robert Walpole, and our genial and learned host was the late John Cornforth (1937–2004). John had been associated with *Country Life* for forty-odd years, and was well known at Houghton. His connections with the

National Trust (NT) went back nearly as long. Serving on various committees for the great and good, and taking a benevolent interest in generations of NT curators, he was widely regarded as a sort of departmental fairy godfather.[8] He had written *Country Life* articles beyond count, as well as a slew of fascinating and perceptive books, and he seemed to know everyone and everywhere. Under his expert eye, I and my new colleagues trooped round the Palladian splendours of Houghton. In room after room, we stopped, gazed around, and were treated to a meticulous dissection of each successive architectural space and everything in it. It was a heady experience for a new boy. Finally – or so it seemed to me – we arrived in the library, a room which was not generally on the public visitor route, and which I had seen only in pictures.

By this stage I was positively fizzing with excitement. Quite aside from the magnificence of the room, with full-height bookcases designed by William Kent, the books themselves bore every impression of having been there since Walpole's day.[9] To all outward appearances, the library of the first British Prime Minister had changed little since his death in 1745. This seemed intriguing on all sorts of levels. In the first place, I already knew that the Trust owned two prime ministerial libraries (at Chartwell and Hughenden), and I had already spent a substantial amount of time looking at Disraeli's books. Second, Houghton is one of a parade of really magnificent Norfolk houses, all with major libraries. Two of them (Blickling and Felbrigg) are in the hands of the National Trust; there is another in private hands at Holkham, a library famed for its manuscripts. Libraries in Norfolk country houses were evidently something of a phenomenon, and one which I was already aware that Susie West (then at the University of East Anglia) was working on. Finally, I had recently visited an apparently rather similar library, that of the 2nd Earl of Warrington at Dunham Massey, just outside Manchester.[10] There, as at Houghton, were the books of a Whig grandee, carefully ranged on the shelves of the room which had been designed to house them: a room, moreover, which was not a showroom, but an integral part of the owner's private apartments. But if I hoped to learn more, my hopes were swiftly dashed, as John Cornforth, his disquisition on panelling and upholstery completed, turned on his heel, and we followed him to the next room.

I hope it is apparent that my story is told not without affection, but it masks a serious point. As Maurice Howard points out in Chapter 1, fashions in country house studies have come and gone in line with the broader intellectual preoccupations of the day.[11] At the same time, a great deal of what is written and published continues to originate outside the university sector. Some of this is scissors-and-paste popular stuff, which necessarily tends to result in the repetition and embroidery of well-known stories. More is rather weightier than that – often the work of professional curators working for organisations like the National Trust, for museums and galleries (the V&A was particularly active, especially in the 1970s and 1980s), and of course staff writers at *Country Life*.[12] But wherever it has come from, certainly one of the odder quirks of mainstream country house scholarship is that libraries, more often than not, have been largely or completely missed out of the story. They have not been the only blind spot (service quarters traditionally got pretty short shrift) but are certainly a very striking one.

In France or Poland, or eastern Germany, this would be entirely explicable. For a range of perfectly familiar reasons – war, revolutions, hostile regimes, invading armies or legal codes inimical to male primogeniture – great houses with their historic contents are now rare there, as they are in many European countries. Intact libraries are rarer still, and historic archives, or any hard information on more recent depredations by the Red Army and the Nazis, can be hard to come by. In Ireland the house burnings of the independence period and the Civil War, together with land reforms instituted by the Dublin Castle administration and continued after 1922, mean that Irish big houses are now few and far between, and extant libraries rarer still.[13] Until recently the tainted legacy of an unlamented colonial past was something which for many held little appeal. Beyond the Iron Curtain, too great an interest in a pre-revolutionary and aristocratic past remained taboo up until 1989. And any contemporary attendee of international conferences on country house studies can easily run into curators from historic houses in central Europe, and, not infrequently, discover that there was a library in such-and-such a castle or palace until 1945 – but that the books then vanished, and their current whereabouts are now unknown. All of this presents a series of daunting problems for anyone wanting to know about private libraries in, say, Silesia or Lithuania.

By contrast, in England, Scotland and Wales, great houses are, despite the losses of the twentieth century, still comparatively numerous. Even given the current preoccupation with 'lost houses', many not only survived but remain in the hands of their traditional owners. A few continue to be resolutely private. But many are open to the public on terms ranging from the generous (the great estate as privately owned visitor attraction) through to the very restrictive (the minimum necessary to obtain grants or tax concessions). Other houses have passed into the hands of private trusts of one kind or another, and a good couple of hundred to the National Trust and the National Trust for Scotland. Despite many library sales, many of these houses still have their original books, sometimes hidden away in private apartments, but often on public view. With the surviving evidence literally staring us in the face – the National Trust, alone has over 300,000 books – it seems little short of extraordinary that the great renaissance of country house scholarship in the 1970s and 1980s very largely bypassed the country house library. For many, books were things to be consulted in research libraries to find out about something else. The idea that they could be – and were – studied in their own right was wholly unfamiliar. The great A. N.

L. ('Tim') Munby's illuminating paper on libraries for the V&A's 'Destruction of the Country House' exhibition of 1974 found surprisingly few successors.[14] He died shortly after, at just sixty-one, but it seems reasonably clear that he would have returned to the subject had he lived longer. Mark Girouard's ground-breaking *Life in the English Country House* (1978) made passing reference to libraries, but since then many have been content to repeat its conclusions rather than develop them. Granted, the great Treasure Houses exhibition held in Washington in 1985 *did* include books, but they were mysteriously omitted from the concluding symposium, whose proceedings were afterwards edited by the National Trust's Gervase Jackson-Stops, and published in 1989 as *The Fashioning and Function of the British Country House.*

At this point, some National Trust history becomes relevant. The Trust acquired its first books in 1907, but with the bequest of Blickling Hall in 1940, it became the owner of one of the most remarkable libraries in Europe. Dozens more followed, but initially the Trust paid little attention to them. It was partly a matter of money, but also of preference and prejudice. At Blickling, James Lees-Milne decided to retain the former private secretary of the donor, the 11th Marquis of Lothian, to catalogue the books. She accepted the offer, while recognising that she was wholly unqualified for the job; the decision set back the Trust's conduct of its greatest library by fifty years. Great man though he was, the Lees-Milne world-view tended to give his own taste primacy over research, and as his diaries show, he thought old books were deadly dull, the preserve of dusty and dreary scholars. Things improved in 1957 with the arrival of Cecil Clarabut to create a catalogue of books printed before 1700, though Lees-Milne's successor Robin Fedden took little interest in libraries, which he regarded to be something of an embarrassment. It is perhaps a measure of their marginal status that in the early 1970s the up-and-coming Martin Drury, who went on to become the Trust's Director General, never actually met its first Libraries Adviser, 'a shadowy figure'.[15] Unfortunately the bibliographical method underlying Clarabut's handwritten card catalogue was fairly shaky, a fact immediately recognised by Edward Miller, recently retired as Keeper of Printed Books at the British Museum, who briefly succeeded him. From there we pass into modern times with the extraordinary person of John Fuggles, Libraries Adviser to the Trust from 1978 to 1991. It was perhaps not altogether surprising that books were not always taken as seriously at the Trust in the 1980s as they might have been, yet its Libraries Adviser was one of the few people employed to work full-time on country house libraries. At the same time the chaos on the curatorial front was matched from the late 1970s by a considerable degree of dynamism in conservation: a potentially dangerous imbalance, though probably better than things being the other way round. As early as 1982, my colleague Nicholas Pickwoad was articulating in print some of the ideas developed elsewhere in this volume.[16] It was largely down to his efforts that the NT's books in the 1980s, though still mostly uncatalogued and unstudied, were neither neglected nor horribly over-restored.

If this seems a rather sorry record, it is perhaps worth recalling that it was played out in a period which largely saw the disappearance of the old-fashioned ducal scholar-librarian, and when other corporate owners of country house libraries were doing far less than the NT. It is also fair to point out that intellectual neglect has been a two-way process. If country house owners and their curators were happy to ignore their books, to a large extent the rare books establishment followed suit. To some extent this was the result of a simple information deficit: I myself remember gasping with astonishment at the richness of the unknown collections described in my predecessor's catalogue of the great NT library exhibition at the Grolier Club in New York in 1999.[17] It was also a matter of fashion. To put things rather crudely, the Anglo-American bibliographical tradition was traditionally about describing books and putting them in order, while the new Frenchified history of the book emerged out of the *Annales* school, hostile to empirical methodologies, broadly left-of-centre, and sceptical about elite history.

Happily, as the contents of this volume indicate, the tide has now turned. The study of material culture as a mainstream historical practice, the increasing appreciation of hand-press books in an age of digital humanities, and the Trust's own efforts to provide far greater intellectual access to its library collections in the last ten years through its online catalogue (on Copac, copac.ac.uk), conferences and publishing programme, are at last allowing the importance and riches of country house book collections and collectors to be visible once again.

The intellectual culture of the country house: books as physical objects and their conservation
Nicholas Pickwoad

It is difficult to talk about country house libraries as a single entity, as the collections, though they will inevitably share between them copies of many works, are so varied in their composition, history and ownership that generalisations are of limited value. The dispersal of many collections, or parts of collections, has also meant that large numbers of books from country house collections are now to be found in collections, both private and institutional, scattered across the world. An overall picture is therefore hard to assemble, but where the books remain in place in country houses, of whatever size and status, most will share some important characteristics. These include minimal use, lack of institutional management and possibly decades of neglect, be that more or less benign. Libraries that remain *in situ* also play a role in our understanding of the history of the building and its occupants, as well as offering the possibility of marrying archival records to the acquisition, binding and reading of the books over the centuries. Two other less easily quantifiable characteristics that come into play are the inertia borne of generous storage space, where it is easier simply to store material no longer of current interest in attics, store rooms, cupboards and outhouses than make decisions about discarding it and perhaps also an unwillingness to disturb the books on the shelves of a great library room once it has been filled.

The differences between institutional and private collections reflect both the editions that might be found in them and the state in which they are preserved. For the private owner there was no need to make the books ready for public access and heavy use, a consideration that allowed books to remain in the state in which they were first purchased or, at least, in the first substantial bindings that might have been commissioned for them when they entered a collection. This means that such libraries often preserve not only large numbers of the first or early bindings in boards and leather that fill many library shelves, but also the more ephemeral bindings in which they might have been first bought. Such collections may also preserve the editions that would not necessarily have been found in institutional collections, such as children's books, school books, 'light' literature of all sorts, guide books, manuals, liturgica, etc., that have an important role to play in our understanding of the print culture of the early modern period. It is also sometimes the case that the scholarly enthusiasms of one individual in a family may not have been shared by his decendants, who may have been content to leave their ancestor's books on the shelves of a grand room or in an attic untouched for generations. It is probably for this reason that the library of Sir Richard Ellys, now in Blickling Hall in Norfolk, rich as it is in terms of the subject matter, rarity and quality of so many of its books, still retains three books in unbound sheets and two volumes bought from Amsterdam as sewn bookblocks without boards or covers. These were perhaps acquired shortly before Ellys's death in 1742, leaving him no time to have them bound, and they therefore survive as rare examples of the state in which many books were acquired at the time. More surprisingly, perhaps, given the seriousness of so much of the content of the library, is the copy of an early eighteenth-century Florentine opera libretto,[18] which retains its format-specific secondary cover of a pink-washed paper blocked with a baroque design in a gold alloy. Although bound collections of such libretti have survived,[19] individual items in the state in which they might have been used in an opera house have largely survived, where they survive at all, by accident, and here serve also as a reminder of Ellys's time in Italy.

The same could be said of the guide books, both local and international, accumulated by generations of individual familes and sometimes annotated. On the return of a young man from his Grand Tour, such books might find their way into a cupboard in a closet off the library (as the Earl of Warrington's guide books at Dunham Massey, near Manchester)[20] or onto the library shelves in the case of the fifth Earl of Exeter, with the paper spines painted brown and tooled in gold to match the other books in his library.[21] These are books that might not usually be kept in the formal library and such books would include the almanacs and pocket books used by members of the family, remarkable collections of which can be preserved in country house collections, either brought into the library at a later date (as at Helmingham Hall in Suffolk) or preserved in the archives (as at Kedleston Hall).

The survival of books in more ephemeral, or certainly cheaper, bindings may also be a reflection of the owners' opinion of the books that were left in this state. The hundreds of paper-covered late eighteenth-century publishers' bindings found in the library cupboards at Tatton Park are presumably those books that the Egerton family did not think worth having bound in leather and elevating (quite literally) to the open shelves above the cupboards. In the same way the large collection of unbound pamphlets from the late sixteenth, seventeenth and eighteenth centuries that was kept in the drawers under the presses in the study at Belton House, survived, it can only be assumed, more through inertia than anything else, until many of them were placed in the newly fashionable solander cases bought for them probably by Sir Brownlow Cust, 7th Bt. (1744–1807) from the London binder James Fraser at the end of the eighteenth century. Inaccessible storage can also have a preservative consequence, as the high shelves in the Billiard Room at Nostell Priory bear witness. Accessible now only by means of a scaffolding tower (the highest shelves are some 15 feet from the floor), the shelves contain some immaculate copies of publishers' bindings and books in paper wrappers.

It should not be thought that it is only the cheaper bindings that have been preserved in these collections, though they can be amongst the least common and most interesting. At Kingston Lacy, the reclusive tendencies of the last owner, Ralph Bankes, meant that the library was little disturbed for the greater part of the twentieth century and allowed for the survival unrepaired and in entirely original condition, of a magnificent copy of Conrad Lycosthenes' *Theatrum Vitae Humanae*, described in 1844 by William John Bankes as being in a 'prodigiously rich binding' for Sir Nicholas Bacon. The book, with its binding by Jean de Planche, was preserved at the house as an heirloom and found in a small cupboard full of photograph albums when the house was given to the National Trust in 1982.[22] A comparable binding, executed for Queen Elizabeth I and now in the British Library, suffered badly at the hands of restorers in the mid-twentieth century, making the Kingston Lacy binding still more important as the only surviving untouched example of De Planche's work at its most sumptuous.

What becomes clear when the collections are examined in detail is that they frequently have an archaeological value as a whole – annotation, provenance, binding and even condition – that can exceed their value as collections of individual editions. This in turn necessitates that their preservation will need to be undertaken with specific reference to these different values. However, preserving them in the condition in which they have come down to us often presents extraordinary difficulties, and requires very careful management of the balance between preservation and access. Collections that have survived in fragile condition as a result of no public access and very light use cannot be opened to readers as an institutional collection might be without suffering immediate and often irreparable loss. Books, for instance, sewn on embrittled tanned leather sewing supports (very common on sixteenth-century northern European books) and perhaps with sun-damaged covering materials on their spines that have survived untouched on shelves for the past two or three centuries will frequently now break in half if opened to more than 90 degrees. On the other hand, denying access to books on account of their fragility will be seen as a contradiction of the purpose of making a library available to researchers and can only be allowed in the most exceptional individual cases.

The only answer to this conundrum is to assess carefully the different values that can attach to a book, of which the text may not necessarily be the most important, and work to preserve those values as carefully as possible. Starting from the archaeological ideal that the best treatment is to do nothing beyond stabilising what is there (which can often best be done most effectively by *in situ* programmes where a small team of conservators clean all the books and carry out minor repairs in the library itself), it may be necessary to devise repairs which interfere as little as possible with the structure and materials of the books (known to modern book conservators as 'minimum intervention repairs') but which will allow at least adequate if carefully controlled access to the text. Where more interventive repairs cannot be avoided, it is absolutely essential that the book and its binding are fully recorded before any work is undertaken and that any material that cannot be re-attached to the books is preserved and kept accessible. It goes without saying that new materials used in the repairs must be of conservation quality.

All repairs can be kept to a minimum if two other factors are also brought into consideration – the use of supports and protective enclosures for the books on the shelves and an insistence on the highest levels of care in the handling of books by all who use them. The former include devices such as the external bookshoe, an enclosure made from thin board which is rather like a slip case without a top but with a textblock support in its base, which was originally designed for the National Trust for books in its historic library rooms but is now in widespread use. It protects the sides of the books (and sides of their neighbours on the shelf if they have metal fittings such as clasps) while at the same time taking the weight of the bookblocks in books with weakened structures, while leaving the spine and head edge of the book exposed on the shelf. They therefore offer a high level of protection and support with minimal impact on the appearance of the room. More recently an 'internal bookshoe' has been developed, made of stiff polyester film, which sits inside the covers of a book while still supporting the weight of the bookblock, and thus takes up much less extra space on the shelf – an important consideration where an historic library arrangement needs to be preserved within shelves that are full. More complex and all-enclosing boxes may be needed in special cases (such as the De Planche binding mentioned above), and occasionally for oversize books, horizontal storage may be the only answer.

Supports such as the foam wedges, which allow a book to open to 130 degrees, are now in common use in rare-book reading rooms, but the provision of cradles that restrict the opening of a book to 90 degrees will allow safe access to the text leaves of those books so fragile that they would otherwise be damaged in use.

The provision of the most benign conditions possible within buildings where the environmental conditions are often complex and difficult to improve without unacceptable interference in their fabric and furniture is also essential. In houses still lived in, there will be the added complication of finding a compromise between conditions that are comfortable for living and optimal for the books (and other contents of the rooms). The levels of heat and light desired by human beings can be very damaging to books.

It is only by such means that the full value of such collections to the modern historian can be preserved.

Notes

1   See Christopher Rowell, *Petworth – The People and the Place* (London: Scala, 2012), for a history of Petworth and its inhabitants.
2   *The National Trust Manual of Housekeeping* (London: Butterworth-Heinmann, 2005), p. 9.
3   Other exceptions to this generalisation are the 2nd Lord Leconfield's purchases of important furniture at the Hamilton Palace sale in 1882 and his occasional commissions of significant Arts and Crafts furnishings (see Rowell, *Petworth*, pp. 139–43).
4   See Christopher Rowell, 'Turner at Petworth – The 3rd Earl of Egremont's Carved Room Restored', *Apollo* (June 2002), 40–7.
5   So-named because their design follows the baroque ironwork by Jean Tijou at Hampton Court Palace.
6   The exhibition Turner's Sussex sold out of tickets in 2013, as did Constable at Petworth in 2014.
7   The Accreditation Scheme, formerly the Museum Registration Scheme from 1988–2004, is now administered by Arts Council England and sets nationally agreed standards for museums in the UK. There are currently around 1,800 participating in the scheme.
8   'John Cornforth' [obituary], *The Daily Telegraph*, 10 May 2004.
9   For illustrations of the room see: *Houghton Revisited: the Walpole Masterpiece from Catherine the Great's Hermitage* (London: Royal Academy of Arts, 2013), pp. 119–22. So far as I am aware, no one has ever published anything on the library itself.

10 Susie West, 'The Development of Libraries in Norfolk Country Houses, 1660–1830', unpublished PhD thesis, University of East Anglia, 2000; James Rothwell, 'Dedicated to Books', *National Trust Historic Houses & Collections Annual*, 2010 (published in association with Apollo), pp. 56–61; Ed Potten, '"A Great Number of Usefull Books": the Hidden Library of Henry Booth, 1st Earl of Warrington (1652–1694', *Library and Information History*, 25, 1 (March 2009), 33–49.

11 See pp. 11–23.

12 There are useful reflections on these themes in: Simon Jervis, 'In Institutional Hands: Ham House, the Victoria and Albert Museum and the National Trust', in Christopher Rowell (ed.), *Ham House* (London: Yale, 2013), pp. 383–94.

13 Mark Purcell, *The Big House Library in Ireland: Books in Ulster Country Houses* (Swindon: National Trust, 2011).

14 Nicolas Barker, 'Obituary: John Fuggles: Eccentric and Uproarious Libraries Adviser to the National Trust', *The Independent*, 19 November 2002; John Saumarez Smith, 'John Fuggles, Bibliomane', *The Book Collector*, 61:4 (Winter 2012), 605–9.

15 Martin Drury, 'The Lily and the Boot: Early Days of the Historic Buildings Department', *Views*, 46 (Autumn 2009), 19–20, p. 19.

16 Nicholas Pickwoad, 'Problems of Conservation', *The Library Association Rare Books Group Newsletter*, 19 (May 1982), 11–14.

17 Nicolas Barker (ed.), *Treasures from the Libraries of National Trust Country Houses* (New York: Royal Oak Foundation, 1999).

18 *Il Domizio, Drama per Musica* (Florence, 1700).

19 Irene Alm, *Catalogue of the Venetian Librettos at the University of California, Los Angeles* (Berkeley, CA: University of California Press, 1992).

20 For example: Zaccaria Betti, *Descrizione di un Meraviglioso Ponte Naturale nei Monte Veronesi* (Verona: Nella stamperia di Marco Moron, 1766) (National Trust, Dunham Massey).

21 Lodovico Vedriani, *Raccolta dei Pittori, Scultori, et Architetti Modenesi più celebri: nel quale si leggono l'opere loro insigni, e doue l'hanno fatte / Cauata da vari autori* (Modena: Per lo Soliani stampator ducale, 1662) (Burghley House).

22 Gervaise Jackson-Stops, *The Treasure Houses of Britain: Five Hundred Years of Private Patronage and Art Collecting* (New Haven, CT and London: Yale University Press, 1985), pp. 404–5, and Nicolas Barker, *Treasures from the Libraries of the National Trust Country Houses* (New York: Royal Oak Foundation, 1999), pp. 82–3.

Index

EU authorised representative for GPSR:
Easy Access System Europe, Mustamäe tee 50,
10621 Tallinn, Estonia
gpsr.requests@easproject.com

www.ingramcontent.com/pod-product-compliance
Ingram Content Group UK Ltd.
Pitfield, Milton Keynes, MK11 3LW, UK
UKHW021911060726
6981IPUK00004B/81